April 13, 2012

For Mat Goldsmith

with much gratitude
for your huge role
in developing the
poverty studies
program described in
the last essay,

Herbert Bardsley

Ethics and Advocacy

ETHICS and ADVOCACY

Bridges and Boundaries

EDITED BY

Harlan Beckley, Douglas F. Ottati,
Matthew R. Petrusek, & William Schweiker

CASCADE *Books* · Eugene, Oregon

ETHICS AND ADVOCACY
Bridges and Boundaries

Cascade Books
An Imprint of Wipf and Stock Publishers
199 W. 8th Ave., Suite 3
Eugene, OR 97401

www.wipfandstock.com

PAPERBACK ISBN: 978-1-6667-0298-9
HARDCOVER ISBN: 978-1-6667-0299-6
EBOOK ISBN: 978-1-6667-0300-9

Cataloguing-in-Publication data:

Names: Beckley, Harlan R., 1943–, editor. | Ottati, Douglas F., editor. | Petrusek, Matthew R., editor. | Schweiker, William, editor.

Title: Ethics and advocacy : bridges and boundaries / edited by Harlan Beckley, Douglas F. Ottati, Matthew R. Petrusek, and William Schweiker.

Description: Eugene, OR : Cascade Books, 2022 | Includes bibliographical references and index(es).

Identifiers: ISBN 978-1-6667-0298-9 (paperback) | ISBN 978-1-6667-0299-6 (hardcover) | ISBN 978-1-6667-0300-9 (ebook)

Subjects: LCSH: Christian ethics. | Religious ethics.

Classification: BJ1261 .E77 2021 (paperback) | BJ1261 .E77 (ebook)

VERSION NUMBER 032222

CONTENTS

CONTRIBUTORS

Harlan Beckley, Professor Emeritus of Religion, Washington and Lee University. His publications include *Passion for Justice* (1992); *Economic Justice* (1996) by John Ryan (editor); *James M. Gustafson's Theocentric Ethics* (1989), edited with Charles M. Swezey; and numerous periodical articles. He founded and directed the Shepherd Program on Human Capability and Poverty and the Shepherd Higher Education Consortium on Poverty. Beckley holds an honorary doctorate from Washington and Lee University and served as President of the Society Christian Ethics in 2001.

James F. Childress, Professor Emeritus, University of Virginia, where he was formerly University Professor, John Allen Hollingsworth Professor of Ethics, and founding Director of the Institute for Practical Ethics and Public Life. He has published numerous articles and several books in ethics and bioethics, including, most recently, *Public Bioethics: Principles and Problems* (2020), and, with Tom L. Beauchamp, *Principles of Biomedical Ethics*, now in its eighth edition (2019) and about a dozen translations. Childress has served on multiple national panels to advise on public bioethics issues, most recently a panel on priorities for vaccinations against SARS-CoV-2.

Gary Dorrien, Reinhold Niebuhr Professor of Social Ethics, Union Theological Seminary Professor of Religion, Columbia University. His publications include *Kantian Reason and Hegelian Spirit* (2012), which won the PROSE Award in 2013, *The New Abolition: W. E. B. Du Bois and the Black Social Gospel* (2015), which won the Grawemeyer Award in 2017, and *Breaking White Supremacy: Martin Luther King Jr. and the Black Social Gospel* (2018), which won the American Library Association Award in 2018.

Stanley Hauerwas, Gilbert T. Rowe Professor Emeritus of Theological Ethics, Duke University. Stanley Hauerwas's most recent books are *The Work of Theology* and *Minding the Web: Making Theological Connections* (2018), with Robert Dean. Retired but continuing to write, his *Fully Alive: The*

Apocalyptic Humanism of Karl Barth is soon to be published by the University of Virginia Press. Hauerwas gave the Gifford Lectures in 2000–2001. They are published in *With the Grain of the Universe* (2001). He was President of the Society of Christian Ethics in 2011.

Rebekah Miles, Professor of Ethics and Practical Theology, Perkins School of Theology, Southern Methodist University. Her publications include *Georgia Harkness: The Remaking of a Liberal Theologian, Collected Essays from 1929–1942* (2010); *The Bonds of Freedom: Feminist Theology and Christian Realism* (2001); *When the One You Love Is Gone* (2012); *The Pastor as Moral Guide* (1999), and numerous articles. She was a co-author of *Wesley and the Quadrilateral: Renewing the Conversation* (1997), was associate editor of the *Dictionary of Scripture and Ethics* (2011), and co-edited, with Steven Long, *The Routledge Companion to Christian Ethics* (2010). She received a Henry Luce III Fellowship in Theology.

Douglas F. Ottati, Craig Family Distinguished Professor of Reformed Theology and Justice at Davidson College. His publications include *A Theology for the Twenty-First Century* (2020); *Theology for Liberal Presbyterians and Other Endangered Species* (2006); and *Hopeful Realism: Reclaiming the Poetry of Theology* (1999). He was president of the Society of Christian Ethics in 2010.

Peter J. Paris, Elmer G. Homrighausen Professor Emeritus, Princeton Theological Seminary. His publications include *Virtues and Values: The African and African American Experience, The Spirituality of African Peoples: The Search for a Common Moral Discourse* (2004); *Black Religious Leaders: Conflict in Unity* (1991); *The Social Teaching of the Black Churches* (1985); *African American Theological Ethics: A Reader*, and *Religion and Poverty: Pan-African Perspectives* (2009), editor. Paris served as President of the American Academy of Religion, the American Theological Society, the Society for the Study of Black Religion from 2002 to 2006, and the Society of Christian Ethics in 1992.

Matthew R. Petrusek, is Associate Professor of Theological Ethics at Loyola Marymount University. His books include *Value and Vulnerability: An Interfaith Dialogue on Human Dignity* (with Jonathan Rothchild) and *Jordan Peterson, God, and Christianity: The Search for a Meaningful Life* (with Christopher Kaczor). Petrusek serves as a fellow in Bishop Robert Barron's Word on Fire Institute.

Marcia Y. Riggs, J. Erskine Love Professor of Christian Ethics, Columbia Theological Seminary. Her publications include *Awake, Arise, and Act: A Womanist Call for Black Liberation* (1994); *Plenty Good Room: Women vs.*

Male Power in the Black Church (2003); *Can I Get a Witness?: Prophetic Religious Voices of African American Women—An Anthology* (1997); and *Ethics that Matters: African, African American, and Caribbean Sources* (2010), edited with James S. Logan and essays on conflict transformation and pedagogy. In 2017–2018, Riggs was Henry Luce III Fellow in Theology with the Association of Theological Schools.

Rubén Rosario Rodríguez, Professor of Systematic Theology, Saint Louis University. His publications include *Racism and God-Talk: A Latino/a Perspective* (2008), which won the 2011 Alpha Sigma Nu Book Award for Theology; *Christian Martyrdom and Political Violence: A Conversation with Judaism and Islam* (2017); *Dogmatics After Babel: Beyond the Theologies of Word and Culture* (2018); and *The T&T Clark Handbook of Political Theology* (2019). He directs the Mev Puleo Scholarship in Latin American Theology, Politics, and Culture, a ten-week immersion experience focusing on liberation theology and social justice, and is Coordinator of Masters Programs in the Department of Theological Studies.

William Schweiker, Edward L. Ryerson Distinguished Service Professor of Theological Ethics, The University of Chicago. His publications include *Religious Ethics: Meaning and Method* (2020), *Dust That Breathes: Christian Faith and the New Humanism* (2010); *Religion and the Human Future* (2008); *Theological Ethics and Global Dynamics: In the Time of Many Worlds*, among others. He has served as Mercator Professor, Universität Heidelberg, Deutsche Forschungsgemeinschaft and holds a Doctorate Honoris Causa from The University of Uppsala, Uppsala, Sweden. Schweiker was President of the Society of Christian Ethics (2016).

Per Sundman, Professor of Ethics, Department of Theology, Uppsala University. His publications include *Human Rights, Justification, and Christian Ethics* (1996); *Egalitarian Liberalism Revisited on the Meaning and Justification of Social Justice* (2016); and several book chapters.

Darlene Fozard Weaver, Associate Provost for Academic Affairs, Professor of Theology, Duquesne University. Her publications include *The Acting Person and Christian Moral Life* (2011); *Self-Love and Christian Ethics* (2002); *The Ethics of Embryo Adoption and the Catholic Tradition: Moral Arguments, Economic Reality, and Social Analysis* (2007), edited with Sarah-Vaughan Brakman; and journal articles and chapters in edited volumes. Weaver is Principal Investigator for a *Catholicism and the Common Good* grant from the Henry Luce Foundation.

INTRODUCTION

Matthew R. Petrusek

HIGHER EDUCATION HAS COME under public scrutiny in recent decades for many reasons—ballooning tuitions, exploited adjunct faculty, exorbitant student loans, seeming diminishment of academic standards, a lack of class/race/ethnic inclusion, and a growing sense that going to college is no longer necessary for, and, indeed, may even be an obstacle to, "getting a good job." However, another challenge walks the halls of the academy and, in fact, our entire society. Not surprisingly, voices are heard on both sides of what has become a wide and deep cultural divide in the nation.

On the one side is heard the explosive charge that activist faculty and administrators have transformed colleges and universities into centers of moral and political indoctrination, hubs of advocacy whose primary purpose is not education but to supply society with political agitators. It was not always like this, the critics insist. In the past, students supposedly used to be taught to think for themselves, not to parrot their professors; to speak well, not to shout; to formulate arguments, not slogans; to understand competing points of view, not to denounce them, *a priori*, as "unsafe" or "dangerous." From this side of the divide, the vocabulary and imagery that is popularly associated with contemporary higher education—trigger warnings, safe spaces, six-figure-plus diversity and inclusion officers, privilege denouncing, speech zones, deplatforming, virtue-signaling, with-or-against-us-silence-is-violence demands on administrators in occupied university buildings—suggest that, at least for wide swaths of the American public, something other than the transference of knowledge, critical thinking, and free scholarly inquiry now defines the American campus. And the same forces, the critique continues, have now seeped through the ivy walls that once contained them are running wild throughout the country.

Yet is such a characterization accurate? Unsurprisingly, it often depends on whom you ask, what zip code they reside in, which candidate they voted for in the last election, and, indeed, what they drive (or whether they drive at all). To those on the other side of the national divide, the recent shifts in university culture reflect a growing awareness of the need to confront what they see as systematic injustices and embedded structures of oppression both inside and outside higher education. They point out that this is not the first time in US history that broader cultural debates have generated and been generated by conflicts in higher education: the civil rights struggle of the 1960s and protests over the Vietnam war in the 1970s not only took place in university settings but, to a significant degree, found their origins there. For many, this tumult was necessary to overturn established values that were antithetical to social progress. As such, the criticism from these quarters is not that the university is heading in the wrong direction nowadays; it is that it is not heading in the right direction fast enough. Amidst the general fog of a cold culture war that is increasingly turning hot on many issues, including higher education, perhaps the only point of agreement about the moral status of the university is that it is contested.

How, then, to proceed? What, if anything, can be done to break, or at least to relax, the gridlock between those who still see the academy as a qualified force for good in society and those who would be content to see the whole system fail and be replaced? Insofar as the academy is a microcosm for the nation, how can we build bridges between people of contrary convictions and mark out appropriate boundaries between the ends that the academy and the nation should pursue? This edited volume approaches the question by engaging one of the fundamental issues in the battle over higher education, recognizing its resonance far beyond university campuses: the role that advocacy should play both inside and outside the college classroom.

The contributors, all academics with various degrees of public engagement, draw on their training as professional ethicists, teachers, and ministers to provide clarification on fundamental questions that inhere in the debate. For example, what, precisely, is advocacy, and what does it mean to be an advocate both within a university setting and outside of it? How does the work of advocacy relate to ethics? Can the study of ethics, both philosophical and religious, be coherently defined independently of advocacy? Can advocacy be coherently defined—not to mention effectively practiced—independently of ethical analysis? Is there a difference between "ethical" and "unethical" advocacy? Is there a pedagogical role for advocacy in the classroom? Should students be taught that they ought to advocate for particular moral and political goals? Might such advocacy itself constitute an ethical violation? What does it mean for a professor to identify herself or himself as an "scholar-advocate"? How does "advocacy" qualify what it means to do "scholarship" and how does "scholarship" qualify "advocacy"? Who (if anyone) has the authority to speak on behalf of whom in both identifying the ends and means of advocacy?

The chapters of this volume take up these and related questions from multiple perspectives. It is important to note at the outset that, though all contributors agree that both ethics and advocacy have an essential role in moral analysis and action, there remain significant disagreements about the precise relationship between the two within both theoretical and applied dimensions of analysis (that is, both at the level of how "ethics" and "advocacy" should be respectively defined, and how those respective definitions should be applied to academic and non-academic contexts). However, three methodological and substantive pillars provide a constituent unity to the viewpoints. First, each contributor reaches the dual conclusions that (a) ethics and advocacy should not be understood as synonymous (even if, according to all, they should be defined in relation to each other), and (b) there ought to be room for both ethical inquiry and advocacy, properly defined, within university education, including, under certain constraints, within the classroom itself. Second, each contributor agrees that, to whatever degree advocacy belongs to the purposes of university education, such advocacy ought to conform to ethical standards, including a commitment to engage competing points of view; in other words, there is a solidarity among the contributors in rejecting attempts to "silence" one's opponents. Third, each chapter, to varying degrees, situates its analysis within, or at least in relation to, the academic field of philosophical and religious ethics broadly and of Christian ethics specifically.

Although the authors employ numerous forms of ethical analysis, both religious and non-religious, there are two basic reasons why engaging the question of the relationship between ethics and advocacy through the lens of Christian ethics is distinctively beneficial. First, as several contributors highlight, Christian ethics, insofar as it has ever constituted a distinct field of study (which itself is a contested claim), has sought to articulate the right relationship, in biblical terms, between *defining* the kingdom of God, on the one hand, and *seeking to build* the kingdom of God, on the other. In this sense, the tension between the poles of "thinking/believing" and "practicing/acting," which occupy the core of the relationship between ethics and advocacy, is something that Christianity has been navigating since the first century CE.

Second, the basic moral character of Christianity, especially as we see it manifested in the Sermon on the Mount and in Matthew 25 (i.e., "that which you did to the least of me, you did to me"), gives the question of Christian ethical reflection an indisputably practical nature. "If you love me, follow my commandments," says Jesus according to John 14:15; those commandments minimally include caring for the hungry, the thirsty, and the naked. In this sense, no matter how rarefied a theory of moral knowledge a Christian ethicist develops or adopts, such theories cannot be understood independently of a concrete call for individual and social action in service of the poor.

Third and related, Christian ethics contains a distinct trove of conceptual resources that are apt for engaging the relationship between ethics and advocacy. They include a robust account of moral reasoning seasoned by a fundamental recognition that reason is neither *sui generis* nor comprehensively exhaustive and thus depends upon, and points to, "faith" both epistemically and volitionally (i.e., "trust"); a conception of humans as beings who deserve unqualified basic moral respect because each is made in the image and likeness of God; a fundamental recognition of universal human depravity in the form of original sin, which both generates a call to individual and communal sanctification while also acting as a limiting principle on what moral improvement human efforts alone can achieve; an affirmation of reality that is structured by hope, based on the principle that God's action in and through the events of creation, incarnation, crucifixion, and resurrection generates inexhaustible opportunities for individual and social moral progress on this side of the eschaton; and a fundamental rejection of special moral knowledge that would assert that the power to build the kingdom resides solely within the esoteric prerogatives of those with specialized training (like ethicists). This is an incomplete list, to be sure, but it gives a sense of why Christian ethics has a special aptitude, a vocation, for articulating and implementing a better understanding of the right relationship between ethics and advocacy.

That is not to say that the volume speaks only to Christians and those interested in Christian moral thinking. There are forms of analysis in the chapters that are equally at home within diverse traditions of reasoning, both religious and non-religious. Indeed, another unifying theme among the chapters is an insistence on the necessity of *making arguments*, broadly construed as defensible claims, to justify—and not only describe or confess or advocate—one's beliefs and actions, both individually and as they relate to social movements and causes. Such arguments should employ all relevant evidentiary methods available, including empirical and sociological analysis. As such, the audience for this book is *anyone* interested in ethics, advocacy, and the relation between them, especially, though not exclusively, within a university and social context in the United States.

The chapters constellate around four themes. The first set identifies and defends theoretical foundations for defining "ethics" and "advocacy" and offers conceptual platforms to explain how the two should be related in both academic and non-academic contexts. For example, William Schweiker, co-editor, argues in "The Rhetorics of Ethics: To Convince the Mind and Move the Heart" that the ethics/advocacy debate requires "reconsider[ing] and theologically rehabilitat[ing] a nuanced account of the rhetoric of ethics with respect to basic human powers (the ability to speak, to act, to feel, and to think) and the needs they entail within actual situations." Recognizing that there is no such thing as a "non-moral" space to existence, Schweiker identifies four dominant rhetorical forms, each of which is necessary to stipulate the proper relationship between ethics and advocacy: the casuistic, the explanatory, the narratival, and the horatory. After analyzing each form in depth, Schweiker concludes that the most cogent way to unite the disparate strands of moral rhetoric and overcome their respective limitations—which is necessary for establishing the proper mutual orientation between ethics and advocacy—is to recognize that "the use of rhetorics . . . must be underwritten, backed, by a claim about how life can and should be understood *coram deo*."

In the following chapter, "Retrieving (Meta)Ethics in an Age of Advocacy," Petrusek draws on work by William Schweiker in the methodology of ethics to argue that the fundamental distinction between "doing ethics" and "doing advocacy" lies in the presence, or absence, of meta-ethical analysis. One of the essential dimensions of specifically *ethical* inquiry—indeed, the most fundamental—is addressing the question, "Is this ethical theory *true*?" In contrast, advocacy, by definition, must *presume* the truth of its cause in order to do the work of implementing a particular moral point of view. There is, therefore, "a categorical difference between *making* a moral argument (or formulating a viewpoint) and *expressing* a moral position (or enacting a viewpoint)." The chapter concludes by critiquing a conceptual confusion between the proper roles of ethics and advocacy that occurs in one branch of contemporary "liberative ethics."

Per Sundman, in his chapter, "Who Am I to Speak?: On Advocacy, Ethics, and Social Critique," closely examines the definition of ethics in relationship to what he identifies as "advocacy," "agitation," and "politics," each of which is conceptually distinct from the others. Sundman argues that ethics is not reducible to any of these categories and reaffirms the centrality of seeking truth in ethical analysis, writing, "Truth and validity need to be established, especially if the ethicist claims that at least some agents sometimes have reasons to adjust their behavior in accord with her or his ideas." Sundman also emphasizes, however, that advocacy has a vital role in improving ethical inquiry. He concludes by drawing on the resources of critical theory, particularly its use, in his words, of the emancipatory possibilities of "ordinary language" to engage moral questions. He argues that the path forward in the debate is to "turn to ordinary language for an explication of important properties of moral concepts revealed in 'ordinary use.'"

The next set of chapters in the volume focus on building normative models for relating ethics and advocacy within the discipline of Christian ethics more specifically, especially in light of the "social gospel" tradition. Another co-editor, Douglas Ottati, for example, draws on the thought of Martin Luther King Jr. and John Lewis—both of whom Ottati categorizes as models of "reflective Christian advocates"—to provide a paradigm for how Christian ethics and advocacy can and should mutually inform and be disposed to each other. As he writes, "Good Christian advocacy intermingles with critical, ethical, and theological reflections, and good Christian ethics is practically disposing."

Gary Dorrien takes a similar approach in his chapter, "Social Ethics for Social Justice: The Legacies of the Social Gospel and a Case for Idealistic Discontent." Offering a deep dive into the history of the diverse strands of the social gospel movement, Dorrien focuses on the thought of three thinkers outside of his own "post-Kantian, democratic socialist, liberationist perspective"—Unitarian Francis Greenwood Peabody, Catholic Fr. John Ryan, and Protestant Reinhold Niebuhr—to argue for a position of "idealistic discontent." This disposition to Christian ethics and Christian social advocacy takes seriously the sharp limitations sin imposes on the possibility of authentic moral progress in history while, nevertheless, maintaining a commitment to struggle for justice in the name of embracing the Christian love ethic. That ethic, he argues, "is always the point, the motive, and the end [of ethics], even when it lacks a concrete meaning."

Stanley Hauerwas, in turn, agrees with dimensions of Ottati's and Dorrien's positions while rejecting others. He writes, "the assumption that there is a tension between Christian ethics as a discipline and advocacy for just causes betrays the history of Christian ethics." Hauerwas proffers his own account of the social gospel movement and its influence on the relationship between Christian ethics and Christian social advocacy by focusing on three institutional centers of theological reflection and their differing view on how theology should relate to public advocacy: Union Theological Seminary, Harvard University, and Yale University (where Hauerwas was educated). Offering critique of all three schools' approaches, Hauerwas concludes that the issue, for him, is not ultimately how Christian ethics should relate to the work of advocacy per se, but, rather, how the "church" should exist in the world, especially when taking into account that an adequate Christology rejects reducing Jesus Christ to a "representative of a liberation movement."

In the section's final chapter, Rebekah Miles explores the limitations of ethical inquiry in persuading others in "Searching for the Center that Cannot Hold: Mediating Advocacy and Christian Ethics." Miles draws on her experience advocating for the ordination of individuals in same-sex marriages as pastors in the United Methodist Church to argue that moral argument itself can, and does, often fail to persuade those with opposing points of view. After offering a history of recent developments in Christian ethics, Miles examines how different forms of advocacy can help continue the conversation when moral argumentation, in her view, fails. However, such advocacy, she maintains, must always remain grounded in a respect for differing points of views. We can conclude, then, that one must engage different perspectives, and especially if these points of view engage each other.

The next group of chapters in the volume analyzes the relationship between ethics and advocacy through the lenses of particular moral issues. James Childress, for example, in his chapter, "Mediated Advocacy in Public Bioethics," draws on his long involvement in public bioethics, which he defines as "doing bioethics with primary attention to public policy." He argues that the paradigm of "mediated advocacy" through the institution of a "public bioethics body" (PBB) provides an apt model for relating ethics and advocacy. In addition to offering an expansive historical and conceptual account of the development of mediated advocacy as a form of moral deliberation in bioethics, Childress concludes by explaining how a board created to develop guidelines for a just allocation of COVID-19 vaccines, on which Childress served, fittingly captures the goals of mediated advocacy in practice.

Peter Paris, in turn, examines the conditions for effective advocacy in combatting racism as they relate to ethical inquiry in his chapter, "The Efficacy of Advocacy." Embedded within a historical analysis of the roots of racism in the United States and the long struggle to overcome it, Paris highlights the form of Christianity practiced among slaves, which emphasized the "parenthood of God and the kinship of all people" as establishing the conceptual foundation for the fight for recognition of the full humanity of African Americans. Later identifying what he calls the "separatist" and "inclusivist" traditions of the fight for equality, Paris concludes that, though distinct movements, both remain necessary for racial advocacy to "preserve the health and expansion of what has been achieved thus far" while marking paths for continued progress.

Rubén Rosario Rodríguez, in the following chapter, examines the interplay of ethics and advocacy for the issue of abortion in "Beyond Binary Moral and Political Activism on Abortion." Noting that "no issue highlights the blurring of lines between the theoretical and the practical—ethics and advocacy—more clearly than the battle over abortion," Rodríguez employs central themes in liberation theology to show how Christian ethical reflection provides an alternative to partisan activism. Employing the teachings of Jesus as a model for framing and addressing the issue, Rodríguez calls for a renewed commitment by both pro-choice and pro-life advocates, Christian and non-Christian, to "move forward with great humility and compassion to make life 'more human' by doing as *little* harm as possible while helping *everyone* whenever possible."

The final set of essays pivots from methodology and theory to the pedagogical issue, "What role, if any, should advocacy play in the classroom?" Darlene Fozard Weaver in her chapter, "Doing Ethics and Advocacy in Higher Education," addresses the question from a Catholic perspective. Taking into account the standpoints of faculty, students, administrators, church officials, and the wider public, Weaver lays out a program explicating how different constituents inside and outside the university can "foster the skills and dispositions needed for managing life together in a morally diverse world." In addition to paying close attention to power relations, especially between professors and students when professors are engaging the class in moral advocacy, Weaver emphasizes the fundamental role *virtue* must play in ensuring that advocacy and ethical analysis remain in the right balance. These virtues include the practice of love, wisdom, and solidarity, in addition to moral courage and the promotion of respect for a strong culture of academic freedom.

In "Teaching Is a Moral Advocacy," Marcia Riggs turns to examining how insights from Womanist theology can help reduce polarization in the classroom, the university community, and the culture more broadly. Decrying what she calls a "culture of absolutism," Riggs argues for relaxing the "binary between rationalism and relativism" and, instead, "to foster a continuum of ethical thinking and responses that we construct through our intercultural encounters with one another." In this sense, Riggs contends, the classroom should serve as a model for civic engagement among diverse peoples more generally.

In the final chapter, Harlan Beckley, another co-editor, employs his long experience founding and directing a poverty studies program at Washington and Lee University, which now includes a consortium of twenty-five institutions. He identifies pedagogical principles that productively regulate the combination of ethical analysis and advocacy in the classroom. In

"Ethics and Advocacy in Pedagogy: An Example in Poverty Studies," Beckley, while granting the essential need for experiential learning from those who are vulnerable, distinguishes the program's pedagogy from purely experiential forms of advocacy that accept, uncritically, perspectives from "the margins" as both descriptively and prescriptively normative. On the other hand, Beckley also argues how a shared commitment to advocacy in the limited but unambiguous sense of diminishing poverty fosters a space for constructive disagreement while benefiting students and poor communities alike. As Beckley writes, "The program is founded on the view that, in the long-run, informed and thoughtful citizens disagreeing will produce better results in diminishing poverty than a uniformity of views that follow faculty expectations."

While this volume, in the end, makes no claim for comprehensiveness in the ongoing debate between ethics and advocacy, it is the hope of the editors that these chapters, individually and read together, shed light on the fundamental questions involved. We also hope it becomes clear that, properly defined, ethics and advocacy—or thinking and acting, analyzing and organizing, making distinctions and making a difference—need not be seen as opposing or unrelated intellectual and moral activities. There is no inherent contradiction between being someone who is both a "scholar" and an "advocate," even if disagreement remains among the authors about whether the two can and should be hyphenated. Finally, and perhaps most importantly, it is our hope that the discourse in the following pages provides a model for how to preserve civility and engage in constructive disagreement, especially when passions run high. As *Christian* ethicists watchful of Jesus' frequent warnings to the hypocritical Pharisees, we hope, minimally, to have practiced what we preach.

—PART 1—

Theoretical Issues

THE RHETORICS OF ETHICS

To Convince the Mind and Move the Heart

William Schweiker

PURPOSE AND PRESUPPOSITIONS

THE PURPOSE OF THIS volume is to consider what relation, if any, moral advocacy, that is, the public expression and championing of a moral and/or political cause, has to ethics, that is, the critical inquiry into and assessment of moral and political beliefs, values, practices, and norms, in order to prescribe proper standards and courses of conduct. On first glance, this seems like a confused topic: ethics is, whatever else it is, a practical discipline and supposedly has its point and purpose in orienting human conduct; advocating for a moral or political cause necessarily includes reflection and so some strategy for defending the case as a just, right, and good one. What then is at issue?

Two things seem at issue. First, while there is a necessary connection between ethics and advocacy, it must be noted, sadly, that a good deal of current moral advocacy is mere sloganeering. Some cause and its popular slogans are sung in the streets or chanted on campuses. Cancel culture has become the fad *de jour* in many places around the world and on the internet. To be sure, protests, like the civil rights movement and others, lived on songs and slogans that helped to embolden the heart for the conflicts to be met. While essential to such movements, these slogans and songs do not provide the best insights into the nuance of our topic. Martin Luther King Jr.'s *Letter from a Birmingham Jail* or any one of his sermons—not to mention John Lewis or Malcolm X—are more subtle examples of moral rhetoric in the service of advocacy than are chants and slogans. And while space will

3

not allow a detailed rhetorical analysis of any one sermon or treatise, I take my cue from these forms of advocacy rather than the thin sloganeering that too often marks current discourse.[1]

Second, Matthew Petreusek, one of this book's editors, has argued that ethics and advocacy as moral discourse are related but ought to be distinguished: advocacy begins with the certainty of the truth of one's cause in order to prescribe some course of human conduct; ethics does not assume the truth of a cause, but must seek to validate it as a proper standard and orientation for conduct for living in truth.[2] Stated more baldly, advocates tell you what to believe and to do; ethics helps one to think about what one ought to be and to do. The issue is, and here readers will find disagreement among the authors of this volume, the degree of certainty one expects about basic ethical questions before advocacy begins. Typically, the advocate, as noted, begins with the truth and goodness of her or his convictions and then acts on them. The ethicist must question and validate claims to truth and justice. As will become evident, I am interested in ethics and rhetoric precisely because I do not believe that persuasion demands certainty, at least in matters of faith and morals. The moral and political life is always risky for us mortals.

Advocacy and ethics are intimately related and necessarily so, insofar as human beings are acting, thinking, feeling, and speaking beings. Yet, the distinction—not separation—between advocacy and ethics is pertinent in order to clarify two sides of moral action: the act of thinking and thoughtful action. Confusion arises, then, when the two are simply equated so that the moral crusader uninterested in moral argument carries the shield of ethics while the ethicist races to the streets resolute in the "truth" of her or his ideas and ideals. Sadly, this confusion in moral reflection and action is prevalent in the age of the massive public demonstrations (#MeToo; Black Lives Matter; Environmental Protests, etc.) with the effect of weakening or discarding ethical analysis or removing it from the actual affairs of life that is the real stuff of ethics.

On my account, if we consider the relation that can and ought to obtain between moral advocacy and ethical reflection, it is helpful to recount some history of rhetoric and morals. This is the case insofar as rhetoric is about the *persuasion* of actual persons to make some judgment or take some action. It is, we might say, the study of persuasive advocacy.[3]

1. See for instance Vail, "The 'Integrative' Rhetoric of Martin Luther King Jr.'s 'I Have a Dream' Speech"; Fulkerson, "The Public Letter as a Rhetorical Form"; Cone, *Martin & Malcolm & America*.

2. See Petrusek's chapter in this volume.

3. One must admit that some people advocate a cause even if it will never be persuasive. We can forego in this essay exploring the moral zealot.

Ethics is about *thinking* and *prescribing* how actual people ought to conduct their lives, personally and socially. As we consider the relation between rhetoric and ethics historically, I hope to show the current division between advocacy and ethics is invidious, wrongly drawn, and, furthermore, poorly practiced. My task in what follows is to reconsider and theologically rehabilitate a nuanced account of the rhetoric of ethics with respect to the basic human powers (the ability to speak, to act, to feel, and to think) and the needs they entail within actual situations.

This argument makes three claims that my argument, I hope, sustains. First, we are concerned with *actual* persons, rather than some idealized moral agent able to act in ways that escape the struggles and dilemmas of any real human situation. There is of course a specific conceptual place for abstraction and "ideal theory" within ethics, but it is not the whole of ethics. To proclaim, for instance, that "capitalism" should come to an end because of its moral failures, of which there are admittedly many, is a high-sounding moral proclamation of ideals rather than a plausible course of action for any single individual or community. And it makes sense within ethics at points to abstract from the particularities of persons in order to make some more general claim, say, about human rights. But, finally, we have to take human beings as they are, even as we think about how they ought to conduct their lives.

Second, this argument advances a picture of human beings, albeit in outlined form, that, I hope, is readily acceptable as a common sense picture of our lives. That is, I presuppose that human beings are creatures with the ability to speak, to act, to feel, and to think. Borrowing from and adding to ancient thinkers like Thomas Aquinas, we can call these the basic human powers.[4] Obviously, these powers, capabilities, or capacities (call them what you like) are intimately related and are always the expression of a whole person, not some distinct faculty: to speak is also to think and to act and even to feel; human feelings have cognitive weight that infuse actions, and often come to explicit linguistic articulation. Human beings think as embodied, feeling, sensing beings who must decide how to conduct their lives and negotiate them within some language community. And human action, as opposed to reflexes or natural events, is purposive and so thoughtfully

4. Thomas notes five powers in the soul, but for action he examines intellect, will, and passions of the soul. See Thomas Aquinas, *Summa Theologiae*, I:78–79. There are of course several positions in current thought focused on human capabilities, one thinks of the works of Martha Nussbaum, Paul Ricoeur's late work, Mary Midgley's many works, and others. It is not the purpose of this essay to sort through the differences among these positions. I simply note that my own argument focuses on human beings as moral agents and thus has naturalistic as well as a humanistic aspects cast within a Christian moral outlook and stance.

intentional, but also moved by desires, feelings, and needs, and is open to explanation to others and even to oneself. What is more, human powers are always exercised within some situation or environment: social, natural, imagined, or felt. If ethics and advocacy are human activities, which I take it they are, then we have to explore the relation among these most distinctively human powers.

The third claim of this essay is that there are distinctly theological reasons to explore the relation of rhetoric to ethics. Christian reflection on the orientation of life draws on various sources (the so-called Wesleyan quadrilateral: reason, Scripture, tradition, and experience) that are open to a variety of interpretations, but the task is always to discern and articulate how the Word and Will of God is known and to be followed within the structures of lived reality. For instance, the Word, as Karl Barth and many others would put it, takes three forms (Christ, Scripture, Proclamation) and, we can say with Aquinas, is the *logos* of the Godhead itself through whom all things are created.[5] Because *logos* means word, speech, and reason, Christian faith, then, is deeply rhetorical and hermeneutical in nature. It holds that the divine spirit is the force that activates truthful understanding and responsible action. Theology, as second order reflection, seeks to discern God's word and will within the structures of reality in order to teach, preach, and persuade people of its truth. We might even affirm, with George Steiner, "that any coherent account of the capacity of human speech to communicate meaning and feeling is, in the final analysis, underwritten by the assumption of God's presence."[6] Astonishing claim, indeed, but one that should be sustained in seeking the relations among rhetoric and ethics within Christian theology.

Not surprisingly, these three claims that back my argument and that I want to sustain can be found in thinkers who are often called "Christian Humanists," a title that I gladly accept.[7] But rather than debate titles, my suggestion in this essay, given these claims, is that if we mean by moral advocacy a collapse of any distinction between rhetoric and action, then it is too often conceptually vapid, and, conjointly, our ethics is argumentatively sterile when it no longer seeks to persuade people to a real course of action. The only path beyond this sad situation, I am arguing, is to reconsider and rehabilitate an account of the rhetoric of ethics with respect to the basic human powers and the needs they entail within actual situations. So, consider

---

5. Barth, *Church Dogmatics* I/1; Aquinas, *Summa Theologiae* I:1.

6. Steiner, *Real Presences*, 3.

7. See Schweiker, *Dust That Breathes*; Klemm and Schweiker, *Religion and the Human Future*.

first some history of thought, and that in hand, I will explore some different ways currently of configuring the rhetoric of ethics before ending with my own recommendation for a way forward. Obviously, I can only tell the history that I know, that being Western intellectual history. I am bold enough to believe that this tradition still holds valid resources for our theological and ethical thinking, even if it must withstand constant criticism.

SOME HISTORY OF RHETORIC AND ETHICS

For most of Western intellectual history, rhetoric was a constant companion of moral and political discourse.[8] To be sure, some ancients, like Plato, pitched a battle against rhetoric in the name of dialectic, or, more generally speaking, philosophy itself. Socrates sparred with the Sophists while Plato kept score. The charge was that the Sophists made the weaker argument appear stronger and thus nothing but grasping for political power and prestige. But the aim of philosophy, as Plato contends, should be the truth and what is good and beautiful. Yet insofar as philosophy was to be a way of life, at least with Socrates and those who followed him, it too had to persuade and move the reader/listener to right conduct.[9] Indeed, in Plato's attack on rhetoric in the *Gorgias*, it is, in the end, Socrates himself who is the true rhetor. Not surprisingly, it was Plato's student Aristotle who set the terms of rhetoric for centuries to come. We will need to return to his argument below.

Rhetoric was also important among early Christian and Jewish thinkers. Consider for instance the rhetorical power of the Hebrew Prophets, the Psalms, the epitome of Jesus' teaching in the so-called Sermon on the Mount, and Paul's epistles. The Church Fathers drew on virtually every form of Greek and Roman rhetoric—diatribes, apologies, epitomes, etc.—to make their case for Christian faith in the often-hostile social world of the Roman Empire. They assumed that their arguments would make sense to that hostile world, insofar as their interlocutors were themselves committed to reasoned discourse, to the *logos*. In the hands of the greatest late Hellenistic philosopher, Augustine, rhetorical form and biblical exegesis were put in the service of Christian caritas.[10] Indeed, his *De Doctrine Christiana* set the agenda for the structure and course of education well into the middle

---

8. The scholarship on this topic is enormous. I have found especially helpful Grassi, *Rhetoric as Philosophy*; Toulmin, *The Uses of Argument*; Perelman, *The Realm of Rhetoric*; and Jaeger, *Early Christianity and Greek Paideia*.

9. Hadot, *Philosophy as a Way of Life*.

10. See Stead, *Philosophy in Christian Antiquity*.

ages.[11] This text, as well as many others penned by Christian authors, relied heavily on the insights of formal rhetoric deployed most famously by Cicero in the courtroom, where talking and action meet before the law. All this is to say, the distinction between ethical reflection and moral advocacy, which today might be construed as a division or even hostility, does not find much ground in the ancient Western world other than in some versions of Platonism. Indeed, Plato himself distinguished between the knowledge associated with education (*paideia*) and *techne* as craft, like rhetoric.

If one looks to the rise of the great medieval universities supplanting the focus in the cathedral schools on Sacred Page, again rhetoric was basic to the *trivium*, along with grammar and logic in the so-called Liberal Arts, and linked to the *quadrivium* (arithmetic, astronomy, music, and geometry). To be sure, the high scholastics, like Thomas Aquinas, conceived of theology as both a *sapientia* and *scientia*, but the study of *Sacra Doctrina* presupposed and also crowned the study of the liberal arts.[12] Theology was Queen. And if one hopes to find the origins of the conflict between ethics and rhetoric with the breakdown of the medieval synthesis of faith and reason, one is again befuddled. The Protestant Reformers as well as Renaissance thinkers insisted on biblical interpretation and rhetoric against what for them was arid scholasticism. Phillip Melanchthon, Luther's great collaborator, the so-called Teacher of Germany and one father of Christian Humanism, revised educational practices in ways that fronted the study of rhetoric and translated Aristotle's *Rhetoric* as well as enjoined biblical study.[13] Erasmusian rhetoric is of course renowned even as many of his *Colloquies* were written for the study of rhetoric.[14] John Calvin was trained and steeped in the humanist and rhetorical traditions, especially of the works of Cicero. To be sure, by the sixteenth century, chairs in moral theology were founded in Catholic universities, and so the distinctions started to harden between theology, ethics (moral theology), biblical studies, canon law, and the liberal arts. Yet given the place of sermons, written and preached, among Protestant thinkers, Joseph Butler no less than John Wesley, Jonathan Edwards no less than other Puritan divines, the art of teaching and persuading remained basic to Christian reflection on the conduct of life.

During the European Enlightenment, things did and did not change even if, for many thinkers today, the Enlightenment is the cause of everything

---

11. See Schweiker, "The Saint and the Humanities." Also see the essays by W. Otten and A. Peperzak in the same volume.

12. For an insightful analysis, see Turner, *Thomas Aquinas.*

13. See Melanchton, *Orations on Philosophy and Education.*

14. See Martin, *Truth and Irony.*

wrong in the modern world. To be sure, the rise of modern natural science among Francis Bacon, Immanuel Kant, and others cast suspicion on any connection between rhetoric and truth. "Truth" should persuade, but the ability to persuade as such cannot be the definition of truth. To convince the mind should be sufficient to move the heart. Yet others, like Adam Smith and Lord Shaftesbury, with their concern for sensibility and taste, held contrary views. Likewise, Enlightened worries about factions and fanaticism among Voltaire, David Hume, and others sharpened and also defanged political and moral rhetoric and also debunked priest-craft and so religious rhetoric. Later, the stylistic flair of Friedrich Nietzsche as well as Karl Marx's dialectic sought not only to liberate the mind, but also to shape the conduct and moral outlooks beyond the suspicion of inherited beliefs.

Finally, despite the famous turn to "language analysis" in the twentieth century and the rise of so-called analytic moral philosophy that sought to examine moral discourse while banishing moral prescription from ethical philosophy, the connection been ethics and advocacy remained. Think of the nuanced reflections and fiery words of Martin Luther King Jr. or Malcolm X. Note as well the discourse of liberation thinkers, religious and non-religious. While often strained and too often neglected, the connection between ethical reflection and moral advocacy has been constant throughout Western history. Necessarily so: moral reflection devoid of action is empty; human action without reflection is directionless; talking without thinking is gibberish; thinking without talking is solitary at best, if it is possible at all.

In sum, the history just traced, no matter how brief or limited, makes it clear that rhetoric and ethics, for all of their antagonisms, need to be related. If ethics seeks to be a normative and prescriptive discipline, then it must be able to move people to act, and that is a rhetorical task. This is found in the formation of virtues and the education of conscience. And rhetoric, if it is to avoid sheer sophism or to be nothing but linguistic window dressing, must always be bound to ethical analysis and reflection. Of course, some have argued that thinking is utterly distinct from talking, acting, and feeling, and, therefore, can occupy the judge's seat on the labors of rhetoric and ethics. The transcendental "I" of the German Idealists or Pure Practical Reason could in fact unhinge the mind or brain from the complexities of actual life. It is doubtable, and cannot be argued here, that such claims to the supremacy of reason have little grip on actual human life where our thinking is ingredient within feeling, speaking, and acting. Pure reason is, of course, a noble idea and ideal, but it is one too distant, I judge, from human affairs to be a live human option on its own. The task of the moral life, on my account, is to live a life worthy of one's humanity and not to escape humanity!

Come what may, thinking, like acting, speaking, and feeling, is purposive and so driven by what people value, their interests, desires, and emotions. It is because of this profound insight that moral conflicts arise such that persuasion and reasoning are thereby needed, and ethics, it appears, is basic even to our claims about lived reality. That is, humanly speaking, there is no "non-moral" space to existence, no value-neutral environment for life. In more than a metaphorical sense, people with different moral outlooks and purposes inhabit different worlds of speaking and meaning.[15] Even Kant, the transcendental Idealist, knew that the vast majority of human knowing is found in experience and, what is more, moral philosophy, and so free and rational human action, is at the core of his thought.[16] Take it as given, then, that we need to consider the right relation for rhetoric and ethics, that is, talking to others and human conduct.

A TYPOLOGY OF CURRENT POSITIONS

The reflections on the history of thought above were meant to validate my contention that the connection between rhetoric and ethics is longstanding, if also contested. And we can stress that the study of rhetoric has always been crucial for Christian thinkers. This is especially the case with Christian Humanists. Why? Because we cannot escape our humanity and that humanity is manifest and concealed in what people do, say, feel, and think, or, put more generally, in history, society, and culture. Be that as it may, we need other means to explore the current debate. In order to do so, we have to reach back into history once again and develop a typology of positions apt for our time.

A deeper reach into the history of thought back to Aristotle's seminal work, *Rhetoric,* shows that for him rhetoric combines logic with the ethical branch of politics, and so the question of the human good. On his account, rhetoric is speaking that is both rational and directed to human action or conduct. It thereby links the basic human powers: thinking, acting, and speaking in relation to human emotions and feelings. Aristotle, like Plato, distinguishes acting from making, *praxis* from *techne*. He noted three kinds of appeals that can be made: to reason (*logos*), to the emotions of the

15. On this, see Schweiker, *Theological Ethics and Global Dynamics*; Abel, *Humanistic Pragmatism*.

16. It is interesting that even Kant, in *Critique of Practical Reason*, includes, under the heading of "method," reflection on moral education. While pure reason alone *ought* to motivate action, creatures such as us also need to be formed to live the moral life even if this cannot be taught in any usual sense.

audience (*pathos*), and to character (*ethos*) within three branches of rhetoric: (1) deliberative or political concerned with human aims for happiness; (2) juridical focused on the justice or injustice of a case; and (3) epideictic rhetoric focused on praise and blame.[17] And, further, the appropriate time *(kairos)* is at play in each kind of rhetoric. Of course, other distinctions were added through the centuries as well as the identification and analysis of rhetorical forms—say, irony or metaphor.

If we accept Aristotle's claim that rhetoric links logic and ethics with our felt sense of being in the world (imaginative or real worlds), then we can explore argumentative forms, the rhetoric tropes, in terms of how they construe a form of reflection with respect to the claims about reason, emotion, and moral matters.[18] In this light, there are four dominant rhetorical forms found in current ethics, what I will call (1) the casuistic, (2) the explanatory, (3) the narratival, and (4) the hortatory. There are, of course, different expressions of each of the types, and so no exhaustive account of any of them is possible in this essay. Likewise, other forms might need to be identified in a longer study.

Insofar as this is meant to be a typology, it seeks to illustrate options in current ethics on a spectrum that moves from an account of what Stephen Toulmin called the non-formal logic of moral judgment (casuistic) to that which is strictly rhetorical in purpose (hortatory). Between these are those rhetorical forms that seek a root metaphor for the coherence of moral inquiry and those that try to give an account of the formation of character or *ethos* (narrative). These types (root metaphor of coherence and narrative) do not map easily onto Aristotle's three branches of rhetoric, although those branches could be used to examine specific arguments about a specific topic within the types noted. Likewise, one could trace appeals to *logos, pathos*, and *ethos* in specific arguments. I will merely note some of those connections. A more detailed analysis is beyond the task of this essay. What matters for the present argument is the way each type links a linguistic *form* with a claim about moral *reason* with respect to articulating a moral argument

17. See Rhetoric. I.3, 1358a37: "The kinds of Rhetoric are three in number, corresponding to the three kinds of hearers. For every speech is composed of three parts: the speaker, the subject of which he treats, and the person to whom it is addressed, I mean the hearer, to whom the end or object of the speech refers."

18. For important discussions, See Aiken, *Reason and Conduct*. Aiken isolates levels of moral discourse: expressive-evocative (near our ideas about advocacy), moral, ethical, and post-ethics. James M. Gustafson, partly drawing on Aiken isolated forms of moral discourse: ethical, prophetic (near our advocacy), narrative, and public policy. See Gustafson, *Intersections*; Weaver, *The Ethics of Rhetoric*. More recently, see Bucar, *Creative Conformity*.

or judgment meant to persuade someone about the orientation of morally responsible conduct.

Casuistic Rhetoric

One of the most explicit relations between rhetoric and ethics in recent thought is the connection drawn between Stephen Toulmin's non-formal logic and the tradition of moral casuistry in Toulmin and Albert Jonsen's famous *Abuse of Casuistry*.[19] Their task in that book was to redeem casuistry from the criticism leveled by René Pascal in his *Provincial Letters*. Toulmin had already sounded the need for attention to real-life ethical judgments and forms of argument over the aspirations of ideal theory in his famous essay, "How Medicine Saved the Life of Ethics."[20] His reflections arise out of work on a medical ethics board. Toulmin's point, developed at greater length in *The Abuse of Casuistry*, was that if reflection focuses, as too much ethics does, on matters of fundamental values or norms, agreement becomes almost impossible among people facing actual medical cases; each will have her or his own basic moral commitments to defend. Careful attention to an actual case provides the occasion to find some points of agreement in prescribing courses of action and treatment. *The Abuse of Casuistry* does a history of case ethics and its connection with rhetoric and the non-formal logic of such reasoning, formal logic being reserved for, say, mathematics.

Adduced from reflection on the centuries of casuistic thinking, especially in Catholic thought, and Toulmin's own work on argument, Jonsen and Toulmin set forth a casuistic method of reasoning. Using the terminology of Toulmin's earlier work, an argument starts with a *claim* that requires some *grounds* in facts or data while making the connection between grounds and claim by means of a *warrant* that can also draw on further *backings*. Additionally, the argument can provide *qualifiers* for when the claim might not be supportable as well as rebuttals of attempts to discount the claim.

The task here is not to examine the details of this analysis of argument, but, rather, to note, as Aristotle did, the connection between *logos*, in this case a logic of argument, and ethics, and so debates about values and conduct, is found in rhetoric. This continued Toulmin's criticism of formal logic in ethics, say, the famous practical syllogism, as too removed from actual life and the fact that we normally do not reason about life situations in deductive ways. Rather, people generally reason inductively from some claim present to its grounds, etc. Further, Toulmin and Jonsen were at pains

19. Jonsen and Toulmin, *The Abuse of Casuistry.*
20. Toulmin, "How Medicine Saved the Life of Ethics."

to avoid naïve moral relativism. It is not the case that moral disagreement will devolve into a war of words and the shouting of slogans. It is possible, on their model, to examine the elements of an argument to see if, in fact, it is or ought to be persuasive. In this way, ethics contributes to rhetoric, or even advocacy, by providing a structure of rational, if not formal, argument, whereas rhetoric indicates the onus on moral claims to be persuasive within complex and shifting situations.

In a word, *The Abuse of Casuistry* and Toulmin's other works advances the debate about advocacy and ethics by providing an account of the logic of persuasive arguments within a commitment to address actual people in actual situations. It avoids not only relativism but also forms of reasoning in ethics and, especially, moral philosophy that are, or seem to be, removed from human affairs. The return of attention to casuistry has been a boon for ethics, and especially applied ethics.[21] *The Abuse of Casuistry* adds to the discussion that the resources of some or other tradition, religious or not, are used to supply claims and backings. Given the fact that casuistry, as Jonsen and Toulmin rightly note, works within and helps develop traditions of moral reasoning, it is not surprising that this kind of ethics thrives in religious communities with strong legal traditions, such as is found within Catholicism, Judaism, and Islam, where law, its application, and authoritative interpretations can supply claims, grounds, and backing in the development of those traditions. What is not clear is how the return of casuistry, understood in this broad sense, provides new constructive theological reflection. We will return to this issue below.

Hortatory Rhetoric

If casuistic rhetoric tends to focus on *logos*, and so a reasoned means to persuade the audience of the rightness of a judgment, then hortatory rhetoric expresses *pathos* and seeks to persuade by moving the interlocutor to action. To be sure, each of these forms of moral rhetoric address the other foci of rhetoric (*kairos* and *ethos*), despite their specific concerns. Some years ago, James M. Gustafson identified four forms of moral discourse in medical ethics, what he called the ethical, the prophetic, the narrative, and the policy discourse.[22] Prophetic discourse, as he notes, entails indictment and

---

21. One need only scan the works of current ethicists like Richard B. Miller, Daniel Sulmasy, Sarah Fredericks, Dawn Nothwehr, Maura Ryan, and those who labor in business, environmental, and legal ethics to see the current impact of such thinking.

22. Gustafson, *Intersections,* ch. 2: "Moral Discourse about Medicine." This chapter was originally published in *The Journal of Medicine and Philosophy.*

also utopian elements often but not always found in the larger category of hortatory rhetoric (e.g., sermons, letters), as I am calling it. The concern, again, is to move people to act by arousing moral *pathos* and connecting this to the character of the agent (*ethos*). If one is a just person, then, all things being equal, in this situation of injustice, one must act for the victims of injustice. Various protests movements and liberation causes rely on hortatory discourse that can, but need not, elide the work of ethical reflection and argument.

Within the work of current Christian ethics, a myriad of forms of liberationist thought (Black, Womanist, LGBTQI+, Feminist, Catholic, Latinx, Asian-American, etc.) employ hortatory rhetoric. It might not be too much to say that, in terms of general theological orientation, liberation is the central category for the majority of people working in Christian ethics today, at least in the USA. Holding fast to a preferential option for the oppressed, this strand of ethics seeks not to determine the validity of that orientation; it is grounded in appeals to the Bible and experience. Rather, the task of "ethics" is to isolate and criticize various forms of oppression, provide strategies to overcome them, labor with those in situations of oppression, and convert or embolden people to see and respond to the situation of oppression. Hortatory ethics, in its liberationist form, must be issued from the perspective of the oppressed since, it is argued, the oppressed have a clearer view of structures of oppression than those in positions of domination and power. Yet the rhetorical appeal to others is also to *ethos* in the sense that the question becomes: Whose side are you on, the oppressed or the oppressor? The task is to provide some diagnosis (so, a form of *logos*) while emboldening people to struggle for liberation by an appeal to their emotions and desires.

Hortatory rhetoric has contributed to ethics in some ways. Within Catholic social thought the triad "see, judge, act" has been used to demarcate related but distinct moments in reflection. Each moment is open, of course, to considerable clarification and elaboration. But even of these moments of reflection are nestled with commitments and strategies of liberation that are accepted as true prior to and outside of seeing, judging, and acting. Many, if not most, liberationist thinkers adopt something like this model of reflection. And they argue, additionally, for the reflexive nature of the process such that action for liberation affords better perception (seeing) of systemic structures of oppression and also informs judgments about conduct. At issue ethically is whether or not the reflexive structure of see, judge, and act can or will ever invalidate the initial commitment, religious or otherwise, to the struggle for liberation.

If *casuistic rhetoric* demarks this typology's closest relative to ethics as such, the *hortatory rhetoric* marks its near opposite on the other end of our typology. It is, we can see, closest to pure advocacy insofar as an agent's basic convictions are neither tried nor (in)validated. The contribution it makes to ethics is in exploring the aspects (see, judge, and act) rooted in human powers and important for motivating actual conduct. Yet, one can also see how hortatory discourse might contribute to the development of a moral tradition, as it certainly has in Christian thought, in ways that could contribute to casuistry. Similarly, the casuist might bring precision to each moment of see, judge, and act, and also provide warrants and backings for judgments about liberating actions. This is merely to say that this typology, like any typology, is not analytically tidy; positions do and must interrelate with others in the typology.

Explanatory Rhetoric

If one returns to the connection between logic and rhetoric, much like casuistic thought, but now with an eye to what have been called "root metaphors," then one can isolate another type of the rhetoric of ethics. As Kaoru Yamamoto has helpfully noted, a "root metaphor is the comprehensive, organizing analogy that helps in making sense of experiences, interpreting the world, and defining the meaning of life."[23] Rather than focusing on the logic of moral argument, *explanatory rhetoric*, as we call it, seeks to provide a more or less comprehensive account of the moral life itself by isolating a specific metaphor judged to be distinctly illuminative and explanatory of the meaning of life.

Metaphors, and also human understanding, have a specific "as structure."[24] That is, a metaphor indicates something *as* something else: my love is like a rose, to use a trite example. More specifically, a metaphor, as a rhetorical trope, creates meaning through impertinent predication, as Paul Ricoeur notes.[25] I come to see and understand the meaning of love *as* or *like* a rose, even if, literally speaking, that is not the case. This makes metaphor (or analogy, to use the logical form) basic to human understanding. That is, a metaphor or analogy enables one to grasp similarities in differences without eliding either the similarity or the difference.

What is the meaning of our lives as moral beings? H. Richard Niebuhr, in *The Responsible Self*, famously argued that three basic synecdoches have

23. Yamamoto, *To Clever for Our Own Good*, 92. Also see Midgley, *The Myths We Live By*; Bellah, *Religion in Human Evolution*.

24. On the "as structure" of human understanding see Hans-Georg Gadamer, *Truth and Method*.

25. Ricoeur, *The Rule of Metaphor*.

been used in the history of thought to depict the moral life: human life as making of character (*homo faber*); human life under law (*homo politicus*); and the human as responder (*homo dialogicus*).[26] One could note how these are related to types of rhetoric, which Niebuhr does not do. For him, the human as responder seeks the fitting response (*kathekon*, from the Stoics for "proper action") is the best image of human life. His point was to argue that seeing human life as a response to actions on one as also God's action is the best account of the meaning of the moral life.

Niebuhr's work has influence generations of Christian ethicists in the USA, many, like this author, represented in the present volume. While true, many of those influenced by him have provided different interpretations of the meaning of the moral life and the structure of ethics. One prominent example, already mentioned, is the work of James M. Gustafson. He formulates the basic ethical question as: "What is God enabling and requiring you to be and to do?"[27] Given a theocentric piety, Gustafson argues that one can reverently state that "nature is God," a theological affirmation that backs a naturalistic ethical position. Given that outlook, one must engage other disciplines, including the natural sciences, in order to discern what God is enabling and requiring. How to do so?

Gustafson draws on the metaphor of "intersections" and also participation. The idea is that the moral and religious life—and so human existence—can be seen *as* an intersection where multiple forms of thought and knowledge meet, must be coordinated, and can inform how one ought to responsibly act as a participant in the dynamics of reality. This means, in ways few other theologians or ethicists admit, that new knowledge from, say, biology or history can radically challenge basic assumptions, beliefs, and values. In fact, one's basic ideas about God and God's will can be changed or at least amended given relevant knowledge. The focus, again, is on *logos*, but now with respect to how one construes the world and not primarily the non-formal logic of moral argument. Equally important, one's character (*ethos*) and with it one's piety must be transformed into a theocentric perspective, and this piety is not merely a rational conviction, but also a matter of one's affections and sensibilities (*pathos*). A moral judgment flows from a process of discernment, an informed intuition, about what to be and to do.

Partly influenced by Toulmin's and Aitken's works noted before, Gustafson outlines the elements of discernment, especially in volume 2 of *Ethics from a Theocentric Perspective*, which includes points to consider, boundary

26. Niebuhr, *The Responsible Self*.

27. In addition to his *Intersections* (see n. 22 above), see *Ethics from a Theocentric Perspective*.

conditions, presumptions, and general rules within some community of faith and discourse. Discernment is how one lives morally and religiously within intersections. Most profoundly, his account construes a human being "as a participant in the patterns and processes of interdependent of life . . ."[28] Thus to interpret or explain human existence *as* a participant in life requires, so the argument goes, the non-formal logic and procedure of discernment in moral reasoning and a construal of ethics in terms of intersections. And all of this account is underwritten by a theocentric piety and perspective.

There are others who also seek to articulate an ethics as an interpretation of human moral being. One thinks of Catholic ethicist Lisa Sowele Cahill's use of the Wesleyan quadrilateral to give an account of sex, but also of war and medicine. H. R. Niebuhr scholar, Douglas Ottati has written a landmark theology for liberal Protestantism that gives a complex picture of human belief and action. One could also follow the new discourse among race theorists on "intersectionality" in order to explore the overlapping and interwoven character of human identities. Other metaphors are thereby possible, say, the human as thrown project (Martin Heidegger), having an ultimate concern (Paul Tillich), facing a crises of decision (Rudolf Bultmann), but also work in Black Theology (Dwight Hopkins) and Feminist Theology (Kristine Culp). The point is that one of the rhetorics of ethics uses root metaphors "in making sense of experiences, interpreting the world, and defining the meaning of life" that is also developed in accordance with some account of moral thinking and judgment.[29] Whether one speaks of discernment, an informed intuition, or practical wisdom, explanatory rhetoric can back casuistic thinking to address concrete moral problems.

Narrative Rhetoric

Also located between the extremes of our typology and yet closer to the rhetoric of advocacy is the turn to narrative in theology and ethics. These thinkers focus on the formation of moral character (*ethos*) by drawing on virtue ethics, but they situate the moral life within some community and the narratives, stories, or history that forms the community and which it bears through time. Yet narrative, as we will see, has also been given expression by thinkers seeking to understand and interpret human being in time and therefore has been adopted by thinkers with purely philosophical concerns.

28. Gustafson, *Ethics for a Theocentric Perspective*, 2:279. See also Gustafson, "Participation," with a response by William Schweiker. Margaret Farley also has a response to Gustafson's essay.

29. Yamamoto, *To Clever for Our Own Good*, 92.

Realizing the ubiquity of narrative on the current intellectual scenes, this type will also be explored through exemplary thinkers.

No doubt the most widely known theologian who adopts narrative in Christian ethics is Stanley Hauerwas, also represented in this volume. Hauerwas has long argued that if ethics is to be theological, then it must be focused on a community, the church, that is formed to proclaim and live out the story of God's action in Jesus Christ. In this sense, as he has argued, the church does not have a social ethics; rather, it *is* a social ethic.[30] Thus a specific rhetorical form (narrative) is basic to the identity and action of the church and of human beings, as well. This claim immediately confronts Hauerwas with ethical and theological problems.

The moral problem is that human beings inhabit multiple narratives (e.g., I am white, a university professor, father, American, lover of soccer, Christian, etc.), and the Bible itself is open to different interpretations about its central "story." If, as a professing Christian, I nevertheless let the story of, say, America shape my character, then I have forsaken Christ and have been formed by a social collective that can order me to die and kill for it. Communities and persons must then strive to be centrally formed by one overarching story rather than negotiating diverse narratives. Indeed, so powerful is the political narrative that it is not clear, unless there is a counter narrative like the church's, that war should ever be eliminated since wars and their histories are how we identify ourselves and form our values.[31] The story of Christ is to form Christian identity and constitute a community, a *polis*, capable of living out an alternate world that in fact identifies the real character of the state as a realm of violence and war. This is accomplished, Hauerwas argues, when Christians realize that because of Christ's life and teaching, they need not fear death or the capacity of that fear to motivate the endless quest to be in control. Yet in order to realize this fact, Christians must form those virtues necessary to proclaim and inhabit Christ's story. In terms of ethical argument and judgment, then, one draws from the story of Christ in order to make the distinctions between the church and the "World." The church is to primarily a servant community dedicated to peaceableness within a violent and oppressive "World."[32]

---

30. See, for instance, Hauerwas, *The Peaceable Kingdom*.

31. Hauerwas, *Should War Be Eliminated?* For a powerful example, see Sledge, *With the Old Breed*.

32. I put "World" in scare quotes to indicate that it is a theological and not geo-graphical concept. For Hauerwas, the world is primarily that domain of reality in oppo-sition to God. There are, however, other understandings of world in Christian thought, say, as that reality that Christ died to save.

The theological problem is a subtler one, and it is why, more precisely, that church rather than narrative is basic to Hauerwas' theology and ethics. That is, Hauerwas *does not* seek to develop a *theory* of narrative because to do so would be to submit Christ and God to a rhetorical form rather than focusing on the gospel itself, the proclamation of God's work in Christ. While narrative is indeed basic to the ethical stance, it is not normatively basic. God in Christ forming the church is basic and therefore Christian character is always oriented to proclaiming the gospel in word and deed. In this sense, the church is defined by its advocacy, and any strong separation between ethics and advocacy is simply misguided.[33]

There are other thinkers who have developed theories of narrative, none so subtle as the work of the late Paul Ricoeur. Having explored symbol, metaphor, and utopia in other works, his three-volume *Time and Narrative* develops an account of narrative to explain the formation and reformation of human character (*ethos*) in history.[34] Ricoeur contends that human beings have a dual orientation in time: towards death as the natural end of life insofar as we are biological beings, and also towards an imagined eternity given our capacity for thought, for *logos*. Narrative, much like other symbolic forms, thereby links meaningfully *logos* and *bios*. This prefigured dual orientation becomes configured in narrative through emplotment that makes possible the use of ancient stories, like the gospel, or fictive works, say, utopian ones, to provide meaning to the human experience of time and to shape character. The act of understanding a narrative reconfigures the life of the one understanding and thereby opens new possibilities for action. These possibilities constitute what Ricoeur calls the "world in front of the text" which manifests the power of language and understanding to escape the transience of mundane time.[35]

Paul Ricoeur has influenced many theologians such as David Tracy, Mark Wallace, David Klemm, K. J. Vanhoozer, Don S. Browning, and the author of this essay, among others. His later works, like *Oneself as Another*, has also had considerable impact on religious and philosophical ethics.[36] Distinct from thinkers like Hauerwas, Ricoeur's works provide a broad hermeneutical framework for examining the meaning and truth of religious discourse. This means that while narrative is the distinctive rhetorical form

33. On this point, see Hauerwas essay in the present volume.

34. Ricoeur, *Time and Narrative*.

35. Ricoeur, like Christian theologians, uses the concept "world" in the hermeneutical sense meaning any defined domain of meaning. Accordingly, we can, and in fact do, live in many worlds. See Schweiker, *Theological Ethics and Global Dynamics*.

36. See Ricoeur, *Oneself as Another*. Also see Wall et al., *Paul Ricoeur and Contemporary Moral Thought*.

for shaping moral and religious character, the theological ethicist can also draw on Ricoeur's work to explore symbol and metaphor for the sake of ethical reflection and moral advocacy. In terms of the topic of this essay, the force of Ricoeur's position is that any claim to meaning, any linguistic or non-linguist act of signification, proposes a "world," or way of life, that anyone might decide to inhabit. In this sense, any strict distinction, and certainly any separation, between reflection and advocacy is impossible to sustain because of how meaning is produced and received. In the same way, absolute certainty in moral matters is beyond the ilk of human beings who, at best, Ricoeur argues in his late work, must use practical wisdom (*phronesis*), along with recognition of duties and life goods, to navigate life's challenges. In this way, "narrative rhetoric" focuses on the formation of *ethos* and is open to casuistic thinking in the development of practical wisdom. It also links ethical reflection and moral rhetoric.

The Rhetorics of Ethics

The typology just developed clarifies diverse ways thinkers relate and also distinguish ethical reflection from advocacy. However, insofar as ethics is a practical discipline, the struggle to become good and not just know the good (as Aristotle put it), the *distinction* between reflection and advocacy ought never become a *separation*. By exploring the various rhetorics used by theologians and philosophers working in ethics, we have seen distinctive rhetorical emphases: casuistry with *logos*; hortatory with *pathos*; explanatory focused on *logos* and *ethos*; and narrative with *ethos* and *kairos*. But these are mere emphases since any rhetoric, to be persuasive, must address each of these foci. On that score, if no other, Aristotle was right. Given this, any ethics in order to be fully practical can draw on all of these diverse rhetorics. And it does so once we realize that each contributes, in distinctive ways, to the formation of practical wisdom whether in casuistic form or not. One seeks to convince the mind and to move the heart.

A WAY FORWARD?

On my understanding, "theological ethics is a way of analyzing and articulating the lived structure of reality in order to provide orientation and guidance for human life. Its distinct character," I have written elsewhere, "is that reality and human life are understood from a theological perspective, existing before God."[37] Given that perspective, the use of the rhetorics explored above, or any other rhetoric for that matter, must be underwritten, backed, by a claim about how life can and should be understood *coram Deo*. I noted before that my argument unfolds within the distinctive, if not unique, powers of human beings, namely, to think, speak, feel, and act that interact in complex ways. I have also tried to show how rhetoric, linking *logos* and ethics, considers these powers in the struggle for persuasion. For instance, if I can show that a specific root metaphor enables one to analyze and articulate the actual structures of life reality, I might be able to persuade one in the orientation and guidance of life. And the same could be said about the other types of rhetoric explored above. The greater adequacy, and so the greater truth of a commitment, depends on which form of reflection and persuasion is not only coherent, but also enables us to understand more completely and better our moral plight.

Again, what about a distinctively theological perspective in ethics?[38] We have seen appeals to a living tradition of moral reasoning to ground a theological claim (casuistic rhetoric), the conviction about God's liberation of the oppressed (hortatory rhetoric), a root metaphor of participation or, to note another, ultimate concern (explanatory rhetoric) and also narrative either forming the church or agent's character (narrative rhetoric). Each of these rhetorics is thereby funded by a specific theological or philosophical outlook. And what about this argument itself?

Recall George Steiner's remarkable claim. Any "coherent account of the capacity of human speech to communicate meaning and feeling is, in the final analysis, underwritten by the assumption of God's presence."[39] Theologically, this must mean that any discourse about moral matters that in fact communicates in ways that convince the mind and move the heart assumes God's presence. Traditionally, this convicting presence—convicting both in the sense of exposing and judging one's sin, but also in securing in the heart a living conviction of the divine reality—is the work of the Holy Spirit, what we might call the divine rhetor. Yet this means, crucially, that theological ethics has another task unacknowledged in philosophical ethics. A theologian must also discern the spirits, as it were, in order to differentiate the true Spirit of God at work against the many wrongful, unjust, and irresponsible spirits vying for people's lives. In other words, a genuinely *theological* ethics

---

37. Schweiker, *Theological Ethics and Global Dynamics*, xxi.

38. There is a mountain of work on this general topic, but see Pelikan, *Divine Rhetoric*. Interestingly, John Wesley also argued that the sum of Christ's message and the order of Christian life is to be found in the so-called Sermon on the Mount.

39. Steiner, *Real Presences*.

seeks to analyze and articulate the presence of the divine Spirit within the structures of lived reality, providing orientation and guidance in life.

What is the criterion for judging that God is indeed present in the midst of the moral challenges of our lives? Is it the peaceable church, God's act of liberation, the wisdom of a tradition, or nature reverentially construed? To be sure, theologians will look to experience, Scripture, history, and rational inquiry in order to carry out that work of wisdom. But the criterion of God's presence must be the glory of God, as theologians through the ages have argued. But what is the glory of God? In short: *"Gloria Dei est vivens homo,"* as Saint Irenaeus put it. Of course, no human, excepting Christ, is fully alive now insofar as our lives are strung between death and hope, between goodness and happiness, between mundane time and the vision of God. Yet whatever does not respect nor enhance the integrity of life, that is, the concord or peace within the self with and for others, is not for Christians of the divine Spirit. Some Christians find this concord, this peace, in love, others in hope, still others in faith. But the criterion is that peace in the self and among people that is the union of righteousness and flourishing as the substance of things hoped for. And that hope is the divine presence needed in order to persuade and vivify responsible human action within the structures of lived reality.

BIBLIOGRAPHY

Abel, Ruben, ed. *Humanistic Pragmatism: The Philosophy of F. C. S. Schiller.* New York: Free Press, 1966.

Aiken, Henry David. *Reason and Conduct: New Bearings in Moral Philosophy.* New York: Alfred A. Knopf, 1962.

Aristotle. *Rhetoric.* London: Penguin Classics, 1992.

Bellah, Robert. *Religion in Human Evolution.* Cambridge: Harvard University Press, 2011.

Bucar, Elizabeth. *Creative Conformity: The Feminist Politics of U. S. Catholic and Iranian Shi'I Women.* Washington: Georgetown University Press, 2011.

Cone, James H. *Martin & Malcolm & America: A Dream or a Nightmare.* 20th Anniversary Edition. New York: Orbis, 2012.

Fulkerson, Richard P. "The Public Letter as a Rhetorical Form: Structure, Logic, and Style in King's 'Letter from Birmingham Jail.'" *Quarterly Journal of Speech* 65.2 (1979) 121–36.

Gadamer, Hans-Georg. *Truth and Method.* 2nd ed. Spring Valley: Crossroads, 1991.

Grassi, Ernesto. *Rhetoric as Philosophy: The Humanist Tradition.* Translated by J. M. Krois and A. Azodi. Carbondale: Southern Illinois University Press, 2001.

Gustafson, James M. *Ethics from a Theocentric Perspective.* 2 vols. Chicago: University of Chicago Press, 1981, 1984.

———. *Intersections: Science, Theology, and Ethics.* Cleveland: Pilgrim, 1996.

———. "Moral Discourse about Medicine: A Variety of Forms." *Journal of Medicine and Philosophy* 15 (1990) 125–42.

———. "Participation: A Religious Worldview, with a Response to 'Participation: A Religious Worldview' by William Schweiker." *Journal of Religious Ethics* 44.1 (Mar 2016) 176–85.

Hadot, Pierre. *Philosophy as a Way of Life*. Oxford: Wiley, 1995.

Hauerwas, Stanley. *The Peaceable Kingdom: A Primer in Christian Ethics*. Notre Dame: University of Notre Dame Press, 1991.

———. *Should War Be Eliminated: Philosophical and Theological Investigations*. Pierre Marquette Theology Lecture. Milwaukee: Marquette University Press, 1984.

Jaeger, Werner. *Early Christianity and Greek Paideia*. Cambridge: Belknap Harvard University Press, 1961.

Jonsen, Albert, and Stephen Toulmin. *The Abuse of Casuistry*. Berkeley: University of California Press, 1988.

Klemm, David E., and William Schweiker. *Religion and the Human Future: An Essay on Theological Humanism*. Oxford: Blackwell, 2008.

Martin, Terence J. *Truth and Irony: Philosophical Meditations on Erasmus*. Washington: Catholic University of America Press, 2015.

Melanchthon, Phillip. *Melanchthon: Orations on Philosophy and Education*. Edited by S. Kusukawa. Cambridge: Cambridge University Press, 1999.

Midgley, Mary. *The Myths We Live By*. New York: Routledge, 2003.

Niebuhr, H. Richard. *The Responsible Self: An Essay in Moral Philosophy*. Louisville: Westminster/John Knox Press, 1999.

Pelikan, Jaroslav. *Divine Rhetoric: The Sermon on the Mount as Message and as Model in Augustine, Chrysostom, and Luther*. Yonkers: St. Vladimir's Seminary Press, 2000.

Ricoeur, Paul. *Oneself as Another*. Translated by K. Blamey. Chicago: University of Chicago Press, 1992.

———. *The Rule of Metaphor: The Creation of Meaning in Language*. Toronto: University of Toronto Press, 1977.

———. *Time and Narrative*. 3 vols. Translated by K. Blamey and D. Pellauer. Chicago: University of Chicago Press, 1984.

Schweiker, William. *Dust That Breathes: Christian Faith and the New Humanisms*. Oxford: Wiley, 2010.

———. "The Saint and the Humanities." In *Augustine Our Contemporary: Examining the Self in Past and Present*, edited by W. Otten and S. Schreiner, 249–66. Notre Dame: University of Notre Dame Press, 2018.

———. *Theological Ethics and Global Dynamics: In the Time of Many Worlds*. Oxford: Blackwell, 2007.

Sledge, E. B. *With the Old Breed: Peleliu and Okinawa*. New York: Presidio, 2007.

Stead, Christopher. *Philosophy in Christian Antiquity*. Cambridge: Cambridge University Press, 1996.

Steiner, George. *Real Presences*. Chicago: University of Chicago Press, 1989.

Toulmin, Stephen. "How Medicine Saved the Life of Ethics." *Perspectives in Medicine and Biology* 25.4 (1982) 736–50.

———. *The Uses of Argument*. Updated ed. Cambridge: Cambridge University Press, 2003.

Turner, Denys. *Thomas Aquinas: A Portrait*. London: Yale University Press, 2013.

Vail, Mark. "The 'Integrative' Rhetoric of Martin Luther King Jr.'s 'I Have a Dream' Speech." *Rhetoric and Public Affairs* 9.1 (2006) 51–78.

Wall, John, et al., eds. *Paul Ricoeur and Contemporary Moral Thought*. New York: Routledge, 2002.

Weaver, Richard M. *The Ethics of Rhetoric*. Brattleboro: Echo Point, 2015.

Yamamoto, Yaoru. *To Clever for Our Own Good: Hidden Facets of Human Evolution*. Lanham: University Press of America, 2007.

RETRIEVING (META)ETHICS
IN AN AGE OF ADVOCACY

Matthew R. Petrusek

[P]rotest [has become] a distinctive moral feature of the modern age and
... *indignation* is a predominant moral emotion ... The self-assertive
shrillness of protest arises because the facts of incommensurability
ensure that protesters can never win an *argument*; the indignant self-
righteousness of protest arises because the facts of incommensurability
ensure equally that the protesters can never lose an argument either.
Hence the *utterance* of protest is characteristically addressed to those
who already *share* the protestors' premises ... This is not to say that
protest cannot be effective; it is to say that it cannot be *rationally* effective
and that its dominant modes of expression give evidence of a certain
perhaps unconscious awareness of this.

—ALASDAIR MACINTYRE, *AFTER VIRTUE*[1]

ALASDAIR MACINTYRE'S BITING ASSESSMENT of the state of moral argument
in the early 1980s—long before Twitter, Facebook, YouTube, and twenty-
four-hour news cycles—is remarkable in its prophetic durability: there may
be many words that aptly capture the signs of our times, but protest in the
key of "indignation" rightly stands among them. Stock definitions have

---

1. MacIntyre, *After Virtue*, 71.

limited usefulness, but the *Oxford English Dictionary's* description remains fitting: "Anger at what is regarded as unworthy or wrongful; wrath excited by a sense of wrong to oneself or, especially, to others, or by meanness, injustice, wickedness, or misconduct; righteous or dignified anger; the wrath of a superior."

The chief characteristic of indignation is anger, and *righteous* anger in particular. To be indignant is to be angry from above. One may be on the losing side of a conflict, weaker in a physical or political sense, but the presence of indignation indicates a certainty of one's *moral* supremacy— a dynamic the *OED* captures in its characterization of indignation as "the wrath of a superior." To be indignant is to know that the object of one's anger is not only mistaken but *bad*; that the ideas of one's opponents are not only misguided but *inconceivable*; that one's ideological rivals must not only be argued against but *destroyed*. Consequently, the indignant does not seek to persuade, to convince, or to reason with (the indignant, qua indignant, demands apologies, but would never write one); rather, she or he organizes, rallies, shouts, pressures, boycotts, shames, cancels, and, in some cases, fights. It is not that indignation signals the absence of reason per se; rather, as the quote from MacIntyre suggests, it is that indignation subordinates reason to the goal of political and cultural conquest. "The truth" of the indignant's cause is a given, a morally obvious and, therefore, undebatable fact. The only remaining questions are thus tactical in nature, questions of attaining power, not consensus.

A quick survey of recent history yields an abundance of high-profile instances of indignant protest in various public and semi-public spheres (e.g., university campuses). Indeed, indignant anger at its extremes has also not only likely contributed to an increase in hate crimes in the past years, as recorded by the FBI,[2] but also specifically to two nationally significant cases of murder and attempted murder: the 2017 death of Heather Heyer, killed by a Nazi sympathizer while protesting white nationalism in Charlottesville,[3] and, the same year, the attempted assassination of Republican members of Congress at a baseball field in Alexandria, targeted by a man who was part of a Facebook group called "Terminate the Republican Party."[4]

More recently, protests against police killings, racism, the policies and person of President Trump, and the results of the 2020 presidential election

2. See, for example, Berman, "Hate crimes in the United States increased last year, FBI says."

3. See, for example, Caron, "Heather Heyer, Charlottesville victim, is recalled as a 'strong woman.'"

4. See, for example, Pearce, "Virginia gunman hated Republicans, and was always in his 'little world.'"

have, at times, degenerated into looting, burning, and rioting, including the January 2021 breaching of the United States Capitol building. These nation-wide incidents have led to the loss of numerous human lives and property damage—which, it is important to remember, translates into severe, if not devastating, financial hardship for real people operating real businesses on tight margins—well exceeding a billion dollars.[5] It is all a chilling reminder of the frighteningly short distance between the indignant words, "You are not allowed to speak" (a tactic often called "no-platforming") to the indig-nant act, "You are not allowed to be."

These angry currents in civic life—which are also virulently active online and in network and cable television—prompt those of us who call ourselves ethicists and especially *Christian* ethicists, to ask how we should respond. The first impulse may be to take sides. To highlight the contem-porary prevalence of indignation is not to say that some of that indignation is not justified. Indeed, one does not have to look hard within the canons of Christian ethics to find support for the claim that anger is sometimes, well, *righteous.* Thomas Aquinas argues, for example, that "if one is angry in accordance with right reason, one's anger is deserving of praise."[6] And Martin Luther, in his colorful style, once remarked, "I have no better rem-edy than anger. If I want to write, pray, preach well, then I must be angry."[7] One can also point to Jesus' cleansing of the Temple, or to the prophetic denunciations of injustice and immorality in Old Testament prophets like Amos and Jeremiah, as paradigmatic examples of righteous indignation. It is important to recognize, in other words, that there are, indeed, events and situations in which it would be morally problematic *not* to experience anger.

Yet the insight in MacIntyre's characterization of indignation is not that all indignation is wrong or that moral responses should not include indignation. Rather, it is that *the expression of indignation is not an argu-ment* and, consequently, cannot by itself *convince* anyone that the viewpoint generating the indignation is rationally superior to any other point of view.[8]

5. See, for example, *Axios,* "Riots Cost Property Damage."

6. *ST* II–II.158.1

7. Luther, *What Luther Says,* 27.

8. It is important to note that, while I agree with MacIntyre's characterization of indignation and its prevalence in contemporary moral discourse, I do not endorse the conclusion of *After Virtue* regarding the meaning and status of "rationality" itself—namely, that there is no universal rationality but, rather, only "traditions" of rationality, each ultimately incommensurable with the other. For an extensive treatment of this dimension of MacIntyre's thought, see MacIntyre, *Whose Justice? Which Rationality?* As I will argue in greater depth, engaging meta-ethical questions about the status of "truth" qua "truth" is not only an essential dimension of ethical analysis, and primarily distinguishes ethics from advocacy, but also necessary for determining the authority

Indignation may make one a passionate advocate for one's cause, but it cannot provide a cogent explanation for which cause or set of causes one should be supporting in the first place.

THE COMPONENTS OF THE ARGUMENT

This chapter examines this recognition that there is a categorical difference between *making* a moral argument (or formulating a viewpoint) and *expressing* a moral position (or enacting a viewpoint). Indeed, I believe this difference between "making" and "enacting" in the moral sphere can also be generalized as the difference between (1) *doing ethics* and (2) *doing advocacy.*[9] This chapter seeks to clarify the definitional lines between these two terms and contend that a sharp distinction between them is essential for the conceptual and practical integrity of both. On the one hand, collapsing ethics into advocacy risks defining ethics as entirely prudential in both methodology and purpose, rendering the fundamental ethical question to be about means (how to implement a moral conclusion) rather than about ends (how to determine which moral conclusion is true). This reduction not only diminishes the depth and breadth of ethical inquiry, but also undermines the efficacy of advocacy, as well: if advocates cannot demonstrate the *truth* of their cause, at least tentatively, using the tools of ethical analysis available, particularly meta-ethical assessment, then they cannot offer any *reason* why anyone should accept their position beyond sheer assertion and, implicitly or explicitly, the threat of coercion.

On the other hand, doing ethics without advocacy risks rendering ethical reflection into an entirely cognitive and theoretical activity, detached from the final goal of ethical analysis—good action in the pursuit of justice. My position is thus not that ethicists should refrain from engaging in advocacy, but, rather, that ethicists should recognize that (1) ethics and advocacy are not the same either in goal or methodology, and (2) all forms of advocacy should be firmly grounded in rigorous ethical analysis, and meta-ethics

---

of any ethical position in relation to competing positions. MacIntrye's meta-ethical conclusions are complex—he does not believe in universal reason but does believe that one tradition can be more "rational" than others in comparison—but it is not necessary, I believe, to endorse those conclusions in order to draw from other aspects of his work. In short, I believe MacIntyre aptly diagnoses a fundamental problem in moral discourse without agreeing with his solution for it.

9. I do not mean to imply that all protests are defined by indignation or that indignation is the only form of protest. What ultimately unites indignation, protest, and advocacy more broadly, I argue, is that all three *start* from the premise of the moral goodness of their position and thus seek to reason *towards* how to implement that good.

in particular. Indeed, advocacy without ethics is *unethical advocacy* because it can only attain its goals by submission or manipulation, not persuasion.

The argument proceeds in three steps. First, drawing on the thought of University of Chicago ethicist and co-editor to this volume, William Schweiker, I defend a definition of, and methodology for, doing ethics based on Schweiker's conception of the three tasks of ethics (critical, constructive, comparative) and five dimensions of ethical inquiry (descriptive, normative, practical, fundamental, and meta-ethical). I build on this taxonomy by contending that the list should also be hierarchically ordered by identifying the meta-ethical dimension as the most *conceptually* fundamental.

Second, I argue how ethics differs from the goal and methodology of advocacy. I contend that, while there are deep similarities between ethics and advocacy, the fault line between the two lies in the recognition that advocates qua advocates have stopped, or at least paused, meta-ethical analysis, which lies at the heart of ethical inquiry. The most fundamental task of ethics, in other words, is to identify "the truth," understood as that which makes an ethical position rationally authoritative. The most fundamental task of advocacy, on the other hand, is to *implement* "the truth," which is to say that, unlike ethics, advocacy firmly *presumes* the epistemological authority of its basic moral truth claims.

Third, the chapter applies this distinction to the field of "liberative ethics" to explain how the epistemological and normative features of one dominant version of this ethical theory blur the boundary between advocacy and ethics. This definitional and practical muddling, I conclude, is problematic from both conceptual and applied perspectives, potentially producing forms of ethics that are not only self-contradictory and authoritarian, but also, and consequently, incapable of providing stable theoretical grounds for authentic advocacy. In sum, while ethics and advocacy can and should be mutually informing, establishing the correct conceptual relationship between the two is necessary to prevent moral argumentation from degenerating into mutual indignation, which, as MacIntyre rightly observes, only leads to moral confusion, political tumult, and, eventually, violence.

DEFINING TERMS: ETHICS

William Schweiker has devoted much of his scholarly work to defining the meaning and purpose of ethics as a conceptually unique form of analysis. In a foundational essay on the definition of ethics, he identifies what he calls the "three tasks" and "five dimensions" of ethical inquiry, particularly religious ethical inquiry. The three tasks are (1) critical, (2) comparative, and (3) constructive. As Schweiker explains, "Religious ethics entails the *critical* inquiry into complex ways of religious and moral life, but often also the *constructive* use of religious sources in meeting current problems [and each] of these tasks . . . is usually bound to the work of *comparison*."[10] To do ethics, in other words, is to engage in the interrelated yet distinct tasks of (a) interpreting traditions in and of themselves, (b) putting traditions in conversations with each other, and (c) using the resources from this engagement and comparison to build constructive responses to discrete questions and issues.

Schweiker specifies that these three tasks are carried out in five dimensions of ethics: descriptive, normative, practical, fundamental, and meta-ethical. Each dimension is grounded in, and motivated by, a particular question. The descriptive dimension responds to the question, "What is going on?" and, according to Schweiker, "draws on a range of resources, experiences, types of discernment, and even beliefs about reality to . . . describe and analyze a situation in terms of its moral meaning."[11] The normative dimension of ethics, in turn, seeks to respond to the question, "What norms and values ought to guide human life?" and is related to identifying values that "orient thinking and action."[12] The practical dimension, in contrast, asks and answers the question: "What ought I or we to do?" This may sound similar to the normative dimension; however, while the normative seeks to identify general moral principles and values, the practical focuses more on how to *act* on those principles and values in concrete situations, highlighting the importance of decision making and judgement.[13] The fundamental dimension, in turn, shifts ethical analysis away from the question of "What is going on and how should I respond to it?" to the question, in Schweiker's words, "What does it mean to be a moral agent within the wider compass of reality?"[14] In this dimension, the focus is on the meaning and power (or lack of power) of the "I" who knows, decides, and acts. Finally, the meta-ethical dimension asks, from the broadest possible perspective, whether an ethical viewpoint is true, and thus reflects on "moral concepts, strategies of validating claims, and forming judgments about the relative weight the evidence and interpretations from other fields of inquiry can and ought to have in guiding life."[15]

10. Schweiker, "On Religious Ethics," 3.
11. Schweiker, "On Religious Ethics," 6.
12. Schweiker, "On Religious Ethics," 6.
13. Schweiker, "On Religious Ethics," 7.
14. Schweiker, "On Religious Ethics," 8.
15. Schweiker, "On Religious Ethics," 9.

THE NECESSITY OF THE META-ETHICAL

As ethicist Maria Antonaccio has observed in an essay on moral truth, it is this last dimension of inquiry, the meta-ethical, that emerges as the most disputed in contemporary ethics, noting, in her words, that "the notion of moral truth is one of the most contested subjects in ethical theory."[16] Yet this is precisely the charge of the meta-ethical within ethical analysis: to assess moral truth, looking beyond what any moral tradition may *say* or *believe* to be true (which would fall in the domain of the descriptive dimension) to determine whether it is, in fact, true.

Given the contested status of *the* truth (as opposed to *a* truth) among contemporary ethicists, the legitimacy of meta-ethical inquiry cannot be taken for granted. Most ethicists will likely agree with Schweiker's argument that a comprehensive account of ethics should include descriptive, normative, practical, and fundamental analysis no matter what tradition they identify with. These combined dimensions seek to ask and answer: "What values and principles should we, as moral agents, act on right now given the nature of the specific problem confronting us in this time and place?" This question identifies an approach to ethical inquiry that is difficult to criticize from a formal or methodological perspective: if doing ethics means anything at all, it at least means devising a method to identify and act in relation to individual and social problems in their varied forms. There are diverse branches of ethics, in other words, that could and do make the case that the meta-ethical dimension is not necessary for doing ethics. However, I not only wish to reaffirm the necessity of including the meta-ethical dimension in ethical inquiry qua ethical inquiry, as Schweiker's account does. I also wish to argue that it is *the most conceptually fundamental dimension*, which Schweiker's account does not.

Let me first defend the claim that meta-ethics is a *necessary* component of ethical inquiry. While Schweiker identifies the normative dimension of ethics as one among the other four dimensions, it is important to recognize that, upon reflection, there is actually a normative dimension to *every* dimension of ethics: the descriptive dimension, for example, is not only seeking to describe moral situations, but to be able to say, with authority, "this is the *right* way of understanding this situation"; likewise, the normative dimension is not only seeking to identify what values and principles ought to guide action, but to be able to conclude "these are the *right* principles and actions"; the practical dimension not only tries to specify how one should act in any given situation, but to affirm that this is the *right* way to act; and

16. Antonaccio, "Moral Truth," 27.

the fundamental dimension does not merely seek to give an account of what it means to be an agent, but to contend a *right* understanding of what it means to be an agent; and finally, the meta-ethical dimension not only tries to identify what someone or some group says is true, but to determine whether that account of truth is the *right* one.

In other words, nestled within each dimension of ethical inquiry is some form of a truth claim—about reality, about values and principles, judgment, the agent who acts, and the truth itself. This, of course, is not to claim that every moral tradition makes the same truth claims within each one of these dimensions, or even that every tradition has the same conception of "truth." But it recognizes that every tradition makes *some* truth claims within each one of these dimensions. Indeed, even those who embrace some version of "anti-realism" in ethics—that is, the belief that moral beliefs do not and cannot contain "true" truth claims because truth does not exist or is impossible to know—necessarily believe that their understanding about reality, values and principles, judgement, and the meaning of the agent who acts is *true*. In the same essay on moral truth, for example, Antonaccio describes the philosophical position of emotivism as affirming that "moral statements do not make truth claims or provide any factual information whatsoever[, but only] express the subjective attitudes of the speaker who utters them."[17] My point is that any emotivist who embraces this position does so because she or he believes it represents the right, i.e., truest understanding of ethics and the components of ethical inquiry. So, too, for the ethical-naturalist and ethical non-naturalist and internal realist and moral nihilist and prescriptivist and any other "ist" we might be able to conjure:[18] none of them agrees with the others, *but all of them think they are right.*

How, then, are we to adjudicate among these competing conceptions of the truth? The question itself points to the necessity of meta-ethical analysis. It is not sufficient from an ethical or epistemological perspective merely to say, "this ethical system affirms this sets of values and has this understanding of reality and this understanding of what it means to be an agent." Put bluntly, we must determine whether the ethical system we examine speaks nonsense, and the way we do that is by engaging in meta-ethical

17. Antonaccio, "Moral Truth," 33.

18. These categories are those which Antonaccio employs to organize different moral theories. According to her analysis, ethical-naturalists, ethical-non naturalists, and another category not mentioned above, reflexive realists, affirm some form of moral realism. Moral nihilist, emotivists, and prescriptivists, on the other hand reject moral realism (See Antonaccio, "Moral Truth," 28–34). My contention here is that whether one rejects or denies moral realism as "true," one believes that one's rejection or denial itself is true; otherwise, it would not be clear why he or she would affirm one position over another one.

analysis—asking not only "What is this ethical system saying about ethics?" but also, "Is what this ethical system says about ethics *right*?" Denying the necessity of this second question, that is, denying the legitimacy of meta-ethical analysis, not only forces us to say "there are incommensurably different moral systems in the world, and that's all I have to say about that," but also, more problematically, "I have no idea even whether my *descriptions* of the incommensurable ethical systems in the world are, in fact, accurate, because I cannot say if those descriptions are true or not—and that's all I have to say about that." This approach to ethical inquiry, abruptly cutting off the analytical arc just before the most important questions, only leads to a radical moral skepticism in which no one can be sure whether any moral claim has legitimacy according to any standard of truth. It is only the meta-ethical, in other words, that equips us to ask and begin to answer the question of whether what we say at the descriptive, normative, practical, and fundamental levels is arbitrary.

THE CONTEXTUAL CRITIQUE AND WHY IT FAILS

One criticism of this defense of the meta-ethical takes the following form: it is still possible to talk about coherent meaning *within* ethical systems in the descriptive, normative, practical, and fundamental dimensions without having to make a meta-ethical case that they are true. Ethicist Kevin Jung holds this position in an article in the *Journal of Religious Ethics*, entitled "Normativity in Comparative Religious Ethics." Jung analyzes the cogency of the claim, made by self-identified "third wave scholars" of religion, that it is possible to split the difference between embracing moral relativism on the one hand and universalism on the other regarding normative moral claims. As Jung writes, "[Third wave scholars] avoid the extremes of both universalist conceptions of comparison and particularist objections to comparison [by] a comparative strategy that uses an '*ad hoc* frame,' which is defined not by claims of universality but by a common question or problem present in individuals and traditions."[19] Third wave scholars, in other words, seek to avoid meta-ethical conclusion on the "truth" of morality, yet still believe it is possible both for moral systems to be internally "true" and in relation to each other when interpreted through shared areas of interest and concern. According to Jung, this approach to normative ethics finds its roots in Jeffrey Stout's contextualist account of moral justification. Quoting Stout, he observes, "contexualism is . . . the view that justification is an activity of 'eliminating relevant reasons for [for doubt]' in the audience to whom the

19. Jung, "Normativity in Comparative Religious Ethics," 643.

justification is addressed concerning a particular propositional belief . . . [which] implies that justification is a status of entitlement to a claim, which 'can vary from context to context.'"[20]

Jung is not convinced that such an approach to justifying normativity in competing ethical systems is coherent, a conclusion with which I agree. While granting the distinction between epistemological entitlement and justification—in short, one may be entitled to believe something from an epistemological perspective, even if the belief itself may not be justified (children, for example, are entitled to believe in Santa Claus even though that belief is not justified)—Jung notes that it is still essential from an ethical perspective not only to ask if it is *understandable* that people hold certain moral beliefs, but also whether the moral beliefs people hold are *true*.

Another way of putting this critique of the contextualist approach is to distinguish between analyzing whether a belief is *coherent* within the belief system it occupies versus whether or not the belief is *true*. While coherence may be a necessary condition for truth, truth is not reducible to coherence. For example, in the difference between valid argument and sound arguments, valid arguments have a conclusion that necessarily follows from its premises and are, therefore, coherent; yet sound arguments have a conclusion that necessarily follows from its premises *and* have true premises. That makes sound arguments both coherent *and* true. Merely coherent arguments can still have false premises. Simply believing something to be true does not make it so, even if the belief coheres with other beliefs within the same contextual belief system. As Jung expresses this point,

> While [contextual] ethnographic and anthropological studies of religious moralities can provide an important service to [comparative religious ethics], it is questionable that they contain the kind of normativity that can be meaningfully used without being vulnerable to epistemic relativism . . . [N]ot everything that individuals or groups claim to be true is a justified belief, no matter how socially rigorous their process of justification may be.[21]

Jung's insights help confirm two conclusions about the necessity of meta-ethical analysis in ethical inquiry: (1) simply examining the internal coherence to ethics and how they may overlap with other contextual ethics

---

20. Jung, "Normativity in Comparative Religious Ethics," 654. Jung quotes Stout, *Democracy in Tradition*, 235. For a much broader examination of Jung's position on meta-ethics—and the field of metaethical study more broadly—see, Jung, *Religious Ethics and Constructivism*.

21. Jung, "Normativity in Comparative Religious Ethics," 662.

does not provide grounds for determining how and why one "context" may provide a better or truer account of morality than another. Indeed, the best contextual analysis can do is to proclaim that a belief system makes sense within itself and *accidently* agrees with another belief system on a specific issue; and (2) such a methodology for doing ethics does not, contrary to its own self-understanding, avoid meta-ethical conclusions on the question of truth, but, rather, *depends upon* a meta-ethical conclusion about the status of moral truth—namely, that all moral truth claims are contextual. Jung suggests this is a *wrong* meta-ethical conclusion (again, a conclusion with which I agree), but, whether right or wrong, *it is still a meta-ethical conclusion* that purports to speak for all ethical systems, because those who espouse this view believe it to be true. In other words, the claim "all truth is contextual" is a *non*-contextual claim whose truth is defended by meta-ethical analysis. Put differently, *even the rejection of meta-ethics engages in meta-ethics.*

The inescapability of meta-ethical truth claims in *moral* theory, coupled with the recognition that adjudicating among competing conceptions of descriptive, normative, practical, and fundamental ethical claims requires meta-ethical analysis confirms that Schweiker correctly includes meta-ethical analysis as a *necessary* component of ethical inquiry. However, I want to make an additional argument, one that Schweiker may not concur with. As a preface to defining the five dimensions of ethical analysis, Schweiker writes, "These questions are not related in a sequential or deductive manner,"[22] meaning he does not wish to identify one dimension as more fundamental or important than another. I agree with this claim from the perspective of how one engages in the actual practice of ethical analysis—a point I will elaborate on below. But I also believe that the same reasons that justify why meta-ethics should be understood as *necessary* also justify why it should be understood as the most *conceptually fundamental* component of ethical inquiry.

My position is rooted in a conceptual distinction: as I argued above, it is ultimately only meta-ethical analysis that determines whether any of the claims in the descriptive, normative, practical, and fundamental dimensions of ethical inquiry have validity. One can put the point this way: meta-ethical analysis and its conclusions possess the *unique* status of serving as the condition for the possibility of making a *true* descriptive, normative, practical, or fundamental claim. The reverse does not hold: making a descriptive claim does not tell us whether what we describe is true; this same observation holds for normative claims about values and principles, practical claims

22. Schweiker, "On Religious Ethics," 5.

about how we should act in a particular circumstance, and claims about being an agent. In short, a deeper analysis of the ethical dimensions in relation to each other demonstrates that every other dimension *should* be deduced from the meta-ethical insofar as it is the exclusive task of the meta-ethical to determine what, in fact, is true.

It is essential to note two qualifications. First, recognizing the conceptual primacy of the meta-ethical does not tell us what "the truth" is. It only demonstrates that without establishing *some truth,* the content of every other dimension of ethical inquiry will be arbitrary. Second, to recognize that the meta-ethical constitutes the ground of all other forms of inquiry from a conceptual perspective does *not* mean that "doing ethics" requires one *to start* with meta-ethical claims. For example, there is nothing contradictory or problematic with beginning ethical reflection by asking what is going on, what principles and values should guide us, what we should do here and now, or what it means to be able to make a moral decision if we *ultimately ask whether our answers to these questions are true.* In other words, the conceptual primacy of the meta-ethical does not lead to the *practical* primacy of the meta-ethical (meaning how one is actually going about doing ethics). One can start from anywhere so long as the inquiry finds its grounding in an analysis of truth.

I emphasize that the argument, up to this point, in no way advances or endorses one meta-ethical theory of truth over another. Like everyone, I have my own beliefs about what is ultimately true about morality and everything else, but this chapter is deliberately agnostic on *what* that truth is and *why* it is true. My only goal is to make the case that *doing ethics* cannot be severed from *doing* meta-ethics—"cannot" both in the meaning of "not able to" and, consequently, "should not." Put more colloquially: if you want to do ethics, you gotta do meta-ethics.

DEFINING TERMS: ADVOCACY

The meaning of advocacy, like the meaning of ethics, can be difficult to pin down, but two articles in the journal *Religion* on the relationship between academic scholarship, which includes the classroom, and advocacy provide a helpful foundation. Scholar of religion Michael Stausberg, for example, defines advocacy as "a defense or support of, preference for or commitment to, some cause, thesis, idea, ideal, worldview, or religion."[23] In a complementary essay, scholar Greg Johnson fills out this definition by distinguishing between "direct" and "indirect advocacy":

23. Stausberg, "Advocacy in the Study of Religion\s," 222.

> [Advocacy is] any intentional action taken by the scholar that in some way—however maximal or minimal—facilitates the political goals of an individual or group, whether directly (e.g., physical action, legal testimony, or publication) or indirectly (e.g., sharing documents, brainstorming about pending issues, or providing transportation to a meeting). Thus construed, advocacy can range from highly visible performances to off-stage actions that are quite mundane.[24]

In both of these definitions, advocacy, however else it might be defined, *begins* with an implicit or explicit normative conclusion—namely, that the goal of the advocate's action, defined as advancing the interest of an individual or group, is *good*.[25] That is, advocacy does not ask, "What is good?" but rather, "How do I advance the good?" This constitutive feature of advocacy recognizes that to be an advocate is to engage in the support or defense of a goal or interest of an individual or group. The advocate has *already arrived* at her or his conclusion about the moral worthiness of the goal; all that remains to be determined is how to implement that goal effectively.

The reason *why* advocacy should be understood in this way, as reasoning *from* a conception of the good rather than *to* a conception of the good, can also be deduced from the above definitions. Minimally, to be an advocate is to act *for* someone or something. The preposition *for* here is essential: advocating means that one is *already* in action, moving *towards* a specific goal. In this sense, it is conceptually (and physically) problematic both to be asking "Is the goal for which I am acting right?" while acting towards that same goal. To be sure, ambivalence, doubt, and skepticism about a goal is possible (and common). But if one is acting for the advancement of the goal *while* doubting the moral rightness of the goal, then one is, by definition, being a *bad* advocate—acting against the very goal that, at the same time, one is acting for. Being a good advocate, and by "good" here I mean being

---

24. Johnson, "Off the Stage, on the Page," 291.

25. Throughout this chapter, I use "right" and "good" interchangeably. In other contexts, they can refer to two substantively different moral realities. "The right," for example, is typically associated with moral theories that, at an epistemological level, deny that morality can be deduced from any conception of "reality," a collection of theories usually categorized as "ethical non-naturalism," which are paradigmatically represented in the non-teleological theory of Immanuel Kant. "The good," on the other hand, is typically associated with moral theories that affirm the possibility of deducing morality from "reality," and are usually categorized under theories of "ethical naturalism." The teleological morality of Thomas Aquinas provides a paradigmatic form of this kind of ethics. This article does not seek to endorse one view of ethics over the other; "right" and "good" in this context are thus synonymous, meaning "true" in the sense of "worthy of belief and acting upon."

an advocate who fulfills the purpose of advocacy, presumes that one reasons *from* a fixed conception of what is good *for* the advancement of that good.

Defined this way, a clear demarcation between the work of advocacy and the work of ethics already emerges. However, it is important to recognize, before further illuminating and defending this demarcation, that it is also possible to identify significant overlap. There is nothing inconsistent for an advocate, for example, to engage in the normative dimension of ethical inquiry. Indeed, this is something that the advocate *must* do: being a good advocate presumes that one clearly identifies the values and principles that motivate one's action. So, too, for the practical dimension of ethical inquiry: a good advocate not only identifies the principles and values that motivate action, but also demonstrates why those principles and values lead to the judgment that the specific action he or she is engaged in is justified. Making justified judgments, in turn, presumes that the advocate believes she or he has a good descriptive grasp of the circumstances she or he occupies. Finally, an advocate, insofar as she or he is acting for a cause, must at least have an implicit understanding of what it means to be able to act, which captures the fundamental dimension of ethics.

But can and should an advocate engage in meta-ethical analysis, as well? It is within this unique dimension, I believe, that advocacy and ethics most definitively reveal their conceptual difference; for while, as argued above, meta-ethics lies at the conceptual heart of what it means to do ethics, advocates, as advocates, must pause, or at least subordinate, meta-ethical inquiry to be good advocates. This does not mean that advocates cannot nor do not offer reasons for why they believe what they believe, and that they believe these reasons to be true. *It means, rather, that the nature of advocacy itself stipulates that the good of the cause's advancement constrains what can count as legitimate meta-ethical inquiry.*

It does so in two ways. First, from the advocate's standpoint, there is no reason to examine what may or may not be true if it cannot be demonstrated how and why the purported "truth" may be helpful to the advancement of the cause; in other words, asking theoretical questions about the nature of the good for the sake of asking theoretical questions is, for the advocate, at best a waste of time and, at worst, harmful to the advancement of the cause. Second, advocates, strictly within the role of advocates, must assume the truth of their cause in such a way that downplays, if not ignores, debates taking place on more fundamental questions undergirding their advocacy. Advocates in the pro-life vs. pro-choice dispute, for example, are not asking themselves whether human life morally begins at conception or not; they each have respectively already *settled* that question, and their goal, as advocates, is to advance their side of the cause culturally and politically.

That does not mean that advocates cannot have nuanced and sophisticated positions or that they are duplicitous or manipulative in their arguments (although that can certainly be the case); it only means that all their nuance and sophistication must rest upon at least *one* firm and foundational assumption about the goodness of their cause, or else they are not fulfilling their role as advocates.

Meta-ethics unconstrained by advocacy, on the other hand, does not seek the truth *so that*; it seeks the truth for the sake of the truth, whatever it may be. To be sure, the conclusions one reaches from a meta-ethical perspective can and likely will point in a particular normative direction, which, in turn, will point towards particular forms of advocacy. Yet it remains the case that the purpose of meta-ethical inquiry is not *for* anything other than the identification of the truth. In short, the advocate must see "truth" ultimately as a tool for the advancement of the cause. The ethicist, on the other hand, sees everything else as a tool for attaining the truth.

COMPLEMENTARITY AND DIFFERENCE

I do not intend this fundamental differentiation between ethics and advocacy to serve as an indictment of advocacy as a legitimate form of moral action. Properly understood, the two are mutually complementary. As argued above, meta-ethical inquiry ultimately determines whether any claim is true. That means that any advocate, no matter what his or her cause, *depends* on an at least implicit meta-ethical analysis to establish both the moral "given," (the platform, *from which* the advocate argues) and the goal *towards which* he or she moves. Absent meta-ethical support, the advocate's cause can be "true" only by luck; otherwise, it is an arbitrary expression the advocate seeks to impose on those who do not share his or her moral premises—precisely the kind of scenario that Alasdair MacIntyre believes describes contemporary moral discourse. Without meta-ethics, every advocate stands on sand or, worse, thin air.

Yet it is also important to recognize that advocacy can complement ethics. While ethics can identify normative principles and how they should be acted upon, the rooting of the ethical in the meta-ethical dimension gives the whole enterprise an inescapable theoretical quality. As Schweiker's taxonomy effectively highlights, doing ethical inquiry, especially doing it as a profession, requires engaging a multi-dimensional analysis of the most fundamental epistemological, anthropological, ontological, and theological questions embedded in deep moral complexity. That nuance and complexity cannot be reduced to a placard, bumper sticker, chant (especially one that rhymes!), slogan, or banner.[26] However inescapable the complexity of ethical inquiry must at least strive for practical relevance, which can take the form of advocacy. After all, the whole *point* of ethical inquiry is to guide concrete, discrete human action, which never takes place at the theoretical level.

In sum, ethicists have good reason to remain committed to theoretical inquiry, especially including meta-ethical inquiry. And advocates have good reason to remain committed to effective action in advancing their cause. The upshot is not that ethicists cannot or should not engage in advocacy or that advocates cannot or should not do ethics. It rather recognizes that being an ethicist means determining what is true, and being an advocate means implementing truth. For the good of both ethics and advocacy, all of us should make the conceptual distinction between the two as bright as possible so that we can have clear understanding of when we do ethics and when we act as advocates. Otherwise, we risk turning ethics into a tool for the advancement of specific causes, and advocacy into an activity of thinking and talking rather than acting.

A TEST CASE FOR ETHICS AND ADVOCACY: LIBERATIVE ETHICS

At the beginning of this article, I noted that at least one branch of "liberative ethics" illuminates a problematic blurring of ethics and advocacy. It is now possible to explain why. First, note that liberative ethics represents an expansive form of ethics that, like any branch of ethics, contains diverse thinkers who disagree with each other. There is danger in characterizing a school of thought by reducing it in a way that distorts rather than clarifies. I

26. Think of the difference this way: an advocate paints a sign saying "Life is precious! Vote 'No' on Proposition Q!" (a proposition I have invented for the purpose of this example). The ethicist, in contrast, who agrees with the advocate on this issue, joins the advocate on the street with another sign, written from the standpoint of an ethicist (in very small letters): "Given that it seems rational to question the legitimacy of Kant's sharp separation between noumena and phenomena and, consequently, the reduction of all 'religion' to the ethical, the possibility emerges of an ethic embedded with the knowable structure of reality itself provided that, first, we develop a hermeneutic principle that separates 'life' in a normative and, therefore, value-conferring sense from what may or may not exist at any particular time and place. This principle, in turn, must find its roots in some conception of subjectivity, which means Kant remains a valuable dialogue partner. Thus, there may be justification to exercise one's agency in the form of a 'No' vote on Proposition Q!" The advocate may, understandably, tell the ethicist that she or he is not helping advance the cause and kindly ask her or him to return to the bowels of the library.

focus this analysis and critique of liberative ethics on one text—in particular, the introduction to that text—so I am aware of this danger.

I have selected *Ethics: A Liberative Approach* as representative because the book explicitly positions itself as an encapsulation of both the methodology and substantive content of liberative ethics and, unsurprisingly, contains numerous authors, including the editor, who are well known for work in liberative ethics. Also, while the book includes a variety of liberative perspectives, all of them find their touchstone in the introduction's foundational and normative claims about the constitutive features of liberation ethics; otherwise, in the introduction's words, "this textbook can only be written as a collection of scholars working from within the context of their own communities."[27] The liberative approach, outlined in the introduction, provides the cohesive foundation uniting these otherwise different ethical contexts.

My first task is to show that the text's approach to ethics can be interpreted as a form of advocacy as this chapter defines it. This interpretation is justified because the introduction openly claims the mantle of advocacy: "[Liberative] ethicists operate as scholar-activists who theorize and theologize for the express purpose of changing oppressive social structures, as opposed to simply better understanding said structures for the sole sake of scholarship."[28] Liberative ethics, in other words, does not require a deep, structural interpretation to uncover an interpretive principle that unlocks its nature and priorities that otherwise might be difficult to detect. To *be* a liberative ethicist is, by definition, *to be* an advocate, which means that the absence of advocacy would signal that one is not, properly understood, a liberative ethicist. The two are intentionally conflated.

The introduction provides additional support to classify liberative ethics as advocacy. Recall the three constitute features of advocacy outlined above: (1) advocacy does not engage in meta-ethical inquiry, and the extent to which it seeks "the truth" is constrained by how the truth helps advance the advocate's cause; (2) the advocate reasons *from* a fixed normative ethical platform *for* advancing that platform's putative good rather than starting from the question: "What should my ethical platform be and what would justify it as 'ethical'?"; and (3) forms of knowledge that are not supportive of the goals of the advocate are deemed unimportant and discarded.

The introduction makes several claims that fit the first criterion of advocacy: most explicitly the assertion that "truth" in a meta-ethical sense is not knowable and, therefore, not the concern of liberative ethics: "A truth

27. De La Torre, *Ethics,* 4.
28. De La Torre, *Ethics,* 6.

beyond the historical experiences and social locations where individuals act as social agents cannot be ascertained whether said truth exists or not."[29] This claims that all truth is contextual; no truth is universal. The introduction confirms this interpretation by also claiming that "all ethics is contextual . . . rooted in the social location of those seeking faith-based responses to their oppressive situations."[30]

With these two claims, the introduction precludes meta-ethical inquiry into the truth status of any contextual claim. To be sure, the introduction and the following chapters make an abundance of truth claims, particularly in the descriptive, normative, and practical dimensions of ethics, and the introduction also *asserts* a standard to determine the relative truth of any claim. However, not only is that standard asserted rather than argued for; it serves as a paradigmatic example of the advocate insistence that only truth that advances the good of the cause is called truth. Consider, for example, the following statements:

- Whatever liberation looks like, it can only be determined by the local people living under oppressive structures.[31]

- [W]hat I (as well as you) believe to be true, right, and ethical has more to do with our social context (our community or social networks) and identity (race, ethnicity, gender, orientation, or physical abilities) rather than any ideology or doctrine we may claim to hold.[32]

- Far from repeating timeless, ahistorical principles, liberative ethics presents itself as a reflection vigorously involved with people's daily experiences. All chosen praxis (actions) is derived from the perspective of the oppressed . . . Before we can do theology, we must do liberation while connecting the spiritual with material realities.[33]

Perhaps it is the claim in the last passage—that we must do liberation before being able to do theology—that most clearly demonstrates the prudential approach that liberative action takes towards the truth. The introduction stipulates, *a priori*, we will be able to say anything is "true" if and only if it falls into the category of "doing liberation," which is additionally conditioned by whether or not any specific truth claim accords with the experiences of those "living under oppressive structures." This epistemological

29. De La Torre, *Ethics*, 4.
30. De La Torre, *Ethics*, 3.
31. De La Torre, *Ethics*, 3.
32. De La Torre, *Ethics*, 1.
33. De La Torre, *Ethics*, 4.

filter ensures that only that which advances liberation can be legitimate knowledge. This claim transforms the meta-ethical question from "Is this claim true?" to "Do oppressed people say this claim is true and does the claim help advance the goals of liberation?" That is not doing meta-ethics.

Second, it is evident that liberative ethics as the text presents it argues from a fixed normative platform, a platform asserted rather than argued for. The passages cited previously support this interpretation, though the introduction also directly states, for example, "Although the common starting point of theological reflection is the existential experience of the marginalized, the ultimate goal remains liberation from the reality of societal misery."[34] The introduction also makes clear that the goal of liberative ethics is, consequently, not to justify the truth of its foundational normative claims from a meta-ethical perspective, but to *implement* its vision of the good: "Liberative ethics is oriented toward the future—what can I do, physically and spiritually, to bring about a more justice-based social order that celebrates life?"[35] The base question for liberative ethics, in other words, is not "What is justice?" but, "How do I bring about more justice?"

Third, and related, the introduction employs the normative and epistemological foundation it asserts for liberative ethics to make it clear that any form of knowledge, any experience, any culture, or any other dimension of human existence that cannot be rendered useful for the advancement of liberation is, *ipso facto*, ethically unimportant (unethical) and even devoid of the divine. As the introduction claims, "liberative ethics focuses on human needs rather than ecclesial dogma"[36] and "God is never found in cathedrals made of crystal, whose ornate steeples serve as monuments to those who reached the pinnacle of wealth on the backs of the poor and disenfranchised. God is only found in the 'least of these.'"[37] Therefore, anything that does not fit this paradigm of knowledge and value—all the architecture, art, poetry, drama, liturgy, Christology, ecclesiology, moral theology, politics, economics, etc., that cannot be interpreted as embodying the "least of these"—is rendered, at best, morally neutral and, at worst, an obstacle to liberation's goals.

34. De La Torre, *Ethics*, 4.
35. De La Torre, *Ethics*, 4.
36. De La Torre, *Ethics*, 5.
37. De La Torre, *Ethics*, 6.

BLURRING TO THE POINT OF DISTORTION:
ADVOCACY WITHOUT ETHICS

These examples, I believe, demonstrate how this version of liberative ethics constitutes a blurring of the lines between ethics and advocacy. It would be more accurate, purely from a descriptive perspective, to rename liberative ethics, "advocacy for liberation." Why is this conflation a problem? For at least three reasons.

First, it undermines ethical inquiry. As explained above, liberative ethics reduces ethics to advocacy in a way that constricts the breadth and depth of what it means to do ethics. Constraining ethical inquiry within the confines of "liberation" prevents it from asking questions and entertaining answers that are not in the service of liberation. This conceptual hemming is not only detrimental to ethics as a discipline; it leads to contradictory and circular ethical outcomes. For example, how can we reconcile the claim, "there is no truth that is not contextual," with the claim, "there is no universal, ahistorical truth"? What if there is a "context" that seeks to affirm a universal ahistorical ethic? Is that context, therefore, by definition "wrong" and thus morally inferior to other "contexts"?

Second, the liberative approach makes a circular argument, which is apparent in the following series of questions and answers about what "liberation" means:

> What is liberation?
> Liberation is what those who are oppressed say it is.
> What defines "those who are oppressed"?
> Those who are in need of liberation.

In other words, liberation is defined by those who are oppressed, and oppression is defined by those who need liberation. It is not clear how liberative ethics breaks free from this circular, self-referential loop, especially considering there is no universal vantage point to which one could appeal to help untie the epistemological knots.[38] One of the dangers of conflating ethics and advocacy is this kind of painting oneself into a conceptual

---

38. This conceptual problem is similar to the one in Aristotle's claim that we derive the definition of virtue (including the virtue of justice) by observing the example of the virtuous man. Aristotle defines virtue, for examples as "[the] state of character concerned with choice, lying in a mean, i.e., the mean relative to us, this being determined by a rational principle, and by the principle by which the man of practical wisdom would determine it" (Aristotle, *Nicomachean Ethics*, 1107a, 1–2). In order to know what virtue is, in other words, one must consult the "man of practical wisdom"—and in order to know who the man of practical wisdom is, one must already know the definition of virtue.

corner, which, in turn, undermines the rational and moral legitimacy of the advocate's position.

Third and related, the underlying epistemological structure of liberative arguments render those arguments impossible to contest and, therefore, impossible to evaluate as worthy of rational assent. Critical to the composition of any argument is not only establishing its validity (that the conclusion follows from the premises), but also its *soundness* (being able to determine if the premises are *true* or, at least, tentatively true). However, arguments founded upon experiential claims alone, claims that take the form of assertions whose "truth" can only be determined by those claiming to have the same "experience," can neither be proven true nor false, even tentatively. Consider, for example, this hypothetical argument from a liberative approach:

> Premise 1: "We" experience exclusion from participation in society.
>
> Premise 2: All forms of exclusion from participation in society are a form of injustice.
>
> Premise 3: Those who experience injustice are victims.
> Conclusion: "We" are victims of injustice.

How can one begin to analyze an argument that takes this form? First, it is important to recognize that one can certainly analyze the *validity* of this argument: temporarily setting aside the truth status of each one of the premises, it certainly is the case that *if* "we" feel excluded *and* all forms of exclusion from participation in society are a form of injustice *and* those who experience injustice are victims, *then* "we" are the victims of injustice. On this basis, it is possible for an "outsider" (someone who does not belong to the group that constitutes the "we") to evaluate the integrity of the argument vis-à-vis its validity. The argument does appear to be valid, which provides a minimal but, at least, epistemically stable foundation to begin to assess its integrity.[39]

39. Several readers of drafts of this chapter have encouraged me to engage the thought of ethical theorist Jeffrey Stout in more depth, especially the account of "immanent criticism" he lays out in *Democracy and Tradition*. My response has been, and remains, that I believe that the account that Stout offers serves as an *example* of meta-ethical analysis and, therefore, does not pose a "challenge" to the argument I seek to advance. In other words, Stout does what I hope all ethicists will do: examining the validity of truth claims within the horizon of an at least putative shared rationality. I do not find the argument Stout makes about the relationship between objectivity and metaphysics ultimately persuasive, though my thinking benefits from it tremendously. But that is irrelevant for this chapter. To put it directly, Stout represents part of the solution to the problem I seek to address.

What about the *soundness* of the argument? Recall that to be sound, an argument must both (a) be valid and (b) have true premises. Yet it is precisely in the necessity of true premises that arguments based on experience break down; for how can those who do not belong to the "we" possibly evaluate the content of the first premise? That is the heart of the problem: if the final authority of the truth of the claim "we experience exclusion" is *the experience* of the "we"—and, moreover, the "we" holds the final authority on who constitutes the "we"—then those outside the group *have no rational basis to determine the truth or falsity of the claims* that the "we" makes.[40]

More specifically, there are two distinct questions embedded in the first premise that anyone outside the "we" group would need to address to evaluate the argument's soundness. First, outsiders would have to determine whether those in the "we" group all *do*, in fact, share the same experience. Someone could say, for example, "we Californians experience exclusion in the federal government because it is unfair that super-populated California has the same number of senators as desolate Wyoming," and yet be speaking for others, like me, who disagree. Others, despite sharing the same external group characteristic (being a Californian), both believe in the wisdom of the Constitution and reject the claim that state residency should dictate one's political point of view.

Indeed, this kind identity-based non-sequitur has dogged my wife, a native Argentinian, ever since she moved to the United States as an adult. Growing up in a lower-middle-class and, periodically, poor household on the edge of the city's most dangerous neighborhood (a requisite disclaimer for anyone trying to discount her perspective as "privileged"), my wife, like everyone else she knew, used to understand the terms "Latino" and "Hispanic" as serving a purely descriptive function. ("Latinx," she has told me, is a neologism that nobody back home would ever dream of saying.)[41] For

40. I am not claiming that "experience" cannot or should not constitute part, even an important part, of ethical analysis. I also recognize that there are whole philosophical systems, phenomenology among them, that seek to systematize a normative understanding of experience, including how experience can and should relate to morality. I would argue that such an investigation and systemization of experience falls squarely into meta-ethical analysis, and thus does not pose a challenge to the position I defend here—namely, experience deliberately *severed* from any possibility of meta-ethical analysis cannot and, thus, should not form the foundation of a moral position, especially moral advocacy.

41. According to a recent Pew Research poll, only 3 percent of Hispanics in the US choose to use the term "Latinx," although 25 percent of Hispanics have heard of the term. Such a statistic once again points to this crucial question embedded in experience-based moral arguments: "Who is speaking for whom and on what authority?" See Noe-Bustamante et al., "About one in four US Hispanics have heard of Latinx but just 3% use it."

her, the designations did not imply any specific normative moral or political beliefs, just as, for example, describing someone as "Anglo" would (or should) tell you *nothing* about that person's beliefs, either. Upon moving to the United States, however, and, in particular, taking classes in American higher education, she quickly realized that most of her professors expected her, as "Hispanic" and a "Latina," to hold and advocate for specific moral, political, and even theological viewpoints, including views that contradicted her lived experiences and carefully reasoned conclusions. To make matters worse, professors—including non-Hispanic professors—have repeatedly implied that she is a "traitor" to her ethnicity for questioning the coherence of basing moral reasoning on ethnicity; even more insultingly, they have implied that the only possible explanation for why she thinks the way she does is because she has been "brainwashed" by her husband—a white heterosexual patriarchal-privileged male, they say, which, she points out, strips her of the agency they claim to be defending. These judgments, moreover, have rolled down exclusively from individuals in positions of institutional and cultural power, and *never once* from the hundreds of middle and lower-class Latinos/Hispanics whom she knows personally and works with closely through her professional ministry.

This example, anecdotal of course, confirms a general conclusion: whether a group defined by a particular set of criteria, especially if those criteria relate to attributes that have historically been considered to be outside of an individual's control (e.g., race, biological sex, country of origin, ethnicity), *actually* share the same experience and, based upon that experience, desire the *same* social or political goal, is something that those making the claim must *demonstrate*, not merely assume. Otherwise, like in the case of my wife (and many others we know), individuals may be appropriated into political and social movements that they fundamentally disagree with—including movements predicated on the assumption that ethnicity entails holding certain moral and political values.

Setting aside this empirical, and, indeed, moral issue with the first premise, there remains, second, the question of whether the experience of the "we" (assuming it is uniform) *accurately reflects reality*. One cannot assume "experience" and "reality" are always the same. For example, those flying coach may experience exclusion standing in a check-in line that snakes out to the curb while they watch first class passengers zip straight to the check-in counter—but is that experience *justified*? Likewise, an atheist attending a university whose mission statement includes commitments to a faith tradition could claim that she or he is experiencing exclusion from full participation in the life of the university community, including its religious life—but, again, would this experience of exclusion correspond with *actual* injustice? Or, to use a classroom example, a student who received a B- may feel that he or she deserved an A, but does that sense of entitlement correspond with the student's actual performance in the class? Note that the challenges these examples point to is not a question of sincerity or authenticity of belief (though those can be at issue, too); rather, they point to a question of *fairness* and, more specifically, the recognition that determining whether an individual's experience of injustice corresponds with a real situation of injustice *requires a definition of justice that is not reducible to experience alone.*

Narrow experiential arguments deny any authority outside of the experience itself, which reduces the avenues for evaluating the position to precisely one: something is true if someone (or some group) says they experience it as true. Period. Applying this standard to the hypothetical argument above, the first premise thus becomes *unassailable*—not because it is incontrovertibly true in the sense of impossible to rationally deny (for example, that one and zero cannot share the same conceptual properties), but because *it is incontestable*: if the experience of the group is the first and final authority, then someone outside the group can neither say "no, you actually do not have that experience (you are deceiving yourself)" nor "even if you do have that experience, that experience does not accurately reflect the way things actually are (your experience is sincere, but it does not correspond with moral reality)." In short, any possible critique of the first premise in an experientially based argument is rendered moot even before it is formulated.[42]

This points to a deeper problem. The authority of the "we" in the first premise in an experiential argument does not stop at the first premise. If experience is the ultimate arbiter of truth, the "we" also assigns itself the authority to give content to the meaning of the terms in the other premises, as well: including the meaning of "society," "exclusion," "injustice," "victim," etc. The upshot is that, if the argument is valid (and in this case, it is), *there is nothing that those outside the group making the argument can say to critique it.* These kinds of experiential arguments leave those outside the self-assigned epistemological and moral circle of authority—the "we"—two options: either *submit* to the argument "we" are making and be on the side of justice as an "ally," or reject (or even critique) the argument "we" are making and be,

---

42. Those advocating for exclusively experience-based moral arguments could contest, "Who are *you* to say what defines moral reality?" Fair enough, but, of course, that question can be turned back around. If, in reply, the answer is ultimately *no one* can define moral reality with any rational authority, then we are, functionally, operating within moral nihilism, which, among other implications, means all forms of advocacy are arbitrary.

at best, tagged as "against us" and/or on the side of the "oppressor"—which, functionally speaking, is difficult to distinguish from "the enemy."

This kind of argument by-way-of submission forms the foundation of what I mean by "advocacy without ethics," and it is, I believe, the kind of argumentation we see in the example of liberative ethics I have examined. It does not appear that those making arguments based upon this epistemic and moral premise believe that the authority of their arguments is limited to the group making them. Rather, they seem to believe both (a) the truth status of what they are saying can *only* be determined by the contextual experience of those who need liberation, and yet (b) *others* must recognize the moral authority of these experiences and alter their behavior accordingly. If we are not part of the pre-determined authoritative group, we must (in the sense having no other epistemological or moral option) shut up and do what we are told. This approach to ethics that explicitly rejects any kind of meta-ethical responsibility to defend the truth of its moral claims devolves into an example of sheer advocacy—that is ultimately impossible to distinguish from tyrannical fiat.

CONCLUSION: KEEP THE SEPARATION SHARP FOR THE SAKE OF JUSTICE

These critiques of liberative ethics seek to demonstrate the danger that advocacy without ethics poses to ethics. There is also a danger to advocacy. One of the achievements of liberative ethics, notwithstanding the problems identified above, is the light it casts on the many shadows of society, the places that few spend time thinking about and even less time fretting about. For all the important work we can do at the ethical level rooting out inconsistencies, establishing of methodologies, and arguing for the superiority of one form of reasoning over another, it remains that many individuals and groups are unjustly ignored, humiliated, oppressed, manipulated, exploited, and even killed by those with greater power. However we might diagnose the causes from an empirical perspective, these individuals are all around us, perhaps invisible, but certainly not faceless or nameless. Liberative ethics says to all of us not only "don't look away," but "stop and behold your sisters and brothers in pain, go among them, and do what you can to help make things better." This is a profound call to conscience that we owe in part to the work of liberative perspectives.

But the problem is that the same perspective that calls us out of our places of comfort and privilege and into the streets, the prisons, the detention centers, the mental hospitals, the courts, and everywhere else there is unjust and avoidable suffering does so in a way that has the effect of creating a new Babel, confounding our language and making it difficult, if not impossible, to understand each other's speech (Gen 11:7). Indeed, ironically, by freeing every "context" to say whatever it wills about the nature of morality under the assertion that all truth is context-dependent, we become *bound* to our identities (or the identities those authorized to speak on behalf of the oppressed assign to us) and lose our capacity to find a substantive common language about justice. This is not a language based on an accidental (and thus temporary) alignment of competing ethical traditions, but one we can agree on because it is true or, at least, tentatively true.

In short, denying those who care about justice the ability to talk about the truth by claiming all truth is contextual and that, consequently, truth is only that which some authoritative groups says it is, can only result in the worst forms of advocacy—advocacy by means of indignation. For how can we convince anyone else *to agree* with us when our argument is premised on the claim that those outside our group identity cannot possibly understand because they have not had our experiences?[43] If this is the ground on which we stake our moral claims, we cease to be either ethicists or ethical advocates. We become self-righteous agitators, members of a mob whose goal is submission, not persuasion. And when this transformation of moral discourse happens—a transition well under way both inside and outside the academy—the best we can expect is shouting, and the worst we should fear is violence.

If we want to avoid this fate, if we want to give justice a chance, the best path forward, I propose, is to give meta-ethics its rightful place back at the head of the table, to take off its blinders, untie its hands, and rip the tape off its mouth.

43. Lisa Sowle Cahill, for example, has recently argued that, while drawing on contextualist accounts of the good is important for Feminist ethics, Feminist ethicists have reason to find their grounding in a universal realism. She states in a recent article. "A historically sensitive but realist approach is also regarded by many feminist philosophers as basic to normative moral discourse, especially if women are to connect globally in making gender equality a social and political reality" (Cahill, "Renegotiating Aquinas," 193). Meta-ethical inquiry is necessary for identifying and justifying such "realism."

BIBLIOGRAPHY

Antonaccio, Maria. "Moral Truth." *The Blackwell Companion to Religious Ethics*, edited by William Schweiker, 27–35. Oxford: Blackwell, 2008.
Aquinas, Thomas. *Summa Theologiae*. Translated by the Fathers of the English Dominican Province. 5 vols. Notre Dame: Christian Classics, 1981.

Aristotle. *Nicomachean Ethics*. Translated and edited by Roger Crisp. Cambridge Texts in the History of Philosophy. Rev. ed. Cambridge: Cambridge University Press, 2014

Berman, Mark. "Hate crimes in the United States increased last year, FBI says." *Washington Post,* November 13, 2017. https://www.washingtonpost.com/news/post-nation/wp/2017/11/13/hate-crimes-in-the-united-states-increased-last-year-the-fbi-says/.

Cahill, Lisa Sowle. "Renegotiating Aquinas: Catholic Feminist Ethics, Postmodernism, Realism, and Faith." *Journal of Religious Ethics* 43.2 (2015) 193–217.

Caron, Christina. "Heather Heyer, Charlottesville victim, Is recalled as a 'strong woman.'" *New York Times,* August 13, 2017. https://www.nytimes.com/2017/08/13/us/heather-heyer-charlottesville-victim.html.

De La Torre, Miguel A., ed. *Ethics a Liberative Approach.* Minneapolis: Fortress, 2013.

Johnson, Greg. "Off the stage, on the page: on the relationship between advocacy and scholarship." *Religion* 44.2 (2013) 289–302.

Jung, Kevin. "Normativity in Comparative Religious Ethics." *Journal of Religious Ethics* 45.4 (2017) 642–65.

Jung, Kevin, ed. *Religious Ethics and Constructivism: A Metaethical Analysis.* New York: Routledge, 2018.

Kingson, Jennifer. "Riots Cost Property Damage." *Axios,* September 20, 2020. https://www.axios.com/riots-cost-property-damage-276c9bcc-a455-4067-b06a-66f9db4cea9c.html.

MacIntyre, Alasdair. *After Virtue.* Notre Dame: University of Notre Dame Press, 2003.

———. *Whose Justice? Which Rationality?* Notre Dame: University of Notre Dame Press, 1989.

Luther, Martin. *What Luther Says: An Anthology.* Vol. 1. Compiled by Ewald M. Plass. St. Louis: Concordia, 1959.

Noe-Bustamante, Luise, Lauren Mora, and Mark Hugo Lopez. "About one in four US Hispanics have heard of Latinx but just 3% use it." *Pew Research,* August 11, 2020. https://www.pewresearch.org/hispanic/2020/08/11/about-one-in-four-u-s-hispanics-have-heard-of-latinx-but-just-3-use-it/.

Pearce, Matt, and Joseph Tafani. "Virginia gunman hated Republicans, and was always in his 'little world.'" *LA Times,* June 14, 2017. http://www.latimes.com/nation/la-na-pol-virginia-shooter-profile-20170614-story.html.

Schweiker, William. "On Religious Ethics." *The Blackwell Companion to Religious Ethics,* edited by William Schweiker, 1–15. Oxford: Blackwell, 2008.

Stout, Jeffrey. *Democracy and Tradition.* Princeton: Princeton University Press, 2005.

Stuasberg, Michael. "Advocacy in the Study of Religion/s." *Religion* 44.2 (2013) 220–32.

WHO AM I TO SPEAK?

On Advocacy, Ethics, and Social Critique

Per Sundman

THIS ESSAY EXAMINES FRUITFUL intersections between advocacy and ethics.[1] The thesis claims that advocacy and ethics are distinctive and yet can be fruitfully interrelated. Advocates can as activists use ethical tools—occasionally, at least—in attempts to evaluate the causes they fight for. Indeed, ethicists sometimes act as advocates, and we would presumably prefer to be justified in thinking that our activity is worthwhile. Yet advocacy is not about the possibility of and conditions for providing a rational evaluation of the causes in which the advocate is invested, at least not primarily so. This presumably belongs to the sphere of ethics.

The argument has two interrelated parts: the content of the role of an ethicist and its possible justification. Of course, one could and perhaps should question the proper order of these questions. Why not start by asking whether it really is a good thing that there are ethicists, i.e., persons who after training perform the societal role of ethicists? Would not the world be better off if these people were dedicated to advocacy for veganism or for sustainable communications or making marginalized beings visible in respectable societal roles, i.e., as deliberating participants in the shared determination of the collective action of democracy? Or, as missionaries for faith doing what we can to safeguard that as few as possible lead meaningless lives, possibly ending up in permanent isolation from God?

1. I am grateful to Harlan Beckley for numerous valuable comments, helpful suggestions, and kind patience with my *Swenglish*.

One may wonder if academic ethics is more important to others than those persons who enjoy reading philosophical texts. Also, ethics is usually performed by academics who are, comparatively speaking, privileged. Many are raised in *respectable* academic families and by white aristocrats, often upper middle class, heterosexual, European men who have been over-represented in this group since Socrates. It is not farfetched to suspect that *our* vision is obscured by taking access to language and time for granted. *We* might be unconsciously involved in attempts to defend privileges, the practice of what Marxists tellingly call "ideology production," while convincing ourselves and others that ethics is important as a discipline. The burden of proof is set. This challenge makes the goals of this essay, to avoid ideology production and to present a defense for ethics as a critical intellectual discipline, interesting.

Let's begin with some general observations about the distinctive traits of ethics by relating it to advocacy, agitation, and politics, and then trace trends in ethics that relate it to societal causes, politics, and, by extension, advocacy. The final section is devoted to the influence of critical theory. It explains that insights from critical theory, with a suspicious eye towards normative ethics, shows how ethics and advocacy can be closely aligned and simultaneously distinctive.

ADVOCACY

There are different uses of the word *advocacy*. Advocacy 1 pleads to support someone else. An advocate typically supports a person or persons in trouble or in a particularly exposed situation. This meaning of advocacy connotes attempts to accomplish things on someone's behalf, usually outcomes difficult or impossible to achieve by the person for whom the advocate speaks.

The meaning and the moral challenges of Advocacy 1 are intertwined. An advocate seeks to assist, which is *ceteris paribus* a good thing. Nevertheless, regardless of selfless intentions, advocacy can be more or less respectful. There might be a mismatch between the advocate's and her "client's" conception of the client's best interest. Moreover, the advocate can be more or less perceptive of her client's situation and wishes. Consensus is one thing. Communication and consent another. Imposing help against the other's will treats the other as if she is inferior or incompetent.

There are complex criteria for success. Besides the moral procedural criteria concerning, e.g., respectful treatment, there are non-moral procedural ones, and moral as well as non-moral outcome-related ones. Non-moral procedural criteria coincide with professionalism, i.e., be knowledgeable of all the means available and pursue them optimally. There are obvious outcome-related criteria. As for any purposive activity, instances of advocacy can be evaluated in terms of the degree to which goals are reached, but also in terms of the relative importance, moral as well as non-moral, of their ends. Perhaps the purpose is to end societal misrecognition of a specific group or the acquittal of an innocent person. The success of the first can be difficult to measure, but both are arguably expressions of morally important ends. However, an advocate can also knowingly work for the acquittal of a guilty person. He can endeavor vigorously to preserve the privileges of, say, white men by referring to their merits and consciously neglecting the extent to which group-related privileges played a role in the creation of their CVs. Nevertheless, the fact that this advocate does no good neither means that he does not perform advocacy, nor that he is not successful. Put in other words, the rightness and goodness of Advocacy 1 is a complex and open ethical problem.

The second meaning of advocacy connotes action for the advancement of a societal cause, say, universal health care, stricter arms regulations, fewer arms regulations, lower taxes, a universal ban on plastic bags, or paid parental leave.[2] In Habermas's words, Advocacy 2 activity is strategic. Its success is determined by its effectiveness *vis-à-vis* the realization of an external goal. The cause is external in virtue of not being implicit in the notion of Advocacy 2.[3] Advocacy 1 differs in this respect. The activity of representing is ingrained with moral concerns. Their relation to the desired outcome does not determine their existence, meaning, and strength. Of course, there can be partly overlapping content between instances of Advocacy 1 and 2, say, between activism for ending prevalent misrecognition of a particular group of people and the societal cause of changing oppressive structures. The principled difference between concrete people (Advocacy 1) and cause (Advocacy 2) remains.

Furthermore, the goals of Advocacy 2 are public, not personal. Acting for the advancement of a private cause, i.e., saving money in order to pay for warm clothes or a good meal, is purposeful activity too, but not something ordinarily spoken of as advocacy. Working for a cause becomes advocacy when the realization of the cause is an integrated part of the politics of a certain community, nation, or federation. These distinctions are crucial from an ethical point of view.

2. *Oxford English Dictionary*, s.v. "activism."

3. Borradori, *Philosophy in a Time of Terror Dialogues*, 4–8. Borradori distinguishes between two models of public participation: Political Activism and Social Critique. Advocacy 2 resembles Political Activism since the chosen form of public participation is not an integral part of her or his profession as, e.g., ethicist.

ADVOCACY AND AGITATION

Advocacy 2 intersects in interesting ways with a common usage of "agitate." I have in mind generating public excitement in order to realize political goals. One can imagine public speeches or social media announcements. A political agitator calculates what kind of enthusiasm among which people would best further the cause. She wants to touch a group large enough to make itself heard and considered a power among rulers. Causing excitement is an instrument, but does not work through a predictable mechanism like starting a bus engine to cause physical movement.

I trust an interesting overlap between agitation and advocacy, version 2, has surfaced. Agitators and advocates both further political causes by influencing people to act. There might be differences in nuance. An advocate might be more optimistic about moving people to act by good arguments while agitation does not place similar restrictions on means. Good agitators use good arguments if an argument is more effective than other strategies. There is no constraint on using partly false propaganda, if it can be most effective. The end may or may not justify the chosen means. Agitation must be approached by further normative analysis by investigating what ends, if any, can justify which means. Perhaps no ends can justify certain means, but some ends can justify morally exceptional means. The point is that without external moral "side constraints" on means or moral evaluation of the chosen end, say, prohibition against the use of manipulation or justice for native Swedes, pure probability analysis determines the rational choice of means, i.e., the means most effectively to fulfill the end. Ethical reasoning will not necessarily contradict, but definitively constrain and transcend, the outlook of the agitator.

DISTINCTIVENESS?

Note that Advocacy 1 connotes the distinctive notion of supporting another by speaking on her behalf, whereas Advocacy 2 does not. Advocacy 2 and agitation both aim at the realization of political goals by influencing a group of people. Furthermore, neither the advocate nor the agitator has power in and of themselves. Employers, judges, or presidents have the power to effect some specific outcomes.[4] Employers can employ or unemploy; judges can execute a sentence; presidents can order a military attack.

4. See Morriss, *Power*, 30: "Benn's bankrupt financier had a certain amount of power *before* his fall, which he lost when his empire collapsed; although his fall possibly affected people more drastically than any of his previous actions, he did not thereby exercise power. To affect something (or somebody) but not effect (accomplish) anything

Advocates and agitators resemble the public role of an influencer or lobbyist. Advocates and agitators, however, are not only about marketing themselves or some commodity. Advocates (2) and lobbyists are most similar. They work for a cause rather than for themselves only, and both try to influence rulers. Lobbyists, however, can do their job as employees for a large corporation or an organization. This is different from Advocacy 2. The advocate (2) works primarily for a cause she is invested in. Some lobbyists can be advocates who use the position and resources offered through employment to further a cause they believe in. Many persons probably work for Amnesty International or the NRA for ideological reasons. Nevertheless, as lobbyists, they limit themselves to the agenda and strategies sanctioned by their employers, which is not the case for freestanding advocates.

Moreover, in a liberal democracy, agitators do not primarily work through strategies to influence those in positions of power. They try to influence people, citizens, and voters in order to influence rulers to adjust their agenda. Thus, the racist agitator tries to influence politicians by evoking racist emotions among voters, e.g., reinforcing low expectations for some groups. Advocacy is more open ended. An advocate can serve a cause by agitating people, but she can function similarly to a lobbyist by petitioning and meeting with relevant political leaders. Nevertheless, this potential difference in who the influencers try to affect does not differentiate them entirely. Within ordinary language, Advocacy 2 and agitation denote the same kind of activities. Advocacy 2, with or without agitation, is the craft of inventing, choosing, and implementing strategies for realizing political goals.

THE POLITICIAN

Let us extend this conceptual map. In the context of the institutions of representative democracies, e.g., contemporary Sweden, there are significant differences between politics, through a publicly recognized role as a politician, and devoting time and energy to a political agenda. There are important overlaps as well as differences between these roles. Politicians have specific roles within the administrative and legislative system of the state and usually within a freestanding "party." The latter organizations aim at participating in the government of society (or to govern in splendid solitude). Some politicians function only in relation to their party. In liberal democracies,

---

seems, then, not to be an exercise of power." See also Schweiker, *Responsibility and Christian Ethics*, 25: "Power is the ability to produce effects in the world and thus the force or energy to act."

the designation of politicians is election-based, though this may be indirect. Ministers, for example, are designated by the prime minister or the president. It remains a (socially constructed) fact, though, that politicians are neither employees only, nor freestanding agitators.

Furthermore, the politician is situated in a system that renders it possible to determine the rulings of a state or a party. Indeed, political decisions through legislation and the ability to enforce rulings altered societal core institutions such as the family and property, hospitals, schools, and universities. To the extent that politicians rule, they have power, in varying degrees. Advocates try to affect rulers.

Another side of designation through election is that politicians can expect to be affected by changing preferences among voters. The politician can either attempt to convince voters about the politician's vision for society or try to "change their minds." Affecting people by convincing arguments and rhetoric in order to stay in office is necessary to realize concrete politics. Thus, politicians are simultaneously influencers and rulers depending on how successful they are as communicators. Politicians therefore can be partly agitators and advocates.

Agitation and politics are interrelated in numerous ways. The freestanding advocate does not, at least not primarily, agitate in order to gain a role as a politician for herself. Advocacy 2 aims to make sure that someone who probably will do the alleged right thing is designated and that the preferred political institution has power to bring about a cause. The motives typical of politicians are more mixed, since furthering the cause and safeguarding a designation is likely intertwined. However, advocates of the second kind also need popularity to be effective. Besides, being publicly recognized, perhaps as a liberatory celebrity, can be self-gratifying. Still, the difference between influencing legislative power and the executive's direct enforcement remains.

THE ETHICIST

How then do the ideal types of the activist, the agitator, and the politician relate to ethics? The question is not what do ethicists do. They might preach, bully a colleague, or write a petition against local infringements on the right to asylum. We need to know how an ethicist is distinguished from other societal role holders. What does Ruben designate when he coherently labels Sondra an ethicist?

For religious persons, ethics is a branch of theology due to how existential and religious questions are related to morality.[5] Others would presumably say that ethics is located in departments of practical philosophy because of its focus on agency.[6] Despite differences in tradition as well as institutional location, ethicists investigate through philosophizing, rather than by empirical investigation, although the latter are often relevant. Let's begin by explicating distinctive properties of philosophy as academic activity.

Delineating the distinctive traits of a philosophical method, and what it means for scientific research to use this method, is complicated. Philosophy has many schools, and there are many views regarding possible common properties that define it. The general concept should help to identify all schools as versions of ethics. Our conception must accommodate relevant differences and yet explicate common properties that distinguish ethical research from other kinds of research.

This approach suggests that ethics is distinguished either by systematic presentations of critical reflections on how human beings ought to live or by critical reflections on the same subject matter.[7] How we ought to live is admittedly vague. The element of evaluation is crucial. It concerns assessment directed towards "conduct, character, or community as good or bad, right or wrong, honorable or dishonorable, just or unjust, as contributing to or detracting from human well-being" and functioning.[8]

Let us imagine instances of ethics. There are many; I will mention two: Immanuel Kant's *Grundlegung zur Metaphysik der Sitten* and some of Kant's unpublished conversations on moral problems with forgotten colleagues. The latter happened, although *we* know nothing about them.

5. See Gustafson, *The Contributions of Theology to Medical Ethics*, 15–25, for an enlighteningly clear account of the relation between theology and ethics.

6. The common institutional difference between practical and theoretical philosophy is constructed from the distinction between problems related to action and problems related to beliefs about reality, e.g., philosophy of science, epistemology, metaphysics, and philosophy of mind.

7. Referring to reflections on morality is an option. However, given how some ethicists distinguish between ethics and morality in which ethics refers to first-person oriented conceptions of the good life and morality to norms that regulate relations between oneself and others, I find that the phrase "reflection on how people ought to live" enables acknowledgment of these differences. See Ricoeur, *Oneself as Another*, 203; Namli, *Human Rights as Ethics, Politics, and Law*, 13. Namli writes: "I view ethics as a philosophical discipline dedicated to the critical study of morality."

8. Stout, *Ethics after Babel*, 69–70. Stout interprets the alleged conceptual core of moral language, what this language needs to be about in order to be recognizable, as an instance of moral language.

The first systematically presents learned reflections on moral problems, the content and justification of the moral *ought*, in particular. The other constitutes learned systematic reflections on how human beings ought to live together as a community from the first-person singular perspective. They share a common focus, i.e., the Socratic question about how we ought to live.[9] They also share use of analytical skills and knowledge about the history of moral philosophy in attempts to accomplish inter-subjectively valid explications of moral problems. Both examples of ethics—one actual and written, the other imagined and oral—are systematic in relating to a methodology. They are not random remarks and aphorisms. Arguably, these qualifiers clarify distinctive conceptual properties.

It might seem controversial to claim that being systematic and explicit are necessary properties of ethics as an academic activity. There are ethicists who do imaginative work while focusing on intersections between art, e.g., literature, and ethics.[10] However, though they can be compared with the fascinating long poem *Alfabet* by the Danish poet Inger Christenssen, neither novels nor poetry must be systematic or explicit about alternative ways of interpreting and solving moral quandaries.

Viewing systematic analysis and interpretation as necessary ingredients of ethical activity need not be controversial. The opposite of systematic activity is not organized according to any pattern or structure and capricious in not adhering to any methodological norms, whether hermeneutical, deconstructive, or logical. A presentation of odd observations about morals, e.g., "I have met more than one moral philosopher who behaved arrogantly towards three theologians," followed by "I have seen one pale faced ethicist who was meticulous about obeying traffic rules," cannot count as ethics. Statements like these do not constitute interpretations of what morality can mean and what function it can have, not to mention how moral beliefs, claims, or judgments can be justified.

Furthermore, systematic thought springs from the necessity of aiming for understanding, which presupposes inter-subjectivity as a goal.[11] Ethics demands the ethicist use her writing skills to ascertain that the most reasonable interpretation for her reader coincides with what she intended to express. The same goes for dialogues aimed at furthering an argument. Claims or observations are only available for critical scrutiny if they are made explicit. The implied need not be incomprehensible, but ambiguity

9. Plato, *Apology*, 38a5–6.

10. See Andersson, *Det etiska projektet och det estetiska*. See also Andersson "Traces of a Half-Forgotten Dog."

11. See Habermas, *On the Pragmatics of Communication*, 93.

and opacity make inter-subjectively shared comprehension comparatively difficult. Poems and novels, like *A Good Man Is Hard to Find* by Flannery O'Connor, are not subject to worries about obscurity. Ethicists are expected to do more than summarize stories, notwithstanding their moral relevance.

Different interpretations of right action or good character can be analyzed without suggesting how they ought to be interpreted, though.[12] Moral language and moral ontology in general can also be described. Some analytical philosophers adopted this stance, believing that moral disputes and judgments are beyond the scope of what can be spoken about with sufficient clarity ("That whereof we cannot speak, thereof we must remain silent").[13] This stance was linked to pessimism about the possibility of inter-subjectively valid arguments for beliefs or judgments about what actually is right or good. Indeed, influential moral philosophers claimed that the best arguments speak in favor of no thought-related beliefs about moral matters, only judgments that express subjective emotions. Moral language primarily expresses attitude. According to them, moral judgments do not express beliefs that can be true, since subjective feelings are not about anything that can be true. This became what Alasdair MacIntyre several years later referred to as "an emotivist turn."[14] Philosophers such as Charles Stevenson, Alfred Ayer, and in Sweden Axel Hägerström represented this trend.[15]

Today there is a great plurality of modes of doing ethics. Specialization occurs in complex fields of application, such as environmental and medical ethics, not to mention artificial intelligence. Recent technical developments have inspired talk about a "design turn in applied ethics."[16] Others are experts in normative political theory. Although some continue to abstain from taking a stand on moral issues, ethics today is often explicitly normative. It contains arguments about what in general or in specific areas is morally right or good.[17]

Implementing valid moral ideas does not belong to the work of the ethicist, per se. We might in different instances of our lives be responsible for acting upon principles that may have originated from an ethicist, ourselves included. But, put bluntly, ethicists are primarily responsible for excelling in the practice of doing ethics.

12. See Kelsay, *Arguing the Just War in Islam.*

13. See Wittgenstein, *Tractatus Logico-Philosophicus,* 7. See also McManus, *The Enchantment of Words,* for an interesting investigation on the significance of Wittgenstein's early work.

14. MacIntyre, *After Virtue,* 18–20.

15. See Grenholm, *Etisk teori Kritik av moralen,* 40–61.

16. See van den Hoven, "The Design Turn in Applied Ethics."

17. See Sen, *The Idea of Justice,* 52.

Doing ethics entails affirming aspirations to master a specific practice of critique. It means that there is a presumption of thinking that it is insufficient to claim that a moral idea is true or valid. Truth and validity need to be established, especially if the ethicist claims that at least some agents sometimes have reasons to adjust their behavior in accord with her ideas.

APPLIED ETHICS

If ethics is critical reflection on morality, what does that entail? Emphasis on critical reflection understands ethics as a specific intellectual activity. It produces communication of theory rather than implementation of care, commands, duties, prescriptions, principles, rights, or virtues. What about other combinations of agency and theory?

The monographs *Animal Liberation* and *Practical Ethics* are widely read and discussed products of a contemporary ethicist. Peter Singer's books were groundbreaking in several respects. The first, in 1975, was originally entitled *Animal Liberation: A New Ethics for Our Treatment of Animals,* and is now marketed as *Animal Liberation: The Definitive Classic of the Animal Movement.* These monographs widened the focus, at least in Western European and North American ethics, towards other creatures than human beings and towards application.

Although this ethics had political implications, it is not the strategic political action typical of Advocacy 2. Rather, it is critical reflection on the implications of a version of utilitarianism for judgments about right action or policy in distinctive fields of human activity. The primary purpose is to provide evaluations of normative arguments and establish critical implications for practices of mass breeding and killing of non-human animals. Singer seeks to implement interpretations of ethical principles that make the consumption of dead animals unlawful by influencing lawmakers to enforce the implications of the principles. Lawmakers are, he hopes, affected by a work of ethics.

Ethicists can participate in movements oriented to the moral implications of animal liberation. However, ethics as a discipline does not determine the movement the ethicist joins. Participating in one movement takes time; participating in many is impractical and may also be contradictory. Being both animal liberation ethicists and advocates for animal liberation is likely determined by the fact that people care about non-human animals, and probably did so before becoming ethicists.

Many objections have been raised against applied ethics. Particularly relevant in this case is its allegedly context-insensitive deductive procedure,

which applies abstract principles in contexts in which they and their origi-
nators are not at home. Deductive applied ethics starts from principles, say
utilitarian ones, whose validity is taken for granted, considered obvious,
or is outlined as less theoretically controversial than alternatives (e.g., deontological ones). The phrase "being at home" might seem strange in this
context. It denotes moral concepts, e.g., a principle that has a recognizable
function among the regulative norms, or standards of excellence, of the
practice or context in question.[18] It connotes having a recognized function
in the language of a specific context or practice. There are, for example, certain norms that determine the distinctive traits of concrete practices, such
as baseball. In order to master baseball, one must not only acquire certain
physical skills, say, to throw a ball, but also learn the rules of the game.
Such rules define the concept of a strike and the meaning of saying "three
strikes and you're out." The concept of a strike is at home in the set of rules
that constitute the game of baseball. Philosophers like Paul Weithman and
Alasdair MacIntyre claim that morality or a conception of virtue built on
norms of excellence resemble games.[19] It has its own distinctive rules and
concepts, and belongs to a particular time and place. In other words, the
rules of baseball are limited in scope by virtue of receiving their rationale
from significantly different kinds of activities. Being not at home resembles
playing rugby amidst a baseball game, which might be harmless, even funny,
but makes limited sense. Perhaps therefore applying the rules of one moral
context to another resembles applying the rules of baseball to a tennis match
or to criminal law.

Though this particular critique of applied ethics depends on naming
morality a game, there is a significant difference between thinking, like
MacIntyre, that there is no common morality but many different local practices, and Weithman who names morality "the social cooperation game," a
game played wherever persons cooperate socially.[20]

---

18. MacIntyre, *After Virtue*, 187–89: "By a 'practice' I am going to mean any coherent and complex form of socially established cooperative human activity through
which goods internal to that form of activity are realized in the course of trying to
achieve those standards of excellence which are appropriate to, and partially definitive
of, that form of activity . . ."

19. MacIntyre, *After Virtue*, 188. MacIntyre here explicates his excellence-oriented
conception of virtue with the help of the rules that make up the game of chess. See
also Weithman, "Constructivism, Baseball, and Ethics," 26, 31. On 26, Weithman writes
about the Constructvist inspired by a Wittgensteinian conception of games: "For we
can read her as likening the practices by which necessary goods are produced and dis-
tributed to a game—call it 'the social cooperation game.'"

20. Weithman, "Constructivism, Baseball, and Ethics," 26.

In contemporary southern Italy there is a Mafioso way of life in which the concepts *omertà* and family honor play important parts. In the same area there are also prevalent Christian Roman Catholic moral practices, articulated in the life of the Priest Don Peppino Diana, who practiced prophetic truth-telling.[21]

According to narrow contextualism, talk about human dignity is not at home in a Mafioso or a neo-fascist corporative way of life. The fact that it nevertheless makes sense to use it, for representatives of the Church, for example, speak in favor of thinking about moral matters in terms of wider contexts than the codes of specific groups. We shall subsequently return to this point.

For now, note that the critique of applied ethics raises important questions. First, is it the task of ethics to produce action-guiding principles, or lists of virtues, for others to follow? The second concerns the ideology critique, i.e., a systematic suspicion of norms whose possible legitimation of current power relations and privileges has not been scrutinized and originate from agents in privileged positions unburdened, for example, by poverty and/or race.[22] A third concerns the scope of the validity of moral norms or principles decisively conditioned by being at home in particular language games or practices. The latter two points are related. If doing ethics is to participate in an academic practice, then *we* might be trapped in ideology production as soon as steps are taken towards claims about the content of moral norms. If so, not only applied ethics, but normative ethics in general might be *morally* questionable. Privileges seems to be entwined with the capability of mastering this practice.[23]

Before addressing this quandary, we need to consider a second influential trend in ethics that seeks to overcome both problems with deductive

21. See Saviano R. 283–311. On Don Peppino Diana.

22. There are, of course, degrees of privilege. Many ethicists belong to the growing group of contingent faculty. Albeit vulnerable, these persons are still privileged in possessing more than average of cultural capital and less so when it comes to social security, yet they have more than unemployed or cognitively disabled people.

23. Young, *Justice and the Politics of Difference*, 57. Ethicists belong to the comparatively privileged group of professionals who, as a group, in Young's terminology, has the opportunity to live a life of respectability. Young writes the following about non-professionals: "The life of the nonprofessional by comparison is powerless in the sense that it lacks this orientation toward the progressive development of capacities and avenues for recognition"; "Nonprofessionals, on the other hand, lack autonomy, and in both their working and their consumer-client lives often stand under the authority of professionals" (Fraser, "Social Justice in the Age of Identity Politics," 23–24). Fraser writes about class-related injustice. It allegedly is caused by the economic structure of capitalism and by misrecognition, neither of which has similar negative effects on the lives of tenured ethicists.

forms of reasoning and the application of principles alien to local practice. This turn to contextual ethics returns to the third and last objection above, the issue of scope.

CONTEXTUAL ETHICS

Moral concepts undeniably come from somewhere. It is another thing to claim that the validity of moral norms is determined by and coincides with the scope of the particular context from which they emerge. If so, moral ideas stemming from a Christian context can be valid among Christians, but not among non-Christians and vice versa. Put starkly, it could be claimed that the scope of the validity of norms that originated from late-eighteenth century Königsberg is limited to that time and place.[24] This is a complicated and potentially controversial claim. The Königsberg example illustrates a possibly interesting difference between originating from a particular place and being part of a philosophical critique formulated in that place. The former contains a plain observation about origin, whereas the latter contains a rigorous attempt to justify the universal validity of human dignity.

Nevertheless, philosophical critiques of Kantian universalism have turned applied and normative ethics towards contextualism, i.e., the meanings of moral ideas are determined in concrete contexts and the justification of moral beliefs are contingent upon those contexts.[25]

Explications of criteria for right action do appear to be difficult to separate from a descriptive analysis of the workings of a particular society. Compare how Jon Elster's *Local Justice* proceeds. Attention to the concrete details of particular life rather than to abstraction, however, does not establish a link between ethics and advocacy. On the contrary, the task of the contextual (applied) ethicist is arguably to explicate norms in actual use. It is not construction of ideal theory. This explains why contextual ethics is burdened by having to show that it is not locked in a stance of mere explication of moral concepts in use or uncritical affirmations of validity. Explication of tacit moral norms can also be of value, of course, when assessment in light of alternative interpretations and norms is left to the reader. Either contextual ethics merely explicates the tacit moral norms in use in a particular place without providing assessments, or the ethicist also argues that some of the explicated norms are valid, and perhaps there are valid contextual

---

24. Pui-lan, *Postcolonial Imagination and Feminist Theology,* 56.

25. See Stout, *Ethics after Babel,* 133–35.

principles that determine the relative strength of each norm, which is useful when claims are in conflict.[26]

However, in order for there to be a predictable link between ethics and advocacy, the contextual ethicist needs to go beyond explication and provide good reasons for thinking that some norms in use at a particular place and time ought to be acted upon by the members of the community in question.[27] The reasons cannot be based only on the fact that the norms are in use, since obviously some are contradictory and some amoral.

A cause worthy of one's political commitment must not be reducible to morally ambivalent custom. It must not only be about things a group of people care about; it must also be worthy of their investment. Advocacy seeks political influence in order to further societal goals that the advocate finds worthy of time and energy. Therefore, it appears that Advocacy 2 could benefit from having access to means for critical evaluation of goals, possibly provided by ethics.

CRITICAL THEORY AND ETHICS AS SOCIAL CRITIQUE

There are other conceptions of ethics. One of particular interest connects ethics and social critique. Perhaps theoretically informed advocacy belongs to critical ethics, ethical theories informed and inspired by critical theory. Although the full complexity of critical theory is beyond our scope, an encyclopedia quotation will suffice for our purposes. Critical theories, broadly considered:

> aim to explain and transform *all* the circumstances that enslave human beings, many "critical theories" in the broader sense have been developed. They have emerged in connection with the many social movements that identify varied dimensions of the domination of human beings in modern societies. In both

26. Walzer, *Thick and Thin Moral Argument*, 49. Walzer writes about the critical potential from within a local thick or maximalist morality. "To construct a theory out of an actual thick morality is mostly an interpretive (rather than a philosophically creative) task. If the purpose is critical, then what is required is a *pointed* interpretation, a localized theory that concludes with a moral maxim the philosophical equivalent of an Aesopian fable."

27. An activist might get inspiration from reading an investigation, say about the history of Human Rights. Although the justification of the conviction about the rightness of respecting Human Rights might and might not be part of the new inspiration, it does not take place in the inspiring text but the mind of the beholder. See William Schweiker's chapter in this volume.

the broad and the narrow senses, however, a critical theory
provides the descriptive and normative bases for social inquiry
aimed at decreasing domination and increasing freedom in all
their forms.[28]

The quotation enlightens in two ways: it reveals a distinctive common property, the focus on emancipation or liberation, and a striking ambivalence among critical theories. Critical theories can be, on the one hand, transformative, and, on the other, be tools ("bases") for socially transformative activities. Critical theory is connected to specific normative principles and a general political cause simultaneously. The theory should serve the emancipation of the structurally oppressed and offer strategies for furthering the chosen cause. So understood, crucial ingredients of Advocacy 2 belong to "critical theory ethics" or ethics as social critique.

Perhaps there are good reasons to assume that ethics cannot avoid taking some general normative (moral) content for granted, say, the rightness of emancipation or the wrongness of oppression. Still, if ethical theory aims at critique it must acknowledge there are many alternative normative concepts that could serve as guiding lights and offer orientation for a political morality. Most of them need interpretation.

The tricky question is to determine what emancipation means. She who claims that oppression is wrong states the obvious. However, she who communicates that oppression is about group related misrecognition primarily, besides saying something ethically interesting, receives a specific burden of proof. The burden consists of the obligation to provide reasons for thinking that, among alternatives, the interpretation is comparatively reasonable.

Taking on this burden requires self-reflective criticism, not merely assertive critique. Besides being critical towards everything that is morally bad, such as injustice or oppression, ethicists should be critical in a thorough and qualified sense. Philosophy identifies, explicates, and sometimes mends inconsistencies, incoherencies, and implied presuppositions. Therefore, critical questions about what normative content a particular theory uses to identify emancipation, oppression, and historical progress necessarily come with the philosophical task. This ethics suggests ways to reason about alternative interpretations of emancipation. Still, critical theory poses challenges to both "traditional" normative ethics and to accounts of moral epistemology, particularly justification. Let us turn to them.

The principal critical question concerns whether normative ethics serves the end of explicating differences between actual structures and more

28. *The Stanford Encyclopedia of Philosophy*, s.v. "Critical Theory."

just ones or if it inevitably will be ideological. Let me explain. Critical theory harbors sensibilities to and explications of the oppressive character of past and present societies.[29] These societies typically instrumentalize and reify in ways that transform persons into economically useful things. Critical theory presumes that principles originating from a place of unfair privileges are more likely to legitimate prevailing social systems than to explicate how, for example, humiliation is reiterated, in new guises. Dominant accounts of ethics arguably exhibit biases and negligence about who counts, how and why. The burden of proof falls upon ethics to show that ideology production is avoided.[30]

So, how shall we determine whether our prerogatives lead us to reproduce abstract theories that inevitably legitimate current societal systems?[31] In the words of Melissa A. Mosko, can we avoid the risk of "reinscribing the patterns of oppression and dehumanization" that we aim to resist, when "we carry those structures with us into our relationships with others . . . ?"[32] This question can be scrutinized empirically, i.e., to what extent is every privileged person, completely or partly, incapable of tracing the impact of his privileges on moral discernment? We can also pose philosophical, theological, or anthropological questions about a general human propensity for narcissism, as when someone cares little about other people but cares a lot about being loved. Or, we might assume a human inability to form thoroughly open-minded and self-critical ideas about moral rightness. Christian theologies have for centuries labelled such shortcomings instances of

29. Habermas, *The Theory of Communicative Action*, 377, 379, 389. On 389, Habermas writes: "Instrumental reason is also 'subjective' in the sense that it expresses the relations between subject and object from the vantage point of the knowing and acting subject and not from that of the perceived and manipulated object. For this reason, it does *not* provide the explicative tools needed to explain what the instrumentalization of social and intrapsychic relations means from the perspective of the violated and deformed contexts of life."

30. Thompson, *Ideology and Modern Culture*, 72–73: "The concept of ideology, according to the formulation proposed here, calls our attention to the ways in which the meaning constructed and conveyed by symbolic forms serves, in particular circumstances, to establish and sustain structured social relations from which some individuals and groups benefit more than others, and which some individuals and groups have an interest in preserving while others may seek to contest."

31. Habermas, *The Theory of Communicative Action*, 370. With the help of Georg Lukács, Habermas formulates the problem of critical self-reflection as follows:: "Lukacs had already conceded that the further the process of reification moved away from the sphere of production and the everyday experiences of the proletarian lifeworld, and the more it changed the qualitative nature of thoughts and feelings, the less accessible it became to self-reflection."

32. Mosko, "Emancipatory Advocacy," 338.

sin which manifests itself as distorted moral cognition, moral rationality, motivation, or a combination of these. Such claims about the human psyche must, of course, be critically evaluated. Coherence with historical facts, i.e., historical traces of weakness of will, moral courage, egoism, or altruistic motivation is an important touchstone.[33] Prevalent inclinations to share, help, and act on the basis of tacit assumptions of trust are hard to reconcile with at least some versions of innate human depravity. Whereas, systemic racism and tribalism are not.

We may conclude that ethicists need to be humble and self-critical as well as self-reflective. We need to learn which patterns of oppression are imprinted in us in order to avoid repeating and legitimating them. However, merely assuming the necessity of professional virtuousness, in the form of humility, does not settle the issue of who is able to practice ethics as researcher and teacher entitled to articulate and defend normative ideas of political relevance.

CRITICAL EVALUATION

One way of evaluating normative arguments is to investigate whether the proposed normative content is biased by investigating whether it legitimates privileges. Comparatively speaking, the world's ethicists, at least those among us safely employed as university professors, are privileged. Our cultural capital is large compared to uneducated and unemployed or to people who do hard physical work, not to mention illegal immigrants.[34] We may never have had to experience how gender, family background, and skin color affect opportunities in our lives. Some ethicists receive free lunches that no one seems to pay for. It might not be farfetched to expect ideology production from such a group. We, in spite of pretensions, produce normative theories that obscure rather than identify actual injustices.

Despite these troubling concerns, there can be remedies of two kinds. The first is an observation, not a remedy. The second addresses the problem of complete or partial blindness due to inability to imagine hardships while seated at the university desk. It is a rudimentary argument about the critical potential of ordinary (natural) language.

Let us start with the observation: there is a significant difference between the meaning of the normative principles of theories of justice and politics expressed in policies and laws. States have the ability to create

33. Glover, *Humanity*, 407–9.

34. See Ledford, "US trust in scientists is now on par with the military," for polls concerning the trust in scientists in the US.

modes of social organization, such as public-sector welfare, a redistributive tax system, and property. Theories of justice can contain ideas about right social organization based on a specific interpretation of justice.[35] Elene Namli's point that "Justice disappears at the very moment someone claims that his action, decision, policy, or interpretation *is* just" is well taken.[36] Still, conflating explications of a preferred conception of justice with descriptive claims about actual social organization, although tempting and hard to avoid, is not necessary.

Libertarian politics differ from libertarian conceptions of social justice. For example, Robert Nozick emphasized: "There are important differences between the model and the model's projection onto the actual world."[37] Nozick labels possible denotations of the preferred conception of justice Utopia, i.e., no actual society is expected to be just. Indeed, representatives of Native American nations imagined different denotations from President Ronald Reagan. Similarly, egalitarian liberal conceptions of justice can be transformed into regulatory property norms through redistributive tax laws and establishment of public schools. The fact that egalitarian liberals have been criticized for not articulating the critical potential of their normative ideas highlights the difference between normative ethical theory and concrete application through societal institutions such as the family, the limited company, money, property, and the university.[38]

This observation demonstrates the difference between arguments about the fit between normative principles and institutional patterns and arguments about the meanings and justification of normative principles. Claiming a faltering fit between majority rule and democratic principles differs from claiming that popular control and political equality explicate the normative core of democracy.[39] Criticizing principles due to faltering fit with actual institutions is beside the point unless it targets the principles for being unrealistic. Assuming principles are the culprit of injustice can be a misplaced critique of the principles when in reality it is institutional applications that falter. As a consequence, the critical potential of, e.g., a

35. See Nozick, *Anarchy, State, and Utopia*, 178–82, for an example of an explication of social justice that contains a conception of an argument for natural (non-conventional) rights to private property.

36. Namli, *Human Rights as Ethics, Politics, and Law*, 60.

37. Nozick, *Anarchy, State, and Utopia*, 307.

38. See Kymlicka, *Contemporary Political Philosophy*, 91: "In short, liberal egalitarianism's institutional commitments have not kept pace with its theoretical commitments."

39. See Beetham, *Democracy and Human Rights*, 5, 18–26, for an enlightening discussion about the relationship between arguably justified democratic core principles and the institutional application of majority rule.

conception of justice that could serve the purpose of explicating shortcomings of actual institutions is overlooked.

What about the "remedy"? It makes use of natural language, a point in need of explication. Let's begin with the distinction between explanation and justification: "The reasons that justify my action, and thus explain why it was the right action to perform, may not be the same as the reasons that explain why I in fact did it."[40] Consider reasons for telling the truth. It can be inconvenient, e.g., when someone else is blamed for something I have done. Then, telling the truth is likely to come with a cost. The explanation for telling the truth may not differ from the reasons that justify truth-telling. My upbringing, what my parents would think of me, might have been the effective motivation; parental approval might name my strongest desire. Yet, the rightness of truth-telling is, in ordinary language, independent of a desire not to disappoint my parents. Indeed, truth-telling appears to be right even if my parents applaud me for avoiding blame. Similarly, the explanation for why I believe that earth is oval differs from the justification of that belief.

In spite of these observations concerning differences between explanation and justification, there are sophisticated attempts to harmonize these distinctive reasons for action. These are often labelled internalist views of practical reason.[41] They insist that motivations are necessary parts of reasons for action. Justifying reasons are closely connected to motivation. Since a belief cannot move us to act unless it is supported by a decisive desire, the belief alone is not a reason for action. One justification for internalism suggests that the strongest reasons for acting coincides with our strongest motivation. Harry G. Frankfurt formulates it as follows: "The most fundamental issues of practical reason cannot be resolved, in other words, without an account of what people love."[42] According to him, if we love doing the right thing, we are justified in giving unqualified priority to moral issues. One might hold that once the meaning of a specific moral imperative is known, then the strength of our motivation will in fact reflect the overriding strength ascribed to *the moral demand*. If so, deciding to act on the moral imperative is practically rational and justified since it attempts to further an end of terminal value, the object of our deepest and most effective motivation, our love.

Is it possible to understand what morality demands, and yet fail to be motivated to act? Bluntly, yes. It is fully possible to care more about showing

---

40. Searle, *Rationality in Action,* 110.

41. *The Stanford Encyclopedia of Philosophy,* s.v. "Reasons for Action: Internal vs. External."

42. Frankfurt, *The Reasons of Love,* 57.

disinterested concern for someone I love, myself for example, than caring about being a good neighbor to fellow human beings.[43] As noted before, many religions contain conceptual resources to identify and explicate such inclinations. The concept of sin is one.[44] This coheres with the observation that morality contains ideas about what we ought to care about, not reliable predictions about what we care about.

The debate about externalism and internalism will not be settled here, but the difference between explaining why I did what I did and evaluating whether or not I did the right thing remains. Failure to account for this difference conflates criteria for right action with criteria for praise and blame. Act-utilitarians pertinently observe that it can be permissible for concrete agents not to perform the right action, the one that actually maximizes utility, since calculating the consequences of numerous mutually exclusive alternatives is often impossibly difficult, perhaps even counterproductive. Trying to do the right thing is, therefore, more relevant for praise than succeeding, which may be attributable to luck. For accounts of justification, however, the role of intention and "trying" is an open question. The deontologist adds that persons who fail to intend to act rightly are blameworthy and breach an obligation.

Where does this lead us, and how do these observations relate to insights borrowed from critical theory? Since justifying or validating reasons can be external to motivation and linked primarily to moral beliefs rather than judgments about how to act, in which desires play a constitutive and executive role, we have to look beyond ourselves for possible validation.[45]

43. See Frankfurt, *The Reasons of Love*, 43: "Among relationships between humans, the love of parents for their infants or small children is the species of caring that comes closest to offering recognizably pure instances of love." The moral problem remains to what extent and in what circumstances it is right to be decisively moved by love. There are obvious cases where being so moved would be an act out of love and problematic favoritism simultaneously.

44. See Grantén. *Utanför paradiset Arvsyndsläran*, 115–26, for an explication of the contemporary relevance of a Lutheran conception of original sin. See also Gustafson, *The Contributions of Theology*, 22: "Thus, relative to the ultimate power, God, humans are finite; relative to God's purposes and activity for the well-being of the whole creation, humans are inordinately curved in upon their narrow self-interests in efforts to find security."

45. The internalist might seek to avoid explicating actual motivation as a valid reason for action. However, if only ideal motivation is a "truly" good reason, then the defining properties of the ideal differ from actual motivation and one cannot refer to actual (decisive) motivation as its constituent source. Therefore, internalism cannot find argumentative support along this route. See also Habermas, *The Theory of Communicative Action*, 390.

Therefore, externalist accounts of justificatory reasons offer a liberatory potential for ethicists.

As stated above, the suggested path is to turn to ordinary language for an explication of important properties of moral concepts revealed in "ordinary use." This path must address valid objections, including one that claims ordinary language is not a neutral ground, but an enabler of ideology. Indeed, present language reveals how previous language expressed humiliating racist and sexist prejudices.[46]

If current language becomes the blueprint for ideas about how the notions of moral obligation and moral rightness ought to be interpreted, would the preferred explications of moral concepts be predetermined as conventional and skewed, captured by an inevitable and increasingly arrogant repetition? My answer starts with a positive reading of another kind of inevitability. Moral ideas are inescapably tied up in language.[47] Any attempt to speak about something outside of language, say, a moral reality, takes place in language. Proponents of accounts of non- or pre-conceptual moral reality have a burden of proof to establish that the meaning of the real object of moral perception is independent of the concept used to identify its distinctive properties. It is similarly difficult to separate the concept in question from constitutive norms imprinted in use of (natural) language. Faced with the inevitability of being trapped in language, we pause and turn to something obvious. Our worry about repeating oppressive patterns is also formulated in language. Observations of how attempts to articulate positive accounts of, say, justice contain injustice and make use of other ideas about justice that are collectively constructed in language. Indeed, the very ideas about theoretical humility and presumptions about complicity in continuing injustices are in language ready to be used.[48]

Moreover, since language constantly changes, so does moral language. Current forms of language allows us to explicate interpretations of those changes and to form hypotheses about various movements that

46. This is not to be confused with thinking about progress as a historical fact, which apparently runs the risk of turning a potentially radical idea into mere legitimation of *status quo*. See Allen, *The End of Progress*, 25.

47. See Habermas, *The Theory of Communicative Action*, 392, on communicative rationality: "And what is paradigmatic for the latter is not the relation of a solitary subject to something in the objective world that can be represented and manipulated, but the intersubjective relation that speaking and acting subjects take up when they come to an understanding with one another about something. In doing so, communicative actors move in the medium of a natural language, draw upon culturally transmitted interpretations, and relate simultaneously to something in the objective world, something in their common social world, and something in each own subjective world."

48. See Block, "White Privilege and the Erroneous Conscience," 374.

effect change. Some of those movements consist of people with comparatively few resources in money and cultural capital. Ethicists who presume
tacit complicity in ongoing injustices would be irrational and unjust if they
did not try to identify people who are the most vulnerable, comparatively
powerless, and construed as anonymous members of inferior collectives,
or worse as things, not persons.[49] We ought to ask: Are there unrecognized
emancipatory potentials in language in different movements of liberation
that we need to attend to? There probably are.

Moreover, language poses no barrier for asking: Who is left out? Who
lives on margins where no movements exist? Languages, even colonial ones
such as Swedish or English, contain resources for thinking about the standing of those who have no access to language, like some cognitively disabled
person. How are we to speak respectfully on their behalf, as their personal
advocates. The question cannot be avoided since severely cognitively disabled and non-speaking non-humans are implicated in how humanity collectively directs its life.

We can now formulate an insight from critical theory that deserves
attention. Justificatory or validating reasons must challenge accounts of
what we actually care about, but also about what we ought to care about.
This must not be done by suggesting that *we* should go beyond good and
evil, and perhaps admire brute force or sublime creativity, but by questioning how given conceptions of the good and the right can be more inclusive
and respectful. Our complicity in everyday moral shortcomings constitute
good reasons to ask: Who are we to say that accounts of morality cannot be
reconstructed and become more "deserving" of being labelled "conceptions
about how we ought to live"? Furthermore, while moral concepts reside in
language, they are never far from application. The ethicist should vigilantly
rework attempts to strike a balance between the political irrelevance of abstraction and the injustice of legitimation. We better not bungle it by being
so caught up in Advocacy 2 and its instrumental reason that we lose our
orientation.

Given the validity of moral principles such as the right of every human
being to equal concern and respect, advocates of both kinds are needed.
For righteousness to reign, some must speak the truth about violations,
and some must try to move people to act by being upset by violations. The
ethicist can provide arguments and warn against dogmatic interpretations
of righteousness. She can connect and evaluate descriptive analyses of social systems with moral principles. Indeed, ethicists can also write petitions,
make speeches, and organize as well as participate in demonstrations. These

---

49. See Pui-lan, *Postcolonial Imagination and Feminist Theology*, 56.

activities can all serve a cause described as "deeply human" or "humane."[50] Everything in its morally justified place.

50. Glover, *Humanity*, 62.

BIBLIOGRAPHY

Allen, Amy. *The End of Progress: Decolonizing the Normative Foundations of Critical Theory*. New York: Columbia University Press, 2017.

Andersson, Helen. *Det etiska projektet och det estetiska: tvärvetenskapliga perspektiv på Lars Ahlins författarskap*. Lund: Symposion, 1998.

———. "Traces of a Half-Forgotten Dog: Suffering and Animal Humanity in Hélène Cixous' Algerian Scenes." *Literature and Theology* 31.4 (December 2017) 420–36.

Beetham, David. *Democracy and Human Rights*. Cambridge: Polity, 2007.

Borradori, Giovanna. *Philosophy in a Time of Terror: Dialogues with Jürgen Habermas and Jacques Derrida*. Chicago: University of Chicago Press, 2003.

Frankfurt, Harry G. *The Reasons of Love*. Princeton: Princeton University Press, 2004.

Fraser, Nancy. "Social Justice in the Age of Identity Politics: Redistribution, Recognition, and Participation." In *Redistribution or Recognition: A Political-Philosophical Exchange*, edited by Nancy Fraser and Axel Honneth, 7–109. London: Verso, 2003.

Glover, Jonathan. *Humanity: A Moral History of the Twentieth Century*. London: Pimlico, 2001.

Grantén, Eva-Lotta. *Utanför paradiset Arvsyndsläran i nutida luthersk teologi och etik*. Stockholm: Verbum, 2013.

Grenholm, Carl-Henric. *Etisk teori Kritik av moralen*. Lund: Studentlitteratur, 2014.

Gustafson, James M. *The Contributions of Theology to Medical Ethics*. Milwaukee: Marquette University Press, 1982.

Habermas, Jürgen. *On the Pragmatics of Communication*. Cambridge: MIT Press, 1998.

———. *The Theory of Communicative Action Reason and the Rationalization of Society*. Vol. 1. Boston: Beacon, 1984.

Kelsay, John. *Arguing the Just War in Islam*. Cambridge: Harvard University Press, 2009.

Kymlicka, Will. *Contemporary Political Philosophy: An Introduction*. Oxford: Oxford University Press, 2002.

Ledford, Heidi. "US trust in scientists is now on par with the military." *Nature*, August 6, 2019. https://www.nature.com/articles/d41586-019-02389-8.

MacIntyre, Alasdair. *After Virtue: A Study in Moral Theory*. 2nd ed. London: Duckworth, 1985.

McManus, Denis. *The Enchantment of Words: Wittgenstein's Tractatus Logico-Philosophicus*. Oxford: Oxford University Press, 2006.

Morriss, Peter. *Power: A Philosophical Analysis*. Manchester: Manchester University Press, 1987.

Mosko, Melissa A. "Emancipatory Advocacy: A Companion Ethics for Political Activism." *Philosophy and Social Criticism* 44.3 (2018) 326–41.

Namli, Elena. *Human rights as Ethics, Politics, and Law Acta*. Universitatis Upsaliensis Uppsala Studies in Social Ethics 43. Uppsala: Uppsala University Press, 2014.

Nozick, Robert. *Anarchy, State, and Utopia*. Oxford: Basil Blackwell, 1974.

Plato. *Apology*. Translated by Benjamin Jowett. Project Gutenberg, 1999. https://www.gutenberg.org/files/1656/1656-h/1656-h.htm.

Pui-lan, Kwok. *Postcolonial Imagination and Feminist Theology*. London: Student Christian Movement, 2005.

Ricoeur, Paul. *Oneself as Another*. Chicago: University of Chicago Press, 1992.

Saviano, Roberto. *Gomorra En resa i Camorrans land*. Translated by Barbro Svensson. Stockholm: Brombergs, 2008.

Schweiker, William. *Responsibility and Christian Ethics*. Cambridge: Cambridge University Press, 1995.

Searle, John R. *Rationality in Action*. Cambridge: Cambridge University Press, 2001.

Sen, Amartya. *The Idea of Justice*. Cambridge: Belknap, 2009.

Singer, Peter. *Animal Liberation: The Definitive Classic of the Animal Movement*. New York: Harper Perennial, 2009.

———. *Practical Ethics*. 3rd ed. Cambridge: Cambridge University Press, 2011.

Stout, Jeffrey. *Ethics after Babel: The Languages of Morals and Their Discontents*. Boston: Beacon, 1988.

Sweeny Block, Elizabeth. "White Privilege and the Erroneous Conscience: Rethinking Moral Culpability and Ignorance." *Journal of the Society of Christian Ethics* 39.2 (2019) 357–74.

Thompson, John B. *Ideology and Modern Culture: Critical Social theory in the Era of Mass Communication*. Cambridge: Polity, 1990,

van den Hoven, Jeroen. "The Design Turn in Applied Ethics." In *Designing in Ethics*, edited by J. Van den Hoven et al., 11–31. Cambridge: Cambridge University Press, 2017.

Walzer, Michael. *Thick and Thin Moral Argument at Home and Abroad*. Notre Dame: University of Notre Dame Press, 1994.

Weithman, Paul. "Constructivism, Baseball, and Ethics." In *Religious Ethics and Constructivism: A Metaethical Inquiry*, edited by Kevin Jung, 21–39. New York: Routledge, 2018.

Wittgenstein, Ludwig. *Tractatus Logico Philosophicus*. Project Gutenberg, 2010. https://www.gutenberg.org/files/5740/5740-pdf.pdf.

Young, Iris Marion. *Justice and the Politics of Difference*. Princeton: Princeton University Press, 1990.

—PART 2—

Normative Models

CHRISTIAN ETHICS AND ADVOCACY

Douglas F. Ottati

As I write, a second wave of the global coronavirus epidemic is spiking, and, in the United States, we have hit well over 150,000 diagnosed new cases per day. Joe Biden has been elected president, but the current president, quite apart from credible evidence, insists the election was stolen. Republican leaders are slow to acknowledge the results, and today armed protesters stormed the US Capitol. A spate of incidents in which African-American men and women have died in police custody and been shot by police has bled into the fall with the shooting of Walter Wallace in Philadelphia. The distressing deterioration of the earth's natural environment at human hands continues, and recent fires in the western US have been ominously intense (as fires also were in Australia). This nation, like many others from Turkey to Finland, struggles with how to deal with migrants and refugees. People in the rural US confronting widespread opioid abuse and problematic economies feel as if educated, urban, and coastal elites have left them behind. Manufacturing jobs continue to decline. Monuments are lightning rods.

Almost everything seems urgent, and the culture is trying to respond. News staffs rethink relationships between reporting and exposing falsehoods and injustices. Social media brim with calls to action and questionable information. Talking heads on proliferating networks almost endlessly debate and commend values, policies, and positions. Many open their programs with rehearsed homilies. What passes for public discourse sometimes resembles a shouting match, and conspiracy theories bloom. Colleges hold forums and invite visitors to address issues from climate change to gender identity and racism, often expecting speakers to champion particular responses. Crisis, contention, and division are the order of the day. Advocacy abounds, but clarity is at a premium.

This essay is about Christian ethics and advocacy. Ethics involves critical reflections on moral reasoning and moral questions. It explores ideas about what is good and bad and about moral duty and obligation. It also asks how we frame our moral cases for actions, practices, and policies. Advocacy supports and recommends specific causes, views, and policies.[1] The two clearly are not the same. Ethics tries to clarify our moral conceptions and arguments, while advocacy commends and exhorts. The two obviously interrelate. Moral advocates commend causes or policies to advance what is good, mitigate or eliminate what is bad, and that accord with understandings of moral duties and obligations. An ethicist's critical reflections on moral reasoning and questions about what is good, bad, and a matter of moral obligation will dispose her to advocate some particular causes and policies.

The first term in the title of this essay introduces a further layer of complexity. *Christian* ethics operates in conjunction with a Christian theology. Like all ethics, it deals with what is good and right, but it does so in the light of a heartfelt Christian theological vision of ourselves, objects, and others in relation to God. This does not make Christian ethics entirely unique since all ethics also interconnect with interpretations of oneself, objects, and others in light possibilities and limits within the nature of things. However, a Christian ethic intentionally interconnects with a Christian piety and theological vision. Advocacy may be called Christian, then, if it is informed by a Christian ethic that commends causes and policies intertwined with understandings of what is good and bad and of moral duty and obligation in relation to God.

This essay argues that while Christian ethics and Christian advocacy may and should be distinguished, they are closely interrelated. Good Christian advocacy intermingles with critical, ethical, and theological reflections, and good Christian ethics is practically disposing. My approach will illustrate rather than be comprehensive or logically constraining. I will analyze terms, arguments, distinctions, and connections in the writings of two Christian advocates and of two Christian ethicists. Then, I will ask what these analyses indicate about Christian ethics and advocacy. I will also suggest that ethical reflections and analyses clarify agreements and disagreements, and so help us to improve the quality of our arguments and debates.

---

1. *Merriam-Webster's English Dictionary*, s.v. "advocacy."

JOHN LEWIS AND MARTIN LUTHER KING JR.: REFLECTIVE CHRISTIAN ADVOCATES

The late Congressman John Lewis clearly was an advocate. Newscasts and eulogies described his experience of being beaten by law enforcement as he and other civil rights activists tried to cross the Edmund Pettus Bridge (named for a Confederate brigadier general) in Selma, Alabama, on "Bloody Sunday," March 7, 1965. They highlighted his life of moral and political involvement, noted that he commended getting into "good trouble," and that he sometimes was called "the conscience of the House of Representatives."

At the beginning of *Across That Bridge*, Lewis says he is often asked, "How did you do it? How did you hold to nonviolence . . . ? How is it possible to be cracked on the head with a nightstick . . . and not raise a hand one time in self-defense?"[2]

He answers in part:

> We believed that if we are all children of the same Creator, then discrimination had to be an error, a misconception based on faulty logic . . . We asserted our right to human dignity based on the solid faith in our divine heritage that linked us to every other human being, and all the rest of creation, known and unknown, even to the heart and mind of God and the highest celestial realms of the universe . . . We had nothing to prove. Our worth had already been established before we were born.[3]

These sentences express a disposing religious vision that developed with Lewis's childhood experiences in church in racially segregated rural Alabama. Lewis says that from an early age he was "not carefree," but had a "sense that something is wrong."[4] Listening to Martin Luther King Jr. on the radio and later meeting and collaborating with King were also critical. So were Lewis's educational experiences at American Baptist Theological Seminary, Fisk University, and the Highlander Folk School (where he and others delved into ideas of the social gospel).[5] His theology articulates a specific piety, an interplay of experiences and believing.

But the passage also outlines an argument. A *theological premise* drawn from a vision of God: "we are all children of the same Creator." *Ethical ideas that bear closely on a significant moral question of the day*: all have worth as well as a "right to human dignity" based in "our divine heritage" and linked

2. Lewis, *Across That Bridge*, 19.
3. Lewis, *Across That Bridge*, 23.
4. Lewis, *Across That Bridge*, 22.
5. Lewis, *Walking with the* Wind, 3–70, 80–82.

to "the heart and mind of God." *An interpretation of the circumstances and conclusion disposing us to advocate for change*: American society discriminates against Blacks, and this is "a misconception based in faulty logic."

Consider another passage:

> Why do we struggle? . . . Why participate in the work of justice at all? Why risk beating, torture, even death to sacrifice ourselves . . . for the sake of progress we may or may not live to see? . . . I believe that we are all a spark of the divine, and if that spark is nurtured it can become a burning flame, an eternal force of light. I believe that the true destiny of humankind is to recollect that it is light, and to learn how to abide in infinite awareness of the divine in all matters of human affairs.[6]

This goes to an advocate's motive. Why participate in a movement for justice that risks "beating, torture, even death . . . for the sake of a progress we may or may not live to see?" Lewis's reply: "We are all a spark of the divine, and if that spark is nurtured it can become a burning flame, an eternal force for light . . . the true destiny of humankind is to recollect it is light," and to live with this awareness "in all matters of human affairs."

Rather than analyze with precision, this religious language symbolizes and evokes. It outlines a theological view of ourselves and our possibilities afforded by the nature of things. It states what orients persons to live in a certain way or to take up a practical stance in life. The vision of what we are (sparks of the divine) and of that for which we are destined (recollecting that we are light) becomes the basis for a calling and a motive. A theologically suffused "is" founds an "ought" that enjoins participation in a risky struggle for freedom and justice.

Turn now to a question that enlists others in the revolutionary work of nonviolent resistance and so explicitly commends a particular style of involvement, practice, and action.

> Living as light means putting away remedies based on fear, retribution and revenge and acting collectively through government to respect the dignity of all humankind . . . All our work, all our struggle, all our days add up to one purpose: to reconcile ourselves to the truth, and finally accept once and for all that we are one people, one family, the human family, that we are all emanated from one divine source and that source is Love . . . You *are a* light. You are *the* light . . . Clothe yourself in the work of love, in the revolutionary work of nonviolent resistance against evil . . . And if you follow your truth down the road to

6. Lewis, *Across That Bridge*, 199–200.

peace and the affirmation of love, if you shine like a beacon for all to see, then the poetry of all the great dreamers and philosophers is yours to manifest in a nation, a world community, and a Beloved Community that is finally at peace with itself.[7]

These lines connect with the passage quoted immediately above. Because we are a spark of the divine, because we are light, we ought to live as light, illumine the truth that all are one family emanated from the divine, and reconcile ourselves to it. With intonations reminiscent of the Apostle Paul's admonitions to live by the Spirit in Romans 8 and Ephesians 6, Lewis exhorts: because "we are all emanated from . . . Love," we ought to clothe ourselves "in the work of love." We ought to clothe ourselves in the "revolutionary work of nonviolent resistance against evil," whose aim is neither retribution nor revenge but reconciliation and "a Beloved Community that is finally at peace with itself."

Lewis's reasoning is theological, symbolic, and reflective, but hardly neutral. It disposes people to participate in a nonviolent struggle for equality and justice. There are unmistakable overtones of the theology of Martin Luther King Jr., especially Lewis's framing his case for "nonviolent resistance." Recall King insisting that "nonviolent resistance . . . is not a method of stagnant passivity . . . not passive nonresistance to evil," but "active nonviolent resistance" that "does not seek to defeat or humiliate the opponent." Why? Because "the end is redemption and reconciliation."[8]

Lewis and King advocate nonviolent resistance, a specific style of involvement that coheres with the character of the desired political community. There are situational and practical reasons to favor nonviolence. For example, neither advocate intends to separate from the wider American society; both pursue an integrated and just society in which all Americans, including blacks, participate with dignity and respect. Nonviolent resistance is an appropriate mode of advocacy because it aims to reach the conscience of the opponent rather than drive an alienating wedge between African and white Americans.[9] Thus, King believes that violence creates "more social problems than it solves." Indeed, "if the Negro succumbs to the temptation of using violence . . . unborn generations will be the recipients of a long and desolate night of bitterness."[10] Here, we see advocates reflecting on practical aims, tactics, and consequences.

7. Lewis, *Across That Bridge*, 207–8.
8. King, *A Testament of Hope*, 17–18.
9. King, *A Testament of Hope*, 83, 118.
10. King, *A Testament of Hope*, 44–45.

But note, too, Christian theological backings for nonviolence intertwined with these tactical judgments, including the relationships that King and Lewis believe obtain between an integrated and tolerably fair society and images of reconciliation, Beloved Community and the kingdom of God. King consistently commends nonviolent resistance as a practical method because it transposes the end of reconciliation into a means-in-action and because it gains support from the teaching of Jesus and the New Testament concept of *agape*. The discipline of nonviolence, he says, allows African Americans to exercise agency and gives "new self-respect" to those who are committed to it.[11] Or, as Lewis says, when Rosa Parks, steeped in "a new theology" that focused not only on ethereal needs, but also "on the lives of believers and on the communities in which they live," refused to give up her seat on a bus in Montgomery, she was "declaring that as a child of the divine, she had a power that no other human being . . . could ever take away."[12] This discipline, says King, enables the movement to conduct the struggle for civil rights "on the high plane of dignity," but also *without "drinking from the cup of bitterness and hatred."*[13] And, *agape*, as a specific form of love, a redemptive good will that recognizes all life is interrelated and aims to restore community, backs this same commitment to nonviolence.[14]

The claim is that nonviolent resistance can be an effective method of advocacy that embodies a theology of reconciliation and a form of love that "discovers the neighbor in every man it meets," and thus reflects the attitude of "the Good Samaritan."[15] Pragmatic considerations enter in, e.g., the aim of "the American racial revolution" is "to 'get in' rather than to overthrow." This argument echoes Reinhold Niebuhr's judgment in 1929 that, due to their minority status, "the emancipation" of blacks "in America probably waits upon the development of" a Gandhian strategy of nonviolent coercion and resistance.[16] But King carefully links nonviolent resistance not only with Gandhi's concept of "truth-force" or "love-force," but also with interpretations of the Sermon on the Mount and the spirit of Jesus, and of Luke 10. It is a method of "Christianity in action" whose "aftermath is the creation of

---

11. King, *A Testament of Hope*, 39. In his last speech, King says, "we are masters in our nonviolent movement in disarming police forces: they don't know what to do" (218).

12. Lewis, *Across That Bridge*, 27, 29.

13. King, *A Testament of Hope*, 218. My emphasis.

14. King, *A Testament of Hope*, 18–20, 38–39, 46–47.

15. King, *A Testament of Hope*, 19.

16. Niebuhr, *Moral Man*, 250–51, 252. Lewis notes the importance of Niebuhr's reflections on nonviolence in Lewis, *Walking with the Wind*, 76.

beloved community."[17] Lewis agrees: if you "clothe yourself in the work of love, in the revolutionary work of nonviolent resistance . . . you shine like a beacon" and the social "poetry of all the great dreamers and philosophers is yours to manifest."[18]

Compare these ideas with Lewis's views of democracy and how to build it in a column published shortly after his death:

> Democracy is not a state. It is an act, and each generation must do its part to help build what we called the Beloved Community, a nation and world society at peace with itself . . . I urge you to answer the highest calling of your heart and stand up for what you truly believe. In my life I have done all that I can to demonstrate that the way of peace, the way of love and nonviolence, is the more excellent way . . . So I say to you, walk with the wind, brothers and sisters, and let the spirit of peace and the power of everlasting love be your guide.[19]

Like any well-conceived advocacy for a cause, the column interprets the circumstances calling for involvement. Lewis interprets the "Black Lives Matter" movement in America during the summer of 2020 as a hopeful sign about "the next chapter of the great American story." He notes that "millions of people . . . set aside race, class, age, language and nationality to demand respect for human dignity." He believes the social movement following the killings of George Floyd and Breonna Taylor—and also Emmett Till—is part of a longer narrative. For Lewis, who visited the Black Lives Matter Plaza in Washington DC, the day before he was admitted to the hospital, the current movement shows that (in a phrase borrowed from King) "the truth is marching on."[20] The column encourages a younger generation to learn that they are involved in a longer, "soul-wrenching, existential struggle." It invites them to take up "the way of love and nonviolence . . . the more excellent way." Less than four months before a pivotal American election, Lewis echoes King once more, stating, "the vote is the most powerful nonviolent change agent you have in a democratic society."[21]

17. King, *A Testament of Hope*, 38–39, 86–87.

18. Lewis, *Across That Bridge*, 208.

19. Lewis, "Together, You Can Redeem the Soul of Our Nation," 3–4.

20. King closes his speech before the state capitol in Montgomery, Alabama, just weeks after "Bloody Sunday" on the Pettis Bridge in Selma by quoting from Julia Ward Howe's abolitionist hymn, "Mine Eyes Have Seen the Glory." The effect is to connect the march to Montgomery with God's truth marching on since before the American Civil War (King, *A Testament of Hope*, 227–30).

21. Lewis, "Together," 3–4. Some ask whether the commitment to nonviolence in Lewis and in King is strategic or absolute. (Neither explicitly condemns all violent

Lewis's column illustrates public Christian advocacy that draws upon and bolsters a theological vision of the good as well as our moral possibilities and limits. With respect to the good, it links democracy with helping to build "the Beloved Community" in each generation. With respect to our moral possibilities and limits, it makes a moving reference to sin and corruption. "We must discover what so readily takes root in our hearts that could rob Mother Emanuel Church in South Carolina of her brightest and best, [and] shoot unwitting concertgoers in Las Vegas."[22]

SOME CONCLUSIONS ABOUT CHRISTIAN ADVOCACY

Note a few conclusions supported by this analysis of Lewis and King. First, their Christian advocacy interconnects with theological-ethical reflections about what is good, e.g., a "Beloved Community" closely connected with reconciliation and the image of the kingdom of God, and what is right, e.g., a "right to human dignity" based in the symbol of God as creator and persons as valued creatures. It interconnects, too, with theological ideas about human tendencies and limits, e.g., sin and persistent corruption, but also hope for redemptive possibilities. These are ways in which Lewis and King's Christian advocacy engages critical ethical and theological reflections.

Again, both men know that they are not elaborating just any sort of Christian theology. They work instead with what Lewis calls the "new theology" that Parks and others encountered at Myles Horton's Highlander Folk School and with the social Christianity that King found in Walter Rauschenbusch and Reinhold Niebuhr. They also say why they prefer it.[23]

We can identify *four elements* in Lewis for participating in a risky nonviolent movement for justice, reconciliation, and a good society that

---

movements for social change.) Is this the only or the best way to put the question? The commitment is strategic as a matter of aim or objective in conjunction with a reading of the circumstances in American society with its minority black and majority white populations. But there are also theological reasons for nonviolent resistance, among them theological ideas that influence Lewis's and King's understanding of the practical aim. That is, there is an interaction of advocacy, conceptions of what is good and right, etc.

22. Lewis, "Together," 2–3.

23. See King's account of his journey from "a rather strict fundamentalistic tradition" to a theological stance influenced by Rauschenbusch and Niebuhr in King, *A Testament of Hope*, 35–38. Lewis's journey from the religion of his youth in Troy, Alabama, to the "new theology" is similar. See Lewis, *Walking with the Wind*, 3–89.

intertwine with his theological vision.[24] There is *an interpretation of the circumstances calling for moral involvement* that draws on judgments about what is going on. Lewis claims that American society is unjustly discriminatory and that, in the nation and its history, there is a movement for justice and a more humane democracy that extends across generations. This view draws on empirical observations, e.g., there is a Black Lives Matter movement, and that Emmett Till was murdered. But it is also value-laden rather than morally neutral; that is, it interconnects with Lewis's understandings of *moral norms and action-guides* such as love (*agape*) and justice as equality. He sees that American society is wanting and systemically unjust partly from the vantage point of these norms.

Lewis's interpretation of circumstances and his specifications of moral norms intertwine with a third element: the primary *good* or *cause* served by the practical involvement. He intends to advance the cause of a good society or Beloved Community where the dignity and worth of all persons are recognized and upheld, a cause closely connected with democratization. Again, his entire case draws on a fourth element: *anthropological assumptions* about the capabilities of human agents, communities, and institutions, their motives, tendencies, and possibilities. Lewis believes, for example, that persons and communities suffer from chronic corruption, but also retain a modicum of conscience or moral sense. Consequently, it is important to resist the skewed interests, commitments, and practices of persons and communities. But encounters with the nonviolent suffering of persons seeking to advance what is right and good may also move others toward better attitudes and social practices.

The four elements of Lewis's case are relatively independent. If it could be shown, for example, that there is no continuity—either historical or ideological—between the civil rights movement of the mid-twentieth century and the Black Lives Matter movement, his interpretation of circumstances would need to be revised. Nevertheless, Lewis's call to nonviolent resistance, his anthropological assumptions, specification of the good, and understanding of the norms of love and justice might remain largely intact. Still, the four elements exhibit important interactions and interdependencies. If Lewis did not understand the good society as one in which the dignity and worth of persons is recognized and upheld, his understandings of love and justice, his sense that there is something wrong with American society, and his exhortation to participate in the nonviolent movement would be

24. See Potter, *War and Moral Discourse*, 23–24; Dyck, *On Human Care*, 33–51; Swezey, "What Is Theological Ethics?," 5–20.

undermined. In short, there are multiple points at which one might agree or disagree with Lewis's case for nonviolent involvement.

One last point: the religious and theological symbols of reconciliation, redemption, the kingdom of God, and the Beloved Community contribute to a specification of the good or the cause that calls for and guides moral involvement. For anyone steeped in the language of the New Testament as Lewis and King were, these terms symbolize a reality present among us, but also not yet—a *telos* coming from heaven, but also lying beyond current societies and nations. They lend an elusive quality to the idea of the good society that more philosophical and univocal vocabularies do not, and they contribute to Lewis's case for participating in a work of justice whose fulfillment we may not live to see.[25]

CHRISTIAN ETHICS AND THEOLOGICAL VISIONS

Turn now to the relationship between ethics and theology in the thinking of Walter Rauschenbusch and Reinhold Niebuhr, figures that Lewis and King found especially helpful. And begin with the premise that there is no generic Christian theology, only particular varieties.[26] The varieties become ethically significant when they dispose us toward different specifications of the elements of moral reasoning.

A Social Gospel

Rauschenbusch, "the real founder of social Christianity" in America, believes the social crisis gripping "industrial and commercial life" is "the overshadowing problem of our generation," that it undermines political democracy and yet motivates people to turn to embrace better ideals.[27] This view of the times shapes his social gospel, but so does his reading of Scripture keyed to "the social Christianity of Jesus," which retains the hope of the prophets.[28] Jesus' teaching, says Rauschenbusch, focuses on a kingdom of God that repudiates "the force revolution," extends beyond Israel, and embodies

25. Lewis, *Across That Bridge*, 199.

26. Often the varieties develop within distinguishable Christian sub-traditions, e.g., Roman Catholic, Lutheran, and Reformed. See Ottati, "How Can Theological Ethics Be Christian?," 6–7.

27. The characterization of Rauschenbusch is Niebuhr's in the preface of *An Interpretation*. See also Rauschenbusch, *Christianity and the Social Crisis*, xi; *Christianizing the Social Order*, 1–6.

28. Rauschenbusch, *Christianity and the Social Crisis*, 71.

an anti-despotic or proto-democratic spirit of mutual service. Jesus insists that the purpose of human life is more than material and economic, but he never "spiritualizes the vitality out of the Kingdom idea" or transfers "the Kingdom hope from earth to heaven."[29] Take the Lord's Prayer, or "the great prayer of social Christianity." "Hallowed be thy name. Thy kingdom come. Thy will be done, as in heaven, so on earth." Rauschenbusch believes these petitions express Jesus' "yearning faith in the possibility of a reign of God on earth . . . They look forward to the ultimate perfection of the common life of humanity . . . and pray for the divine revolution which is to bring that about."[30] The kingdom focus means that "the purpose of all that Jesus said and did and hoped to do was always the social redemption of the entire life of the human race on earth."[31]

That this is an ethically significant variety of theology becomes apparent when we compare it with more individualist and privatized spiritualities. Rauschenbusch insists that the doctrine of the kingdom "is itself the social gospel."[32] This means that, while "personal religion has supreme value," and while "spiritual regeneration is the most important fact in any life history," "religious individualism" risks inappropriate selfishness.[33] Personal devotion needs to be reconsidered "from the point of view of the Kingdom," or of "humanity organized according to the will of God."[34] The social gospel aims to evangelize "a new type of Christian" whose wider horizon extends beyond individual souls to "social salvation" and "a vision of a true human society."[35] The kingdom message produces a new sort of faithfulness,[36] i.e., persons who understand themselves enmeshed in interdependent interrelations working together to bring about a more just and humane society, not as discreet individuals anticipating the redemption of their souls on another metaphysical plane. The contrast helps explain King's and Lewis's journey from the more fundamentalist traditions in which they were raised toward a social Christianity.

---

29. Rauschenbusch, *Christianizing the Social Order*, 48, 52, 57, 58, 66.

30. Rauschenbusch, *Prayers*, 18, 23.

31. Rauschenbusch, *Christianizing the Social Order*, 67.

32. Rauschenbusch, *A Theology*, 131.

33. Rauschenbusch, *Christianizing the Social Order*, 104, 111.

34. Rauschenbusch, *A Theology*, 142, 144.

35. Rauschenbusch, *Christianity and the Social Crisis*, 352, 354, 356. This pastoral interest is also visible in Rauschenbusch, *The Social Principles*, a book with study questions written for the YMCA and YWCA.

36. Rauschenbusch, *Christianizing the Social Order*, 111.

A Case for Social Reform

Rauschenbusch advocates a raft of progressive reforms: a living wage, compensation for job-related disability and death, sick benefits, maternity care for working women, improvement and inspection of working conditions, the organization of labor, prohibition of child labor, excluding the young from night labor and hazardous employment, old-age pensions, improved care for the aged, better housing and urban sanitation, labor co-partnerships with capital and profit-sharing, tax reform, and the extension of education, libraries, museums, parks, and playgrounds.[37] These contribute to his "practical socialism," a political stance that pursues a more humane society by ameliorating disparities in wealth produced by capitalism and improving the condition of laboring classes and the poor.[38]

An *interpretation of circumstances* informs these recommendations. Industrial machinery, says Rauschenbusch, sends a shock wave through the economic order with staggering results. Rents increase and land is becoming monopolized. Labor is at "a fearful disadvantage" in relation to capital. Workers are displaced, their families are only "weeks removed from destitution," and they live with constant insecurity. Labor disputes are costly and violent; "poor food and cramped rooms lower the vitality of the people"; nervous disorders, tuberculosis, and alcoholism are increasing; and industries oppress immigrants. While he has confidence in the basic design of American political and judicial institutions, Rauschenbusch asserts that, under then-current conditions of severe economic disparity, the courts and representative assemblies have become tools for the dominant class. Again, a new orientation is discernible among socialists, workers, progressive politicians, college students, seminarians, and ministers. There is a social gospel movement in place working in partnership with social and psychological science as well as the democratic spirit.[39] The competitive system divides rich and poor, leads to class conflict and the loss of approximate equality, and threatens the stability of political democracy. Conspicuous injustices

---

37. Rauschenbusch, *Christianizing the Social Order*, 341–51, 412–29. Rauschenbusch doesn't pass muster by all moral standards. See his complaint in Rauschenbusch, *Christianizing the Social Order*, 278, that the immigration of cheap labor from south and central Europe encouraged by industrialists cost native American jobs, "checked the propagation of the Teutonic stock; radically altered the racial future of our nation," and could result in Catholics outnumbering Protestants.

38. Rauschenbusch, "Dogmatic and Practical Socialism," 310–21.

39. Rauschenbusch, *Christianity and the Social Crisis*, 215–79; *A Theology*, 1–5.

cry out for reforms to check economic interests through institutions that represent all the people and not just an economic aristocracy.[40]

Salient *anthropological assumptions* support this view. Humans are inherently social, an idea Rauschenbusch gleans from fundamental tenets of socialists and reformers and the economist Richard Ely's contention that social solidarity implies the mutual interdependence and a unity of human interests.[41] Rauschenbusch also draws this apprehension from biblical and theological resources, e.g., the implications of addressing God as "*Our* Father" and the social reality of God's kingdom.[42] He maintains that people are endowed with a social instinct that comes through in sexuality, family life, neighborhood, and nation, and that humanity forms an organic whole or family in accord with the teaching of Jesus.[43]

We cannot understand persons—their possibilities and limits—apart from social relations and institutions. Consider temperance. Rauschenbusch does not believe an alcoholic in Hell's Kitchen represents a simple individual failure of will. Rather, it is likely that he is encountering a person broken by persistent insecurities and strains, which accompany the competitive system of capitalist industry, and whose desires have been skewed by the idealization of intoxication in social circles and advertising. Resentments and conflicting interests that characterize workers and factory owners also largely result from an industrial system that sets capital and labor against each other.

Rauschenbusch does not believe social reforms will eliminate all conflict and establish a utopian society.[44] He thinks self-interest "a necessary part of human nature," and that "it would be a calamity to rob this instinct of its incentives and its motive force." The issue is whether a given institutional structure systematically pits the interests of individuals against the public welfare and leads to inherent conflict. Notice that here a moral norm impacts both anthropological assumptions and a reading of circumstances. Justice protects the community against the selfishness of individuals; as approximate equality, it "is the condition of good will" between people, and deep-seated injustice throws the foundations of society out of plumb.[45]

---

40. Rauschenbusch, "Dogmatic and Practical Socialism," 309; *Christianity and the Social Crisis*, 284; *Christianizing the Social Order*, 311–40, 352–64.

41. Ely, "Social Solidarity," 187–92, 235–41.

42. Rauschenbusch, *Social Principles*, 22–23.

43. Rauschenbusch, *Social Principles*, 17–30.

44. Rauschenbusch, *Christianity and the Social Crisis*, 420–21.

45. Rauschenbusch, *Christianizing the Social Order*, 290, 330, 333.

Rauschenbusch emphasizes that, with more social justice, the interests of individuals and classes will better harmonize with the broader public good. He assumes the capacity to manage important social relations and conditions. But his confidence is not unbounded. The ideal society is one in which "self-interest and the common interest run in the same direction," though the forces at work in history make it difficult to predict the future, and "at best there is always but an approximation to a perfect social order."[46]

These observations already involve *norms* and *guidelines*. When he appeals to *justice*, Rauschenbusch focuses on economics and politics, e.g., inequities in the industrial system and oligarchic control of courts and legislatures. Justice approximates equal opportunity and the fair distribution of wealth, benefits, and burdens. "[T]he establishment of social justice by the abolition of unjust privilege" moves us toward a better society.[47] This connects with the *freedom* to pursue opportunity, which Rauschenbusch links with organizing associations that enable people to control their livelihoods. He calls this "economic democracy," and it goes hand-in-hand with political democracy.[48] A related norm, *respect for persons*, Rauschenbusch calls the "value of life" and "the worth of human personality." Indeed, "the conservation of life," which he associates with reforms that improve basic conditions and meet human needs, is "the first duty of every Christian factor of the social order."[49]

The chief moral excellence is love, "the society-making quality" that "creates fellowship," the social instinct that binds people together in mutual interdependence. Love "runs through all our relations and is the foundation of all our institutions." One discerns it, says Rauschenbusch, in friendship and common devotion to a cause and in the lives of families, neighborhoods, unions, and nations. Love is "the central law of life . . . the social instinct which binds man and man together and makes them indispensable to one another. Whoever demands love, demands solidarity. Whoever sets love first, sets fellowship high." Here, we find a direct connection with the anthropological claim that humans are inherently social. As "the chief law of Christianity," love "expresses and reinforces" the social nature of humans. The teaching and example of Jesus strengthen and intensify our social sensibility, and the mission of the church is to promote and extend the horizons of social affection. Jesus' kingdom preaching energizes "the

46. Rauschenbusch, *Christianizing the Social Order*, 272, 326; *Christianity and the Social Crisis*, 421.

47. Rauschenbusch, *Christianizing the Social Order*, 337.

48. Rauschenbusch, *Christianizing the Social Order*, 352–64.

49. Rauschenbusch, *Social Principles*, 1–16; *Christianizing the Social Order*, 388–389, 412–18.

faculty and habits of love" and stimulates "the dormant faculty of devotion to the common good."[50]

The primary *cause* or *good* supporting Rauschenbusch's reading of current circumstances, his anthropological assumptions, and his norms or guidelines is a deep loyalty to the *common welfare of humanity*. Competitive conditions and injustices threaten this good, which is advanced by progressive reforms and approximations of a perfect society. It gains support from his anthropological assumptions; commitment to the common human welfare is appropriate for interdependent creatures endowed with impulses of social affection. Loyalty to the common good, the cause behind the emergent orientation toward social reform, accords with the value of human personality and norms of justice and love.

This loyalty also receives decisive support from the key doctrine of the social gospel: the kingdom of God.[51] The basic direction of Jesus' mind and life is, for Rauschenbusch, the revelation of God's will, and the kingdom of God is the center of Jesus' teaching and mission. Jesus points to a humane society that is both task and gift, and that attends to the plight of the poor and the vulnerable. He heralds a social order that guarantees the worth of human personality, establishes justice, and represents the progressive reign of love and the unity of humanity. "The Kingdom of God is humanity organized according to the will of God."[52] Jesus initiates the kingdom, the single best indicator of God's purposes, and shows that "the will of God is identical with the good of mankind."[53]

These specifications of the four elements, like those in Lewis's case for advocating racial justice, are relatively independent. Thus, empirical information that counts for and against Rauschenbusch's estimates of urban conditions and the plight of labor does not impact decisively the anthropological assumption that we can manage important social consequences. Nevertheless, Rauschenbusch's specifications, like Lewis's, *interact*. For example, assumptions that people can manage some social consequences, that social feeling may be extended, and that interests of persons and groups may be brought into greater harmony encourage his belief that the situation may be improved. Altering a key specification could change Rauschenbusch's entire case. For example, a belief that we are unable to manage social consequences would hamper his case for progressive reform. Why reform

50. Rauschenbusch, *Christianity and the Social Crisis*, 67–68; *Christianizing the Social Order*, 262; *Social Principles*, 17, 25, 28.

51. Rauschenbusch, *A Theology*, 131.

52. Rauschenbusch, *A Theology*, 142–43.

53. Rauschenbusch, *Social Principles*, 128.

economic structures if the results will be unintended and unanticipated? Thus, one might share Rauschenbusch's loyalty to the common good of humanity and his judgment that present economic structures work against it, but support a different practical stance due to our limited abilities to manage social consequences.

Worldviews and Theologies

What is the place of humans in the wider world or universe? Is the wellbeing of a human community intertwined with other communities and with ecosystems and nonhumans? To what extent do persons and groups honor the interests of others? How effectively can they influence or direct historical outcomes? Are things moving toward a discernible *telos*? *Worldviews or visions of humans and the world* intimate answers to such questions, and so they influence the ways we understand the elements of moral reasoning.[54] Some worldviews are *theological*; they portray us, objects, and others, as well as possibilities and limits afforded by the nature of things, in relation to God or the gods and divine purposes.

The commitments of Lewis and King to justice as equality are bolstered by a theology of creation (e.g., all people are valued children of the one creator), the pronouncements of prophets (e.g., "Let justice roll down like waters"), and the teachings of Jesus (e.g., the Golden Rule). Their cases for nonviolent resistance reflect the story of the Good Samaritan, and biblical ideas of *agape*, sin, and reconciliation. The symbol of God's kingdom shapes Rauschenbusch's case for reform. So do biblical images of human sociality and solidarity (e.g., "*Our* Father"), prophetic insistences on justice for the poor and vulnerable, and Jesus' focus on love and the interests of others. But it is also possible to identify theological themes that will allow us to track with greater precision how Christian visions and elements of moral reasoning intertwine.

I glean five themes from reading H. Richard Niebuhr's classic, *Christ and Culture*. Other schemes are possible. (Let many flowers bloom.) But these are sufficiently illuminating.[55]

54. John P. Reeder Jr. argues religions furnish visions of the good and the real that locate us in relation to what is important and to the possibilities afforded by the nature of things, and that we may compare and contrast the worldviews of different religious communities and their traditions. We may also compare them with pictures of what is important and possible offered by Marxists, existentialists, and others. See Reeder, "What Is a Religious Ethic?," 164, 171–73.

55. Niebuhr, *Christ and Culture*. The typology of stances Niebuhr presents remains controversial, though the theological themes that inform it are rarely fully appreciated. See Niebuhr, *Christ and Culture*, 121–31.

1. *Reason and revelation.* What are the valid sources of knowledge and insight and how are they distinguished and related?

2. *God and world.* What is God's will (the true good), and how does it relate to the processes of nature and history, including human institutions?

3. *Sin and good.* How radical and extensive is the human fault, and how does it relate to true virtue or moral goodness?

4. *Law and gospel.* What are the true standards for guiding and judging our actions, and how do they relate to gospel grace and forgiveness?

5. *Church and world.* How does the community that explicitly acknowledges God and God's purposes relate to other communities and institutions, and to the wider culture?

One may plot Christian theological visions, including Rauschenbusch's, with reference to specific resolutions of these themes and their interrelations.

Rauschenbusch's Theology and the Elements of Moral Reasoning

Rauschenbusch claims that God's chief purpose, the kingdom, is "the good of mankind," the truly humane and good society. The best socialized or "Christianized" institutions, such as democratic political structures and public schools, pursue this end. *Thus, God's purpose harmonizes with the purposes of the best cultural institutions.* By contrast, the worst institutions, those that are "unChristianized," such as autocratic business, oppose the kingdom.[56] This resolution of *the God and world theme* furnishes the main theological support for Rauschenbusch's specification of the chief good or cause to be served by the reform movement.

Revelation, or Jesus' message of the kingdom, is not the only source of insight for the true good; Rauschenbusch also appeals to the best cultural reasoning in the form of emerging disciplines of sociology and economics, as well as the best ideas furnished by social reform movements. But corrupted cultural reasoning, e.g., *laissez-faire* economics captivated by "the law of profit" and competitive individualism, leads to dehumanization. *Thus, revelation in Jesus Christ harmonizes with the best available cultural reasoning and opposes the worst.* This understanding of *the key sources of insight* becomes crucial when Rauschenbusch ponders the chief good to be served by our moral involvements, but is also vital for identifying appropriate moral norms and interpreting current circumstances. His anthropological

56. Rauschenbusch, *Christianizing the Social Order*, 128–68, 180–201.

assumption that people are social and interdependently interrelated also owes much to what he considers the best cultural reasoning of the time (e.g., Ely's idea of social solidarity) and harmonizes with Rauschenbusch's reading of key biblical and theological symbols.

Rauschenbusch thinks principles that should guide and judge our actions, such as love as mutuality and attention to others (especially the poor and vulnerable) and justice as approximate social equality, represent a confluence of the best insights of modern culture from democratic and socialist currents and the teachings of Jesus and the prophets. *The gospel of Jesus Christ harmonizes with the best cultural norms and opposes the worst, e.g., capitalist endorsements of unbridled self-interest.* This resolution of the *law and gospel theme* does not emphasize the need for grace and forgiveness, though grace plays a part in Rauschenbusch's hope for the spiritual regeneration of corrupted individuals and institutions. And his estimate of how social structures and expectations shape persons' interests and attitudes tempers his moral judgments of corporate leaders who enact destructive practices.[57]

Rauschenbusch develops a conception of "super-personal forces" of *sin* resident in *laissez-faire* and autocratic structures that skew social practices and corrupt persons and communities.[58] The idea emanates partly from Jesus and the prophets and New Testament images of principalities and powers that oppose Christ's kingdom. By contrast, structures that advance the kingdom help to form people in *true virtue* (a social type of faithfulness). Thus, sin's corruption, while socially embodied and transmitted, is neither entirely radical nor universal, and this resolution of *sin and good* contributes to Rauschenbusch's overall stance. Sin is less virulent among those who reason socially and participate in "Christianized" aspects of the social order than it is among those whose reflections are dominated by "unChristianized" commercial and libertarian ideas that oppose the kingdom's advance.

A similarly uneven distribution of sin characterizes the church, where progressive elements—those informed by a deep commitment to the kingdom and strong appreciation for mutuality and social justice—differ from those mired in privatized spirituality coopted by commercial capitalism. This distinction lies near the heart of Rauschenbusch's calls for the church to awaken to the work of reconstructing society. He wants a church that forms prophetic minds whose spirit comes to expression in social creeds, denominational offices, para-church organizations, and seminary professorships of social ethics. For the apostle of the social gospel, the church's best elements

57. Rauschenbusch, *Christianity and the Social Crisis*, 244–46.
58. Rauschenbusch, *A Theology*, 69–76.

make common cause with the best institutions and movements of the wider culture that address ills of industrialism in order to usher in a more humane society.

Revising American Social Christianity

Rauschenbusch's theological ethic finds favor with Lewis and King, but their social Christianity and their advocacy cannot be understood with reference to Rauschenbusch alone. King tells us that, upon reading Reinhold Niebuhr, he became more "aware of the complexity of human motives and the reality of sin." He also felt that Rauschenbusch "had fallen victim to the nineteenth century 'cult of inevitable progress,'" and had come "perilously close to identifying the kingdom of God with a particular social and economic system."[59]

Consider King's first point. Niebuhr holds that human creatures have significant abilities, but that many things remain beyond our control. Immensities of nature and perils of history threaten our needs, loves, and aims. We become anxious and insecure, and so, despite the fact that we are unable to control all relevant outcomes, we try to establish our security by exercising power. The pursuit of security through power tempts us to overreach, to embrace a will-to-power at the expense of other persons and communities. This is sin as pride; caught in its grips, we pretend to be something more than we are, and bad consequences follow.[60] Occasionally, these consequences help us to recognize sin's destructive and immoral presence even in ourselves, though, when we do, too often we double-down and concoct self-serving justifications.

Prophetic religion therefore speaks truth to power. "A dominant class must be told that there is no security in increasing oppression of a resentful oppressed class. Sooner or later injustice will create the force of vengeance by which it is destroyed." Similar things must be said to strong nations and egotistic individuals.[61] "Every civilization and every culture is . . . a Tower of Babel," rife with pretensions to finality, universality, and divinity, loathe to acknowledge its finitude and limitations.[62]

In later writings, Niebuhr also explores sin as sensuality.[63] Rendered anxious and insecure by threats, real or imagined, we may relinquish attempts to secure imperiled interests and values in favor of more easily

59. King, *A Testament of Hope*, 35–37.

60. Niebuhr, *Beyond Tragedy*, 102.

61. Niebuhr, *Beyond Tragedy*, 106.

62. Niebuhr, *Beyond Tragedy*, 28.

63. Niebuhr, *The Nature and Destiny*, 228–40.

attainable satisfactions, e.g., acquiring excessive possessions. Is this yet another attempt to make oneself god, or is it an escape from the tensions of life and an uneasy conscience? The key point for our purposes is that, whether we probe pride or sensuality, the temptation to sin and sin itself remain features of our human predicament. Social structures and practices contribute to the malformation of persons, but sin does not reduce to social conditioning. Its roots go deeper; it cannot be corrected merely by altering social structures and systems.

Commenting on racism in 1945, Niebuhr says the roots of prejudice, hatred, and contempt lie deeper than ignorance. They are bound up with fears of competition from the other, as well as with the tendency to imaginatively elevate ourselves, our race, or our culture into the ultimate defining standard, and then to anxiously defend this concocted and false superiority against those who differ. Even intellectually accomplished reasoners succumb because "race bigotry" is "something darker and more terrible than stupidity." It is a "form of original sin" that "must be broken by repentance and not merely by enlightenment."[64]

Now to King's second concern: the perils of naïve beliefs in progress and identifying the kingdom with a particular socio-economic system. "My kingdom is not of this world"—Niebuhr says Jesus' statement before Pilate in John 18:36 is profoundly true. Why? Because the world is alienated from its true character, people make themselves god and so do not know themselves truly in relation to God. The kingdom, or "the picture of what this world ought to be," consequently is not of this world.

Nevertheless, this picture impinges on our consciences, subjects the world to criticism, and constantly enters into the world as a "dangerous peril to the kingdoms of the world." That is, the kingdom of God, as the moral element of conscience, de-legitimates present kingdoms and powers, points toward other possibilities, and prompts challenges and conflicts that result in steps toward a new justice. Nevertheless, sin continues; the new justice also falls short of the kingdom's "perfect justice."[65] The new regime must therefore also come in for criticism, and "the sinful world is not as easily transmitted into the kingdom of God as modern theology had supposed."[66]

Indeed, as he ponders prospects for a new international order following the Second World War, Niebuhr says that modern bourgeois political theory, which sprang from Enlightenment rationalism, is dangerously naïve just because it has no equivalent to the doctrine of original and persistent

64. Niebuhr, *Love and Justice*, 128.

65. Niebuhr, *Beyond Tragedy*, 285–86.

66. Niebuhr, *Beyond Tragedy*, 282.

sin. This is why, though it gave birth to the democratic ideal, it remains unable to fathom the darker impulses that democratic polities must struggle to check and balance. Thus, it entertains optimistic ideas of moral progress.[67]

For Niebuhr, then, sin is radical and universal in a way that, for Rauschenbusch, it is not, and, God's primary purpose, the kingdom or good society, while historically relevant, remains profoundly more elusive than Rauschenbusch imagined. There are other differences, but this is enough to suggest why Niebuhr favors Christian realism and affirms a message of *hope beyond tragedy*. This message draws on a mythos of crucifixion and resurrection, which cannot be pressed "to yield too detailed knowledge of the future." But those who reject the conceptions implicit in the mythos tend toward either moral nihilism or utopianism, and "since there are few moral nihilists, it follows that most moderns are utopians."[68]

Niebuhr's estimates of the darker recesses of sin and a kingdom that functions as both judgment and promise, primarily impact anthropological assumptions and specifications of the good or the cause to be served. Moreover, these revisions of social Christianity come to the fore when King and Lewis emphasize nonviolent *resistance*. Because radical and universal corruption persists and the kingdom, while relevant, remains beyond our grasp, and because the truth is hope beyond tragedy, the road to racial justice is long. Indeed, it calls for a distinctive stance that applies pressure to structures, entails confrontation and civil disobedience, and occasionally leads to being "cracked on the head with a nightstick."[69]

Nevertheless, for King the "neo-orthodox" corrective is too pessimistic. He recognizes that, in our fallen state, estranged from our essential nature, "men are not easily moved from their mental ruts or purged of their prejudiced and irrational feelings." But he adds that even in this estranged state, the nonviolent approach gives those committed to it "new self-respect" and "reaches the opponent and so stirs his conscience that reconciliation becomes a reality."[70] Here, partly influenced by Paul Tillich's existential theology and Gandhi's idea of "soul force," we see a correction of Niebuhr's correction! Should we describe it as a stronger emphasis on the continued functioning of conscience, even among sinners, a different reading of the persistence of good in created human nature? Its immediate impact is on King's anthropological assumptions about our possibilities, limits, and tendencies. Borne by practical experiences and requirements of

67. Niebuhr, *The Children of Light and the Children of Darkness*, 16.
68. Niebuhr, *Beyond Tragedy*, 304–05.
69. Lewis, *Across That Bridge*, 19.
70. King, *A Testament of Hope*, 39.

the civil rights movement, he fashions a more realistic social gospel than we find in Rauschenbusch and a more hopeful Christian realism than we find in Niebuhr.

This brings us to a significant theological point—King's elaboration of hope beyond tragedy. Following important criticisms of white theologians, including Niebuhr, James Cone claims that "the cross and the lynching tree interpret each other," and that they need to be remembered together. The cross apart from the lynching tree is in danger of succumbing to false pieties, and "yet the lynching tree needs the cross, without which it becomes simply an abomination. It is the cross that points in the direction of hope." Only when the evils of the cross, the lynching trees, and the many other "Calvaries" are remembered together is there hope "beyond tragedy."[71] This is profound theological wisdom gleaned from the longsuffering experience of African-American Christian communities. It is part and parcel of Lewis's insistence that the Black Lives Matter movement should be seen in the context of a longer narrative that includes Emmett Till. It is also integral to King's historically resonant claim, in the words of Julia Ward Howe's abolitionist hymn, and as he stood before the capitol in Montgomery, Alabama, just weeks after "Bloody Sunday" on the Pettis Bridge, that "the truth is marching on."

We understand King's elaboration of hope beyond tragedy more thoroughly if we focus on his last public address at the Mason Temple, headquarters of the Church of God in Christ, the largest African-American Pentecostal group in Memphis on April 3, 1968, where he had traveled to support a sanitation workers strike.[72] The speech begins with King imagining himself before a panoramic view of history and the Almighty asking him, "Which age would you like to live in?" King says he "would take . . . mental flight by Egypt . . . across the Red Sea, through the wilderness on toward the promised land." He would move on by Greece and great philosophers, past Rome, the Renaissance, and the Reformation; he would watch Abraham Lincoln vacillate and finally sign the Emancipation Proclamation. But he wouldn't stop in any of these places. "Strangely enough, I would turn to the Almighty, and say, 'If you allow me to live just a few years in the second half of the twentieth century, I will be happy.' Now that's a strange statement to make, because the world is all messed up." King continues, "I see God working in this period . . . something is happening . . . people are

---

71. Cone, *The Cross and the Lynching Tree*, 161, 164, 167. See also Ottati, *A Theology for the Twenty-First Century*, 489–90.

72. King, "I See the Promised Land," in King, *A Testament of Hope*, 279–86.

rising up" and saying they want to be free, and now "we are determined to gain our rightful place in God's world."

Next, King says the issue is injustice, and that, like the beaten man on the side of the road, the sanitation workers in Memphis need us to develop "a kind of dangerous unselfishness." They need us to ask, much as the Good Samaritan did, "If I do not stop to help the sanitation workers, what will happen to them?" He notes that he almost died after being stabbed in New York City, and says how happy he is to have lived to see so many important events in the civil rights movement, including the sit-ins at lunch counters, the Birmingham Campaign, and the march in Selma.

King mentions his flight from Atlanta, delayed while the bags and the aircraft were meticulously checked because he was on board, and then he says, "But it doesn't matter with me now. Because I've been to the mountain-top." God has "allowed me to look over. And I've seen the promised land. I may not get there with you. But I want you to know tonight, that we as a people will get to the promised land. And I'm happy tonight . . . not worried about anything . . . not fearing any man." The last line is from the abolitionist hymn once again: "Mine eyes have seen the glory of the coming of the Lord." An assassin killed King the next day.

The address begins and ends with references to the story of the Exodus and the journey to the promised land, a story often interpreted by African-American Christians by being remembered together with their own story of suffering, lynching, oppression, and discrimination. King's rhetorical reference to himself as the leader who sees but does not enter into the promised land brings the very long journey from Pharaoh's Egypt to Memphis and beyond directly into the Mason Temple. Just here, the speech articulates hope in a biblical and realistic key, a bittersweet hope requiring patience and commitment across generations. We see the same acknowledgment of a movement that spans generations in Lewis's farewell column. We see it also in his invitation to participate in a movement "for the sake of progress we may not live to see."[73] This realism does not guarantee we ourselves shall enter the perfectly good society, but it remains hopeful that the struggle will yield progress over time. There is no naïve optimism, but no surrender to pessimism or despair.

It can be difficult to know what King and Lewis mean by the Beloved Community. The term, which was used by James Lawson of the Fellowship of Reconciliation, originates with the American philosopher Josiah Royce, who says that "all morality" is to be "judged by the standards of the Beloved Community, of the Kingdom of Heaven." Indeed, "the central doctrine

73. Lewis, *Across That Bridge*, 199.

of the Master," says Royce, was "So act that the Kingdom of Heaven may come." This means helping to make humanity "one loving brotherhood," acting so that humanity "comes more and more to resemble the ideal of the beloved, the universal community."[74] Lewis says that, for King and for Lawson, the Beloved Community is "nothing less than the Christian concept of the Kingdom of God on earth."[75] But he also writes, "democracy is not a state. It is an act, and each generation must do its part to help build the Beloved Community, a nation and world at peace with itself." In the second instance, the term doesn't quite look like another name for the kingdom. Does it refer to an intermediate community of reconciliation that is incomplete but points to the kingdom? Is it a name for genuine democracy, though democracy itself is never perfect, and the nation and the world are never truly at peace? From Royce to King to Lewis, the rhetorical ambiguity is important for preserving the tensions resident in genuine hope.[76]

Advocates and Ethicists

Lewis and King are important, even exemplary Christian advocates; Rauschenbusch and Niebuhr are important, even exemplary Christian ethicists. But besides these four there are many more who advocate and reflect at many different places and times. So, our conclusions should be tailored to the illustrative character of the argument presented.

First conclusion: to a significant degree, good Christian advocates also appear to be their own ethicists and theologians. This seems true when we examine King's revisions of both Rauschenbusch and Niebuhr. His anthropological assumptions, his reading of the good to be served, and his distinctive interpretations of important theological themes, e.g., sin and the good and his vision of hope beyond tragedy do not repeat what we find in these earlier exponents of social Christianity. Indeed, King's understandings of important elements of moral reasoning, as well as of crucial theological themes, are strongly influenced by African-American piety and his practical experiences as an advocate for civil rights. And again, even if Lewis's reflections on elements of moral reasoning and theological themes are not as sustained and detailed as King's, we see them at work in his appeals to the

74. Royce, *The Problem of Christianity*, 199–200.

75. Lewis, *Walking with the Wind*, 78.

76. Lewis, "Together," 3. A similar rhetorical ambiguity seems present in The King Center's statement of what King meant by the term. See "The King Philosophy," thekingcenter.org.

worth of God's children, justice as equality, suffering in resistance, living as light, and hope for reconciliation.

Second, good Christian ethicists appear to be their own theologians, and also to recognize that, in certain circumstances, their theological ethics dispose them toward specific policies and views. They engage in critical reflections, but they also know that their disciplined ethical and theological reflections finally are not morally neutral. This seems apparent when we consider Rauschenbusch's theology, e.g., his social understanding of sin and his interpretation of the kingdom, together with his case for social reform, and his policy preferences in an age of industrial capitalism, urbanization, and immigration. It seems true when we consider Niebuhr's understandings of sin, the kingdom as judgment and promise, racism, and the shortcomings of liberal political theory.

Third, the traffic between Christian piety and advocacy on the one hand, and Christian theological ethics on the other, runs in both directions. This is surely true of King's ecclesial and activist involvements, and his interpretations of the kingdom, the good society, and hope. It is true, too, of Lewis's experiences of struggle, his references to sin, and his claim that we should live as light. Participation in a movement for social reform influences Rauschenbusch's politics, his understandings of circumstances, goods, anthropological assumptions, and norms, as well as his interpretation of Jesus and the prophets. But his understanding of Jesus and the prophets also influences his politics and his specifications of the elements of moral reasoning. Again, Niebuhr's understanding of the radical and universal character of sin draws on exegetical and theological arguments, and also reflects his estimates of political possibilities and limits in a troubled world.

Finally, this essay suggests there is something to be gained from stepping back to reflect critically on the conceptualities and arguments of both Christian advocates and ethicists, namely, the increased clarity about our theological ethics and our advocacy that disciplined analysis brings. Critical analyses will not produce complete agreement, but they may help us to locate where we agree and disagree, and then to ask what counts for and against the stances and positions we prefer. Think, for example, of the many ways one might disagree with Rauschenbusch's case for social reform. One might formulate, as Niebuhr did, different theological estimates of sin, the kingdom, and the relationship of God's purposes to human communities and aims. One might reject Rauschenbusch's assumption that we are able to manage significant social consequences. Maybe one will disagree with his estimate of economic inequalities and their causes in his industrial age. Perhaps we shall develop a different understanding of justice. The list goes on, but in each instance different arguments and evidence count for and against the judgments we make, and the quality of our judgments may be improved by added precision. It may be predictable that, in a contentious and disturbing time, the balance between ethics and advocacy shoud tip toward the latter and often largely apart from critical reflection. But from where I sit in early 2021, we have pretty nearly demonstrated the dangers to Christian faithfulness, to politics, and to culture of walking down that path too far.

BIBLIOGRAPHY

Cone, James. *The Cross and the Lynching Tree*. Maryknoll, NY: Orbis, 2011.

Dyck, Arthur J. *On Human Care: An Introduction to Ethics*. Nashville: Abingdon, 1977.

Ely, Richard T. "Social Solidarity." In *The Social Gospel in America 1870–1920: Gladden, Ely, Rauschenbusch*, edited by Robert T. Handy, 235–41. New York: Oxford University Press, 1966.

King, Martin Luther, Jr. *A Testament of Hope: The Essential Writings of Martin Luther King, Jr.* Edited by James Melvin Washington. San Francisco: Harper & Row, 1986.

Lewis, John. *Across That Bridge: A Vision for Change and the Future of America*. With Brenda Jones. New York: Hachette, 2012.

———. "Together, You Can Redeem the Soul of Our Nation." *New York Times*, July 30, 2020. https://www.nytimes.com/2020/07/30/opinion/john-lewis-civil-rights-america.html

———. *Walking with the Wind: A Memoir of the Movement*. With Michael D'Orso. New York: Simon & Schuster, 1998.

Niebuhr, Reinhold. *Beyond Tragedy: Essays on the Christian Interpretation of History*. New York: Scribner's, 1937.

———. *The Children of Light and the Children of Darkness: A Vindication of Democracy and a Critique of Its Traditional Defense*. Hoboken: Prentice Hall, 1960.

———. *An Interpretation of Christian Ethics*. New York: Harper & Row, 1963.

———. *Love and Justice: Selections from the Shorter Writings of Reinhold Niebuhr*. Edited by D. B. Robertson. Louisville: Westminster John Knox, 1992.

———. *Moral Man and Immoral Society*. Louisville: Westminster John Knox Press, 2013.

———. *The Nature and Destiny of Man*. Vol. I, *Human Nature*. Louisville: Westminster John Knox, 1996.

Niebuhr, H. Richard. *Christ and Culture*. New York: Harper & Row, 1975.

Ottati, Douglas F. "How Can Theological Ethics Be Christian?" *Journal of the Society of Christian Ethics* 31.2 (Fall/Winter 2011) 3–21.

———. "Christ and Culture: Still Worth Reading After All These Years." *Journal of the Society of Christian Ethics* 23.1 (Spring/Summer 2003) 121–31.

———. *A Theology for the Twenty-First Century*. Grand Rapids: Eerdmans, 2020.

Potter, Ralph B. *War and Moral Discourse*. Richmond: John Knox, 1970.

Rauschenbusch, Walter. *Christianity and the Social Crisis*. New York: Macmillan, 1912.

———. *Christianizing the Social Order*. New York: Macmillan, 1913.

————. "Dogmatic and Practical Socialism." In *The Social Gospel in America 1870–1920: Gladden, Ely, Rauschenbusch*, edited by Robert T. Handy, 308–22. New York: Oxford University Press, 1966.

————. *Prayers of the Social Awakening*. Boston: Pilgrim, 1909.

————. *The Social Principles of Jesus*. New York: Methodist Book Concern, 1916.

————. *A Theology for the Social Gospel*. Louisville: Westminster John Knox, 1997.

Reeder, John P., Jr. "What Is a Religious Ethic?" *Journal of Religious Ethics* 25.3 (1997) 157–81.

Royce, Josiah. *The Problem of Christianity*. Chicago: University of Chicago Press, 1968.

Swezey, Charles M. "What Is Theological Ethics? A Study of the Thought of James M. Gustafson." PhD diss., Vanderbilt University, 1978.

SOCIAL ETHICS FOR SOCIAL JUSTICE

The Legacies of the Social Gospel
and a Case for Idealistic Discontent

Gary Dorrien

I BELONG IN THIS book only for believing that social ethics should mediate how social ethicists conduct advocacy, not for believing that social ethicists conduct too much advocacy. My regret about social ethics is that it drifted from its originating concerns for much of its history, settling for complacency, celebrations of US American success, and mere academic description. The social gospel founders of social ethics did not worry that too much advocacy would ruin their field, much as they strove to provide an empirical basis for it. Neither did the founders of Christian realism and liberation theology worry that advocacy would undermine their field; it was more like the opposite. I would not be a social ethicist had I not learned decades ago of the US American and European Christian socialist traditions, which did not reduce Christian ethics or the kingdom of God to socialist politics—except when they wrongly did. I conceive social ethics as a tradition of academic, ecumenical, and public discourse that analyzes the relations of power at multiple sites of exploitation, exclusion, harm, and oppression, taking up the public struggle for social and ecological justice.[1]

The field of social ethics was invented in the 1880s by white, middle-class, reformist, ecumenical, Protestant, social gospel academics—Francis

---

1. This chapter contains capsule summaries of detailed arguments I have made in *Soul in Society*; *Social Ethics in the Making*; *Economy, Difference, Empire*; *The New Abolition*; *Breaking White Supremacy*; *Social Democracy in the Making*; *In a Post-Hegelian Spirit*; and *American Democratic Socialism*.

Greenwood Peabody, William Jewett Tucker, Graham Taylor, and Richard Ely. It bore all the limitations in this description, yet the social gospel was a revolution in Christian thought that reached far beyond the tame progressivism of that group. It was revolutionary in Christian theology for contending that the church operated for centuries with the wrong hierarchy of topics. The teaching of Jesus resounds with social ethical maxims and concerns never mentioned in the ancient Christian creeds. The social gospel protested that the church expunged the prophetic heart of biblical faith, forgetting what it means to pray, "Thy kingdom come." The white social gospel had a reformist mainstream that changed what Christian ethics was about and a socialist flank that linked the capitalist system to racism, militarism, sexism, and imperialism. More important, there was a black social gospel with reformist and radical flanks of its own. Both helped to create a new abolitionist politics and theology.

The justly renowned white social gospel recovered the social justice emphasis of Hebrew Scripture and the centrality of the kingdom of God in the teaching of Jesus. It created the ecumenical movement and put social justice on the agenda of the churches. The white social gospel responded to the ravages of industrialization and urban corruption and did not recoil from European socialism and European Christian socialism. Even the squishy mainstream of the white social gospel that placated the capitalist class and avoided the s-word supported producer cooperatives, the socialization of natural monopolies, and other forms of economic democracy. The American difference was that the social gospel was an evangelical earthquake crossing the color line that should be called the Third Great Awakening. It preached that only a spiritual awakening would save the nation from its sins.

The black social gospel arose in response to the abandonment of Reconstruction and an upsurge of racial terrorism. It combined the abolitionist faith in the God of the oppressed with an explicit political agenda to recover the Fourteenth and Fifteenth Amendments to the Constitution and enact a federal statute against racist lynching. It enlisted the churches in the struggle for racial justice, co-founded protest organizations opposing America's racial caste system, and devised its own theologies of social salvation with socialist and progressive language of social justice. The early black social gospel had an assimilationist stream revolving around Booker T. Washington, a nationalist stream that considered white America hopelessly hostile to black Americans, a radical protest stream revolving around W. E. B. Du Bois and Reverdy Ransom, and a synthetic stream that fused other traditions. It yielded a generation of protest leaders who espoused social gospel socialism, combining progressive theology and social justice politics—Mordecai Johnson, J. Pius Barbour, Benjamin E. Mays, and Howard Thurman. These third-generation social gospel leaders were mentors of Martin Luther King Jr., providing neo-abolitionist theology that shaped King and the civil rights movement.

In the social gospel, society became a subject of redemption. Social justice became intrinsic to salvation. Salvation must be personal *and social* to save; the church has a mission to transform the structures of society for social justice. On both sides of the color line, the social gospel was divisive and controversial, compelling leaders to fight their own denominations. Social gospel leaders were admonished constantly that the church had never talked like this. They admitted it was true; no one had known there was a social structure. A bad society makes ordinary people do bad things. A good society makes people less selfish and violent.

I have long admired the founders of the social gospel and favored those in the socialist flanks. Social gospel socialism, especially in the black church, was the wellspring of liberation theology, holding struggles for economic and racial justice together. It caught my attention that the white social gospel had leaders who vehemently opposed anti-black racism: Albion Tourgée, George Gates, George Herron, W. D. P. Bliss, Herbert S. Bigelow, Celia Wooley, Mary White Ovington, Harlan Paul Douglass, and Kirby Page. It puzzled me that historians did not mention them and claimed that the social gospel looked away from racial injustice. These neo-abolitionists, it turned out, were also socialists, feminists, and anti-imperialists, which hooked me into exploring the radical social gospel. In black communities excluded from the labor movement, socialism was a heavier lift, yet the black social gospel had socialists who opposed all sites of oppression: Ransom, Johnson, Mays, George W. Woodbey, George Slater, Robert Bagnall, George Frazier Miller, Pauli Murray, and King.

The founders of the white social gospel were shamed by the Knights of Labor—a radical, Christian, industrial union with no color bar. The Knights arose in the 1870s with almost a million members by 1886. They were predominantly Protestant until Catholics poured into the union in the mid-1880s. The Knights blasted churches for siding with the ruling class, but they got pulled into strikes and were violently suppressed by state militias. They were surpassed by the American Federation of Labor (AFL), a federation of mostly craft unions. Industrial unionism organizes all the workers in an enterprise into one union. Craft unionism splits the workers into separate crafts. The AFL had a few industrial unions, and two in particular: miners and garment workers. They were the basis of its socialist wing. But the AFL was overwhelmingly a bastion of conservative, insular, racist, sexist, craft unionism that barred black Americans and immigrants, especially Asians. The rise of the AFL was a colossal victory for racist divide-and-conquer.

The social gospel emerged during the rise and fall of the Knights and the ascendance of the AFL. Union organizers blasted the churches for doing nothing for poor and working-class people. It was obvious to them that the churches took the side of the ruling class no matter what they said about taking no side. In Protestant churches, they said mainline Protestants were middle class. In Catholic churches, there were working-class unionists, but Catholicism was a struggling immigrant faith trying to assimilate, and the Vatican feared the rise of socialism in Europe. The founders of the social gospel chafed when union organizers said the church was the enemy of working people. They knew it was true and founded the social gospel to enlist churches into struggles for justice, extended the social gospel into the academy, and are justly remembered for it.

The original idea of socialism goes back to Charles Fourier and Robert Owen in the 1820s, in France and England. Both sought to achieve the un-realized demands of the French Revolution, which never reached the working class. Instead of pitting workers against each other, a cooperative mode of production and exchange would allow workers to collaborate. Socialism was about organizing society as a cooperative community. Early traditions of socialism conceived it as producer cooperatives or cooperative guilds. Other kinds of socialism soon arose: radical democracy, a form of populism; Marxism, a theory of proletarian revolution; anarcho-syndicalism, a call for worker syndicates; Fabianism, a theory of democratic state collectivism; Social Democracy, a blend of Marxism and democratic state socialism; and guild socialism, a blend of cooperative and Syndical ideas. These movements blamed capitalism for all of society's ills, but Christian socialists did not, so there were Christian versions of every socialist tradition.

The rich British tradition of Christian socialism exemplifies the ethical cast of the Christian socialist difference. British Christian socialism was founded by Frederick Denison Maurice, John Ludlow, and Charles Kingsley in the late 1840s. Maurice argued that cooperation is the moral law of the divine moral order. Socialism reflects the divine order by creating a cooperative society. Ideologically, the first Christian socialists were in the cooperative tradition of Owen, sometimes with a French inflection. Fatefully, they clashed with each other over consumer cooperatives, state financing for producer cooperatives, and cooperative syndicates. Is socialism only about the mode of production? Should the state finance cooperatives? Shouldn't socialism be less divisive than capitalism? These questions thwarted the first wave of Christian socialism.

The mighty second wave in the 1880s was mostly Anglo-Catholic. Many Anglican socialists were stubbornly cooperative in the Owen and Maurice mode; some joined the Fabian movement after it arose in 1884; some joined the Social Union reformers who came out of Oxford; some gave highest priority to socializing land; many joined the Workers Party movement after 1893; and some championed the Guild Socialist movement. But the Christian socialists led with ethical claims that qualified their commitments to these ideologies. They were committed to an ethic of equality, freedom, and cooperative community. They denied that a Fabian or Syndical or Social Unionist or Marxist ideology was more binding than their ethical convictions. The leading British Christian socialists fit their ideology to their ethical convictions and swallowed the taunt that this moralistic impulse made them poor socialists. Even those who joined the Fabian Society fought for the ethical difference. It arose repeatedly over imperialism and racism, because Sidney Webb and other Fabian leaders did not regard anti-imperialism and anti-racism as socialist causes. Charles Marson, Stewart Headlam, Conrad Noel, Scott Holland, Charles Gore, and others excoriated the old patriotic imperialism, the new capitalist-rivalry imperialism, and the plunder of Africa. They were anti-imperialists because their deepest convictions were ethical-religious. They loathed the patriotic racism they were taught in school.

THE EVANGELICAL IN THE SOCIAL GOSPEL

Since both US American social gospel traditions grew out of evangelical traditions, a great deal of early social ethics operated principally on a social gospel interpretation of Scripture: pay attention to the Exodus narrative, the prophets, Luke 4, and Matthew 25! This bright thread runs through the entire history of the social gospel and liberation theology. In the early generations of the social gospel, it resounded through the theologies of Washington Gladden, Reverdy Ransom, Richard R. Wright Jr., Walter Rauschenbusch, W. D. P. Bliss, Alexander Walters, George Herron, Vida Scudder, Nannie Burroughs, Harry Ward, and Adam Clayton Powell Sr.

Wright and Rauschenbusch were similarly quotable on the biblical basis of the social gospel. Wright told his national readership in the African Methodist Episcopal Church that the prophetic religion of Jesus is "the basis of any true Christian theology," centering on the kingdom of God—a radically expansive present and eschatological reality that brings God into everything. The kingdom can be entered, as Jesus taught in Matthew 19:23 and Mark 9:47. Human beings are to seek it, as Jesus taught in Matthew 6:33

and Luke 12:31. The kingdom or commonwealth of God is a society that people join under the rule of God. It is within and among human subjects, though Wright preferred the social rendering. It starts small, like a mustard seed, but grows into the greatest thing in the world, the moral and spiritual commonwealth of God.[2]

Rauschenbusch was famously quotable on this subject. He taught that the church falls away from the gospel whenever it reduces the heavenly, inward, communal, social ethical, and eschatological kingdom to only one or two of its dimensions, as the church usually did. He argued that the justice-oriented prophetic faith is the beating heart of Scripture, the prophetic spirit rose from the dead in the social ethical teaching of Jesus, and Christianity should transform society in the kingdom-bringing spirit of Jesus. Rauschenbusch knew about the apocalyptic turn in recent German history-of-religions scholarship and acknowledged it was correct but exaggerated. The Gospels are strewn with social ethical teaching, even though the early church was apocalyptic. Thus, it seemed to Rauschenbusch that the social gospel of Jesus had a strong scriptural basis and the early church spilled some apocalyptic coloring over him. But Rauschenbusch allowed that Jesus believed in devils and other things out of play for modern Christians.

Social gospel theologians sometimes conflated the kingdom of God with the socialist or liberal democratic politics of the social kingdom. Herron was a chief offender of the former type, and Shailer Mathews of the latter type, until Mathews decided that German scholars were right about the apocalyptic Jesus. Then he launched the Chicago School tradition of sacralizing social process without any sure word from Jesus. Rauschenbusch was not always careful to elaborate his own multi-dimensional theology of the kingdom, sometimes opting for social gospel shorthand with a rhetorical flourish. But when he wrote carefully, he insisted that the divine kingdom partly eludes our grasp and condition, lying before and beyond us. We shall never achieve the kingdom or see it realized, but every approximation to its social salvation is worthwhile.

This evangelical line resounds through every generation of social gospel and liberationist witness with adjustments geared to scholarly and cultural fashions of the day. Consider the two classic books of the past generation, each entitled *The Politics of Jesus*, by John Howard Yoder in 1972, and by Obery Hendricks Jr. in 2006. These were very different books, yet both centered on Luke 4 and Luke 6, sharing a profound insistence that the substantive norms of Christian ethics are *in* the gospel.

---

2. Wright, *Outline of the Teaching of Jesus*, 9.

Yoder said the history of modern Christianity is a trail of reasons not to make Jesus the norm of Christian ethics. Jesus taught an ethic of love perfectionism offering no help for the problems of social ethics (Reinhold Niebuhr). Or, Jesus was a simple rural figure who personalized all ethical issues (Tolstoy). Or, Jesus was indifferent to social and political issues, caring only about individual salvation (evangelical revivalism). Or, Jesus was a radical monotheist who pointed people away from local and finite values (H. Richard Niebuhr). Or, Jesus entered the world to die for the sins of humankind, which lifted him beyond the category of teacher or exemplar (Catholic and Protestant orthodoxy). Yoder blasted these options as different ways of evading actual norms *in* the gospel. Jesus is embarrassing, so we find a way to get around him.

Yoder argued that Jesus espoused a new spiritual community and way of living together. The gospel is about the new aeon of the kingdom. In the old order, sin and death ruled under the signs of vengeance and the state. In the new aeon, the rule of vengeance and the state are overthrown. Luke 4 is the platform of the politics of Jesus and Luke 6 is the gospel reaffirmation of the platform.

Hendricks similarly interpreted Luke 4 as the platform and Luke 6 as the reaffirmation, with no reference to Yoder. The gospel tells us right at the beginning of Jesus' ministry that it is good news for the poor, as a collective or class identity. The point of his ministry was to struggle for radical change necessary for the poor and oppressed. Jesus said that captives are to be released referring to political prisoners and people whose grinding poverty landed them in jail. Jesus advocated liberation for those oppressed by the crushing weight of empire. Hendricks admonished readers not to say "bruised" by the empire—the Greek is stronger. Jesus ended by proclaiming the year of the Lord, so, the mission of Jesus was good news for the poor: struggling for radical change, freeing people from jail, opposing the oppressive empire, and land reform.

Hendricks marched through Micah, Amos, and Matthew 25 in similar fashion, spelling out passionately that the church should stand on *mishpat, sadiqah,* and *hesed.* The principles of Jesus and biblical faith are justice, righteousness, and steadfast love for the hungry and hurting. Despite these affinities, Yoder and Hendricks got very different things out of the scriptural passages on discipleship, justice, the kingdom of God, the cross, and the Christian community. Yoder made a nearly unique case from an ecumenical, broadly-Anabaptist standpoint for the social relevance of the radical politics of Jesus. Hendricks epitomized the convergence between the radical social gospel of King and the liberation theology of James Cone.

The Yoder argument, especially as refashioned by Stanley Hauerwas, had immense influence in the 1990s, speaking to the sense of loss, diminishment, dislocation, and alienation of churches previously accustomed to a custodial role in American society. Hauerwas affirmed Yoder concerning how Christians should relate to politics and society: the gospel alternative to activist churches aiming at social reform, and conversion churches focusing on individual souls, is to form confessional communities of the cross that practice love of enemies, suffering for righteousness, and worshipping Christ. Hauerwas advised white US American church leaders to shed their Christendom agenda. He knowingly said that seminaries produced young pastors lacking any idea of helping congregations be the church. He quoted pastors besieged by a culture that had turned against them. He luminously revived social gospel arguments about the evisceration of kingdom Christianity in Constantinian Christianity, stressing that churches should be formative communities. But Hauerwas did so by faulting the social gospel for luring modern churches into social activism. Freedom and justice, he fatefully claimed, are bad ideas for Christians.

Hauerwas taught in a field that had almost no history apart from the social gospel conviction that Christian communities should join struggles for social justice and peace. Reinhold Niebuhr blasted the idealism, romanticism, rationalism, and pacifism of the field he entered, but never questioned its social gospel basis, as Hauerwas frequently observed. Once Hauerwas set himself against the social gospel concern about the right ordering of the world, he contended that his field of social ethics had asked the wrong questions. He became the nation's leading Christian ethicist by issuing broadsides against liberalism, Reinhold Niebuhr, and ecumenical ethics.

But the dichotomy between the faithful church and the pagan everything else that Hauerwas borrowed from Yoder was not what social ethics needed. It smacked of religious exclusivity, convicted that other religions are worthless. It undercut Christian struggles for a just social order. It reduced the theology of the kingdom God to a my-group binary, misrepresenting the gospel-centered faith of Rauschenbusch and King. Above all, it evaded the critical force of every liberation theology, claiming "nonviolent us" status distinguished from unrighteous others—masking the oppressions named in liberation theologies. Hauerwas's brilliant work helped pastors scale back to something they could preach and manage in a time of cultural fragmentation and upheaval, economic globalization, and ecological catastrophe. But Christian social ethics propels us into that world, not rationalized insularity.

POST-KANTIAN, CHRISTIAN SOCIALIST, LIBERAL-LIBERATIONIST

Everything I have written about modern theology and social ethics bears the marks of how I came to write. I organized three national social justice organizations through my twenties and halfway through my thirties. I joined a church when I was twenty-eight years old and became an academic at the age of thirty-five. I would be nowhere near the church had there been no social gospel movement, no Christian socialist flanks of it, and no Martin Luther King Jr. I wouldn't be in the classroom either without these influences. But I don't believe that Christian communities are only as good as whatever they do for justice and peace, and in class, my aim is to help students understand multiple perspectives, not to persuade them of my position. Theologically, I am a post-Hegelian, Anglican, liberal-liberationist who believes that theology should be interested in everything, employing all the disciplines, accepting criticism from all quarters, and risking metaphysical audacity. Faith is a form of daring.

I developed my religious philosophy in *In a Post-Hegelian Spirit* (see bibliography). For all the clashing between varieties of rationalism and empiricism that consume philosophical types, nearly all of us are empiricists, taking a stand in the stream of our own experience—a fog privileging particular kinds of experience, and, for metaphysical thinkers, striving to be as comprehensive, rendering nothing human as foreign. Metaphysical reason, in my conception, is about trying, fallibly, to show how different aspects of experience fit together. Love divine creates and calls out from created things the love that all things were created to be and express. The mind emerges through the process of apprehensions and adjustments. The fact that the world gives rise to minds that apprehend the world tells us something important—there is a kinship between mind and the world. If mind is part of nature, nature must be grounded in mind; otherwise nature could not contain it.

Realistic theologies are keyed to what is said to be actual. Idealistic theologies are keyed to claims about truths, transcending actuality. I oppose lifting realistic actuality above idealistic discontent, even as I acknowledge that idealism poses the greater danger. A wholly realistic theology would be a monstrosity, a sanctification of mediocrity, inertia, oppression, domination, exclusion, and moral indifference. Christianity is inherently idealistic in describing the being or movement of spirit as ultimate reality and holding to transcendent truths. But an idealistic theology lacking a sense of tragedy, real-world oppression and exclusion, and the danger of its own prideful intellectualism would be worse than theological realism. The only kind of idealism that interests me is liberationist—privileging the critique of oppression, linking tragedy with the struggle for justice, expressing idealistic discontent, and admitting what it does not know.

The critiques of sexist oppression and exclusion developed in feminist, womanist, and ecofeminist ethics of the past half-century deeply shaped my liberal-liberationist perspective. Beverly W. Harrison was just beginning to formulate a feminist social ethic when I studied at Union Theological Seminary in the 1970s. She taught a generation of seminarians to privilege gender as a category of analysis and implored them to oppose capitalism vehemently. At Union in those years, all the black theologians we studied were male, and the female theologians were white. This chasm did not go unnoticed. We speculated about how black women would change the discussion in theology and ethics. We had no way of knowing what the change would be, but Jacquelyn Grant, Katie Cannon, and other womanists found an answer by fending off the question whether race or gender was the "higher priority." The discursive tradition they founded refused to make an either/or answer, teaching the theological field to interrogate the intersections of race, gender, and class, and later, of sexuality and ecology.[3]

Holding together the multiple forms of domination has never come easily. The classic works of liberation theology are vague and thin on political economics, and a great deal of cultural leftist theory dispenses altogether with economic justice. Economic justice and cultural recognition must work together. Every form of injustice is rooted simultaneously in the political economy *and* the status order. No struggle for justice can succeed lacking a politics of redistribution, a politics of recognition, *and,* today, a new global politics of politics itself, no longer run by sovereign Westphalian states.

Conceived as a theory of justice, Marxism is a redistributive theory focusing on capitalist exploitation. John Rawls elaborated a theory focused on the fair distribution of primary goods. Amartya Sen and Ronald Dworkin developed theories focused respectively on equal capabilities to function and approximate equality of resources. These theories offer ways to account for racial, gendered, and sexual harm, but in derivative fashion. Redistribution theories silence or marginalize the most pressing causes of harm for denigrated groups. Cultural accounts of injustice are symbolic, rooting injustice in social patterns of interpretation and representation. Here, the defining injustices are disrespect, being rendered invisible, and being judged by norms alien to one's culture. But recognition strategies try to mitigate unjust outcomes without changing the underlying economic structures.

3. Harrison, *Making the Connections;* Cannon, *Black Womanist Ethics.*

Both of these orientations have reason to safeguard the priority of their claims, and there is a structural conflict between them. Recognition promotes group differentiation while the logic of redistribution abolishes it. Nancy Fraser, devoting much of her career as a feminist social theorist to this problem, devised a social spectrum bordered at one end by the redistribution model and at the other end by the recognition model, construing gender and race as hybrid modes in the middle combining features of an exploited class and an oppressed sexuality. Both forms of injustice are primary and co-original.

Fraser ended with a four-celled matrix placing redistribution and recognition at opposite ends of a vertical axis, and affirmation and transformation remedies at opposite ends of a horizontal axis. Affirmation remedies operate within the system; transformation remedies abolish it. Two combinations came out better than the others. The welfare state meshes consistently with mainstream multiculturalism, since both are affirmation strategies. Democratic socialism and cultural deconstruction also go together, since both are transformation strategies. Fraser argued that only combining democratic socialism and cultural deconstruction can do justice to all struggles against injustice. Affirmative strategies assume a zero-sum game and do not promote coalition building. The conflict between redistribution and recognition is especially acute across collectivities, such as gay and working class, or black and female. Affirmation strategies work additively and conflict with each other. Transformation strategies try to promote synergy, not being zero-sum.

I have thought with and against Fraser for many years. I admire her expansive vision and her emphasis on socialist transformation; I do not accept her harsh critique of the welfare state and multiculturalism and oppose undermining the gains of progressive politics in these areas. The right is out to destroy the welfare state, affirmative action, and multicultural education; I am not for helping it. For the same reason, I do not accentuate the cleavage between democratic socialism and social democracy. At least social democracy achieves universal healthcare and solidarity wage policies. I believe that Social Democratic parties lose their soul when they don't fight for new and old forms of economic democracy.

Globalization changed the debate over justice and Fraser's response to it by exposing that problems of representation are as fundamental as the problems of distribution and recognition. Who is included and what are the rules? Distribution and recognition are political in contesting for policy objectives, but politics *itself* determines how the state organizes itself and structures struggles for justice. The image of justice as a scale held by a blindfolded judge evokes an enduring test of justice: impartiality. In the modern period, the image of justice as a Westphalian map evokes the problems of the bounds of justice as the framing issue. What is the scale of justice on which contested heterogeneous claims might be impartially weighed? Fraser observes that the image of the scale has been stretched to the breaking point because parties no longer fight over something that can be weighed on a single scale. Movements demanding economic redistribution clash with defenders of the economic status quo, with movements defending specific groups, *and* with representational claims on behalf of the global poor, refugees, the global environment, and world peace. When groups clash over these claims, the threat of partiality is exceeded by the specter of incommensurability. The framing question supersedes the questions of how much inequality is tolerable and what constitutes equal respect: Who are the subjects entitled to just distribution or reciprocal recognition?[4]

Politics, defined by the issue of representation, furnishes the *stage for* movements of redistribution and recognition. We need politics more than ever now that it is failing us. The defining political injustice is to be misrepresented—to be wrongly prevented from participating equally with others. The deepest form of it is when the boundaries of a community are drawn to wrongly exclude some people from participating in contests over justice. Fraser calls it "misframing," the denial of a right to have any rights. I believe, with Fraser, that it must begin with the socialist principle that all who are affected by a given structure or institution should hold moral standing as subjects of justice. National governments are too selfish not to fail this test, and today nationalism is escalating. There are two fronts of the struggle to achieve the principle of all-affected moral standing. One is the prosaic political struggle to secure mere decency and generosity in government policies. The other is the global fight led especially by environmentalists, indigenous peoples, and feminists to claim their standing as subjects of justice. There is a right to make a claim of injustice against any power that causes harm.

EMPIRICISM, CATHOLIC ETHICS, AND NIEBUHRIAN REALISM

I do not want to suggest that my approach to social ethics simply combines an old school democratic socialism with the liberationist movements of the past half-century. I teach the history of social ethics every other year because I want seminarians to know the history, and I am deeply influenced by three long-running traditions of Christian social ethics outside my own post-Kantian, democratic socialist, liberationist perspective. These three

4. See Fraser, *Scales of Justice*.

traditions are especially important to me in brokering the "too much advocacy" concern.

The first is the inductive study of social crises and reform movements that social ethics took at its birth, which yielded empirical traditions of social ethics at Union Theological Seminary, Yale University, the University of Chicago, and the womanist movement. The second is the tradition of Catholic social teaching, which first allied with the social gospel in the work of John Ryan and showed the importance of having a philosophical underpinning. The third is the Christian realism of Reinhold Niebuhr, especially his critique of the Christian ethical failure to grapple with power.

Peabody put social ethics on the academic map. He was a Unitarian who emphasized the teaching of Jesus, but when Peabody taught social ethics, he said the field had to have its own method in order to become a field. In disciplinary terms, social ethics was a successor to courses in moral philosophy that nearly every American college and university taught into the 1880s. Students customarily studied moral philosophy from a ministerial president in the first and last semesters of their program. Usually, the presidents did not say they taught Scottish commonsense moral theory, though they did, since the whole idea of moral philosophy was to instill virtue and think about the good life. Theology is inherently divisive and prescriptive. Even homogenous American colleges puzzled over their own cultural and religious diversity. Moral philosophy was the solution to the problem of how colleges should talk about the moral good and produce virtuous graduates. It worked until the late 1870s, when the academy exalted the natural sciences above other disciplines and the schoolmaster *ethos* of moral philosophy became quaint.

Social ethics was originally a dream of a unified social science that analyzed society and helped to solve its problems. Nearly from the beginning, it named a specific academic field and a way of thinking about Christian ethics that transcended the academy. Peabody dreaded that social science was breaking into multiple disciplines that would leave ethics behind. The new Christian ethics sought to hold together the *is* and the *ought*, working with the emerging social sciences to improve American society, replace the old moral philosophy, enlist the churches in progressive social change, and hold together the teetering social sciences. This was the idea that Peabody took to his classes at Harvard College and Divinity School.

He approached ethics inductively as the study of social movements addressing social problems. No doctrine, scriptural tradition, ethical system, or teacher knew beforehand what should be undertaken. The reform movements provided the sites and subjects of what needed to be studied, guiding students to places where people suffered from neglect, exclusion, ignorance, prejudice, exploitation, or oppression. Peabody's early classes focused on the temperance movement, the labor movement, the plight of Native Americans, and the rising divorce rate. He stressed that his inductive social approach engaged the problems of real life, unlike the old, deductive, individualistic, boring moral philosophy. At first, he called it "practical ethics," a parallel to "applied Christianity," which the social gospel was called for thirty years. Peabody kept tinkering with the name, changing the title of his trademark course. Finally, after twenty years of name changes, his friend William James suggested, "Why not call it 'social ethics'?"[5]

His method had three steps—observation, generalization, and correlation. Peabody generated data, assembled and analyzed it, and discerned the underlying moral unity in nature. Somewhere between the second and third steps, science passed into a new moral philosophy. The hard part was the third step of drawing ethical principles from the data. Every social problem had its own history and quirks, but Peabody pressed students to glean the interrelationships. It was not enough to describe a problem, or even to propose a solution to it. Description and analysis were fine, but merely academic. Solutions were good, but piecemeal. Social ethicists had to aim for the underlying unity of the whole, including its ethical character and principles.

That launched a distinct approach to social ethics that morphed into many variations in theological institutions and did not slow—except at Harvard—social scientific specialization. In 1884, the American Historical Society declared its independence. The following year, social gospel economist Richard Ely founded the American Economic Association with a reform agenda, but by the turn of the century it dropped ethics and reform. The American Statistical Association was founded in 1888 and the American Academy of Social and Political Science in 1889. In 1905, sociologists launched the American Sociological Association, the kiss of death for Peabody's unifying American Social Science Association, which went out of business in 1909. The new disciplines declared the method, boundaries, and status of a science, taking leave of squishy ethical concerns. The phase in which the social sciences had a social philosophy was over. If sociology was a science, it did not need a philosophy, even a moral one.

Peabody-style social ethics helped deprive Harvard sociologists of a department of their own until 1931, and got bad press from them. The usual charge was that Peabody draped the faith of the social gospel in academic dress or refashioned moral philosophy with a social scientific gloss. He

5. Peabody, *Jesus Christ and the Social Question*; *The Approach to the Social Questionl*; *Reminiscences of Present-Day Saints*, 136.

supposedly eschewed the social scientific mission to discover new truths, using scientific induction to serve religious or ethical beliefs. The noble burden of secular social science was to overthrow the progressive idealism that Peabody-types imposed on it. But true-versus-fake induction was not the real issue. Peabody did not assume his moral principles; he worked seriously at finding them. He used the inductive method to develop general moral principles, not to isolate problems and solutions. His secular critics misrepresented him on this point. Peabody did not hide his ethical intent in doing inductive research. He dreaded both sides of the prevailing debate between *laissez-faire* capitalists and Marxian materialists. Both promulgated pessimistic, degrading, reductionist conceptions of the self. Though Peabody oozed the bourgeois conceits of his time and group, he pioneered an approach to social ethics that got the main thing right—tracking reform movements is always a good way to proceed.

Many have said so with a keener critical eye than Peabody. Harry Ward was an apostle of Peabody's approach at Union Theological Seminary. Ward was a united-front radical who battled for socialist and anti-militarist causes. Politically, he was far to the left of Peabody and Graham Taylor, yet he was a stickler at Union for their inductive method, drilling prospective social ethicists in it. Ward, not Reinhold Niebuhr, mentored most of the doctoral students at Union. They explained that Ward trained them in a field, whereas Niebuhr's students majored in Niebuhr. Ward taught students to adopt a stripped-down activist version of Peabody's questions: What are the facts? What do they mean? What should be done? Induction as a substitute for advocacy was furthest from his mind. Ward based class discussions on student field research. Union students always knew where he stood, and he taught for a verdict—as many of them preferred. In the 1920s, Ward's united-front leftism compelled him to apologize for Soviet communism. Twenty years later, he destroyed his reputation by refusing to back down, unlike Niebuhr, who drifted to the anti-Communist Old Left and subsequently to Democratic Party liberalism. But the Peabody method of allowing social movements to determine what social ethics is about had a long run at Union through Ward.

At Yale the inductive option was creatively refashioned by H. Richard Niebuhr, who opposed the activist orientation of Union Seminary and the social gospel tradition. Niebuhr taught that the value of justice, like other values, exists in the reciprocal relations that selves have to each other. There is no value apart from the relation of selves. To be an ethical self is to be a responsible participant in a network of relationships. Christian ethics is best conceived as the *ethos* or distinctive character of a Christian community's moral life, not as normative prescription. Instead of asking, "What should we do?" Niebuhr advised students to ask "What is going on?" and "What is God doing?" Finding the answer is each person's moral responsibility; Christian ethics is Christian self-knowledge within the context of Christian community. Instead of organizing Christian ethics around the monotheistic-idealistic command to remember God's plan or the deontological reduction to moral rules, Niebuhr commended an ethic of monotheistic responsibility advising responsible selves to respond to the action of God in all actions upon them.[6]

This rendering of the social ethical meaning of Christianity shaped two generations of students at Yale, notably Paul Ramsey and James Gustafson. It was also adopted by a diverse array of social ethicists *not* sharing Niebuhr's aversion to social activism, notably Charles Curran, Gibson Winter, and Emilie Townes. Curran put Niebuhr's analysis at the center of his constructive position, an alternative to physicalist natural law versions of Catholic moral theory. Winter developed a social theory of self-hood based on Chicago School pragmatist George Herman Mead and French phenomenologist Maurice Merleau-Ponty, supplemented by Niebuhr's relational theory of experience. Townes developed a womanist ethic of responsibility centered on Niebuhr's discussion of personal accountability and his question: "What is going on?" The inductive approach, as at its inception, is a protean option fueling powerful examples of ethical advocacy in the cases of these ethicists.[7]

John Ryan, the pioneer of Catholic social teaching in the US, exemplifies my conception of social ethics as a field centered in the analysis of relations of power and the struggle for social justice. For twenty years, he was a lonely figure. A single papal encyclical, *Rerum Novarum* (1891), made his career possible, but its scathing critique of capitalism was out of play in American Catholic seminaries. Ryan allied with social gospel Protestants on socio-economic issues, especially Richard Ely, while shuddering at liberal Protestant theology. He argued in his first book, *A Living Wage* (1906), that the rights to live and marry inhere in all persons, the right to a living wage is derivative and secondary, and the USA needed living wage legislation. Ryan advocated an eight-hour workday, state government unemployment and health insurance, national and state government ownership of railroads and telephone companies, municipal ownership of essential utilities and streetcars, national ownership of forestlands, and progressive taxes on income and inheritance. He claimed not to worry, in 1899, when Leo XIII

---

6. See Niebuhr, *Radical Monotheism*; *The Responsible Self.*

7. Curran, "Moral Theology," 446–67; Winter, *Elements for a Social Ethics*, 215–53; Townes, *Womanist Ethics*, 5–6.

condemned Americanism by name, since Ryan stood on the authority of *Rerum Novarum*. Eight years later, Pius X exhaustively condemned all forms of modernism, including evolutionary theory and biblical criticism, and biblical scholar Francis E. Gigot warned Ryan that he might be the next scholar to be shut down by the Vatican. Ryan fretted about it until 1911, when an Irish Franciscan with Vatican connections told him he would be okay as long as he stuck to I-oppose-socialism. Ryan asked Socialist Party leader Morris Hillquit for a debate in which he attacked socialism and Hillquit responded.[8]

Hillquit vowed to defend only the actual socialist movement of the Second International, brushing off Fabian socialism and Christian socialism. That suited Ryan. Hillquit argued that anarchy reigned supreme under capitalism, energy and resources were wasted on a monumental scale, pauperism was rampant, the working class got poorer, and the US stood helpless before mighty economic trusts. Ryan said Hillquit trafficked in exaggeration and half-truths. How could Hillquit know that reforming the trusts is pointless? The great trusts were barely twenty years old, and American politics was just beginning to corral them. Far from getting poorer, American workers had more discretionary income, leisure, recreation, and access to culture than their parents or grandparents. Capitalism is wasteful and anarchic, Ryan allowed, but these were small evils compared to Hillquit's remedy of abolishing individual liberty and making everyone a servant of the state. It was better to reform capitalism with progressive-populist legislation. Hillquit replied that he prized individual freedom and opposed despotic bureaucracy—why did Ryan insist on caricaturing socialism? Ryan countered that most socialists were not urbane like Hillquit; the threat of left-wing dictatorship was plainly evident. Ryan predicted that future generations would condemn the greed, materialism, labor oppression, and severe inequalities of capitalism, a truly barbaric system. There had to be a way to reform capitalism, just as the social gospel progressives contended.[9]

The Ryan-Hillquit debate won a national audience for both, demonstrating that Protestants did not own the social gospel. Ryan went on to a distinguished teaching career at Catholic University and directed the Social Action Department of the National Catholic War Council, which morphed in 1923 into the National Catholic Welfare Conference. He was a major player in policy and political fights over the New Deal, especially the controversial National Industrial Recovery Act of 1933, which advocated a forty-hour workweek, minimum wage rates, the right of labor to collective

8. See Leo XIII, *Rerum Novarum*; Ryan, *A Living Wage*.
9. See Hillquit and Ryan, *Socialism*.

bargaining, and a substantial measure of industrial self-government. Ryan called it a weak version of Catholic social teaching. The Supreme Court shot down the NRA in 1935 and Ryan implored Franklin Roosevelt to fight back, rescuing as much of it as possible, which occurred in the Wagner Act of 1935, an historic victory for union rights. Ryan was constantly accused of betraying his duties as a priest, an academic, and a moral theologian by battling for social justice causes. He justly replied that his career was buttressed by two encyclicals backing everything he said about the rights of labor, the role of government, and worker self-government: *Rerum Novarum* of 1891 and *Quadragesimo Anno* of 1931.

I treasure the modern Catholic tradition of social teaching because it focused from the beginning on the problem of capitalism and labor. It is based on one of the great philosophical traditions, with a method that works in various cultural contexts and reaches beyond Christianity. Every Catholic institution teaches some version of it. The focus on capitalism and labor institutionalized the colossal problem of economic justice in a way that has few parallels in non-Catholic traditions. A philosophical basis is far better than eschewing one, the default of Protestant traditions that run from metaphysics and ontology. The same is true of practicing a method that applies to multiple contexts. Catholic institutions will be teaching *Rerum Novarum* long after the Protestant social gospel is forgotten.

The third long-running social ethical tradition that I engage as a source of framing and correction is the Christian realism of Reinhold Niebuhr. Here I shall swing back to the social gospel, setting up the concept of power in Niebuhrian ethics. The problem of power has an awkward history in Christian social ethics, as Niebuhr harshly said.

The Christian gospel is about claiming and bearing the cross of Christ, while social ethics was founded on the hope of creating a good society. To the founders of social ethics, the concept of power smacked of monarchical theology, oppression, aggressive self-assertion, and, especially, the violence of war. The social gospel founders preferred to talk about democracy, faith, progress, peace, the common good, and the way of Christ. But the commitments to democracy and economic justice drew social ethicists into the hard-edged sphere of power. Moreover, these commitments opened to an understanding of power that was in the social gospel: power as inclusive transformative capacity, the ability to achieve a purpose.

The reformist mainstream of the social gospel was proudly middle-class, optimistic, and moralistic in supporting the progressive movement, cooperatives, and sometimes, municipal socialism. The socialist left-wing spoke the customary language of progressive idealism while advocating radical economic democracy. Some figures in the latter group advocated a Social Democratic fulfillment of social contract liberalism, construing power as managed by good politics. Others were straightforwardly Marxist in construing power as quantified, bought, owned, given, exchanged, or stolen. In both cases, social gospel radicals contended that economic justice is the precondition of individual opportunity. Debates over pacifism were not field dividing; the politically liberal and radical wings of the social gospel both had numerous pacifists and non-pacifists. The dividing issue pitted liberal idealists, who spurned class analysis and talk about power, against social gospel radicals, who fixed on democratizing power.

Social gospel radicals did not say that middle-class idealism could transform society. Rauschenbusch said emphatically that idealists alone never achieved *any* social justice cause. Class *happens* when socially awakened workers *make* it. It is made when exploited people articulate their interests in distinction from other classes, and justice requires that they fight for their rights. Rauschenbusch worked hard at persuading his church-going readers not to dread the Wobblies—the anarcho-syndicalist Industrial Workers of the World who dreamed of one big union. Few theologians write like that, which is why I stubbornly remind readers that a century ago there was such a thing as radical social Christianity.

Every social gospel moderate and nearly every social gospel radical contended that cooperative ownership is the ideal. The cooperative idea instilled Christian virtues, required virtues to succeed, and promoted community and fellowship. For twenty years, Washington Gladden advocated profit-sharing as a realistic half-way house to achieving the ideal. Fighting is bad, he implored. Sharing is much better and more reasonable. In the 1880s and early 1890s, Gladden gave the same sermonic lecture about good will and the common good to union and business groups. The church had a role to play as an honest broker that helped labor and capital come together. Gladden won much applause, which compounded his aversion to choosing sides. Every Sunday morning, he preached to the capitalist class of Columbus, Ohio. Gladden did not want to say that the social gospel could achieve its economic ends only by aligning itself with a fighting, striking, fractious, pro-labor, usually racist, usually anti-clerical left. But he moved reluctantly in that direction because the struggle between labor and capital turned into a rout.

Rauschenbusch said it robustly: democracy is radically transformative. In the age of monarchs, God was construed as a monarch. In the age of democracy, God had to be conceived as relational and fellow-suffering, the justice-demanding Spirit of love divine. The "kingdom" or commonwealth of God is social, ethical, indwelling, *and* eschatological here-and-not-yet, not to be passively awaited. Rauschenbusch got many things wrong, and the movement he championed famously got more things wrong. He employed the terms "Christianize," "moralize," "humanize," and "democratize" interchangeably, which was already quaint in his time; he said nothing about racial injustice for most of his career and was painfully conflicted about feminism. But he was prophetic about economic power without reducing Christian ethics to merely oppositional discourse.

The root of the problem was the predatory logic of capitalism, which theologians addressed too timidly. In Catholicism, the dominant power was the dogmatic mythology of a priestly class. In Protestantism, it was the financial and cultural power of a ruling capitalist class. Rauschenbusch applied the same test to the political and economic spheres: Does a given system reward cooperation and the common good or selfishness and will to power?

He answered that capitalism is essentially corrupting. Capitalism saps its own foundations by degrading the cultural capital on which economic success depends, turning labor and nature into commodities and reducing citizens to small-minded consumers. It gives autocratic power to owners and managers unrestrained by democratic checks. To Rauschenbusch, it was incredible that a worker could labor for thirty years and possess no more rights over property than a medieval serf. Workers labored on industrial property that was too expensive for them to own, but was financed by their savings and labor. The law was on the side of the capitalists because they made it.

Reinhold Niebuhr, when pressed on the question, sometimes admitted that the social gospel had advocates who were not moralistic and averse to power politics. But whenever Niebuhr wrote on this subject, he opted for ridicule. Social gospel liberals were stupid, he said, and usually meant that liberal idealism made them stupid. *Moral Man and Immoral Society* said it scathingly. Politics is about struggling for power. Human groups never willingly subordinate their interests to the interests of others. On occasion, individuals rise above self-interest, motivated by compassion or love, but groups never overcome the power of self-interest and collective egotism that sustains them. Liberal idealists failed to recognize the brutal character of groups and their resistance to moral suasion. Secular liberals like John Dewey appealed to reason; Christian liberals appealed to reason and love; both were maddeningly stupid.[10]

Niebuhr took most of the field of social ethics with him, moving, as he put it, to the left politically and the right theologically. He not only took for granted the activist cast of the social gospel; he accentuated it, at first with

10. See Niebuhr, *Moral Man*.

further-left politics. Liberalism and capitalism were finished and no amount of New Deal tinkering would save them. Mass production needed mass consumption, but capitalism was too predatory and class-stratified to sustain mass consumption. Thus it was a disintegrating system that required, but could not accommodate, continually expanding markets. There was no third way; there was only the choice between revolutionary state socialism and reverting to fascist barbarism. Economic democracy was serious only if it meant government control of the economy.

Niebuhr revived the radical wing of the social gospel, but not wisely. Wrongly, Niebuhr and the radicals of the 1930s equated socialization with nationalization and rejected production for profit. Wrongly, they claimed that state planners could replicate the pricing decisions of markets. Wrongly, they wanted government planners to organize an economy. In the late 1940s, when Niebuhr gave up on socialism, he made his peace with welfare state liberalism, joined the Democratic Party establishment, and stopped writing about economic justice—a pretty good summary of the field that he influenced.

On these issues, Rauschenbusch was better than the entire generation of Niebuhrians that panned him for being too idealistic. Rauschenbusch advocated mixed forms of worker, community, and state ownership. He contended that democratic control was the heart of the matter and that markets cannot be abolished in a free society. He had a strong concept of personal and collective evil coupled with a message of social salvation. On the other hand, even Rauschenbusch recycled the totalizing rhetoric of state socialism and claimed that prices under socialism would be based on services rendered. He could be sloppy, failing to distinguish between different kinds of social ownership and to critically analyze problems that come with them. Above all, Rauschenbusch trusted too much in the tide of social idealism.

Niebuhr was the towering corrective to social idealism, teaching social ethicists to view the world as a theater of perpetual struggles among competing interests. In foreign policy, realism sought a balance of power among regimes and a stable correlation of forces. In domestic policy, after Niebuhr dropped socialism, realism conceived government as a countervailing power mediating between corporate capitalism and the trade unions. Theologically, realism accentuated human egotism and the social irrelevance of the teaching of Jesus. Jesus taught an ethic of love perfectionism, which says nothing about how to maintain a relative balance of power. According to Niebuhr, the teaching of Jesus had social relevance only in affirming that a moral ideal judges all forms of social order. It's good to have an ideal, but the ethic of Jesus offers no guidance on holding the world in check. The highest good in the political sphere is to establish justice, which depends on resorts to violence. Even Gandhian nonviolence is a form of coercive violence, although Gandhians advisedly never put it that way. Today we have debates about whether Martin Luther King Jr. was a true-believing Gandhian, a Niebuhrian, or somehow both.

Niebuhr's attentiveness to irony and paradox, his insistence on the inevitability of collective egotism, and his sensitivity to complex ambiguities inherent in all human choices made permanent contributions to Christian thought. His passion for justice roared through his work in all these changes of position. But his polemic against the idea of a good society was costly for ethics. The idea of a good society emerges from discussion and is always in process of revision. To let go of it undercuts the struggle for gains toward social justice, negating the elusive but formative vision of what is worth struggling for. Without a vision of a just society that transcends the prevailing order, ethics and politics remain captive to the dominant order, restricted to marginal reforms. The borders of possibility remain untested.

The social gospel tried to moralize the public square, but Niebuhr replied that politics is a struggle for power driven by interests and will-to-power. The social gospel taught that a cooperative commonwealth is achievable; Niebuhr replied that the idea of a good society ideal must be surrendered. He got the first thing right, allowing for his polemical exaggerations against the social gospel, and the second thing wrong. Social ethicists have struggled ever since with both legacies.

Most who love Niebuhr, like me, hold some notion about when he was at his best. I believe it was in the early 1940s, when he pushed to get the Union for Democratic Action (UDA) off the ground, stopped attacking the New Deal, synthesized his mature theological position, and still pressed for economic democracy. The Niebuhr of *The Children of Light and the Children of Darkness* (1944) would have had a different legacy had he stuck with the politics of that book. As it was, he became more and more like the Cold War liberals of the Americans for Democratic Action (ADA) until he became one of them. Yet the smoothest transition that Niebuhr ever made was the one in which he folded UDA into the ADA. All of his other changes involved an emotional drama. The one by which he joined the Democratic establishment was unruffled by comparison. Afterward, he never took an ethical position that conflicted with a US American national interest. Realism was a bulwark against doing so, or even raising the possibility.

I have the same fourfold regret about Niebuhr and Paul Tillich. In their later careers, both opted out of solidarity movements for social justice and postcolonial liberation. Both ridiculed social gospel socialists and religious idealists who battled in solidarity movements. Both basked in the applause of the American empire. And both justified these positions with Marxist reasons. They burdened Christian socialism with Marxist requirements and expectations, contending that ethical Christian socialism is pointless; only the Marxian proletarian version deserves respect. That gave the later Niebuhr an excuse to drop Christian socialism and Tillich an excuse to do nothing for it. Both defended the American empire whenever it had an interest at stake in the so-called Third World, and both were scathing in ridiculing ethical socialists battling for "lost" causes.

The figures who pulled the ecumenical movement into global solidarity struggles for social justice and postcolonial reordering were the scorned religious idealists who never accepted Niebuhr's framework: Mordecai Johnson, Benjamin E. Mays, Howard Thurman, Martin Luther King Jr., Pauli Murray, Myles Horton, and Walter Muelder. It's the left wing of the black social gospel and its white allies. Those who stuck with social gospel radicalism did not believe that struggles for justice were optional or that the welfare state eliminated the need for economic democracy. Quitting the struggle was not considered.

I never end on that note, however, and will not here. For many years, Niebuhr blasted everyone who tried to get a social ethic out of Jesus, admonishing that Jesus is no help with problems of proximate means and ends, necessary violence, and calculated consequences. But something nagged at him. Something was missing in his dichotomizing between love and justice. The later Niebuhr realized what it was: the love ethic kept him and others in the struggle, whether or not they succeeded. *That* was its relevance.

In the 1930s, Niebuhr equated justice with equality, or an equal balance of power. Later he stressed that justice is a relational term, depending on the motive force of love, and it cannot be defined abstractly. There are no definitive principles of justice, for all such instruments are too corrupt to be definitive. But Niebuhr judged that three regulative principles are useful: equality, freedom, and order. Social justice is an application of the law of love to the sociopolitical sphere, and love is the motivating energy of the struggle for justice. The meaning of justice cannot be taken directly from the regulative principles. It is determined only in the interaction of love and situation, through the mediation of equality, freedom, and order.

The upshot, this being Niebuhr, was paradoxical. Love is uncalculating concern for the dignity of persons; it asserts no interests. But because love motivates concern for the dignity of persons, it motivates a passion for justice overflowing with interests and requiring principles of justice. I think that is exactly right. The love ethic is always the point, the motive, and the end, even when it lacks concrete meaning. Love is not merely the content of an impossible ethical ideal, but the motive force of the struggle for justice.

Love makes you care, makes you angry, throws you into the struggle, keeps you in it, helps you face another day.

BIBLIOGRAPHY

Cannon, Katie G. *Black Womanist Ethics*. Atlanta: Scholars, 1988.
Curran, Charles E. "Moral Theology: The Present State of the Discipline." *Theological Studies* 34 (September 1973) 446–67.
Dorrien, Gary. *American Democratic Socialism: History, Politics, Religion, and Theory*. New Haven: Yale University Press, 2021.
———. *Breaking White Supremacy: Martin Luther King Jr. and the Black Social Gospel*. New Haven: Yale University Press, 2018.
———. *Economy, Difference, Empire: Social Ethics for Social Justice*. New York: Columbia University Press, 2010.
———. *The New Abolition: W. E. B. Du Bois and the Black Social Gospel*. New Haven: Yale University Press, 2015.
———. *In a Post-Hegelian Spirit: Religious Philosophy as Idealistic Discontent*. Waco: Baylor University Press, 2020.
———. *Social Democracy in the Making: Political and Religious Roots of European Socialism*. New Haven: Yale University Press, 2019.
———. *Social Ethics in the Making: Interpreting an American Tradition*. Chichester: Wiley Blackwell, 2009.
———. *Soul in Society: The Making and Renewal of Social Christianity*. Minneapolis: Fortress Press, 1995.
Fraser, Nancy. "From Redistribution to Recognition? Dilemmas of Justice in a 'Postsocialist' Age." *New Left Review* (1995) 68–93.
———. *Scales of Justice: Reimagining Political Space in a Globalizing World*. New York: Columbia University Press, 2009.
Fraser, Nancy, and Kevin Olsen, eds. *Adding Insult to Injury: Nancy Fraser Debates Her Critics*. London: Verso, 2008.
Harrison, Beverly W. *Making the Connections: Essays in Feminist Social Ethics*. Edited by Carol S. Robb. Boston: Beacon, 1985.
Hendricks, Obery M. Jr. *The Politics of Jesus: Rediscovering the True Revolutionary Nature of the Teachings of Jesus and How They Have Been Corrupted*. New York: Doubleday, 2006.
Hillquit, Morris, and John A. Ryan. *Socialism: Promise or Menace?* New York: Macmillan, 1914.
Leo XIII. *Rerum Novarum: The Condition of Labor (1891)*. In *Catholic Social Thought: The Documentary Heritage*, edited by David J. O'Brien and Thomas A. Shannon, 12–39. Maryknoll: Orbis, 1992.
Niebuhr, H. Richard. *Radical Monotheism and Western Culture*. 4th ed. New York: Harper & Row, 1960.
———. *The Responsible Self: An Essay in Christian Moral Philosophy*. New York: Harper & Row, 1963.
Niebuhr, Reinhold. *Moral Man and Immoral Society: A Study in Ethics and Politics*. New York: Macmillan, 1932.

Peabody, Francis Greenwood. *The Approach to the Social Question*. New York: Macmillan, 1909.

————. *Jesus Christ and the Social Question*. New York: Macmillan, 1900.

————. *Reminiscences of Present-Day Saints*. Boston: Houghton Mifflin, 1927.

Ryan, John A. *A Living Wage*. New York: Macmillan, 1906.

Townes, Emilie. *Womanist Ethics and the Cultural Production of Evil*. New York: Palgrave Macmillan, 2006.

Wright, Richard R., Jr. *Outline of the Teaching of Jesus*. 6th ed. Nashville: AME Sunday School Union, 1946.

Winter, Gibson. *Elements for a Social Ethic: The Role of Social Science in Public Policy*. New York: Macmillan, 1968.

Yoder, John Howard. *The Politics of Jesus: Vicit Agnus Noster*. 2nd ed. Grand Rapids: Eerdmans, 1994.

CHRISTIAN ETHICS AND ADVOCACY

Stanley Hauerwas

THE BACKGROUND

To BEGIN, THE ASSUMPTION that there is a tension between Christian ethics as a discipline and advocacy for just causes betrays the history of Christian ethics. It is important to remember that Christian ethics as a discipline is a rather recent development in Protestant theology. The beginnings of Christian ethics as a distinct area in seminaries emerged in the late nineteenth century with the social gospel. The advocates of the social gospel, such as Walter Rauschenbusch, would simply not recognize a division between advocacy and ethics.

The social gospel began with the ambition to address the political and economic inequalities that characterized American society. Advocates of the social gospel were quite critical of the presumption that theology could be done as if unjust social and political realities did not exist. They were often criticized for not being real theologians, but they quite rightly argued that "real theology" and social ethics could not be separated from one another.

The theology that informed the social gospel was the liberal theology of the German theologians of the Enlightenment. Though these theologians were quite different, there was an emphasis on the kingdom of God that was central for the great figures of the social gospel. They sought nothing less than to enact the kingdom by working for the democratization of American society and, in particular, democratization of the economy. What they worked to enact was determined by their understanding of the gospel, so they had little reason to distinguish their theological commitments and their advocacy of various reform proposals. For example, I am confident that they would have thought their advocacy for the democratization of the economy and their stress on Jesus' preaching the kingdom to be closely interrelated.

Given that the first home of Christian ethics was the social gospel, it is not surprising that Christian ethicists have always identified and participated in various causes. One of the insights of those representing the social gospel was often the injustice they protested was not just the work of individuals but was structural. They sought in response to develop alternative institutions.

This did not change with the advent of Reinhold Niebuhr. Niebuhr was quite critical of the social gospel, but he was anything but politically and socially passive. He was as engaged as those influenced by the social gospel, but the character of his engagement had a different feel than the work of those associated with the social gospel. Niebuhr's focus on United States foreign policy was quite distinctive when compared with the social gospel. There is a sense that Niebuhr represented the transition of Christian ethicists to become more attentive to social and political policy issues. For example, Niebuhr served on the Policy Planning Committee of the State Department. One doubts any advocate of the social gospel could have served on such a committee.

Over the last century, Christian ethicists had no hesitation to take sides in the movements of the day. For example, they were quite willing to work to end child labor, for the just wage, the right to unionize, support of the family, the end of war, the right to vote for women, justice for African-Americans—the list is endless. Yet at the same time, they sought a theology commensurate with their pursuit of causes. "Commensurate" is a way to say they sought a theology that would justify their activism.

It has to be said, however, that the kind of advocacy represented by the developments in Christian ethics shaped by the social gospel has changed, but then so has the character of the church and American society. Most of the "ideals" the social gospelers worked to accomplish in fact have been accomplished. Child labor has been abolished, but that does not mean all forms of child misuse have been eradicated. I think it fair to say that the primary advocacy causes today center around race, women, and the environment. Deeply influenced by liberation theology, Christian ethicists make justice for the outcast the center of their work. But it is one thing to make certain causes the defining character of Christian convictions and quite another to be actually engaged in the attempt to see this or that cause through to fulfillment.

WHAT HAPPENED

My account of the development of Christian ethics as a discipline that re-flected the influence of the social gospel can be misleading. By focusing on the social gospel, some may think that there was no tension between the development of Christian ethics as a sub-field in theology and advocacy of certain causes. But that was not the case. The difference can be illustrated by the different stance students brought to their work in ethics at the three major doctoral granting institutions in the middle of the last century; that is, Union, Harvard, and Yale.

I can illustrate the difference by relating how we, that is, those of us educated at Yale in the second half of the twentieth century, understood how we were different from those at Harvard and Union. I should say I was at Yale from 1962 to 1968, and the generalizations I am about to make are gross but nonetheless make the point that there was little agreement about what the field of Christian ethics should look like between the three schools. The difference between the schools reflected the strong figures who taught Christian ethics at their respective institutions.

Nowhere was this more the case than at Union, where Reinhold Niebuhr reigned supreme. Even though Niebuhr died in 1971, his influence on questions concerning the character of Christian ethics remained strong. As I noted above, although Niebuhr was an activist, he brought to his work a "realism" that made him seek a theological alternative to the "idealism" of the social gospel. There was what might be characterized as a theoretical side to Niebuhr that was missing in the social gospel. That does not mean that Union graduates were not agents for social change, but they represent-ed more an "insiders" perspective. In that respect, they reflected Reinhold's certainty about specific policy matters that were fortunately matched by his genuine humility. But Niebuhr produced students who were sure they knew what justice entailed. Accordingly, students at Union were "activist" in ways that Harvard and Yale students were not. For example, Union students in the name of justice would picket a bank because the bank had investments in South Africa.

Students at Harvard studied with James Luther Adams. Adams was the great scholar of Christian ethics, knowing Troeltsch and the German theological tradition in a manner that made his students scholars in a field that could be tempted to be superficial. Students at Harvard were schooled to know every side of an issue, but that often resulted in their knowing so much they were rendered silent in the face of the complexity of the issue be-fore them. They could be quite sympathetic with Union students but would not necessarily join them in their protests. The Union student would be shouting we want justice and we want it now. The Harvard student would be muttering, "I wonder what concept of justice they are using."

There is a remarkable exception to this account of Harvard. That exception had a name: Charlie Reynolds. Reynolds led the protest movement against Nixon and the war in Vietnam. Schooled on the forms of nonviolent protest, Reynolds was arrested for demonstrating against the war at a Billy Graham rally. For Reynolds, such demonstrations were internal to the work of Christian ethics. But Charlie was not only an activist; he was also the founder of *The Journal of Religious Ethics*, which became the journal for scholarly articles in the field.

If Harvard was Adams and Union Reinhold, Yale was clearly Reinhold's brother, H. Richard Niebuhr. He had long had the reputation of being the intellectually deeper of the two brothers. H. Richard was not given as his brother was to social engagements. At Yale, we did not join movements for this or that cause. Nor did we worry who seemed to be on the right side or represented the just response. Rather, we took as our task to help those engaged in social change to better understand the ethical presuppositions that they assumed but did not justify. Thus, the typical Yallie position: "If you make these criteria the heart for what you take Justice to be, then these are your alternatives, but if you make these the heart of what you mean, then these are your alternatives."

H. Richard died in 1962, but his legacy was continued by James Gustafson. Gustafson was the master teacher who represented what I can only describe as the attempt to make Christian ethics a university subject. Accordingly, his graduate students began to read philosophical texts in a manner that made work in Christian ethics more disciplined. In some ways, Gustafson made Christian ethics into a "field." That does not mean students directed by him were not engaged in forms of protest, but such behavior did not come from the work they were doing in theological ethics.

I used to joke that those of us from Yale were not unlike the old TV show, *The Gunfighter*. The gunfighter had a card to identify himself that said, "Have gun, will travel." Those from Yale graduated with a card that said, "Have Conceptual Skills, will travel." By travel, we meant we would go anywhere to have a job. Like the gunfighter, we were open to serve almost any tradition.

There is just one problem with this account—Vietnam and the civil rights struggle. Even Yallies could not avoid those realities. But again, at Yale we were as concerned to clarify just war thinking as we were protesting the war. David Little had come from Harvard, having studied with Adams. He brought a strong emphasis on just war considerations. Because of Little, the work of Max Weber also became important.

I have called attention to the three programs that stood out at the time, but not to be missed is the importance of Paul Ramsey. Ramsey makes such an interesting example of how the doing of Christian ethics was integral to certain forms of advocacy. Ramsey was not an activist, but he was very concerned with policy matters. He was at once *the* just war thinker who was engaged in public discussions about the conduct of war. He took as his task to discipline the moral judgments being made about the war. Yet Ramsey insisted that he was making no strategic suggestions about whether the war should be fought in terms of foreign policy considerations. His perspective, he argued, was entirely about the morality of the war. Though labeled a conservative—his opposition to abortion earned him that title—he was a much more complex figure than that label can do justice. To be against abortion can be understood to be committed to a cause.

Besides the temptation to overlook Ramsey, there is one other program that should be named. It reflects the limits of a Yale perspective that in the account I have just given omits the midwest. Those of us at Yale knew there was something called the University of Chicago "out there," but we were not quite sure what was happening there. Of course, what was happening was Gibson Winter, who represented the engagement with the social sciences that in many ways made Chicago the institution in the deepest continuity with the social gospel. By studying how societies were put together, it was assumed you might better know how to enact fundamental changes. Of course, the work of G. H. Mead also existed at Yale.

But change was coming. The civil rights struggle commanded the attention of everyone. Martin Luther King Jr. was obviously shaped by work that had been done by the social gospel. Many who worked in Christian ethics soon found themselves engaged in sit-ins and other forms of civil disobedience. These forms of direct action were extremely fruitful for generating theoretical issues. For example, Jim Childress wrote a very important dissertation on civil disobedience, and Joe Hough wrote a defense of the black power movement. Engagements produced thought and thought produced engagements. Figures such as William Stringfellow and Dorothy Day were also studied in order to understand their social witness.

HOW I UNDERSTOOD WHAT I WAS DOING

If advocacy means direct action, most of us at Yale were not so engaged. I was writing a dissertation trying to reclaim the importance of character and the virtues for Christian ethics. I was by no means unsympathetic with those engaged in forms of social action, but I did not think such action to be

intrinsic to work done in Christian ethics. I assumed that those working in
Christian ethics had much to learn from those engaged in social policy considerations and forms of social protest. I just did not understand that such
activity was necessary for the constructive work that needed to be done in
theological ethics.

Whether we were right or wrong, most of us at Yale were fascinated
to watch Gustafson extend some of the directions begun in H. R. Niebuhr's
work, how Barth's work might be appropriated, the beginnings of taking
seriously developments in Roman Catholic moral theology, what to do with
Ramsey, and the list could be much longer. We assumed our task was to do
theology in a manner that could illumine in what way it might be said that
the theological convictions could be true.

We did not ignore practical issues such as bussing to achieve integration of public education, but most of us were struggling to understand what
it might mean for ethics to be a theological discipline. This question was
complicated because we were, thanks to Charlie Reynolds, a good friend at
Harvard, introduced to the continually revised manuscript of John Rawls's
A Theory of Justice. Reading Rawls did not turn us into social activists.
Reading Rawls turned us into committed liberals.

Some of us were engaged in conventual politics. William Lee Miller, a
largely forgotten figure in Christian ethics and politics, was running for city
council and some of us were supporting him by helping get out the vote. We
also took courses from him in ethics and public policy. But the organized
protest movements against the war and segregation were just beginning. I
do not remember participating in those events. I was trying to finish a dissertation. Nor did my first teaching position at Augustana College provide
encouragement to be socially active. I thought my job at Augustana was to
try to help Lutherans see there were other alternatives to the Law/gospel
distinction.

It was not until I was teaching at the University of Notre Dame that I
became engaged in what might be thought of as a cause. I became a friend
of a biologist who served on the board of the local Council for the Mentally
Disabled. His name was Harvey Bender, and he was a secular Jew. I admired
his commitments, but more importantly he drew me into the work of the
council. Soon I was on the board and was very active supporting the people
we served. The more I learned from those that were labeled disabled, the
more I thought they represented important commitments that should involve work in Christian ethics.

I am not sure how to describe the significance for me of such involvement, but I assume that my being drawn into the world of disability would
count as some form of social activism. It is not the kind of activism that

King sponsored, but work to sustain a shelter workshop is not that easy, either. At the time, those of us working on behalf of the mentally disabled had no sense that we might be at the beginning of a field now called disability studies, but that has happened. I call attention to that development because it is an illuminating example of how action can produce theory.

What I hope to suggest by calling attention to work with mentally disabled persons is that different forms of engagement will have correspondingly different theoretical implications. The civil rights movement is rightly seen as the paradigm of what it means for Christian ethicists to become agents for social change. But there are clearly different forms of advocacy. For example, it is not clear why Christian ethicists who are opposed to abortion are not counted among those who are social activists. But to be socially active does not make one a theologian or ethicist.

I have been criticized for not writing more in support of African-American demands for recognition. I acknowledge I might have done more, but that criticism sometimes fails to attend to the complexity of the world in regard to race in the late sixties. We might have wanted to write about race, but that desire could result in letting the white voice assume a "know-it-all position" in a manner that failed to attend to the black voice. It was hard not to think it was for the white folk to simply stay silent and listen for a change. That seemed like good advice for white people.

There is a passage in the autobiography of Malcolm X that I have always found illuminating. Malcolm X gave a lecture in New York City in which a young white co-ed was present. She was so impressed with Malcolm, she followed him in a taxi as he found his way to Harlem for a meal. The young woman confronted him as he was eating, declaring she would do anything to support the cause. Malcolm dismissed her, saying there was no place for people like her in the movement. A harsh but true judgment. That encounter strikes me as a paradigmatic exemplification of the complexity of the civil rights struggle.

LIBERATION THEOLOGY

Given the struggle to end segregation and racism, it is not surprising that freedom or liberation became for many the concept that determined what Christian ethics was about. I confess I am not sure what happened when, but the civil rights movement and the development of liberation theology soon were joined in a common effort to end domination and oppression. Under the banner of liberation, the work of ethics was now seen by many as supporting the movements for liberation. The women's movement, which can raise quite different understandings of liberation than the question of race, soon became part of the general struggle for liberation.

I think it fair to say that although I was and am sympathetic, a word that betrays white privilege, I was and am critical of the appeal to liberation as the concept that determines what Christian ethics is about. Such a view not only does not do justice for those working in biomedical ethics and the environmental crisis, but also often misses explorations of fundamental philosophical questions. But then that is what one would expect someone educated at Yale to say.

Equally if not more troubling is the assumption by some that appeal to liberation as the primary focus for moral behavior needs no justification. The assumption that certain movements are self-justifying I take to be deeply problematic. The kind of criticisms developed by John Milbank that call into question the liberal presuppositions that inform those that are rightly protesting against injustice I think are extremely important. It is hard to make such criticism because what is rightly identified as oppression is oppression. But the language of protest can often mislead those working for a better alternative. For example, the use of the phrase "social justice" may be misleading because it implies there is a form of justice that is not social.

In an interesting way, appeals to liberation as the defining character of Christian ethics can be an invitation to self-righteousness that functions as an appeal to authority. Too often, I fear appeals to justice on behalf of the oppressed are assumed to be self-validating. Accordingly, appeals to experience are assumed to be valid, which makes argument impossible. It is not surprising, therefore, that some people who once might have described their work as Christian ethics now claim to be doing social ethics. The latter they take to be a more basic description than the more parochial notion of Christian ethics.

The issues for me are Christological. Appeals to Jesus as the representative of a liberation movement is far too singular to do justice to the Jesus who was crucified. In an odd way, in spite of my criticisms of Reinhold and H. Richard, I have worked as they did to make Christian ethics a theological discipline. That has entailed developing an understanding of the significance of the church that I should like to think is a form of advocacy. One of the crucial questions raised by those who represent a liberation perspective is one of audience.

My emphasis on the significance of the church for how one should understand Christian ethics has earned me the description of being a "sectarian." I am allegedly trying to convince Christians they should withdraw from the world. I do not think such a characterization accurate. I am not asking Christians to withdraw; I just want them to be in the world as Christians.

That Christians must call to task the current rise in nationalistic sentiment I take to be a given, but the givenness draws on the catholic character of the church. The same kind of reasoning is where Christians should begin their thinking about immigration.

How Christians think about the fundamental narratives that define America is a witness that waits enactment. America is a slave country that remains to be acknowledged. Americans tend to think slavery and racism were overcome by the civil rights movement. The latter is seen as the embodiment of liberal ideals. Thus, the presumption that slavery and racism have been overcome justifies an attitude of indifference. Christians have a quite different story to tell. It is a story of sin that requires repentance. Christians must struggle with the question of what do you do when what was done was so wrong it cannot be made right.

These kinds of considerations, of course, involve my commitment to non-violence or pacifism. Many assume that such a commitment makes one politically irrelevant. I have tried to show, however, the opposite is the case. The non-violent must be the most political of animals seeking to come to agreements that make violent conflict less necessary. At the very least, the non-violent must be those who have learned to listen. Listening, moreover, is a virtue that makes politics possible. I cannot imagine, therefore, how my theological emphasis is not a form of engagement.

As I have suggested elsewhere, it is not at all clear to me that Christian ethics will survive as a distinct field within the discipline of theology. Christians will, however, continue to discover that there are Christian ways of life that are surprising. Many of the behaviors associated with the liberation movements are of that kind. That such is the case means there will need to be some set aside to think and say what that means for a people so constituted. Let us agree to call them theologians. That is what I have tried to be.

SEARCHING FOR THE CENTER THAT CANNOT HOLD

Mediating Advocacy and Christian Ethics

Rebekah Miles

THE VOCATION OF THE CHRISTIAN ETHICIST

IN 1977, AS MANY Christian ethicists were engaged in a long-running effort to bring greater coherence and definition to their discipline, Glenn Stassen asked if there was, after all, any center to the field, something that "gives it direction and definition." Or perhaps, instead, the field of Christian ethics, like Don Quixote, "simply jumps on its horse and rides off in all directions."[1] Over the last sixty years, the field has been shaped, in part, by questions of coherence. Is there a center to the field? If so, what is it? And how does any one contender for the center of the field relate to other possible contenders, as well as other adjacent fields and practices? The place of advocacy in ethics is linked with this larger question of coherence and the relation of the various parts to the whole.

Now, many decades later, the question of coherence is still unresolved and, almost surely, unresolvable. The field has no obvious, accepted center, but neither is it like Don Quixote. A more apt persona for the field of Christian ethics might be, not Don Quixote, but Walter Rauschenbusch, Reinhold Niebuhr, Georgia Harkness, Martin Luther King Jr.—peripatetic church leaders, advocates, scholars, preachers, and teachers—or any

1. Stassen, "Editorial Notes," 1.

number of contemporary Christian ethicists whose lives and work, though not well-known, are also spread across multiple institutions, commitments, and practices.

One of the inevitable problems in the field of Christian ethics, a problem that drives the ethicist toward multiple tasks and vocations, is that Christian ethics is done, almost entirely, by Christians. Indeed, often Christian ethicists are not only Christians, they are Christian leaders whose faith has driven them toward activism and advocacy; toward participation in the life and order of the church; toward teaching, research, and service. They teach, write, advocate, and lead as Christians and as ethicists. And they do ethics as people who have been formed by their faith and by their various vocational responsibilities. Many of us have taken vows for leadership and service to church and world as ordained clergy. In this volume alone, most of the contributors are clergy—United Methodist (Beckley, Schweiker, and Miles); African American Episcopal Zion (Riggs); Episcopal (Dorrien); African United Baptist Association (Paris); and Presbyterian Church USA (Ottati and Rodriguez). Other contributors to the volume are active laypeople in their churches.

I suspect that many ethicists were driven by their faith first to advocacy and then, by way of their social commitments and projects, they entered the field of Christian ethics. And many of us have moved back and forth between the various tasks given to us as church leaders, citizens, advocates, and scholars and to the many institutional structures in which those tasks are lodged and by which they are fostered. That is not a bad thing. The multiple tasks and callings of our lives mutually cohere; they cohere and are integrated not around an abstract center to the field of Christian ethics, but around human vocations and the groups, conversations, and institutions in which those Christian ethicists and their vocations find a home.

This integration has shaped my work and that of many—perhaps even most—Christian ethicists. My primary areas of advocacy have been in the church and political realms. On the political side, I have engaged in electioneering for the Democrats off and on, beginning with initial forays at thirteen when I leafleted and canvassed in advance of the 1974 Democratic primaries for David Pryor running in the Arkansas governor's race against much despised Orval Faubus and then stretching more recently to registering voters, writing letters, and canvassing (by phone and door to door) for Beto O'Rourke, Jon Ossoff, Joe Biden and Kamala Harris, and others.

My primary area of advocacy has been in the United Methodist Church, where I have been active as an elected clergy delegate to our General Conference since 2004 and in the past few years have been a part of an organized United Methodist resistance movement, working, so far with little success, to bring the United Methodist Church to greater openness on LGBTQ issues. Years ago, I was a member of the United Methodist Genetic Science Taskforce and the General Board of Church and Society where I worked with others—church leaders and ethicists—on statements and church policies on cloning and genetic science, helping to shape policies of the church that are still in effect. Most of my vocational life has been spent in the preparation and formation of candidates for ordained and lay ministries and advocating, by way of tedious and often unsuccessful legislative processes, committees, and task forces, for the reform of the church and theological school structures through which that preparation takes place. Being an advocate has made me a better ethicist and being an ethicist has made me a better advocate. And all of it, whether it is helpful or successful, is driven by my vocation as a Christian.

I take on these integrated tasks as a member of the larger United Methodist Church family and my own family of origin, which includes many United Methodists who have been similarly engaged. Christian social ethicist, activist, and churchman Walter Muelder liked to tell the story of his elderly mother, who, after reading his book *Methodism and Society in the Twentieth Century*, basically a book on Methodist social ethics and advocacy, told him, "Why, Walter, that's the story of our family!"[2] A central part of the story of my Methodist family, as well as the story of the discipline of Christian social ethics in the United States, includes a commitment to advocacy, not as ancillary to moral life and reflection, but at its center.

Some of the essays in this volume leave me benignly puzzled and others encouraged. In my work and life as a Christian ethicist, reflection and advocacy are integrated into one thing. Indeed, my work as a Christian ethicist, United Methodist pastor, activist, professor, canvasser, and church reformer are all bound up together, and advocacy runs through it all. Advocacy, for me, is at the heart of ethics, and ethics is at the heart of advocacy.

This integrated view of Christian ethics is not an aberration but the norm through a large portion of the history of our field, certainly for much of the history of Christian social ethics in the United States and especially within the Methodist tradition. Advocacy has not been ancillary or even just closely aligned to ethics, but at its center. Both the field and the world are enriched if many of us keep reflection and advocacy together at the center of ethics, just as the field and the world are enriched when Christian ethicists understand and do their work in a variety of ways. Whether it is enriching or not, that diversity of understanding is not likely to change.

2. Lincoln and Deats, "Walter G. Muelder," 2. Lincoln and Deats refer to Muelder's *Methodism and Society in the Twentieth Century*.

I show how the inclusion of advocacy at the heart of ethics fits well within the history of the field—including the early days of Christian social ethics and in the early years of the Society of Christian Ethics (SCE). I explore the place of advocacy and the search for coherence in Christian ethics, especially in the 1960s and 1970s, as ethicists were seeking clearer boundaries and definitions for the field. This integration of advocacy and ethics is also fitting to the current context of the SCE and its stated goals, as well as the larger social and political contexts. We need scholars working with different models of ethics, including contrasting ideas about the center of ethics or even whether there is a center, and we need them to be engaged with one another for the sake of the world and our shared vocations for healing and transformation.

THE CURRENT CONTEXT OF CHRISTIAN ETHICS

In his 2018 Presidential Address to the SCE, David Gushee spoke passionately of the fracturing of the field, describing his address as a "*cri de coeur* concerning our internal divisions and the imperiled state of our discipline."[3] After mapping the field of Christian ethics and seven contrasting types he sees within it, Gushee offers these summary reflections: "Christian ethics as a discipline now has multiple layers and lineages. There is no consensus, and no imaginable recovery of one . . . There will never again be a consensus way of doing Christian ethics."[4]

How should Christian ethicists best respond to this fracturing, especially in a time of national and global disorder? Gushee laments the divisions and acrimony among Christian ethicists and urges reconciliation and an appreciative forbearance, and even charity, for different ways of doing ethics. He calls on Christian ethicists to listen to one another and to work together without attempting to resolve the differences of approach. This is a valuable way forward, not only because consensus is not an option, but also because the field and world are better when the different lineages can continue and can work side by side. With the nation and world in disarray, Gushee reminds his colleagues, "we need all strands of Christian ethics to do their best work, in conversation with one another."[5]

A current point of tension within the field, and the subject of this volume, is the place of advocacy. This volume was prompted in part by recent

3. Gushee, "Christian Ethics," 3.

4. Gushee, "Christian Ethics," 14.

5. Gushee, "Christian Ethics," 14. Gushee engages in activism and is sometimes called a scholar activist.

discussions in the SCE about the future of both the Society and the field and the proper place of advocacy within them. Over the last two decades, strategic planning committees—the Twenty-First Century Committee and Initiative, the 2020 Committee, and several other groups—helped engage the Society in reflection on the nature of the discipline and ways the field and the Society were changing.[6] This period has parallels with the Society's first two decades, in the 1960s and 1970s, when similar questions were asked about the nature of the discipline and the place of advocacy within it.

An emerging emphasis of recent discussions within the SCE gives greater attention to changing demographics within both its membership and the United States, and asks what those changes might mean for the Society and the field. The Twenty-First Century Initiative recommended, among other things, that the Society seek greater inclusion and participation from "historically underrepresented groups" and that it work toward the "expansion of ethical conversations" within the Society through working groups and sessions that focus on several areas, including Latinx Christian ethics and African-American Christian ethics.[7]

One of the conversations that emerged from those initiatives was a pre-conference workshop at the beginning of the 2016 annual meeting of the SCE, entitled "Got Ethics?: Envisioning and Evaluating the Future of our Guild and Discipline." Panelists Stacey Floyd-Thomas, Gary Dorrien, Miguel De La Torre, Agnes Chiù, and Gloria Albrecht were invited to reflect on "the implications that a diverse demographic and discipline as well as the developing global context may pose for the future of our scholarship and society."[8]

Several panelists emphasized the central place of activism and advocacy in the field of Christian ethics. Angela Chiù described Christian ethics as a discipline that "intersects and calls for Christian engagement with the world."[9] Miguel De La Torre highlighted ethicists who are "scholar activists, concerned with changing the world toward more just social structures" and noted that this dual commitment was more common among ethicists of color and ethicists embracing liberationist perspectives.[10] Gary Dorrien linked the vocation of today's scholar-activists, including himself and all the other

---

6. These include the SCE Twentieth-First Century Initiative and the 2020 Committee.

7. O'Connor, "Report of the 21st Century Committee," rec. 5(a).

8. Floyd-Thomas, "Got Ethics?," 195–203; "Setting the Context"; see also "Ordering Our Steps."

9. Chiù, "Forging and Fumbling Our Way Through," quoted in Floyd-Thomas, "Got Ethics?," 196.

10. De La Torre, "WTF," 6.

panelists, with the long tradition of Christian social ethics with its roots in the social gospel movement. Noting this link and the activist thrust that pervades much of the Christian social ethics tradition, Dorrien concludes, "Today, as in previous generations, some ethicists work hard at straddling the divide between social justice activism and disciplinary scholarship."[11]

De La Torre highlighted a tension in the field between those who emphasize ethics as reflection and those who emphasize ethics as advocacy and a means to change the world. He is clear that both reflection and advocacy are valuable and necessary. De La Torre objects, instead, to those who would dismiss scholar activists and who question the value of advocacy as a part of the discipline of Christian ethics, scorning it as "lacking academic rigor."[12] Note that De La Torre is claiming that Christian ethics, by definition, includes both reflection and advocacy. Although both are needed, De La Torre is clear in the end about what matters most: "the first task of Christian social ethics is to make the 'world' better and more just."[13] Ethics developing on the margins, in solidarity with those who suffer, is the future of the field.[14]

The essays in this collection center around this distinction "between the work of 'ethics,' as critical reflection on and response to moral questions and social activism and moral advocacy."[15] Some of the authors distinguish Christian ethics from advocacy; ethics is critical reflection that informs and enriches advocacy, but is not identified with it. Others seek to flesh out the close connection between them.

HISTORICAL REFLECTIONS

This is not a new discussion in the discipline of Christian ethics or in the SCE. The connection between ethics and advocacy extends back into the field. The SCE is rooted in the Christian social ethics tradition, which has often seen advocacy not simply as an outgrowth of ethics but as integral to it. The Society was organized by professors of Christian social ethics who, in many cases, strongly identified with the social ethics tradition, and who had belonged to a predecessor body, the Association of Seminary Professors of Christian Social Ethics. Edward Long writes, "Most of the participants in that group felt a kinship of some kind with Walter Rauschenbusch and others of an earlier period who stressed the necessity of a social emphasis

11. Dorrien, "Got Ethics?," 7.

12. De La Torre, "WTF," 6–7.

13. De La Torre, "WTF," 8.

14. De La Torre, "WTF," 9–10.

15. From the proposal for this volume.

in Christian thought."[16] This historical link between the SCE and the older tradition of Christian social ethics is unsurprising. This was the dominant tradition in the development of Christian ethics as a field in the US among Protestants. And within this tradition, advocacy had a key role.[17] Of course, this is also true of the Catholic Social Teaching tradition, which may have made the subsequent integration of Catholics and Protestants within the SCE much easier.

Gary Dorrien's monumental study of the field of Christian social ethics traces the beginnings of Christian social ethics and the social gospel movement to the same point in the early 1880s. They began with "the distinctly modern idea that Christianity has a social-ethical mission to transform the structures of society in the direction of social justice."[18] Both the social gospel movement and the emerging field of Christian social ethics were unapologetically activist, and Reinhold Niebuhr, whatever his many criticisms, "simply assumed the activist orientation of the social gospel" movement that had preceded him. In Dorrien's telling, much of the Christian social ethics tradition, before and after, has been "political, activist, and pragmatic."[19]

Although advocacy has been prominent throughout this history, it became a point of tension—both in the field and in the SCE. The Society was founded in 1959 in part to bring greater focus and coherence to the field, and a piece of that discussion was the "relative importance of being an academician and being a social activist."[20] The Society emerged from two predecessor bodies. The social ethicists had initially met in a larger group— the Association of Seminary Professors in the Practical Fields. In the 1950s, the social ethicists within that body, wanting to distinguish themselves from the professors in the practical fields and to focus on their own field, formed the American Society of Seminary Professors of Christian Social Ethics in the United States and Canada.[21] That Society, like its predecessor body, was closely tied with church leaders and institutions, schools of theology, and practical aspects of ministry, Christian life, and political/social realities.

---

16. Long, *Academic Bonding*, 2.

17. Dorrien, *Social Ethics in the Making*; Dorrien, *Soul in Society*.

18. Dorrien, *Social Ethics in the Making*, 1.

19. Dorrien, *Social Ethics in the Making*, 2. The SCE was originally named the American Society of Christian Social Ethics; the arguments for eliminating the word "social" centered not around a denial of the social realities or a rejection of social ethics, but from a recognition that "the use of the adjective 'social' to modify Christian ethics involved a redundancy." See also Long, *Academic Bonding*, 2. Several name changes have been considered.

20. Long, *Academic Bonding*, 9–10.

21. Long, *Academic Bonding*, 1–6.

When the American Society of Christian Social Ethics was founded in 1959, its members made a conscious decision to be a professional, scholarly organization, focused on research and teaching in Christian social ethics.[22] In its initial founding, they created a tension—or perhaps simply amplified an already existing one—within both the Society and field. The Christian social ethics tradition had strongly emphasized its links to the church and to advocacy. In their effort to define a scholarly discipline and to distinguish it from the practical fields, the members of the American Society of Christian Social Ethics began to rethink the relationship between ethics and advocacy. The search for definition as a specialized scholarly field and the tensions around advocacy were evident throughout the 1960s and 1970s and continue today.[23]

One part of the ongoing debate has been the role of the SCE itself as an organ for advocacy. Over time, the Society has, as a body, advocated on various social issues. Most recently, the Society's leadership initiated and many members signed a statement calling for the removal of President Donald Trump from office following the US capital riots of January 2021, as the annual meeting was underway. Since the early 1970s, the Society has considered statements in opposition to racism and the Vietnam War, in support of academic freedom and colleagues Charlie Curran, Hans Küng, and Daniel Berrigan, and in relation to US immigration policy, needle exchange programs, the 1990–91 Gulf War, and US immigration policy.[24]

Members of the SCE have often disagreed about whether it was appropriate to make these public statements.[25] The various resolutions and disagreements about resolutions often led to renewed discussion about the place of advocacy not only within the Society, but also the field itself. One example is a discussion about racism following the Society's creation of a Task Force on White Racism in 1970.[26] Over the next several years, as Society members engaged in conversations about racism and considered various recommendations from the Task Force, including the possibility of public statements, the larger question of the place of advocacy within the field and the Society came to the fore.[27] In response, in 1973, the Task Force on White Racism was turned into an interest group with a broader focus:

22. Long, *Academic Bonding*, 4–8.

23. Long, *Academic Bonding*, 162–63.

24. Gudorf and Long, "History of the Society of Christian Ethics," 55–58. See Long, *Academic Bonding*, ch. 3.

25. Long, *Academic Bonding*, 43–44.

26. Long, *Academic Bonding*, 42–43.

27. Long, *Academic Bonding*, 43–44.

the Action Reflection Interest Group, charged to "examine how action and reflection interrelate in the life and work of the Christian ethicist."[28] The Interest Group considered, among other things, papers by John Bennett and Gayraud Wilmore, speaking from "their own experience about 'Social Action in the Vocation of the Social Ethicist,'" and a paper by Charles Brown on "Action Reflection as a Way of Doing Ethics."[29] Bennett, Brown, and Wilmore were all scholar activists, Wilmore a leader in the civil rights movement. A few years later, around the time that the Action Reflection Interest Group was failing, Brown would help form and then convene the Society's Interest Group on Ethics and the Black Liberation Struggle.[30]

In these same years, members of the field and the Society discussed the boundaries and definition of the discipline of Christian ethics. Max Stackhouse, in a paper at the Annual Meeting of the American Society of Christian Ethics in 1965 published the following year, wrote, "ethics is becoming a distinct discipline." He gave as an example of the increasing disciplinary focus "the rapid and recent growth of an independent scholarly society, The American Society for Christian Ethics."[31] Stackhouse reported that in the process of becoming a distinct discipline, the field's relationship to theology was changing; ethics was still interdependent but no longer a sub-set of theology. Stackhouse notes the lament of some ethicists that, having freed itself of dependence on theology and dogmatics, Christian ethics had become instead "a branch of sociology."[32] Stackhouse examined the proper place and use of data from the social sciences in interdisciplinary Christian ethical reflection, but also referenced the changing relationship of the field to other areas of study and practice. Ethicists were eager to address these tasks, especially the interdisciplinary ones. As Stackhouse wrote, "[I]t is terribly exciting to be an ethicist today."[33]

Not everyone was excited. In 1968, University of Chicago PhD student Richard Mouw wrote of the disappearance within Protestant institutions of the "old scheme" where the "moral implications of Christian faith" were considered within many disciplines—moral theology, biblical ethics, theological ethics, and casuistry. In its place is what purports to be a simpler new scheme, considering the material of all of these fields under one

28. Long, *Academic Bonding*, 47.
29. Long, *Academic Bonding*, 48.
30. Long, *Academic Bonding*, 50.
31. Stackhouse, "Technical Data," 200.
32. Stackhouse, "Technical Data," 200.
33. Stackhouse, "Technical Data," 191.

umbrella—Christian ethics.[34] The point of Mouw's essay was to "get clear about the nature of Christian social ethics," and he was not enthusiastic about some aspects of the "new scheme."

Stackhouse and Mouw may have been right in the 1960s that Christian ethics was growing into a distinct discipline, but it does not appear to have been an even or easy process. In the years following Stackhouse's paper, there were many laments about the lack of coherence. In a 1969 essay, for example, Beverly Harrison, just three years into her long tenure as a professor at Union Theological Seminary, described a "discipline of Christian ethics in disarray," mentioning particularly the disagreement over the place of theology and expressing prescient concern that the discipline would become obsessed with methodology.[35]

One key juncture in this discussion of the definition of the field and the place of advocacy was a 1972 essay by Ralph Potter, which generated a productive debate lasting through most of the 1970s, as I describe below. Potter's essay was written for a festschrift, *Toward a Discipline of Social Ethics*, assessing the field of Christian social ethics and honoring Walter Muelder on the occasion of his retirement as Dean and Professor of Social Ethics at Boston University School of Theology.[36] Paul Deats, the volume editor and Muelder's faculty colleague and former student in Christian social ethics at Boston, opened the volume with an essay, "The Quest for a Social Ethic," in which he began by noting, "There is, at present, no coherent discipline."[37] This is a recurring theme of the book.

Muelder, the volume's honoree, did not appear to be bothered by a lack of settled coherence or focus in the field; indeed, his understanding of Christian social ethics was characterized by breadth, not focus. Muelder envisioned a model of Christian social ethics that is interdisciplinary and, thus, in his words, "difficult to define."[38] It "commits its practitioners to undertake joint, supplementary, or complementary theoretical and empirical studies in theology, philosophical ethics, behavioral and historical sciences. Christian social ethics seeks emergent coherence."[39] In contrast to Karl Barth, Paul Ramsey, and Paul Lehmann, who found the coherence of ethics in Jesus Christ, Muelder argued that "as an interdisciplinary field Christian Social Ethics should be coherent, scientifically, philosophically, and

34. Mouw, "The Task of 'Christian Social Ethics,'" 3.

35. Harrison, "Earnest Ethics," 4.

36. Deats, *Toward a Discipline of Social Ethics*.

37. Deats, "The Quest for a Social Ethic," 21.

38. Muelder, "Christian Social Ethics Bookshelf," 1336.

39. Muelder, *Moral Law*, 20.

theologically, no one discipline dictating coherence." The search for fixed, stable coherence was misguided; any coherence "must be found continually as emergent."[40]

Many Christian social ethicists shared Muelder's emphasis on the inter-disciplinary nature of the field. Phillip Wogaman noted that it was Muelder's interdisciplinary focus that helped Muelder to navigate more responsibly the tension between reflection and activism within ethics. Wogaman wrote that Muelder's "insistence on correlating the insights of the normative dis-ciplines with those of the social sciences has, moreover, helped to protect his work from both unthinking activism and intellectual aloofness from the world of action."[41] Note that this volume of essays on ethics and advocacy has taken shape around the very question to which Wogaman pointed. How are reflection and advocacy combined in an intellectually and socially re-sponsible way within the field of Christian ethics?

Muelder's definition of the task of Christian social ethics also prompt-ed criticism. Richard Mouw quoted at length Muelder's description of the interdisciplinary task of Christian ethics and mocked Muelder's ethicist as "the advance-guard of a new kind of intellectual. The prerequisites rival those necessary for entrance into the sparsely populated ranks of both the class of Platonic philosopher-kings and the ancient order of Melchizedek."[42] Mouw applied G. E. Moore's criticism of casuistry to Muelder's model of Christian ethics. "It has failed only because it is far too difficult a subject to be treated adequately in our present state of knowledge."[43]

Note that a key part of Mouw's criticism was that if one focuses on the complexity of ethical discernment, requiring knowledge across multiple disciplines, Christians can be hindered from making tough judgments on social issues for which there are no easy solutions. In other words, a highly complex interdisciplinary model can undermine the work of moral advo-cacy. He wrote, it

> is often necessary for the Church to take an unequivocal stand against prevailing economic, social, and political conditions, even where it is practically impossible to offer any solution rooted in sound 'theoretical and empirical' analysis. If the Church commits itself to always offering the latter, it will of

40. Muelder, *Moral Law,* 153.

41. Wogaman, "The Dilemma of Christian Social Strategy," 191.

42. Mouw, "The Task of 'Christian Social Ethics,'" 4.

43. Mouw, "The Task of 'Christian Social Ethics,'" 4.

necessity remain silent at times when it has a prophetic obligation to speak.[44]

Mouw was not the only critic. In a festschrift largely complimentary
of Muelder and his interdisciplinary model of Christian social ethics, Potter
was the sharp naysayer. Potter rejected both a broad, interdisciplinary vision of Christian ethics and the central place of advocacy, focusing instead
on moral reasoning and logical argument. His essay prompted a heated
discussion in the field that lasted through the 1970s and has contemporary
parallels.

If the field lacked coherent focus, Potter's essay was an attempted
remedy. Potter, just seven years out of his PhD program and into his long
tenure at Harvard Divinity School, focused on Muelder's work as a negative
example, a model of what Christian ethics ought not to be. Potter charged
that the field of Christian social ethics had grown unwieldy as it drew on
multiple disciplines, including not only theology and philosophy, but also
behavioral and social sciences. A broad definition of Christian social ethics left the ethicist in an "embarrassing and impossible position"[45] with "an
immodest stance within the Church and a ridiculous appearance in the
academic community."[46] Christian ethicists are seen as "ridiculous dabblers
and dilettantes, eager for interdisciplinary work but unable to define their
own discipline."[47] Potter's main stated target may have been Muelder, the
honoree, but this was also a broadside against John Bennett, Gibson Winter,
and the Niebuhr brothers, among others.

Potter's remedy to the immodesty of the dabbling and dilettante ethicists was to focus the attention of the field more narrowly. He described four
broad areas often associated with doing ethics: (1) empirical, social scientific facts, i.e., the interdisciplinary aspects; (2) theological points of view;
(3) "decisions about fundamental loyalties," i.e., the interests and causes to
which people commit themselves; and (4) "modes of ethical reasoning."
Potter wanted to focus, and even limit, the task of the ethicist to this fourth
area of specialization.[48] As the title of his article suggests, ethics is about
the logic of moral argument, "the critical analysis and justification of the
logic of moral discourse employed by Christians."[49] Christian ethicists are to
clarify and maintain the "apparatus of moral discourse," helping to "resolve

44. Mouw, "The Task of 'Christian Social Ethics,'" 5.
45. Potter, "The Logic of Moral Argument," 110.
46. Potter, "The Logic of Moral Argument," 98.
47. Potter, "The Logic of Moral Argument," 98.
48. Potter, "The Logic of Moral Argument," 109.
49. Potter, "The Logic of Moral Argument," 105.

moral arguments"[50] and to "ferret out sources of disagreement."[51] This is a sharp reversal from the interdisciplinary model of Christian ethics.[52]

Christian ethicists might be of service in maintaining the apparatus of moral discourse, but they are not to jump into the fray as advocates or activists. Potter challenged the common focus on advocacy that had been central to much of the Christian social ethics tradition, whether from a social gospeler like Rauschenbusch, a realist like Niebuhr, or a Methodist liberal like Muelder.[53] The ethicist's role is not to engage directly in key ethical issues as an advocate or even to speak to them directly, unless invited. The ethicist's role, instead, is to specialize in the logic of moral reasoning.

Although advocacy is not primary, an ethicist may properly serve in a secondary capacity as a consultant to Christians and their churches regarding issues they cannot sort out on their own. The Christian social ethicist is to guide the perplexed, aiding "reflection upon action, to assist believers and citizens in overcoming perplexity."[54] The ethicist has "no independent, self-initiating task within the church," but a secondary role to respond in situations of perplexity when called upon.[55] Max Stackhouse would later describe the ethicist in Potter's model as the "trouble-shooting ethicist" or the "logical and linguistic trouble-shooter."[56]

Potter granted that there might be social and political emergencies where Christian ethicists would be called to speak directly to an issue and even to become advocates. But these were rare exceptions and always entailed a loss, because the ethicist, being occupied elsewhere, was not able to give full attention to the real focus of Christian social ethics—the logic of moral reasoning. Note that Potter, too, was concerned about advocacy; he simply thought it was best done not by the specialized ethicists, but by civic

---

50. Potter, "The Logic of Moral Argument," 106.

51. Potter, "The Logic of Moral Argument," 107.

52. It is likely that Stanley Hauerwas, in his 1975 essay, "The Ethicist as Theologian," was referencing the Potter essay and the discussion it prompted. Note especially the parallel language. "We do not even know clearly what theological ethics is. To be an ethicist seems to make one the eternal dabbler—one dabbles a little in theology (of various kinds), in philosophy (of various kinds), in political science (of various kinds), in practical problems (of various kinds), and so on. Not only will ethics not keep one out of hell; there is no assurance even that the discipline has sufficient integrity to save one from being an intellectual whoremonger." Hauerwas expressed disinterest both in ethics as activism and in the project to "ferret out the 'ethical core'" (Hauerwas, "The Ethicist as Theologian," 408).

53. Potter, "The Logic of Moral Argument," 103–6.

54. Potter, "The Logic of Moral Argument," 105.

55. Potter, "The Logic of Moral Argument," 105.

56. Stackhouse, "The Location of the Holy," 65.

and ecclesial leaders in better position to make a difference, leaving ethicists to focus on *their* proper task and to offer support to advocates, as needed.

Reaction to Potter's essay was strong and lasted through the remainder of the decade. An important moment was in October 1974 at the first session of the Religious Social Ethics Group at the American Academy of Religion. Potter's article was circulated beforehand, along with a critical response by Douglas Sturm, a professor at Bucknell. It does not seem, given what we know of his unpublished response, that Sturm was troubled by Potter's caricature of the dabbling, dilettante Christian ethicists who sketched a broader field than any ethicist could master. On the contrary, Sturm noted that many fields encompass multiple tasks and areas, more than any one person could master. That is the nature of most fields of study; they are broad—which is likely why they are called "fields"—and scholars find areas of specialization within them. The field of Christian ethics is no different.

This first session of the Religious Social Ethics Group in 1974 prompted a series of conversations about Potter's essay and its implications for the field, supported by several grants, including one from the National Endowment for the Humanities. For the most part, the members, at least in the first few years, joined Potter's task, which had been a shared undertaking of many Christian ethicists through the 1960s and early 1970s, of seeking greater definition for the field, but there the unanimity ended; they disagreed about the direction of that definition and focus.

In the 1974 conversation of Potter's essay, the attendees considered his assessment of the four broad tasks often associated with the field (the social sciences, theology, ideology and interest, and moral reasoning), but they ran into a dispute over which should be primary. It was quickly apparent that Potter's argument to center the field on the logic of moral reasoning was not a crowd favorite. The attendees took a straw poll for the proper focus of the field, with Potter's four broad areas as the balloting options. We know from Glenn Stassen's report that of the fifty-six ethicists present and voting, seven agreed with Potter (probably including Potter himself) and wanted "to focus on the mode of moral reasoning dimension, ten wanted to focus on the empirical and social science dimension, nineteen on the theological or quasi-theological dimension, and twenty on common loyalties, ideologies, and interests."[57] In other words, only 12.5 percent sided with Potter that the center should be moral reasoning, with 18 percent of the attendees wanting a focus on the social sciences; 34 percent on theology; and 36 percent on ideologies and interests.

57. Stassen, "Editorial Notes," 4.

It appears that the winners of the straw poll gained the right to set the agenda, agreeing to center their discussions over the following years around two areas—those two garnering the most votes—"the theological dimension" and "the dimension of loyalties, interests, and ideologies," sidelining Potter's focus on the logic of moral reasoning. Out of this meeting, members formed four working groups on the topics of economics; medical ethics; socialism; and war, peace, violence, and revolution. The working groups, initially supported by external grants, met at the American Academy of Religion Religious Social Ethics Group through the rest of the 1970s and into the early 1980s.[58]

Potter's proposal, though faring poorly in the straw poll, was not forgotten. Within these working groups, members attempted to deal with some of Potter's four categories and with the issues he raised about the proper focus of the field and the place of advocacy. Some of the scholarly responses to Potter's work, especially from the initial 1974 meeting of the Religious Social Ethics Group, were published in the spring 1977 *Journal of Religious Ethics*, a special issue, entitled "Analysis and/or Advocacy: Critical Engagement with Ralph Potter on the Scope of Christian Social Ethics."[59] Several other critical assessments were published in the *Journal of Religious Ethics*, including an article in 1976 by Max Stackhouse, who had been a part of the conversations of Potter's essay, and another by June O'Connor in 1979.[60]

The essays in the special issue of the *Journal of Religious Ethics* were written by an impressive roster of Christian ethicists, including Glenn Stassen, who was just beginning his tenure at Southern Baptist in Louisville; James Childress at Georgetown; Alvin Pitcher at the University of Chicago; Gibson Winter at Princeton; Richard Roach at Marquette; William Everett, who would go to Emory and then to Andover Newton; and Joseph Hough, then at Claremont and later at Vanderbilt and Union in New York. (The list of scholars seems impressive now; at the time, many were early in their careers.) All joined Potter's task of seeking greater definition for the field but took that definition in different directions.

Stassen, the chairperson of the Religious Social Ethics group and the presider at many sessions, was the editor of this special issue of the *Journal of Religious Ethics* and described the discussion over the previous three

---

58. The programs of the annual meetings, going back to 1964, are found through the website of the American Academy of Religion and hosted at the Pitts Theology Library at Emory.

59. This narrative is recounted in Stassen, "Editorial Notes," 1–7; O'Connor, "On Doing Religious Ethics," 81–96; and Hicks, "Divergences in an Expansive Discipline."

60. O'Connor, "On Doing Religious Ethics," 81–96; Stackhouse, "The Location of the Holy," 63–104.

years as centering around two questions. First, the group asked whether there is "a coherent center to the discipline." And second, if there is to be a central focus, what candidates "have more promise and less pernicious bias than others."[61]

Not everyone agreed with Potter and the majority opinion on the need for, or the possibility of, a coherent center to the field. Alvin Pitcher and Gibson Winter, in a presentation similar to Gushee's 2018 presidential address, outlined several fundamentally different models in religious social ethics that they believed could not be reconciled. They argued then for the acceptance of a radical "pluralism of perspectives."[62]

Although these perspectives could not be reconciled, the field could still be held together by shared common concerns, including a common purpose, that is "the transformation of human existence and institutional life in the direction of justice and human fulfillment." This transformation included practical "outcomes in renewed *ethos*, just policy and right decisions,"[63] outcomes that overlap with advocacy. Although the different models of ethics present this practical dimension differently, the shared purpose provides some cohesion for the field and its institutions. Pitcher and Gibson wrote, "[R]eligious social ethicists share common concerns which inform such a body as the American Society of Christian Ethics." The field can be held together as well by its "common function" in human social life: "illumination and disclosure through dialogue."[64] The pluralism of perspectives within the field parallels a similar pluralism in modern society, and the mutually enhancing engagement between the different points of view is critical for both the field and the larger society.

Joseph Hough and Richard Roach disagreed even more forcefully with Potter on the place of advocacy. Roach, a Jesuit ethicist, argued for an understanding of "social ethics broadly as critical advocacy" and insisted that this vision was a key part of Roman Catholic social teaching, which emphasizes "an obligatory social role."[65] Roach had recently returned from Chile and noted that his remarks and their urgency were shaped in part by brutality he had witnessed under Augusto Pinochet following the 1973 coup d'etat against Salvador Allende."[66]

61. Stassen, "Editorial Notes," 1.

62. Pitcher and Winter, "Perspectives," 84–85.

63. Pitcher and Winter, "Perspectives," 84.

64. Pitcher and Winter, "Perspectives," 85.

65. Roach, "A New Sense of Faith," 136.

66. Roach, "A New Sense of Faith," 152.

Hough argued not only that advocacy had a place in Christian ethics, but was its main purpose. In his article, "Christian Social Ethics as Advocacy," he wrote, "The purpose of Christian social ethics is primarily that of advocating particular positions on social policy based on Christian Ethical Criteria," or as he insisted later in the article, its primary role is "the *relentless* advocacy of ethical positions."[67]

Hough noted that his rejection of Potter's position and his own insistence on the place of advocacy emerged from pivotal experiences working in the early 1970s against white racism with Project Understanding, a group of seminary professors, students, and other church people—lay and clergy—organizing congregations and training religious leaders to address racism in their local communities. Hough was especially eager for the field of Christian ethics to focus on this primary purpose of advocacy because of factors in the immediate social context—brutal realities of racism in the US and trends among conservative and liberal Christians, i.e., a growing conservative impulse within churches to avoid political action[68] and a waning activism on the left, spurred in part by an innervating and malignant tolerance that undercut moral judgment. Any attempt to "make faith a-political," Hough wrote, "is an ill-concealed return to sanctifying the status quo . . . and even appears to be acquiescence in repressive measures, creating new injustices in society in the name of reconciliation."[69]

Given these trends, as well as the moral and political crises of the time, Hough found Potter's move to center Christian ethics on the logic of moral reasoning untenable. Christian ethicists needed to step up their advocacy, not sideline it. Potter's proposal

> to restrict the major focus of Christian social ethics to a reflective task and consultative style only adds to the likelihood that apathy and retrenchment will increase in both the churches and society. It may well be that the ethicist's function now is to add to perplexity and to shatter the self-confidence of the community—without shattering its faith.[70]

Potter's proposal is ill advised, especially given the context, and "its basic conservative flavor hardly squares with any of the traditional emphases of significant leaders in the field in our recent past."[71] Note that Hough is not

67. Hough, "Christian Social Ethics as Advocacy," 115, 123. My emphasis.

68. This was in the very early days of the emerging political religious right, which Hough clearly did not foresee. The Moral Majority began a few years later in 1979.

69. Hough, "Christian Social Ethics as Advocacy," 117.

70. Hough, "Christian Social Ethics as Advocacy," 117.

71. Hough, "Christian Social Ethics as Advocacy," 124.

just calling for a close alliance between ethics and advocacy, but claiming that Christian social ethics *is* advocacy.

The ongoing discussion of Potter's article concentrated, as Stassen described it, around whether the field had a center and, if so, what was the best candidate for that center—the one with the most promise and the least "pernicious bias." One candidate was advocacy. The program books of the American Academy of Religion and the accounts of the meetings of the SCE for the remainder of the 1970s, as well as the tables of contents for the *Journal for Religious Ethics* and the *Selected Papers from the Annual Meeting of the Society of Christian Ethics* reveal that the discussion of 1974 propelled a series of conversations formative for the field and for the ethicists. And, of course, Potter's framing of the question came out of prior discussions about ethics and advocacy in the 1960s that were fostered and held together by the new SCE.

WHAT IS MISSING, DISTORTED, OBSCURED, OR INCOMPLETE?

Some responses to Potter's essay and to the subsequent discussions, focused on what had been left out. In a 1979 article in the *Journal of Religious Ethics*, June O'Connor, who was at University of California Riverside, reviewed Potter's argument and the discussion that followed and observed that the conversation had often focused on reason and "rational processes of justifying actions," but had neglected the role of feeling. O'Connor promoted the role of feeling in ethics as a source of moral knowledge, and she outlined the limits and gifts of both feeling and rational processes. And in 1977, Max Stackhouse responded to Potter and to an earlier essay by Gustafson, saying that both of their attempts to map the field into component parts were negligent in their omissions—for Stackhouse, this was the grounding of the field in the holy.

Stackhouse, in the middle of his three-decade tenure at Andover Newton, which preceded his move to Princeton, was responding to a 1965 essay by James Gustafson. In this essay, "Context versus Principles: A Misplaced Debate in Christian Ethics," Gustafson criticized and attempted to ameliorate the sharp division and even antagonism within Christian ethics between those emphasizing context or situation and those emphasizing formal principles.[72] Among the contextualists, he placed H. Richard Niebuhr, Paul Lehmann, Joseph Sittler, Joseph Fletcher, Gordon Kaufman, Charles West, and himself. Among the critics of contextualism who emphasized

72. Gustafson, "Context Versus Principles," 171–202.

formal principles he placed John Bennett, Paul Ramsey, Alvin Pitcher, Clinton Gardiner, and Edward Long.

Gustafson, who had finished a PhD and taken a position at Yale a decade prior, insisted that the division along the lines of principle and context was misplaced and no longer fruitful; the two branches were so large and diverse that the scholars on one side of the divide were as different from each another as they were from the scholars on the other side. Moreover, the similarities between thinkers on opposite sides were often as striking as the differences. When the comparisons and distinctions are drawn based on one or two points—like context and principle—scholars miss the complexity of each position; they are unable to see a wider field of view.

Gustafson may have been thinking here about his mentor, H. Richard Niebuhr, who insisted that the difficulty with dividing a field into types is that you can only compare one set of factors at a time. That may be helpful pedagogically, but it never matches the reality of the complex, multifaceted positions held by real scholars; indeed, it can even lead to misunderstandings of the various positions and to a constricted vision that misses altogether some aspects of the field and its questions.[73]

Moreover, wherever Christian ethicists begin—with context or principle or something else—they will eventually have to consider a wider array of factors—which Gustafson called base points, which include context/situational analysis, moral principles, "fundamental theological affirmations," and "the nature of the Christian's life in Christ and its proper expressions in moral conduct."[74] Christian ethicists, including those in the two groups under discussion in his article, might begin from or strongly emphasize one of these base points, but "necessarily move toward some consideration of other base points."[75] They are all necessary components of the field.

In her 1998 Presidential Address to the Annual Meeting of the SCE, Lisa Cahill, a professor at Boston College who had been a Gustafson student at the University of Chicago, referenced Gustafson's article and made a parallel argument under a similar title: "Community Versus Universals: A Misplaced Debate in Christian Ethics."[76] She argued that the entrenched debate in Christian ethics between the universalists and the communitarians, like the one three decades earlier between Christian ethicists who emphasized principle and those who emphasized context, was misplaced and obscured another issue that was ultimately more important.

73. Niebuhr, "Types of Christian Ethics," xxxvii–lv.

74. Gustafson, "Context Versus Principles," 192.

75. Gustafson, "Context Versus Principles," 201.

76. Cahill, "Community Versus Universals," 3–12.

Cahill linked the contextualists of the 1960s with the communitarians of the 1990s. The communitarians, who "discredit the continuities among contexts," are the heirs of the contextualists, but reversed in at least one way; in the 1960s, the contextualists were the more focused on moral action and advocacy. In this case, the communitarian heirs have become more taken with theory and less focused on advocacy.

Cahill proceded to try to bring the two groups closer together by offering a softer, more contextual version of the universalist position, focused on basic human needs and goods while admitting that these are always expressed contextually. She also attempted to change the focus to a deeper issue, often overlooked. Much of the debate had centered around how norms were grounded; the hyper-focus on that point made the field neglectful of and even blind to a deeper point. The primary issue in Christian life and ethics, insisted Cahill, was less about the grounding for basic human goods and more about who they were extended to. She wrote, "The real issue of social ethics, as of Christian distinctiveness, is the circle of concern or solidarity within which human persons are willing to extend a share in basic goods . . . The real scandal of Christianity is not the particularity of its moral vision, but the vacuousness and contradictions of its moral life."[77]

In a similar argument, fifty years after Gustafson's "Misplaced Debate," Karen Guth lamented another sharp division in the field of Christian ethics—between realist and ecclesial ethics, the heirs of Reinhold Niebuhr on one side and of Yoder and Hauerwas on the other—and made a sustained argument that the debate is misplaced, unfruitful, and even destructive.[78] Guth, also in that H. Richard Niebuhr/Gustafson lineage[79] by way of her mentor Charles Mathewes, who worked with Gustafson student William Schweiker, argued that the two groups of scholars more often relate negatively against one another, caricaturing each other without truly engaging the other, without seeing the nuance of the other side or the great diversity of perspectives. Each group would find assistance in remedying its internal weaknesses by engaging seriously with the other group, because what scholars on one side neglect, scholars on the other side emphasize.

The tendency to divide along realist and ecclesial lines also blurs people's vision. They may be less likely to see the nuance and complexity of the members of a group of which they are not a part; they may overlook the vast differences among people within that group. She also noted that these

77. Cahill, "Community Versus Universals," 7.

78. Guth, *Christian Ethics at the Boundaries*. I explored this material in Miles, "Beyond Typologies."

79. Many contributors to this volume, myself included, are also in that H. Richard Niebuhr lineage by way of Gustafson or one of his students.

kinds of divides have another cost. Scholars tend to overlook any scholars not identified with either group. Her example is feminist theology, largely ignored by both the realist and ecclesial camps, which is a loss for all parties, because the ignored group would also enrich the conversation, often at points of weakness in the other positions.[80] Guth called for greater engagement at the boundaries of various perspectives—realist, ecclesial, feminist, and many others.

In a recent article in a special issue of *Modern Theology* devoted to changing boundaries in the realist and ecclesial camps, I wrote about the science of human categorization that illuminates the problems raised by Niebuhr, Gustafson, Cahill, and Guth. Within the scientific field of human categorization, scholars argue that the capacity to categorize was an important part of primate and then early human development, making it easier for early humans and proto-humans to distinguish quickly between edible and poisonous foods or between animals that were dangerous and those that were not. The benefit to human development was even greater if the categorization could be taught and passed from one generation to the next.

There are two types of categorization—exemplar and prototype. In exemplar categorization, which is common in non-human primates and human children, something new in the environment is compared, mentally, with an array of similar things that are already familiar.

In prototype categorization, which is unique to humans, something new in the environment is compared not by mentally scanning for similarities and difference with things that are already known to experience, but by creating an ideal type that summarizes the similarities among things in that category (the class of poisonous berries, for example). Prototype categorization gives an evolutionary advantage, because it is faster and more efficient; the person simply compares the new thing to the ideal type. It also has the advantage of being more easily taught, thus allowing early humans to pass knowledge across generations. But prototype categorization has serious dangers; it is subject to greater error. When comparing a new thing in the environment with an ideal type, the human mind tends to attribute, often falsely, to this new thing all of the characteristics of the prototype. The mind sometimes fails to perceive the new thing as it is, missing the ways that it is different from the prototype.[81]

80. Among her exceptions, she includes Miles, *The Bonds of Freedom*.

81. Miles, "Beyond Typologies," 564–67. See also Anderson, "The Adaptive Nature," 409–29; Smith et al., "Categorization," 24; Couchman et al., "Rules and Resemblance," 172–82; Stafford, "Is Race Perception Automatic"; and Smith and Minda, "Prototypes in the Mist," 1411–36.

The study of categorization has resonance with Niebuhr's 1942 reflections on types, mentioned previously. Niebuhr had cautioned that setting up types necessarily shortchanges complexity; the inevitable pattern of comparing thinkers in relation to one set of factors—such as the connection between Christ and culture—however pedagogically helpful, distorts one's vision of the nuance of the complex arguments made by actual scholars. As Niebuhr wrote, "every individual man or movement has a unique character."[82]

CONCLUDING REFLECTIONS

In this essay, I have narrated an account of the field of Christian ethics, especially over the 1960s and 1970s, as ethicists attempted to delineate the discipline, both in its boundaries and center, and to discern how the various possible centers of the field related to each other, as well as to adjacent fields and practices, including advocacy. As I noted above, the place of advocacy in ethics is linked with this larger question of coherence and the relation of the various parts to the whole. I find an array of striking points in this account, some of which illuminate recent conversations in the field, specifically at the SCE.

First, the search for a fixed center has failed. As Muelder called for a broad definition in the 1960s and Pitcher and Winter recommended a radical pluralism of perspectives in the 1970s, so Gushee urged in 2018 the embrace of a multiplicity of models and traditions, arguing not only that we do not need a common center, but that, even if we did, we would never successfully find one.

Second, if the search for a fixed center failed in reaching its object, it succeeded in furthering a discussion; in the 1970s, the field was centered and propelled forward by engaged conversation around Potter's essay. His insistence that the field should focus on the "logic of moral argument" and avoid advocacy found little traction. It is surprising that an article perceived by so many to be wrong could go on to have a shaping impact on the field—though not in the direction intended by the author. Then, as now, the field finds a fluid coherence through conversations engaging scholars from an array of positions.

Third, the search for a center may have moved the field, but it tended to distort the vision of the scholars within it. Scholars have tended to focus on and divide across a few factors, missing the underlying complexity and a wider array of factors in the field. Both Gustafson and Cahill, echoing

82. Niebuhr, "Types of Christian Ethics," lv.

Niebuhr, pointed to misplaced debates, where scholars, hyper-focused on a particular polarity, overlooked key features of other positions, the field, and its broader context.

Fourth, Gustafson offers a remedy as he describes base points that ethicists, whatever their focus, must consider. That helps broaden the vision, but even his helpful delineation fails to do justice to the complex nature of a practical, interdisciplinary field. Muelder described a coherence that was always emerging, not only from the kinds of factors to which Gustafson pointed, but also from the field's engagement with multiple disciplines, and I would add multiple institutions and practices, including advocacy. Christian ethics is not only interdisciplinary, but also inter-institutional and inter-practice. Fluid coherence continually emerges out of engagement with multiple factors.

Fifth, to make sense of the nature of Christian ethics as interdisciplinary, inter-institutional, and inter-practice, it helps to remember that Christian ethics was once counted among the practical fields. Christian social ethicists were a part of the Association of Seminary Professors in the Practical Fields. Within many seminaries, the field of Christian ethics was located in the same department or division with the practical, pastoral disciplines. Christian ethics centers on practices, including, and perhaps especially, advocacy. Indeed, Don Browning argued that Christian ethics should be the "center" and "premiere region" of practical theology, in part because ethics helps to "establish the principles, methods, and procedures necessary to undergird" social practice, which includes advocacy.[83]

Sixth, how can a field that that is interdisciplinary, inter-institutional, and inter-practice hold together? It is evident in my narrative of the field that Christian ethics holds together not only by discussions of shared questions, but also by the institutions and structures that foster those discussions, such as societies, working groups, journals, grant making bodies, and universities.

If we took a poll on what holds Christian ethics together and provides coherence, I cannot imagine a less promising candidate than the institutional structures that support it and provide avenues for conversation. The discussions described in my account and in the larger field of Christians ethics have been shaped by institutional structures that have held the conversations together—whether the structures that led to the SCE, those that precipitated the discussions during the 1970s such as the Religious Social Ethics Group and the *Journal of Religious Ethics*, or the structures within the SCE that fostered the discussions of this volume.

83. Browning, "Practical Theology," 80.

If the field is held together in part by institutional structures, then the recent erosion of trust in institutions imperils the field. Substantial evidence points to recent sharp decline in trust and participation in institutions to much lower levels than in the 1970s.[84] Academic institutions are not immune. Scholars participate less in their academic guilds. My account of the field of Christian ethics illustrates the central place of academic institutions and structures; without them, the engagement I have described would not have been possible.[85]

Seventh, this decline highlights another point of coherence: the field has been shaped by its unique participants and their interest and proclivities. It was shaped by those who showed up, especially those who were invited into the discussion and given voice through conference presentations and articles. It was shaped by the ways leaders set up the conversations, by the topics and papers that formed its center. It was shaped, then as now, by what and who were not included, by the absence of some perspectives. This point gives greater urgency to recent efforts of the SCE to reach out and engage more fully scholars from diverse demographic groups. Given the important place of academic institutions and structures within this narrative, it is evident that when scholars of any demographic are not present and fully participating, it hurts both the field and its scholars.

Eighth, Stassen was not offering all the options when he wrote playfully of the two possibilities facing Christian ethics. The first option is that the field has an obvious center. The second is that the field is like Don Quixote and "simply jumps on its horse and rides off in all directions." The second may be closer to the truth, but it is not Don Quixote riding off in all directions, but, instead, ordinary Christian ethicists carrying on their work and lives through the multiple institutions, communities, and practices to which they have been called. This, too, is a point of coherence in the field. It is, admittedly, coherence at the microcosmic level, but it points to and reflects a kind of fluid, emergent coherence at the macrocosmic level. The coherence is found through vocation.

The contributors to this volume explore the relationship between ethics and advocacy. Perhaps the clearest mediation between the two is found in these points of coherence—in the lives of Christian ethicists trying, not always successfully, to live out of their vocations; in the multiple institutions, structures, and communities of which they are a part, not only academic institutions, but also churches, social movements, and political parties, all of

84. Vallier, *Trust in a Polarized Age*; Dimrock, *How Americans View Trust*; and Putnam, *Bowling Alone*.

85. Hall and Battaglio, "Bowling Alone, Rigor, and the Decline of Social Capital in Academic Service."

which are sites of advocacy; and in the practices which are centered within these institutions and communities. Advocacy is not simply one among an array of practices, but a current running through them.

One of the complications in the field of Christian ethics is that it is done, almost entirely, by Christians. Christians are called to do justice and actively love and care for others—which necessitates advocacy. Potter lamented the loss to the field when ethicists turned from their primary task of analyzing the logic of moral arguments toward advocacy. On the contrary, ethics and advocacy are mutually enriching. But even if advocacy did not enrich the work of Christian ethicists, it would still be theirs to do.

BIBLIOGRAPHY

Anderson, John. "The Adaptive Nature of Human Categorization." *Psychological Review* 98.3 (1991) 409–29.

Browning, Don. "Practical Theology and Religious Education." In *Formation and Reflection: The Promise of Practical Theology*, edited by Lewis Mudge and James Poling, 79–102. Philadelphia: Fortress, 1987.

Cahill, Lisa Sowle. "Community Versus Universals: A Misplaced Debate in Christian Ethics." *Annual of the Society of Christian Ethics* 18 (1998) 3–12.

Chiù, Agnes. "Forging and Fumbling Our Way Through: Professionally Developing Our Future Selves." Panel presentation, Society of Christian Ethics Annual Meeting, Toronto, Canada, January 7, 2016.

Couchman, Justin, et al. "Rules and Resemblance: Their Changing Balance in the Category Learning of Humans (Homo sapiens) and Monkeys (Macaca Mulatta)." *Journal of Experiential Psychology: Animal Behavior Processes* 36.2 (April 2010) 172–82.

Deats, Paul, ed. *Toward a Discipline of Social Ethics: Essays in honor of Walter Muelder.* Boston: Boston University Press, 1972.

———. "The Quest for a Social Ethic." In *Toward a Discipline of Social Ethics: Essays in Honor of Walter Muelder*, edited by Paul Deats, 21–48. Boston: Boston University Press, 1972.

De La Torre, Miguel. "WTF, What Gives, and Who Cares?: The Hopelessness of Our Discipline and Future." *Journal of Race, Ethnicity, and Religion* 7.5 (November 2016) 1–10.

Dimock, Michael. "How Americans View Trust, Facts, and Democracy Today." *Pew Research Center Trust Magazine*, February 19, 2020. https://www.pewtrusts.org/en/trust/archive/winter-2020/how-americans-view-trust-facts-and-democracy-today.

Dorrien, Gary. "Got Ethics? How History has Shaped Us." *Journal of Race, Ethnicity, and Religion* 7.5 (November 2016) 1–8.

———. *Social Ethics in the Making: Interpreting an American Tradition.* Chichester: Wiley Blackwell, 2009.

Floyd-Thomas, Stacey, ed. "Got Ethics?: Envisioning and Evaluating the Future of Our Guild and Discipline." *Journal of the Society of Christian Ethics* 36.2 (2016) 195–203.

———. "Setting the Context." *Journal of Race, Ethnicity, and Religion* 7.5 (November 2016) 1–4.

———. "Ordering our Steps, Engendering Ethics, and Race-ing Forward: The Promise and Peril of Organizations and Human Development." *Journal of Race, Ethnicity, and Religion* 7.5 (November 2016) 5–9.

Gudorf, Christine, and Edward Long. "Society of Christian Ethics: History and Practice." *Council of Societies for the Study of Religion Bulletin* 32.2 (2003) 55–58.

Gushee, David. "Christian Ethics: Retrospect and Prospect." *Journal of the Society of Christian Ethics* 38.2 (2018) 3–20.

Gustafson, James. "Context Versus Principles: A Misplaced Debate in Christian Ethics." *Harvard Theological Review* 58.2 (April 1965) 171–202.

Guth, Karen. *Christian Ethics at the Boundaries: Feminism and Theologies of Public Life.* Minneapolis: Fortress, 2015.

Hall, Jeremy, and R. Paul Battaglio. "Bowling Alone, Rigor, and the Decline of Social Capital in Academic Service." *Public Administration Review* 79.5 (2019) 625–28.

Harrison, Beverly. "Earnest Ethics." *Union Seminary Tower* 15.3 (Spring 1969) 4–5.

Hauerwas, Stanley. "The Ethicist as Theologian." *Christian Century* 92 (April 23, 1975) 408–12.

Hicks, Jane. "Divergences in an Expansive Discipline: How Should We Study Christian Ethics." *Currents in Theology and Mission* 39.5 (October 2012) 359–67.

Hough, Joseph. "Christian Social Ethics as Advocacy." *Journal of Religious Ethics* 5.1 (1977) 115–23.

Lincoln, C. Eric, and Paul Deats. "Walter G. Muelder: An Appreciation of His Life, Thought, and Ministry." In *Toward a Discipline of Social Ethics: Essays in Honor of Walter Muelder,* edited by Paul Deats, 1–20. Boston: Boston University Press, 1972.

Long, Edward. *Academic Bonding and Social Concern: The Society of Christian Ethics, 1959–1983.* Notre Dame: Religious Ethics, Inc., 1984.

Miles, Rebekah. "Beyond Typologies: At the Boundaries of Realist and Ecclesial Ethics." *Modern Theology* 36.3 (July 2020) 561–68.

———. *The Bonds of Freedom: Feminist Theology and Christian Realism.* Oxford: Oxford University Press, 2001.

Mouw, Richard. "The Task of 'Christian Social Ethics.'" *Christianity Today* 12 (January 5, 1968) 3–5.

Muelder, Walter. "Christian Social Ethics Bookshelf." *Christian Century* 30 (October 30, 1963) 1336.

———. *Methodism and Society in the Twentieth Century.* New York: Abingdon, 1961.

———. *Moral Law in Christian Social Ethics.* Richmond: John Knox, 1966.

Niebuhr, H. Richard. "Types of Christian Ethics." *Christ and Culture,* xxxvii–lv. 50th anniversary ed. New York: HarperCollins, 2001.

O'Connor, June. "On Doing Religious Ethics." *Journal of Religious Ethics* 7.1 (1979) 81–96.

———. "Recommendations of the Twenty First Century Committee." *Society of Christian Ethics,* October 10, 2000. https://soce.memberclicks.net/index.php.

Pitcher, Alvin, and Gibson Winter. "Perspectives in Religious Social Ethics." *Journal of Religious Ethics* 5.1 (1977) 69–89.

Potter, Ralph. "The Logic of Moral Argument." In *Toward a Discipline of Social Ethics: Essays in Honor of Walter Muelder*, edited by Paul Deats, 93–114. Boston: Boston University Press, 1972.

Putnam, Robert. *Bowling Alone: The Collapse and Revival of American Community*. Revised and Updated. New York: Simon and Schuster, 2020.

Roach, Richard. "A New Sense of Faith." *Journal of Religious Ethics* 5.1 (1977) 135–54.

Smith, David, et al. "Categorization: The View from Animal Cognition." *Journal of Behavioral Sciences* 6.2 (June 15, 2016) 24.

Smith, J. David, and John Minda. "Prototypes in the Mist: The Early Epochs of Category Learning." *Journal of Experimental Psychology: Learning, Memory, and Cognition* 24.6 (1998) 1411–36.

Stackhouse, Max. "Technical Data and Ethical Norms: Some Theoretical Considerations." *Journal for the Scientific Study of Religion* 5.2 (Spring 1966) 200.

———. "The Location of the Holy." *Journal of Religious Ethics* 4.1 (Spring 1976) 63–104.

Stafford, Tom. "Is Race Perception Automatic." *BBC News,* April 23, 2013.

Stassen, Glenn. "Editorial Notes." *Journal of Religious Ethics* 5.1 (1977) 1–7.

Vallier, Kevin. *Trust in a Polarized Age*. Oxford: Oxford University Press, 2020.

Wogaman, Phillip. "The Dilemma of Christian Social Strategy." In *Toward a Discipline of Social Ethics: Essays in Honor of Walter Muelder*, edited by Paul Deats, 167–93. Boston: Boston University Press, 1972.

—PART 3—

Particular Applications

MEDIATED ADVOCACY
IN PUBLIC BIOETHICS

James F. Childress

INTRODUCTION: MEDIATED ADVOCACY

MANY ACADEMIC FIELDS ENCOUNTER tensions between scholarship and advocacy, between standing on the sidelines (observing, analyzing, and even evaluating what's taking place) and taking sides in moral, social, and political conflicts. A health policy scholar, Harold Pollack, has powerfully described these tensions in his own life.[1] Beyond his scholarly work, his "day job," he mounted a strong public defense of the Affordable Care Act and of universal health care coverage. His political advocacy featured op-eds, position papers, petitions, and social media messages. Then in 2016, he called for nonviolent civil disobedience if the Trump administration decided to deport immigrants in the Deferred Action for Childhood Arrivals (DACA) program, and he indicated he would chain himself to a federal courthouse if that happened.[2]

Two years later, in "The Responsibility to Advocate—and to Advocate Responsibly," Pollack reflected on frictions between "health policy scholarship" and "health policy advocacy."[3] This article stresses that concerned persons may pursue advocacy in different ways than dramatic nonviolent civil disobedience or even op-eds, petitions, and the like. For instance, they may

1. Pollack, "Responsibility to Advocate," 44–47.
2. Pollack, "Thinking."
3. Pollack, "Responsibility to Advocate," 44–47.

choose to advise political candidates or office holders—such advising is still advocacy. While Pollack affirms a responsibility to advocate, he views *how* to advocate as a choice. Whatever mode of advocacy is selected, it should embody certain virtues and respect certain constraints, including some that are applicable to scholarship, as well. For instance, Pollack contends that we should hold advocacy to standards of "integrity" and "transparency" no less rigorous than academic scholarship. The relevant standards also include "judiciousness" and "civility," as well as non-manipulation of readers or listeners—and I would add non-deception.[4] Still tensions persist between advocacy and scholarship, with its presumed objectivity, detachment, rigor, etc., even though advocacy often enriches scholarship. It is the action of taking sides, as well as how sides are taken, that creates tensions.

Tensions also arise for Christian moral theologians or ethicists, for moral, social, and political philosophers, and for others who are scholars or specialists in normative disciplines. While advocacy may appear to be less problematic for normative disciplines that include, at a minimum, frameworks for the ethical evaluation of persons, actions, and policies, tensions still surface. This chapter focuses mainly on normative bioethics[5] and public bioethics. It looks first at bioethics' origins and evolution, including the early dominance of religion-informed thinkers before the influx of philosophers. In dialogue with Stephen Toulmin and Albert Jonsen, it examines debates about the role of principles versus case judgments in the work of the National Commission for the Protection of Human Subjects, the first public bioethics body in the US. As a counter, it then provides an in-depth case study of advocacy and advice in building an ethical framework for the allocation of vaccine against COVID-19. This framework incorporates and advocates several principles, including the mitigation of health inequities, and proposes practical criteria and phases for allocation. I conclude with reflections on mediated advocacy as a way to think about the ethicist's work on public bioethics bodies, which need both ethics scholarship and ethics-informed advocacy.

4. Nonviolent civil disobedience also falls under rigorous standards. See Childress, *Civil Disobedience*.

5. Van Rensselaer Potter coined the term "bioethics" in 1970, with a broader meaning than it eventually developed in common discourse. See Potter, "Bioethics," 127–53. I generally prefer the language of "biomedical ethics." See Beauchamp and Childress, *Principles of Biomedical Ethics*, vii. However, in light of the pervasiveness of the term "bioethics" and the value of its breadth, I use it here. For clarification: I do not consider myself to be a "bioethicist" but rather a specialist in ethics and public policy with particular attention to the biological sciences, biotechnology, medicine, health care, and public health. See Childress, "Never Solo," 419–20.

What exactly is *public bioethics*?[6] It is doing bioethics with primary attention to public policy, defined as "whatever governments choose to do or not to do."[7] Scholars and advocates in public bioethics direct their attention to public policies regarding medicine, health care, biotechnology, research involving human subjects, and public health. Even though their main target is public policy, they also attend to public discourse and public culture, not only as ways to shape public policy, but also as important in and of themselves. Public bioethics includes more than the work of individual—or teams of—scholars and advocates. It encompasses commissions, committees, councils, task forces, and similar structures that are usually governmentally established, sponsored, or funded for purposes of collective deliberation about bioethical issues, again with a primary goal of analyzing, assessing, and making recommendations about actual, proposed, and possible public policies.[8]

Public bioethics often involves *mediated advocacy*, that is, advocacy mediated through participation in a public bioethics body (hereafter PBB). Here ethicists function both as specialists in ethics and as advocates. In addition to providing scholarly ethics input as appropriate, they also advocate general moral principles and particular policies, deliberate with others about whether these principles and policies or others would be ethically acceptable and preferable, and then join in (or dissent from) the PBB's collective recommendations to policy makers. This is not simply individual or group advocacy, but advocacy mediated through a PBB's formal processes to inform or advise policy makers.

There is a tendency to overlook or disregard some forms of advocacy, especially if advocacy is primarily viewed as single-minded, uncompromising, and forceful activism, or if it is mainly considered a form of prophetic discourse that presents a broad indictment or utopian vision, as distinguished from policy or regulatory discourse.[9] Of course, activist

6. My late colleague, John Fletcher, probably coined the phrase "public bioethics." See Fletcher, "On Restoring Public Bioethics"; Fletcher and Miller, "Promise and Perils." For an attribution of this phrase to Fletcher, see Briggle, *A Rich Bioethics*, 182 n. 15.

7. Dye, *Understanding Public Policy*, 2. Slightly different statements of this definition appear in different editions.

8. For an examination of three major types of public bioethics bodies, see Childress, *Public Bioethics*, 2–4. For a view of public bioethics as actual governance, rather than committees, commissions, etc., advising policy makers, see Snead, *What It Means*, 6: "the governance of science, medicine, and biotechnology in the name of ethical goods."

9. For distinctions in medical ethics and bioethics between prophetic discourse and policy discourse and between prophetic discourse and regulatory discourse involving oversight bodies, see, respectively, James M. Gustafson, "Moral Discourse," 41–49, and Daniel Callahan, "Why America Accepted Bioethics," S8.

and prophetic discourses are dramatic and important forms of advocacy, but, as Pollack reminds us, advocacy may also appear in rather undramatic discourses, such as making specific recommendations about public policy to policy makers.

The subject of this chapter is *mediated advocacy*, more specifically, advocacy that is mediated through participation in a PBB established to address ethical issues in public policy related to the biological sciences, biotechnology, medicine, health care, public health, and so forth. While such PBBs take different forms, in practice—and at their best—they become moral communities engaged in deliberative democratic processes[10] as they consider general principles and specific policy recommendations, both of which may be the subject of advocacy to the PBB by individual participants as well as, in the end, by the PBB itself. I have found this to be true in a number of PBBs on which I have been privileged to serve, including the 2020 National Academies Committee on Equitable Allocation of Vaccine for the Novel Coronavirus, which I will discuss in detail later. Similarly, I have found that mediated advocacy can best be pursued in relation to critical ethical inquiry, what we often label "ethics," including ethical theories, methods of reasoning, and so forth. In my view, the ethicist can and should engage in scholarly ethics and in advocacy on PBBs, indicating how each informs the other, but, as we will see, tensions often arise.

THE EMERGENCE OF BIOETHICS AS AN APPLIED/ PRACTICAL FIELD

Over centuries the two main—often connected—sources of ethical guidance for physicians (and other healthcare providers) have been religion-based directives and codes developed by organizations of caregivers. Religious communities have historically provided ethical guidance for their members as patients, family caregivers, and professional caregivers. And the Hippocratic Oath is only one example of many codes of ethical guidance prepared by physicians for their guilds. However, by the mid-to-late 1960s, health care professionals and policy makers faced serious moral perplexities as they dealt, for example, with new medical technologies that could prolong life beyond previous limits and expectations, transplant organs from one person to another, and enable new reproductive options. Faced with the limitations and limits of traditional codes of medical and nursing ethics and of religious guidance in a pluralistic society, especially, but not only, for public policy, a new field of applied or practical ethics emerged—"biomedical

10. Gutmann and Thompson, "Deliberating about Bioethics," 38–41.

ethics" or "bioethics." While this reflective and practical field has been multi-disciplinary and multi-professional from its beginning, theologians and other religious thinkers (and philosophers with religious sensibilities) played significant roles in its origins.[11]

Comparing the roles of theologians and philosophers in the origins of bioethics, Albert Jonsen, a former Jesuit and an early contributor to bioethics, stressed: "Theologians were the first to appear on the scene."[12] And one of the field's founders, the Hasting Center's Daniel Callahan, a philosopher with a rich background in religion and religious thought, emphasized: "When I first became interested in bioethics in the mid-1960s, the only resources were theological or those drawn from within the traditions of medicine, themselves heavily shaped by religion."[13] Even when early participants in bioethics did not directly appeal to religious beliefs and practices, those beliefs and practices were usually not far in the background.

Some accounts of the origins of bioethics mark and even lament the field's subsequent secularization, which in part reflects the increased importance of philosophy and philosophers.[14] Factors in this putative process of secularization include not only the increased involvement of philosophers but also—and connectedly—the perceived difficulty of doing religion-based bioethics in an increasingly pluralistic society, whether at the bedside or in the public square, and the increased interest in bioethical issues in public policy in a democratic society, often expressed in public bioethics. To achieve its goals, as Callahan put it, bioethics had to "push religion aside."[15]

A well-known article by philosopher Stephen Toulmin examines "How Medicine Saved the Life of Ethics" by returning to ethics "a seriousness and human relevance which it had seemed . . . to have lost for good."[16] The article's title needs qualification. It really discusses how medicine saved philosophical ethics or moral philosophy, not religiously-based ethics, because the latter did not need saving. Scholars in Christianity and Judaism,

---

11. Early contributors to the field included Joseph Fletcher (whose first works in medical ethics displayed religious influences), John Fletcher (then an Episcopal priest), Paul Ramsey, James Gustafson, Richard McCormick, SJ, Immanuel Jakobovits, William F. May, and Leon Kass (a scientist, physician, and philosopher attentive to religious perspectives), among many others.

12. Jonsen, *Birth of Bioethics*, 34. See also Jonsen, "A History of Religion and Bioethics," 23.

13. Callahan, "Religion and the Secularization of Bioethics," 2.

14. Callahan, "Religion and the Secularization of Bioethics," 2. See also Callahan, "Social Sciences," 280.

15. Callahan, "Why America Accepted Bioethics," S8.

16. Toulmin, "How Medicine Saved the Life of Ethics," 750.

for example, were already seriously engaged in applied or practical ethics, as Toulmin himself recognized.

Exactly how did medicine save philosophical ethics? Not primarily by creating more academic positions in philosophy in medical schools and elsewhere, though it did that. Instead, the turn to medicine directed attention to situations, particular kinds of cases, professional enterprises, and Aristotelian themes of *epieikeia*, which Toulmin thinks corresponds more closely to our modern term "equity" than to "reasonableness," as it is sometimes translated, and *philia*, which he thinks corresponds to our modern notion of "personal relationship," not only to "friendship."[17] He stresses the way medicine directed ethics to the concrete, and underlines the resemblance between ethics and clinical medicine, i.e., the "art of clinical diagnosis and prescription."[18]

This turn of philosophers to medical ethics was somewhat surprising in view of dominant conception of moral philosophy up to the 1960s. To a great extent, moral philosophers eschewed practical or applied ethics and even general normative ethics in order to focus on non-normative metaethics, which addresses the meanings of concepts such as right and obligation, moral epistemology, the logic and patterns of moral reasoning and justification, and so forth.[19] Rather than developing normative moral reasons, metaethics was designed to map the terrain of moral debates by distinguishing moral reasons from non-moral reasons. As Toulmin observes, the philosopher's metaethical task

> was no longer to organize our moral beliefs into comprehensive systems: that would have meant *taking sides* over substantive issues. Rather, it was his duty to stand back from the fray and hold the ring while partisans of different views argued out their differences in accordance with the general rules of the conduct of "rational debate" or the expression of "moral attitudes" as defined in *metaethical* terms.[20]

When by the early 1970s philosophers increasingly engaged in applied or practical ethics, their concerns and agendas were significantly shaped by current events as was also true for religious or religion-influenced ethicists. These included civil rights and war, especially the threat of nuclear weapons, as well as unfolding developments in medicine and healthcare. Several changes in the philosophical agenda were evident in the first issue of

17. Toulmin, "How Medicine Saved the Life of Ethics," 746–48.
18. Toulmin, "How Medicine Saved the Life of Ethics," 743.
19. Beauchamp and Childress, *Principles*, 2.
20. Toulmin, "How Medicine Saved the Life of Ethics," 749.

Philosophy & Public Affairs in 1971, which included articles on why World War II was different, the relevance of Nuremberg, abortion (two articles), and labor, alienation, and social class in Hegel's philosophy.

When philosophers turned their attention to medical ethics, Toulmin notes, this often led to a restatement of the debates that theologians and others had started in more philosophical terms, frequently in relation to utilitarian, Kantian, and other moral theories. These approaches could be fittingly labeled "applied ethics," in which a practical judgment is derived from one of those theories about, for example, whether a physician should lie to a particular patient about a diagnosis of terminal cancer.

Toulmin sharply criticizes such approaches, preferring what might be better described as "practical ethics" or "practical philosophy."[21] The logic of Toulmin's critique of ethical theories and principles makes the language of "practical ethics" more appropriate than the language of "applied ethics," which he still often used in a nod to current usage. As medicine saved the life of ethics by directing philosophy to medical ethics, Toulmin also thought that medicine revived ethics by nudging it in a more Aristotelian direction, away from general theories to "a more direct analysis of the practical cases themselves, using methods more like those of traditional 'case morality' . . ."[22] This turn to medicine and to medical ethics produced "spectacular and irreversible effects on the methods and content of philosophical ethics."[23] In practical philosophy, "[r]ational judgments of practical adequacy are timely not timeless, concrete not abstract, particular not universal, local not general."[24] Practical ethics also featured cases and taxonomies of cases.

ADVOCACY OF CASE JUDGMENTS VERSUS PRINCIPLES: THE EXPERIENCE OF THE NATIONAL COMMISSION

In arguing for the priority of case-based or casuistical approaches over principles-based approaches in moral reasoning, Toulmin (and Jonsen-Toulmin) frequently appealed to the experience of the National Commission for

21. Toulmin also uses the broad language of "practical philosophy," for example, in indicating that the body/mind problem is better examined in the context of medicine, specifically psychiatry. See Toulmin, "Recovery of Practical Philosophy," 349. For his suspicion of the language of "applied ethics," see Toulmin, "Casuistry," 310–11, 314.

22. Toulmin, "How Medicine Saved the Life of Ethics," 749.

23. Toulmin, "How Medicine Saved the Life of Ethics," 749.

24. Toulmin, "Recovery of Practical Philosophy," 341. See also Toulmin, *Uses of Argument.*

the Protection of Human Subjects of Biomedical and Behavioral Research (1974–1978) as it reasoned to its conclusions and recommendations.[25] Jonsen was a commissioner and Toulmin a staff philosopher and consultant for the National Commission, which was established to examine ethical conditions for research involving human subjects, such as children and prisoners. As the first PBB in the US, the National Commission set the model for subsequent commissions.

Following is how Jonsen and Toulmin describe the National Commission's deliberations, reasoning, and practical judgments:

> [T]he locus of certitude in the commissioners' discussions did not lie in an agreed set of intrinsically convincing general rules or principles, as they shared no commitment to any such body of accepted principles. Rather it lay in a shared perception of what was specifically at stake in particular kinds of human situations.[26]

And yet, despite the Jonsen-Toulmin claim, the National Commission did prepare and release the very influential *Belmont Report*, which articulated three fundamental principles for the ethical analysis, assessment, and guidance of research involving human subjects: beneficence (which includes what some others call non-maleficence), respect for persons (which includes respect for autonomy), and justice.[27] These principles are still widely employed in guiding research involving human subjects.

So what are we to make of the apparent inconsistency between the Jonsen-Toulmin claim, on the one hand, and the National Commission's preparation of the *Belmont Report,* on the other? In the first place, Jonsen and Toulmin stress that the *Belmont Report* was prepared late in the National Commission's deliberations, after it had already made its major ethical recommendations about various types of research involving human subjects.[28] Accordingly, these principles were not as important in the commission's actual deliberations as some suppose, whatever their later impact on researchers and institutional review boards. In any event, these "shared

---

25. Toulmin appeals to the experience of the National Commission in support of his case-based approach to practical ethics in several different writings. See Toulmin, "How Medicine Saved the Life of Ethics," 741; "Medical Ethics," 14; "Tyranny of Principles," 31–32, 37–38; "National Commission," 599–614, where Toulmin discusses it most fully; and Jonsen and Toulmin, *Abuse of Casuistry*, 16–19.

26. Jonsen and Toulmin, *Abuse of Casuistry*, 18.

27. National Commission, *Belmont Report*. See also Childress et al., *Belmont Revisited*, 253–65, Appendix: "The Belmont Report."

28. Jonsen and Toulmin, *Abuse of Casuistry*, 356, n. 14.

notions were too comprehensive and general to underwrite specific moral positions."[29]

Second, defenders of the Jonsen-Toulmin claim could argue that the *Belmont Report* was prepared only because the legislation that established the National Commission called for it to identify the principles underlying research involving human subjects. Hence, the *Belmont Report* resulted from the commissioners' effort to comply with its legislative mandate, rather than from the commissioners' felt need for a framework of principles in order to address difficult cases.

These two points—the time of the preparation of the *Belmont Report* relative to the commission's judgments about types of cases and the legislative mandate—support the Jonsen-Toulmin claim about the primacy of case judgments in the commission's work. However, another interpretation of the origin, place, and significance of the general principles in the *Belmont Report* is plausible: these principles were already embedded in the commission's consensus about ethically acceptable and unacceptable research involving children, prisoners, and other populations. From this perspective, the *Belmont Report* identified and articulated principles that were at least implicit in the commissioners' judgments about types of cases in research involving human subjects. Not only did the formulation of these underlying principles illuminate the commission's judgments about types of cases; these principles also provided a way to test the acceptability, adequacy, and consistency of these judgments and to educate and guide others, both at the time and in the future, who were not participants in the deliberations of the National Commission.

It is also important to observe that the National Commission's analyses and judgments about a range of types of cases in research involving human subjects did not emerge *de novo*. They rather occurred within a general and strong consensus about (a) negative paradigm cases, that is, types of cases that evoke universal moral condemnation, and about (b) several principles and rules that support such universal moral condemnation. The negative paradigm cases were the heinous Nazi experiments on non-consenting, vulnerable, captive human subjects. These experiments included horrific high altitude, freezing, malaria, and mustard gas experiments, among others, which caused countless serious injuries and deaths. After the defeat of the Nazis, twenty-three people were tried for these experiments, fifteen were found guilty, and seven received death sentences. Promulgated by four American judges at the Doctors' Trial at Nuremberg, *United States of America v. Karl Brandt et al* in 1946–1947, the Nuremberg Code articulates ten "basic principles" that capture many of the

29. Jonsen and Toulmin, *Abuse of Casuistry*, 356, n. 14.

basic duties and responsibilities of researchers and institutions to protect the rights and welfare of research subjects.[30]

While the Nuremberg Code built on expressed moral outrage about the horrendous Nazi experiments, it would be a mistake to suppose that historically or chronologically the moral principles pertinent to judging human experimentation emerged only out of and after a negative judgment about the Nazi experiments. The relations among particular moral judgments and general moral principles are more complex than such a picture recognizes. Moreover, when the National Commission reached its judgments about different types of human subjects research, about thirty years after the Nuremberg trials, those judgments were inevitably shaped by the moral prohibitions and requirements built into the code. The general negative and positive moral duties in the code provided an important pre-existing, albeit incomplete, moral framework for research involving human subjects. This general consensus certainly made it far easier for the National Commission to address cases that were not fully covered by the negative paradigm case of the Nazi experiments.

Despite some of their points and language, Jonsen and Toulmin in fact do recognize and employ principles (or their equivalents). In one place, they indicate their support for "good casuistry," that is, good case-based ethics, which "applies general rules to particular cases with discernment [in contrast to] bad casuistry, which does the same thing sloppily."[31] In their individually authored works, Jonsen is generally more receptive to principles than Toulmin is. However, in a modest concession to principles, while simultaneously railing against the "tyranny of principles," Toulmin admits that principles may be relevant in relations between strangers in a way they are not in relations between intimates.[32] This admission opens up a debate about how best to characterize contemporary relations in medicine, healthcare, research, and public health. For example, do relations between physicians and patients in modern, bureaucratized health care more closely resemble relations between strangers or relations between intimates? And how should we characterize interactions between public health officials and the public in a pandemic? To avoid oversimplification, we can note

30. Childress, "Nuremberg's Legacy," 349–61.

31. Jonsen and Toulmin, *Abuse of Casuistry*, 16. At one point, Toulmin observes that applied ethics "cannot get along on a diet of general principles alone" (Toulmin, "Tyranny of Principles," 38). This suggests that general principles could be part of the diet of applied ethics; furthermore, virtually no one in applied ethics would claim that general principles are sufficient by themselves—there must be bridges to concrete cases.

32. Toulmin, "Tyranny of Principles," 31–39. Toulmin often draws on Aristotle's discussion of friendship in making these points.

that both types of relations exist, but also recognize that much of medical practice, healthcare, human subjects research, and public health is more like relations between strangers—at least, it is close enough to warrant a substantial role for principles. Moreover, the main example that Toulmin and Jonsen-Toulmin adduce is not a clinical relationship between a physician and a patient, but rather the National Commission's work on public policy concerning research involving human subjects, a topic less likely to be reduced to personal relationships.[33]

The fundamental problem is Toulmin's limited conception of principles. He opposes principles as "tyrannical" largely because he characterizes them as "absolute," "universal," "unchallengeable," "without exception," "unconditional," and "invariant."[34] No wonder then he believes that, in contrast to casuistical methods, they inevitably produce "standoff," "deadlock," and "stalemate." His opposition is less warranted—and even largely misplaced—in regard to ethical frameworks that view principles and rules as *prima facie* or presumptively binding and that incorporate balancing and specification, among other ways to interpret and connect principles and rules to concrete situations of decision making.[35] It is often possible and frequently important for PBBs to advocate both general principles, i.e., general moral considerations, and particular judgments about types of cases, as I will illustrate through the work of the Committee on Equitable Allocation of Vaccine for the Novel Coronavirus which featured the interaction and dialectical relation of principles, goals, criteria, and specific prioritizations in vaccine allocation.

CONSTRUCTING AN OVERARCHING FRAMEWORK FOR EQUITABLE ALLOCATION OF VACCINE FOR COVID-19

Debates About The Allocation of Scarce Medical Resources In The Pandemic

Having co-taught courses on *Confronting Epidemics* several times over the years with colleagues in medicine and public health, I was not surprised

33. I discuss Toulmin's and Jonsen-Toulmin's use of the National Commission as a model for casuistry elsewhere, including Childress, "Ethical Theories," 190–191, from which I have drawn some ideas and formulations.

34. Toulmin, "Tyranny of Principles," 31–39; Jonsen and Toulmin, *Abuse of Casuistry*, 1–10.

35. See Beauchamp and Childress, *Principles*, 13–25.

when in March 2020 the COVID-19 pandemic forced hospitals and physicians to ration limited medical resources, such as personal protective equipment (PPE), beds in intensive care units (ICUs), and ventilators. These dire circumstances led to a cascade of ethical debate about the fair and equitable allocation of scarce medical resources. Limitations of space preclude an extended discussion of the issues raised in that context, including how to specify and balance several principles, such as medical utility (maximizing the probability of successful outcomes, including saving lives or life years), narrow social utility (protecting important roles and functions for societal welfare), and social justice (reducing health inequities and their effects).[36]

The last, social justice, is particularly important because of this pandemic's "distinctive personality," to use historian Frank Snowden's fine phrase.[37] SARS-CoV-2, the coronavirus that causes COVID-19, is strikingly undemocratic. Just as influenza in 1918 struck unevenly, mainly killing healthy adults ages 20–40, children under 5, and others over 65, SARS-CoV-2 does not equally target people of all ages and from all segments of society. Early and subsequent data indicate that older adults and people with underlying health problems and co-morbidities are most likely to become very sick and die, even with hospitalization. Moreover, in the US people of color and poorer people are particularly vulnerable because the pandemic feasts on existing health disparities, including co-morbidities, that make recovery from COVID-19 more difficult. And they are more likely to be infected with this coronavirus because of their living and working conditions.

The debates about social justice in the allocation of scarce medical treatments re-surfaced when attention turned to the possibility of vaccination as an upstream, preventive measure. Any approved vaccines would almost certainly be extremely scarce for several months after Food and Drug Administration (FDA) emergency use authorization. Hence, the need to build in advance an ethically acceptable framework for the allocation of vaccines for COVID-19.

The US Centers for Disease Control and Prevention (CDC) and the National Institutes of Health (NIH) asked the National Academies of Sciences, Engineering and Medicine (NASEM, hereafter National Academies), in partnership with the National Academy of Medicine (NAM), to convene an *ad hoc* committee to "develop an overarching framework" for allocation of vaccines against SARS-CoV-2. The sponsors wanted such a framework to "assist" both domestic and global policy makers in their planning and to

---

36. Childress, "Rationing Health Care," 5–14. See also Emanuel et al., "Fair Allocation," 2049–55.

37. Gonzalez, "Historian Frank Snowden."

"inform" decisions by health authorities, including the CDC's independent Advisory Committee on Immunization Practices (ACIP). The statement of task for the National Academies committee also called for the development of "criteria" for use in "setting priorities for equitable allocation of vaccine" and guidance on how they should be applied in "determining the first tier of vaccine recipients."[38] This statement of task was further amplified in a virtual meeting with officials from the CDC and NIH, one of whom, Francis Collins, the director of the NIH, indicated that the "overarching framework" should include "foundational principles."[39]

Foundational Principles

The National Academies committee sought to formulate foundational principles by considering principles embedded in US social institutions and culture, rather than derived from any particular ethical theory (though, ideally, compatible with several ethical theories). It sought principles that are clear, sound, and broad enough to address a pandemic of a magnitude not witnessed in a century, a pandemic producing disastrous effects for the public's health and, concomitantly, the economy, education, and other important aspects of social life.

Rather than identifying a set of principles and then deriving particular judgments about priorities from them, the committee moved back and forth between the formulation of principles and the formulation of goals, criteria, and priorities. And the committee took seriously the critiques and suggestions offered in the rigorous preliminary and subsequent review processes, as well as in a public hearing and written public comments. It divided the following six principles into three substantive ethical principles and three procedural principles.

- *Ethical principles*
  - *Maximum benefit*—obligation to protect and promote the public's health and its socioeconomic well-being
  - *Equal concern*—requirement that every person be considered and treated as having equal dignity, worth, and value
  - *Mitigation of health inequities*—obligation to explicitly address the higher burden of COVID-19 experienced by the populations

38. National Academies, *Framework*, 20–21.
39. National Academies, *Framework*, 91.

affected most heavily, given their exposure and compounding
health inequities

- *Procedural principles*

  ▫ *Fairness*—requirement of engagement with the public, particularly
  those most affected by the pandemic, and impartial decision making and application of the allocation criteria

  ▫ *Transparency*—obligation to communicate with the public openly,
  clearly, accurately, and straightforwardly about the allocation
  framework as it is being developed, deployed, and modified

  ▫ *Evidence-based*—requirement to base framework on the best available and constantly updated scientific information and data[40]

These principles overlap significantly with principles in other frameworks
for the allocation of scarce medical and public health goods in the current pandemic. These frameworks vary in how they arrange, distinguish,
or combine clusters of general ethical considerations. However, virtually
every framework has a principle, variously worded, on the maximization
of benefits. And most frameworks include principles like the committee's
relating to equal concern, respect, or regard and to equity, fairness, and
justice, which are also stated in various ways. Transparency, a common requirement, is often incorporated into a larger principle. Similarly, a basis in
evidence is often assumed even when not explicitly singled out.[41]

Mitigation of Health Inequities and Their Effects

All of the committee's principles were important in its efforts to develop and
justify its goals, criteria, and priority phases for vaccine allocation—again,
there was interaction rather than one-way derivation. Here I will concen-
trate on a striking and demanding principle of social justice—the mitigation
of health inequities—that directs attention to a primary characteristic of
this pandemic's "personality": the disproportionate and devastating impact
on communities of color. At the time of the committee's report, CDC's data
indicated dramatic differences in rates of COVID-19 cases, age-adjusted
hospitalization, and death among different populations:

> Compared to White, non-Hispanic persons, American Indian
> or Alaska Native (non-Hispanic) persons had a case rate that

40. National Academies, *Framework*, 92–99.

41. For a comparison of four such frameworks for vaccine allocation for COVID-19,
see Table 3:1 in National Academies, *Framework*, 93.

was 2.8 times higher, a hospitalization rate that was 4.6 times higher, and a death rate that was 1.4 times higher. Hispanic or Latinx persons had a case rate that was 2.8 times higher, a hospitalization rate that was 4.7 times higher, and a death rate that was 1.1 times higher. Black or African American (non-Hispanic) persons had a case rate that was 2.6 times higher, a hospitalization rate that was 4.7 times higher, and a death rate that was 2.1 times higher.[42]

In view of these data, it is tempting to focus on race or ethnicity in vaccine prioritization. However, there is no scientific evidence that people are more susceptible to infection or severe disease because of their race or ethnicity. Furthermore, an allocation framework based on race and ethnicity would be subject to a variety of ethical and legal challenges, and it could undermine public trust. A closer look at the data indicates that the SARS-CoV-2 disproportionately affects individuals and populations who, under the burden of structural or systemic injustice like racism, experience major negative social determinants of health.[43] As the committee put it,

> This disproportionate burden largely reflects the impacts of systemic racism and socioeconomic factors that are associated with increased likelihood of acquiring the infection (e.g., frontline jobs that do not allow social distancing, crowded living conditions, lack of access to personal protective equipment [PPE], inability to work from home) and of having more severe disease when infected (as a result of a higher prevalence of comorbid conditions or other factors).[44]

Hence, the committee drew heavily on the principle of the mitigation of health inequities and their effects.

Many ethical frameworks for vaccine allocation in this pandemic include equity in one or more ways.[45] This sense of equity goes well beyond the Aristotelian conception of *epeiekeia* that Toulmin interpreted as "equity" or "reasonableness." Much of what is currently examined under the rubric of equity captures what has often been discussed under categories of justice, with particular attention to health disparities and their connection with systemic and structural injustice.[46]

---

42. National Academies, *Framework*, 3.
43. See also Gayle and Childress, "Race, Racism, and Structural Injustice."
44. National Academies, *Framework*, 95.
45. See Table 3:1 in National Academies, *Framework*, 93.
46. See Braverman, *What Is Health Equity?*; Powers and Faden, *Structural Injustice*.

Goals, Criteria, and Phases of Vaccine Allocation

Based on the principle of maximization of benefit and the "personality" of the pandemic, the committee proposed the following goal: "Reduce severe morbidity and mortality and negative societal impact due to the transmission of SARS-CoV-2."[47] Pursuit of this goal also requires attention to the other principles.

In light of these principles and its overall goal, the committee developed several risk-based criteria for prioritizing potential vaccine recipients:

- Risk of acquiring infection

- Risk of severe morbidity and mortality

- Risk of negative societal impact in the event of infection or severe morbidity or mortality

- Risk of transmitting infection to others

These criteria have an *indirect* but nonetheless *important* connection with the mitigation of health inequities and their effects:

> The first criterion addresses health inequities insofar as individuals subject to them are more likely to live and work in dense settings, where exposure to the virus is more likely. The second criterion addresses them indirectly insofar as those inequities have increased individuals' risk of disease (e.g., social disadvantage is linked to having more disease and more severe disease). The third criterion addresses them indirectly insofar as workers who have been subject to health inequities play essential roles in jobs with greater societal impact (e.g., health and elder care).[48]

This framework of principles, goal, and criteria would be incomplete without the specification of priority groups. The statement of task for the committee's work described priority groups as "tiers," a commonly used term in this context. However, the committee rightly adopted the term "phases" because the term "tiers" is too hierarchical and static.[49] The overall aim is to vaccinate everyone who will accept vaccination as soon as possible. But, given the inevitable early shortage of vaccine, it is necessary and ethical to phase in vaccination, in successive deployments.

Drawing on the risk-based criteria, in light of the substantive and procedural principles and the framework's allocation goal, the committee

---

47. National Academies, *Framework*, 100–102.

48. National Academies, *Framework*, 104.

49. National Academies, *Framework*, 8, 105.

proposed four phases of allocation under conditions of scarcity. The first phase concentrates on those at highest risk, commencing in Phase 1a with frontline health and first responders (a "jumpstart phase"), particularly because of their risk of exposure, and then in 1b people of all ages with comorbid and underlying conditions that put them at *significantly* higher risk for severe disease and death, and older adults in congregate settings. Subsequent phases prioritize vaccination from highest to lowest risk categories. Phase 2 encompasses many different groups based on risks of exposure and of severe illness: K–12 teachers and school staff and child-care workers; critical workers in high risk-settings—workers in *essential* industries and at *substantially* higher risk of exposure; people of all ages with comorbid and underlying conditions that put them at *moderately* higher risk for severe outcomes; people (and staff) in homeless shelters or group homes for individuals with various disabilities; people (and staff) in prisons, jails, etc.; and all older adults not included in Phase 1. Phase 3 turns to young adults; children; and workers in industries *important* to social functioning and at *increased* risk of exposure (not already included in earlier phases), while the final phase, Phase 4, includes all US residents who do not have access in the earlier phases.[50]

Equity as a Cross-Cutting Principle

In presenting these four phases, the committee states: "Equity is a crosscutting consideration: In each population group, vaccine access should be prioritized for geographic areas identified through CDC's Social Vulnerability Index or another more specific index."[51] It is important to distinguish *allocation* from *delivery* and *access*. An equitable framework for allocation identifies priority groups in each phase. In practical terms, one way to implement equity as a cross-cutting principle is to use the CDC's Social Vulnerability Index or another index to identify geographical areas that should be prioritized for access for the designated priority groups.[52] Focusing on a community's resilience in a natural disaster or infectious disease outbreak, the SVI identifies factors, such as socioeconomic status, household composition, minority status, and transportation, that affect a community's resilience. It can help identify people's vulnerabilities and risks in order to facilitate special efforts to reach areas where there are significant needs for and barriers

50. National Academies, *Framework*, 105–38. A figure summarizing this paragraph appears on p. 112.

51. National Academies, *Framework*, 112.

52. National Academies, *Framework*, 132–34.

to access to vaccination. Merely being assigned to an early phase or priority group for vaccination does not ensure access to it where there are barriers to healthcare, transportation, computer and internet capability, etc. Special efforts may also be required to address vaccine resistance and hesitancy.

Other recommendations also seek to promote equity. One is providing vaccination at no cost to the recipient (either for the vaccine itself or administrative fees). Another is attending to equity implications in defining each priority group in each phase. To take one example: in Phase 1a, the category of health care workers should not be limited to those who are paid or better paid, such as physicians or nurses, but rather should include all staff at risk of becoming infected through their exposure in the context of health care. Hence, this category includes workers who clean patients' rooms, transport patients, deliver meals, and so forth. In short, as a matter of equity, all those in a group facing similar risks should have equal priority.[53]

Achieving public health goals through vaccination requires public trust. To be worthy of trust, the allocation criteria and phases must not only satisfy the substantive principles, but also the procedural principles of fairness, transparency, and evidence-based. Fairness, to take one example, requires that policy makers engage with the public, particularly those most affected by the pandemic, on the development, deployment, and revision of the allocation criteria, including the several phases of the vaccine rollout. These procedural principles are also helpful for guiding efforts to overcome vaccine resistance and hesitancy, which are understandably widespread in some minority communities. Health equity cannot be achieved unless efficacious vaccines are actually made effective through vaccinations.

Finally, equity extends beyond US borders. The committee went beyond its statement of task, which focused on domestic vaccine allocation, to recommend that the US support equitable allocation of vaccine for COVID-19 globally by several measures, including deploying a portion (e.g., 10 percent) of its vaccine supply for global allocation and engaging with the World Health Organization.[54]

This case study of the National Academies committee indicates how, in contrast to Toulmin's and Jonsen-Toulmin's reported experience with the National Commission, public bodies have worked with ethical principles and case judgments (in this instance, about prioritization), along with goals and criteria, engaging these dialectically, moving back and forth between them and making refinements in each as appropriate, and engaging members of the committee dialogically to develop a coherent framework

---

53. National Academies, *Framework*, 132.

54. National Academies, *Framework*, 20.

consisting of several interconnected parts. The National Academies committee's framework was intended to "assist" and "inform" the work of policy makers and other decision makers such as the ACIP,[55] which has since made specific recommendations about priority groups, based on the currently approved vaccines (under FDA emergency authorization). The states, especially through their departments of health, and local, tribal, and territorial jurisdictions set out and modified priority groups based on availability of vaccines, specific population needs, and efficiency and equity in vaccine allocation and distribution.

REFLECTIONS ON MEDIATED ADVOCACY

Ethics and Ethicists

These reflections on ethics and mediated advocacy in PBBs begin with some points about ethics and ethicists. Public bodies addressing bioethical issues usually number among their members one or more ethicists. Of course, ethical reflection and discourse, even critical ethical reflection and discourse, are not limited to these professionals, even though that is what they focus on in their day jobs. Hence, we should not overemphasize the role or contribution of professional ethicists to public bioethics.

Based on my experience on several PBBs, I would stress that practical moral insight and wisdom are not the exclusive province of any one professional group. In multidisciplinary deliberations—on a body operating on the model of a deliberative democracy—we should never suppose that the professional role of *ethicist* exhausts the role of *ethics* in advice and recommendations about public policy. Nevertheless, the professional role of ethicist remains useful for public bioethics. Ethicists can and often do make significant contributions to the deliberations of PBBs, particularly through two types of knowledge and skills.

First, ethicists are expected to be familiar with different concepts, traditions, methods, and patterns of moral reflection, including a variety of theories that can cast light on current ethical controversies, possibilities, and limits, and that can, thus, facilitate collective deliberation. Of course, this knowledge must be dispensed judiciously—the public deliberative body is not an academic seminar for long disquisitions on Rawlsian or communitarian thought, for example. Second, ethicists can bring practiced skills in analyzing the logic and rhetoric of moral discourse, formal and informal, to bear in the examination of issues in bioethics.

55. McClung, "Advisory Committee."

The work of bioethics, especially on PBBs, needs to be multidisciplinary and multi-professional. Varied backgrounds and perspectives are vitally important. Ideally, the PBB's processes actually become interdisciplinary and interprofessional. The academic or professional ethicist can and should contribute rigorously, creatively, openly, and humbly to this work and these processes. What the ethicist can and should contribute is not limited to scholarly points about ethics or to neutrally presenting options and their implications for the PBB to ponder. The ethicist's role also includes ethics-informed advocacy in the sense of proposing or recommending the principles the committee should adopt, the findings it should accept, the conclusions it should draw, and the specific recommendations it should make.[56]

In short, the ethicist seeks to persuade other members of the PBB of relevant general principles and values and of particular recommendations which are subject to further revision and adjustment. Indeed, the ethicist's own preliminary, provisional, or initial views may be significantly clarified or even substantially modified through this dialogical process. In this mediated advocacy, the PBB's final recommendations almost certainly will not exactly match any individual participant's—including the ethicist's—own views.

One risk must be acknowledged: the ethicist's participation on a PBB may serve mainly to legitimate that body's work rather than to contribute substantially to ethical analysis and mediated advocacy. Most ethicists who participate on PBBs or other bodies, such as institutional committees designed to address bioethical issues, worry about being co-opted. Sometimes, the ethicist may even need to decline an appointment to a PBB or to withdraw from it when there seems to be no way to contribute significant scholarly input or to offer appropriate advocacy.

Advocacy: General and/or Particular?

On some complex matters, such as mitochondrial DNA transfer, many ethicists and other participants may not know exactly what they think about these matters in advance of the PBB's deliberations. The PBB may consider broad principles to help identify the ethical issues at stake and to determine how to resolve them. A major difference between my account and Toulmin's and Jonsen-Toulmin's is whether "moral considerations," which

56. Some of the content and language of the previous four paragraphs derives from Childress, *Public Bioethics*, 4.

they admit in taxonomies of case judgments, can also be "general moral considerations," that is, principles.[57]

In contrast to the Toulmin and Jonsen-Toulmin conception of how PBBs work by securing consensus on taxonomies of cases apart from principles, the deliberative processes of PBBs often involve moving back and forth between principles, such as mitigation of health inequities, and types of case judgments, such as prioritization of vaccine recipients, as occurred when the National Academies committee constructed its framework for equitable allocation of vaccine for COVID-19. Ethicists and other participants advocate for both general moral considerations and particular judgments, and the PBB, following collective deliberation, advocates for both its framework and policy recommendations. While not commonly considered advocacy, this is properly a form of advocacy. It is mediated advocacy through collective advice and recommendations to policy makers and other relevant parties.

Public Justification

PBBs normally pursue and depend on a process of public justification, in which they present their findings and offer their reasons for recommending—i.e., advocating—particular policies. In contrast to Toulmin, who held that such justifications, particularly when appealing to principles, tend to erect walls and separate and divide,[58] I have found that principles—i.e., general moral considerations—often play a central role in public justification, especially when these are embedded in the society's institutions and culture and are drawn out and specified for the tasks at hand, as occurred in the deliberations of the National Academies committee on vaccine allocation.

The public's role is often important for PBBs, in contrast to Toulmin's claims about its limited role in the work of National Commission.[59] For governmentally appointed bodies, virtually all meetings are open to the public and all deliberations are transparent; for committees under the National Academies of Sciences, Engineering and Medicine, or the National Academy of Medicine, meetings are generally closed to the public, but, on occasion, public sessions are held. For example, the National Academies committee on vaccine allocation held a public hearing and also received a large number of written comments on its draft framework; these were important as the

57. See above and, for example, Toulmin, "National Commission," 606–12.

58. See Toulmin, "Tyranny of Principles," 32. Of course, broader appeals to human rights, for example, may also be important to correct a country's myopia.

59. See Toulmin, "National Commission," 607–10.

committee developed its final report and recommendations. In any event, PBBs generally aim at public justification for their recommendations. Public justification was deemed to be particularly important for a framework for vaccine allocation, because a successful vaccination program depends on public trust, generated in part by procedural fairness, public engagement, and transparency.

Public justification, which appeals to both facts and principles/values as reasons for particular policies, usually does not rest on proof in a strict sense. To take one example: years ago, the Task Force on Organ Transplantation offered several reasons for recommending that the federal government provide funds for heart and liver transplants, just as it does for kidney transplants through the End-Stage Renal Disease Program of Medicare. Those reasons included (a) the continuity of these transplants with other medical procedures, including kidney transplants, that are already covered or should be covered, and (b) the distinctiveness or uniqueness of organ transplantation, especially the social practices that solicit and obtain organs for transplantation through public "gifts of life." Organ transplantation cannot occur without the public's willingness to donate the organs that are essential for the procedure. Building on (b), the task force argued that it is unfair and even exploitative for the society, through the media, health professionals, and public officials, to ask all people, rich and poor alike, to donate non-renal organs if poor people would have little chance to receive such organ transplants if needed.[60] And yet, in our context, access to non-renal organ transplants is determined by ability to pay (directly or through medical insurance) rather than by medical factors.[61]

Philosopher Frances M. Kamm offers a number of important criticisms of the task force's arguments, but in the final analysis she imposes an unduly rigid philosophical model of argument onto public justification, rejecting or downplaying arguments that fall short of "proof."[62] That sets an inappropriate standard for public justification. Indeed, as Toulmin constantly reminded us, we should not expect adequate public argumentation and justification to conform to a rigid geometrical, theoretical model of proof.[63] In a similar vein, O. Carter Snead recently insisted that what should be sought and expected in public bioethics is not "apodictic philosophical proof," but rather "political persuasion."[64]

60. Task Force, *Organ Transplantation*, 104.

61. Herring et al., "Insurance Status," 641–52.

62. See Kamm, "Report," 207–20.

63. See the discussion of Toulmin's argument above.

64. Snead, *What It Means*, 12.

Such persuasion depends significantly on the state of public discourse and public culture. For instance, it's not surprising that the principle of mitigation of health inequities and their effects has gained considerable traction in the era of Black Lives Matter. Widespread and vigorous public advocacy of social justice in words and deeds has doubtless changed the context for public justification, creating a new moment for persuasive appeals for the mitigation of health inequities.

As William Foege and Helene Gayle, the co-chairs of the National Academies committee on vaccine allocation, noted in their preface to the committee's report:

> Inequity has been a hallmark of this pandemic, both locally and globally. Inequities in health have always existed, but at this moment there is an awakening to the power of racism, poverty, and bias in amplifying the health and economic pain and hardship imposed by this pandemic. Thus, we saw our work as one way to address these wrongs and do our part to work toward a new commitment to promoting health equity that is informed by but lives beyond this moment.[65]

Truth or Consequences?

On occasion, members or staff of PBBs may face another hard choice, which we can properly label "truth or consequences." This stems from a conflict between an ethicist's beliefs based on his or her critical scholarly work in ethics and his or her judgment about what, in the circumstances, would be the most ethical recommendations by the PBB. In "Truth or Consequences," philosopher Dan Brock reflects on his experiences in the early 1980s on the staff of the President's Commission for the Study of Ethical Problems in Medicine and Biomedical and Behavioral Research, an important and influential PBB.[66] His insightful reflections resonate with my own experiences on PBBs.

"Truth is the central virtue of scholarly work," Brock writes—indeed, the goal of scholarly work is "an unconstrained search for truth, whatever the consequences."[67] Yet the goal of public policy advice is to provide recommendations for ethically justifiable and feasible public policies in particular

---

65. National Academies, *Framework*, xviii.

66. Brock, "Truth or Consequences," 408–16.

67. Brock, "Truth or Consequences," 408–10.

circumstances. This requires attention to consequences (and other ethical considerations).

By the time the President's Commission prepared its major and influential report on *Deciding to Forego Life-Sustaining Treatment*,[68] it was commonly held that it is morally permissible to allow patients to die, to let nature take its course, as long as we do not kill them. Brock's rigorous philosophical analysis reached a different verdict: conceptually, the difference between killing and allowing to die "is not in itself morally important, and . . . stopping life-sustaining treatment is often killing, though justified killing."[69] By contrast, the majority of the members of the President's Commission rejected this view. It is possible, perhaps even probable, that in the name of "truth," based on his rigorous philosophical analysis, Brock could have convinced the commissioners that, contrary to their operative beliefs, there is no sharp distinction between allowing to die and killing, and that letting die is often killing. However, if he had succeeded in doing so, the effects on public policy and practice would probably have been very detrimental for dying patients.

Under the circumstances, the commissioners, if persuaded by Brock's philosophical analysis, more than likely would *not* have drawn the same conclusion he did: "letting die is the same as killing and, therefore, we should permit both of them under some conditions." Instead, they more than likely would have said, "letting die is just as bad as killing, and, therefore, we should prohibit both of them in all circumstances." The practical results would have been devastating for many patients at the end of their lives—these patients would have been deprived of their right, by then increasingly recognized in both ethics and law, to refuse in some circumstances treatments that could conceivably extend their lives. These patients would have been both wronged and harmed. Hence, the dilemma: if Brock had convinced the commissioners of the "truth" he held on philosophical grounds, this "truth" as mediated through the President's Commission would probably have had terrible effects in the real world.

Similar issues or dilemmas may arise for commissioners as well as for staff who are working with commissioners. The case can be made that a compromise of scholarly "truth" is sometimes warranted for ethical reasons. Under some circumstances, ethicists may legitimately choose for ethical reasons to sign onto a committee's collective recommendation that does not fully reflect or is even in some tension with their scholarly views or choose to refrain from pressing their scholarly ethical views when a committee's

68. President's Commission, *Deciding to Forego*.
69. Brock, "Truth or Consequences," 411.

adoption of those views would probably have unacceptable ethical consequences.[70] Even if such conflicts are not common, they can certainly arise for PBB participants and staff who then have to decide how to respond.

Conclusion: Mediated Advocacy

In conclusion, this chapter has sought to illuminate and illustrate mediated advocacy in PBBs established to inform and advise policy makers. Mediated advocacy is a neglected form of advocacy, overshadowed by more dramatic, activist, and prophetic forms. It raises many of the same issues as other forms of advocacy for ethicists who bring both their scholarship in ethics and their advocacy to the table, but it raises distinctive issues as well. This chapter argues for the ethicist's advocacy, as a member of the PBB or its staff, for principles, i.e., general moral considerations, often rooted in the society's institutions and culture, and for particular case judgments in the form of policy recommendations. It draws on the recent work of the National Academies committee on vaccine allocation, over against the portrait Toulmin and Jonsen paint of the work of the National Commission, to indicate how principles and case judgments can and do interact in collective deliberations, and how the ethicist's responsible advocacy is mediated through the PBB's recommendations to policy makers. This is mediated advocacy.

70. For discussion of Brock's discussion of "truth or consequences" in the context of debates about conceptions of death and organ donation, see Childress, *Public Bioethics*, 164–65, from which some of the ideas and formulations in these paragraphs have been adapted.

BIBLIOGRAPHY

Beauchamp, Tom L., and James F. Childress. *Principles of Biomedical Ethics*. 8th ed. New York: Oxford University Press, 2019.

Braveman, Paula, et al. *What Is Health Equity?: And What Difference Does a Definition Make?* Princeton: Robert Wood Johnson Foundation, 2017.

Briggle, Adam. *A Rich Bioethics: Public Policy, Biotechnology, and the Kass Council.* Notre Dame: University of Notre Dame Press, 2010.

Brock, Dan W. "Truth or Consequences: The Role of Philosophers in Policy-Making." In *Life and Death: Philosophical Essays in Biomedical Ethics*, 408–16. Cambridge Studies in Philosophy and Public Policy. Cambridge: Cambridge University Press, 1993.

Callahan, Daniel. "Religion and the Secularization of Bioethics." *Hastings Center Report* 20.4 (1990) 2–4.

———. "The Social Sciences and the Task of Bioethics." *Daedalus* 128 (1999) 275–94.

———. "Why America Accepted Bioethics." *Hastings Center Report* 23.6 (1993) S8–S9.

Childress, James F. *Civil Disobedience and Political Obligation: A Study in Christian Social Ethics*. New Haven: Yale University Press, 1971.

———. "Ethical Theories, Principles, and Casuistry in Bioethics: An Interpretation and Defense of Principlism." In *Religious Methods and Resources in Bioethics*, edited by Paul Camenisch, 181–201. London: Kluwer Academic, 1994.

———. "Never Solo: Gratitude for My Academic Journey." *Journal of Medicine and Philosophy* 45 (2020) 410–26.

———. "Nuremberg's Legacy: Some Ethical Reflections." *Perspectives in Biology and Medicine* 43 (Spring 2000) 347–60.

———. *Public Bioethics: Principles and Problems*. New York: Oxford University Press, 2020.

———. "Rationing Health Care in the COVID-19 Pandemic: Implementing Ethical Triage." In *Medicine and Ethics in Times of Corona*, edited by Martin Woesler and Hans-Martin Sass, 5–14. Münster: LIT, 2020.

Childress, James F., et al., eds. *Belmont Revisited: Ethical Principles for Research with Human Subjects*. Washington, DC: Georgetown University Press, 2005.

Dye, Thomas. *Understanding Public Policy*. 15th ed. New York: Pearson, 2016.

Emanuel, Ezekiel J., et al. "Fair Allocation of Scarce Medical Resources in the Time of COVID-19." *New England Journal of Medicine* 382.21 (2020) 2049–55.

Fletcher, John C. "On Restoring Public Bioethics." *Politics and the Life Sciences* 13 (1994) 84–86.

Fletcher, John C., and Franklin Miller. "The Promise and Perils of Public Bioethics." In *The Ethics of Research Involving Human Subjects: Facing the 21st Century*, edited by Harold Vanderpool, 155–84. Frederick: University Publishing Group, 1996.

Gayle, Helene, and James F. Childress. "Race, Racism, and Structural Injustice: Equitable Allocation and Distribution of Vaccines for COVID-19." *American Journal of Bioethics* 21.3 (2021) 4–7.

Gonzalez, Susan. "Historian Frank Snowden: May We Be 'Forever Changed' by Coronavirus." *Yale News*, April 8, 2020. https://news.yale.edu/2020/04/08/historian-frank-snowden-may-we-be-forever-changed-coronavirus.

Gutmann, Amy, and Dennis Thompson. "Deliberating about Bioethics." *Hastings Center Report* 27.3 (1997) 38–41.

Gustafson, James F. "Moral Discourse about Medicine: A Variety of Forms." In *Intersections: Science, Theology, and Ethics*, 35–55. Cleveland: Pilgrim, 1996.

Herring, Andrew A., et al. "Insurance Status of U.S. Organ Donors and Transplant Recipients: The Uninsured Give, but Rarely Receive." *International Journal of Health Services* 38.4 (2008) 641–52.

Jonsen, Albert R. *The Birth of Bioethics*. New York: Oxford University Press, 1994.

———. "A History of Religion and Bioethics." In *Handbook of Bioethics and Religion*, edited by David E. Guinn, 23–36. New York: Oxford University Press, 2006.

Jonsen, Albert R., and Stephen Toulmin. *The Abuse of Casuistry: A History of Moral Reasoning*. Berkeley: University of California Press, 1990.

Kamm, Frances M. "The Report of the U.S. Task Force on Organ Transplantation: Criticisms and Alternatives." *Mount Sinai Journal of Medicine* 56 (1989) 207–20.

McClung, Nancy, et al. "The Advisory Committee on Immunization Practices' Ethical Principles for Allocating Initial Supplies of COVID-19 Vaccine—United States, 2020." *Morbidity and Mortality Weekly Report* 69 (2020) 1782–86.

National Academies of Sciences, Engineering, and Medicine and the National Academy of Medicine. *Framework for Equitable Allocation of COVID-19 Vaccine.* Washington, DC: National Academies Press, 2020.

National Commission for the Protection of Human Subjects of Biomedical and Behavioral Research. *The Belmont Report: Ethical Principles and Guidelines for the Protection of Human Subjects of Research.* Washington, DC: DHEW, 1978.

Pollack, Harold. "The Responsibility to Advocate—and to Advocate Responsibly." *Milbank Quarterly* 97 (March 2019) 44–47.

———. "Thinking about Committing Civil Disobedience in the Age of Trump." *Nation.* December 21, 2016. https://www.thenation.com/article/thinking-about-committing-civil-disobedience-in-the-age-of-trump/.

Potter, Van Rensselaer. "Bioethics: The Science of Survival." *Perspectives in Biology and Medicine* 14 (1970) 127–53.

Powers, Madison, and Ruth Faden. *Structural Injustice: Power, Advantage, and Human Rights.* New York: Oxford University Press, 2019.

President's Commission for the Study of Ethical Problems in Medicine and Biomedical and Behavioral Research. *Deciding to Forego Life-Sustaining Treatment: A Report on the Ethical, Medical, and Legal Issues in Treatment Decisions.* Washington, DC: U.S. Government Printing Office, 1983.

Snead, O. Carter. *What It Means to Be Human: The Case for the Body in Public Bioethics.* Cambridge: Harvard University Press, 2020.

Task Force on Organ Transplantation. *Organ Transplantation: Issues and Recommendations.* Bethesda: U.S. Department of Health and Human Services, 1986.

Toulmin, Stephen. "Casuistry and Clinical Ethics." In *A Matter of Principles: Ferment in U.S. Bioethics*, edited by Edwin R. DuBose, Ronald P. Hamel, and Laurence J. O'Connell, 310–18. Valley Forge: Trinity Press International, 1994.

———. "How Medicine Saved the Life of Ethics." *Perspectives in Biology and Medicine* 25 (Summer 1982) 736–50.

———. "Medical Ethics in Its American Context: An Historical Survey." In *Biomedical Ethics: An Anglo-American Dialogue*, edited by Daniel Callahan and G. R. Dunstan, 7–15. New York: New York Academy of Sciences, 1988.

———. "The National Commission of Human Experimentation: Procedures and Outcomes." In *Scientific Controversies: Case Studies in the Resolution and Closure of Disputes in Science and Technology*, edited by H. Tristram Engelhardt Jr. and Arthur L. Caplan, 599–614. Cambridge: Cambridge University Press, 1987.

———. "The Recovery of Practical Philosophy." *American Scholar* 57 (Summer 1988) 337–52

———. "The Tyranny of Principles." *Hastings Center Report* 11.6 (December 1981) 31–38.

———. *The Uses of Argument.* Updated ed. Cambridge: Cambridge University Press, 2003.

THE EFFICACY OF ADVOCACY

Peter J. Paris

INTRODUCTION

THE PURPOSE OF THIS essay is to discuss the necessary conditions for the efficacy of advocacy without which there could be no such activity. The aim of all advocacy is to influence those who have the authority to actualize certain desired ends, goals, or purposes. Advocates are those who plead the case for specific causes such as some particular philosophy, social program, form of government, economic system, civil or human rights, to name only a few. Consequently, lawyers are often viewed as advocates because their primary function is to defend the claims of their clients.

All advocacy implies a dispute between two opposing sides that share a common set of basic values to which both sides appeal as the basis for their conflicting claims. For example, advocates for civil rights, whether for themselves or for others, claim a common citizenship with those who already enjoy such rights. In other words, they advocate for what they believe belongs to them, the denial of which they view as unjust.

With a broad brush, so to speak, this essay will describe and analyze the long journey that African Americans and their allies have undertaken in their as-yet-unfinished struggle for civil rights and human dignity. As we will see, that struggle necessitated an ancillary battle for the affirmation of their status as human beings.

THE STRUGGLE FOR THE HUMANITY OF BLACKS

At the beginning of the American republic, most European settlers, including those who signed the Declaration of Independence and wrote the Constitution, believed that they did not share a common humanity with African peoples. Consequently, despite earlier debates on the continent over the morality of slavery,[1] most settlers in this so-called new world felt no moral obligations whatsoever towards enslaved Africans. Further, notwithstanding the country's economic dependency on the institution of chattel slavery, the writers of its constitution took every precaution to avoid any mention of the words "slavery" or "African" in its founding document. Most important, both Thomas Jefferson, the principal writer of the constitution, and Benjamin Franklin, the future president of the Pennsylvania Abolition Society, believed in the natural inferiority of African peoples and, hence, the necessity of colonizing the latter either to Africa or elsewhere should they ever be emancipated because they could not imagine the two races living together in social harmony. Further, their belief in the natural inferiority of African peoples correlated to a corresponding belief in the natural superiority of European peoples who, incidentally, first came to view themselves as white[2] people only after encountering black Africans.

Since the middle of the twentieth century, what had hitherto been known as the science of race was designated pseudoscience because it had been initiated, supported and promoted by a social and political claim that certain phenotypical differences were markers of either generic states of inferiority or superiority among the world's races. Consequently, such distinctions constituted the basis for the unequal treatment of black Africans who were brought to this country unwillingly as chattel slaves and maintained as such for two and a half centuries. After the institution's demise following a bitter Civil War and the brief period called Reconstruction, it morphed into what historians have called the "Jim Crow" era of racial discrimination and segregation, which endured for three-quarters of a century thereafter.

Let none suppose, however, that the pseudoscience of racism has disappeared completely. Rather, it has steadily gained momentum at least since the early nineties when Charles Murray published *The Bell Curve*,[3] which rapidly became a best seller and launched a fierce debate that endures to the present day in psychological studies pertaining to various indexes of racial inequalities in education, poverty, drug addiction, and incarceration.

1. See Thomas, *The Slave Trade: The Story of the Atlantic Slave Trade*, 1–15, 21–25, 786–801.

2. See Painter, *The History of White People*.

3. See Evans, "The Unwelcome Revival of Race Science."

Now, despite the general debunking of all such pseudo-scientific theories, many white Americans continue to believe in the anthropological doctrine of white supremacy and the consequent inferiority of African peoples. Similar attitudes permeated the thinking of most white South Africans throughout the twentieth century and provided the basis for the development of its apartheid state.

A few years before the beginning of the Civil War, the Supreme Court bestowed legal status on the doctrine of white supremacy in its 1857 *Dred Scott v. Sanford*, case wherein Chief Justice Roger Brooke Taney wrote the majority opinion which stated unequivocally that the reason blacks were not included as citizens in the Constitution was because whites had always considered them "a subordinate and inferior class of beings." The following clearly states his thinking on the subject:

> They had for more than a century before been regarded as beings of an inferior order, and altogether unfit to associate with the white race, either in social or political relations; and so far inferior that they had no rights which the white man was bound to respect; and that the negro might justly and lawfully be reduced to slavery for his benefit . . . This opinion was at that time fixed and universal in the civilized portion of the white race. It was regarded as an axiom in morals as well as in politics, which no one thought of disputing, or supposed to be open to dispute; and men in every grade and position in society daily and habitually acted upon it in their private pursuits, as well as in matters of public concern, without doubting for a moment the correctness of this opinion.[4]

Immediately following the Civil War and the brief period of Reconstruction, the Southern states rapidly institutionalized the practice of racial discrimination and segregation for all people of African descent, thus constituting what historians have called, the "Jim Crow era" in American history. That system of racial inequality became the law of the land in the 1896 *Plesy v. Ferguson* Supreme Court decision that established in law the *separate but equal doctrine* pertaining to race relations that was destined to endure for almost six decades thereafter, when it was overturned by the 1954 *Brown v. Board of Education* Supreme Court decision.

Since the United States Constitution provided no sustained support for the claims of equal citizenship rights for blacks prior to the 1954 Supreme Court's *Brown v. Board of Education* decision, blacks and their allies frequently appealed to the Declaration of Independence as the political

4. Bell, *Race, Racism, and American Law,* 840.

basis for their status as human beings. In that document, Thomas Jefferson had based his view of a common humanity on the laws of nature, which he claimed were self-evident to all. Thus, the opening sentence of that Declaration, "We hold these truths to be self-evident that all men are created equal and endowed by their Creator with certain unalienable rights among which are life, liberty and the pursuit of happiness," became for blacks a sacred principle. Though Jefferson probably believed the principle was not intended to apply to them, blacks laid claim to it nonetheless by evoking its authority in support of their humanity and all consequent rights pertaining to it.

After effectively conquering its indigenous peoples, white Americans believed for many generations that both the country and the Christian faith rightfully belonged to them alone. Their claim to the latter inheritance, however, was challenged round the middle of the eighteenth century when the first of several waves of Christian evangelists held emotional open-air campaigns that historians have called "Great Awakenings," which turned the British North American colonies into a mission field for the conversion of the masses to the Christian faith. That evangelical spirit was revolutionary in the sense that it considered all people as equal beings before God and, wittingly or not, laid a theological foundation for democratic governance in all their social, political, and religious associations. Thus the church's celebration of the Lord's last supper, when reserved for believers alone, exemplified all the marks of an egalitarian society which implied a major threat to a slave-holding society. The churches that grew out of those evangelical campaigns soon began raising questions about the compatibility of Christianity with the institution of slavery.[5] Eventually, that same spirit led to the nascent Baptist, Methodist, and Presbyterian denominations eventually splitting into Northern and Southern jurisdictions during the antebellum period over the issue of slavery: divisions that endured for more than a century after the Civil War. Needless to say, perhaps, racial discrimination and segregation remained normative practices in both the Southern and Northern jurisdictions of those denominations for many years in the future.

Not surprisingly, slave owners quickly discerning the dangerous threat of the evangelical teaching prohibited their slaves from attending the revivals and converting to the Christian faith because they feared its implications for the preservation of the system. Since many of the slave owners themselves were at the same time converting to the Christian faith, they rightly feared

5. It should be noted however, that in the fifteenth century, Pope Pius II had condemned the enslavement of Christians by Christians, but not slavery as such, even though that decree went unheeded by most Catholics in the slave trade. See Thomas, *The Slave Trade*, 71–72.

that if their slaves were to share a common spiritual status with them, they would soon begin raising questions about their civil status. The response of the evangelists, however, to those concerns was to persuade many of them that allowing their slaves to convert to the Christian faith would not imply any change in their status as slaves. Rather, they admonished them that the conversion of their slaves to Christianity would lead them to forsake their uncivilized customs and, accordingly, become better slaves. In other words, the anticipated eagerness of the slaves to become faithful Christians would improve their moral natures by reducing such troublesome behaviors as lying, stealing, quarreling, and the development of hateful dispositions. In fact, they even argued that conversion to Christianity would require them to be more obedient to their masters as the Apostle Paul in Ephesians 6:5 had admonished them so to be. Thus, the encouragement of slaves to convert to Christianity also served as a management tool for their owners.

Further, since evangelicalism taught that all Christians should be evangelists, most converts, whether free or enslaved, tended to proclaim the gospel to their respective families and everyone they encountered. Most important, they soon began assuming leadership functions at their respective meetings, which enabled them gradually to rely less and less on the teaching and leadership of the white evangelists. By assuming such roles for themselves, they set in motion the novel pattern of lay leadership in their churches, which freed them from the tyranny of the ecclesial hierarchy. Soon, on the plantations where slaves were not allowed to worship, or were permitted to do so only in the presence of their owners or the latter's duly appointed overseers, the slaves soon began meeting secretly in the so-called *hush harbors*, where they created unique forms of worship, music, and songs that they called *spirituals*. Gradually, ring dancing, testimonies, praying, shouting, creative preaching, and caring for one another became distinctive marks of their devotion. Biblical teachings about faith, love, hope, justice, freedom, and equality were primary themes in their gatherings because they comprised the essence of their deepest longings. For example, the *spirituals,* composed and arranged by the worshippers themselves, often exhibited what some have called *double entendre,* i.e., double meanings: one for the slave owner and the other for the slaves themselves. That type of trickery enabled them to sing openly in the fields about a forthcoming secret meeting, a planned escape via the under-ground railroad, mockery of their owners, as well as the joys of freedom and equality in heaven, without arousing their owners' suspicions. Thus, their creative genius led to the creation of some of America's unique forms of song, music, and dance. The exercise of their poetic imagination and musical talent enabled them to signal their rejection of slavery and its accompanying misery along with their hopes for freedom someday in the future. Accordingly, they wrote countless lyrics based on biblical teaching with both plaintive and celebratory tunes derived from African memories, such as the following:

> When Israel was in Egypt's land,
> Let my people go;
> Oppressed so hard they could not stand,
> Let my people go;
> Go down Moses,
> 'Way down in Egypt's land,
> Tell ol' Pharaoh,
> Let my people go.
>
> . . . .
>
> Swing low, sweet chariot,
> Coming for to carry me home.
> Swing low sweet chariot,
> I ain't got long to stay here.
>
> . . . .
>
> I've got shoes,
> You've got shoes,
> All God's children got shoes,
> When I get to heaven,
> Gonna put on my shoes,
> Gonna walk all over God's heaven.
>
> . . . .
>
> Steal away,
> Steal away to Jesus,
> Steal away,
> Steal away home,
> I a'int got long to stay here.

In many opaque ways, the spirituals depicted the troubles and misery of slavery along with their hopes for deliverance. Thus, despite their pain and sorrow, the slaves trusted in Jesus as their divine deliverer both in this life and the life to come. In fact, they felt a special bond with Jesus because of their common suffering. Accordingly, they sang,

> Nobody knows the trouble I've seen,
> Nobody knows like Jesus.
> Nobody knows the trouble I've seen,
> Glory Hallelujah.

And, with a touch of exuberance and evangelical zeal, they also sang,

> Git on board, little chillun'

> Git on board little chillun,
> Git on board little chillun,
> There's room for plenty a more . . .

Contrary to the thinking of many, when the slaves sang about their love for heaven, they were not engaged in any escapist flight from the realities of this world. Rather, in doing so, they drew a contrast between their present misery and the spiritual vision of freedom in eternity. Thus, on the one hand, the image of heaven functioned as a principle of criticism on their present condition while, on the other hand, it enabled them to sing with a touch of humor about "walking all over heaven," since there was no segregation there, and about the expectations of their Christian masters who talked about heaven, but were not going there because of their evil ways. Thus, they put those thoughts in the following spiritual:

> Heab'n, heab'n,
> Evr'y body talkin' about heab'n
> Ain't a goin' there;
> Heab'n, heab'n,
> Gonna walk all over God's heab'n.

Now, the substance of the Christian gospel as taught by the white evangelists was reimagined by the slaves themselves, especially through the poetic imagination and extraordinary oratory of their black preachers coupled with the musical genius of their people, constituted the bedrock of the world that blacks were beginning to build for themselves even in the cauldron of chattel slavery itself. Since their ancient African heritage had taught them there was no radical separation between the sacred and the profane or between the religious and the secular, they considered both their religious devotion and socio-economic activities as integrally united. Thus, they had no problem embracing both the Christian understanding of humanity and the constitutional principles of liberty, freedom, and equality because both contradicted the practice of slavery and the doctrine of white supremacy. Hence, as I had concluded elsewhere, the single most important contribution that the black churches have given to the world lies in their explication of the "black Christian tradition," which proclaimed "the parenthood of God and the kinship of all people."[6] Consequently, black Christians have always abhorred slavery and all forms of racism.

Suffice it to say, however, that even under the conditions of slavery, both free and enslaved blacks established churches, denominations, and various mutual aid organizations, the amazing beauty and meaningfulness

---

6. See Paris, *The Social Teaching of the Black Churches*, ix.

of which undoubtedly manifested their humanity and contradicted all the ways whites viewed and treated them. Most importantly, the evangelical spirit that informed the world that blacks built under the conditions of slavery was not only expansive in nature, but eventually produced enduring organizations, emancipatory thought and missionary practices that eventually extended back to their ancestral homelands on the continent of Africa.

Nothing illustrates more clearly the effective communication system between blacks in the Northern and Southern states than the underground railroad that sheltered and facilitated countless numbers of refugee slaves fleeing the misery and oppression of chattel slavery in the eighteenth and nineteenth centuries. In fact, their struggle for freedom produced such paradigmatic figures as Richard Allen, Absalom Jones, Daniel Payne, Alexander Crummell, Harriet Tubman, Sojourner Truth, Edward Blyden, Frederick Douglass, W. E. B. DuBois, Martin Luther King Jr., and countless others. A recently acclaimed HBO movie, entitled *Harriet*, vividly portrays the escape, heroism, and accomplishments of that legendary icon, Harriett Tubman herself, whose life began in Cambridge, Maryland, in 1820 and ended in Auburn, New York, in 1913.

Long before William Lloyd Garrison and other whites in England and America became abolitionists, blacks had hoped and striven for deliverance from slavery. Their strivings towards that goal gave both national and international visibility to the cause. In 1829, David Walker, a free black man in Boston, self-published a small book that demonstrated not only sympathetic concern for his enslaved brethren in the Southern states, but the courageous skills he had honed at that time in communicating with them across the wide divide between the free and slave states. His book was entitled *An Appeal to the Colored Citizens of the World*. Known as "Walker's Appeal," historians have praised it as one of the greatest documents of the nineteenth century. Cleverly transported to the South through various creative channels, its impact affected not only the entire abolitionist movement throughout the century, but also influenced such iconic black leaders as Henry Highland Garnet, Booker T. Washington, and Frederick Douglass in the nineteenth century, as well as such notable twentieth-century leaders as W. E. B. DuBois, Thurgood Marshall, and Martin Luther King Jr. Its revolutionary tone explicitly called for the immediate emancipation of all slaves and full citizenship rights for all. It blatantly condemned the hypocrisy of white Christians whose faith in the one universal God was contradicted daily by their unjust practices towards both enslaved and free blacks alike. And the most radical notion of all was his call for blacks to rebel against the system of slavery.

Though not directly influential on the thought of Gabriel Prosser, whose planned rebellion in 1800 was thwarted by an informant, or that of Denmark Vesey, whose conspiracy to revolt was similarly stymied in 1822, Walker's thought helped to justify those attempts long after their demise. Though the limited success of Nat Turner's rebellion in 1831 greatly shocked the entire slavocracy, many viewed it as the paramount example of what Walker's appeal had advocated. It is interesting to note, however, that both Vesey and Turner were clergymen and Gabriel Prosser was also well read in the Bible. Those facts helped to cement both the reality of human agency among the slaves and the constant fear of white slave owners of rebellion by the slaves.

Little did the slave owners know, however, that their omnipresent fear of slave revolts was an implicit recognition of the humanity of the slaves themselves, because resistance to oppression is a primary indicator of human subjectivity. This was acknowledged by many, including the twentieth-century French existentialist philosopher and novelist Albert Camus, much of whose thought centered on the subject of resistance, and who was a source of inspiration for James H. Cone, the progenitor of the Black Theology movement in the United States.[7] As early as the latter part of the nineteenth century, the stellar abolitionist leader, Frederick Douglass, himself a runaway slave, issued the motto for all who are bereft of their humanity to "agitate, agitate, agitate," because he was convinced that the agitation itself signified their humanity.

Despite all the endeavors of whites to prove that blacks were not wholly human, there is not a shred of evidence that the latter ever doubted their membership in the human family. Rather, in countless ways, they resisted every endeavor by whites to define them as inferior beings by teaching their children otherwise, by resisting their oppression either directly or indirectly, and by their actions of love and respect towards one another, including their master's children whom they birthed after brutal rapes either by their masters themselves, their kinsmen, or their overseers. The love of enslaved black women for their children revealed the spirit of maternal empathy that never blamed those innocent ones for the sins of their fathers. Yet, blacks were never naïve in thinking that whites would easily abandon either the institution of slavery or the doctrine of white supremacy, both of which had benefited them abundantly.

---

7. See Camus, *The Rebel*, and Cone, *Black Theology and Black Power*, 6, 13–14.

THE BLACK SEPARATIONIST AND INCLUSIVIST
TRADITIONS

In the middle of the twentieth century, the iconic African-American nation-alist leader, Malcolm X, converted to the Islamic faith that had been taught to him by a disciple of the honorable Elijah Muhammad, the founder of The Black Muslims in America, now known as the Nation of Islam. Impressed by his loyalty, devotion, and excellent speaking ability, Muhammad soon elevated him to the position of official spokesman for the organization. One of the pillars of his teaching was the absolute futility of African Americans to argue for civil rights, because he claimed that the overwhelming major-ity of white Americans rejected any notion of human equality between the two races. Thus, as Elijah Muhammad's spokesman, Malcolm X concluded whites were incurable racists and, hence, incapable of ever changing their minds on that subject. In his mind, the doctrine of white supremacy that became the law of the land in the 1896 Supreme Court *Plesy v. Ferguson* decision rightly depicted the true nature of white Americans and, hence, its overturn by the 1954 Supreme Court's *Brown v. Board of Education* decision was a blatant contradiction. Further, he argued that the subsequent struggle for civil rights by African Americas, which they thought was supported by the law, made no sense. Malcolm's passion, humor, and fiery rhetoric made an indelible impression on all blacks who heard him, whether or not they were Muslims. Yet, the *Brown v. Board of Education* decision pumped new blood into the various endeavors of the three major civil rights organiza-tions at that time, namely, the National Association for the Advancement of Colored People (NAACP), the National Urban League (NUL), and the Congress of Racial Equality (CORE).

In Montgomery, Alabama, however, that inherent spirit of black resis-tance, emboldened by the 1954 decision, was bent on bringing a case before the courts challenging racially segregated seating in public transportation. Months later, Rosa Parks, the secretary of the local chapter of the Mont-gomery NAACP, refused to give up her seat on a bus to a white man, as was the custom when the reserved seats for whites were all occupied. The arrest of such a respectable person as Parks aroused the anger and disgust of all blacks in the city, including Ed Nixon, the president of the local chapter of the NAACP who, along with Joanne Robinson, the secretary of the Wom-en's Political Action committee, called for a protest meeting at the Bethel African American Methodist Church. Since Nixon, a porter on the train, was required to report to work that day, he strategically asked the Rev. Dr. Martin Luther King Jr. to chair the meeting in his stead. King was a twenty-six-year-old newcomer to the city, pastor of the Dexter Avenue Baptist

Church, and already respected for his education and speaking ability. For the first time anywhere in the South, the meeting decided to organize a mass boycott of the buses under the auspices of the newly formed Montgomery Improvement Association (MIA). Thirteen months later, after the bombings of several homes, including that of Martin Luther King Jr. himself, their courageous action resulted in the Supreme Court decision *Browder v. Gayle* that declared the Alabama and Montgomery laws that segregated buses unconstitutional.

Soon thereafter, with the assistance of Northern sympathizers and such experienced activists as Bayard Rustin, Ella Baker, and others, a conference of black clergy was organized at the Ebenezer Baptist Church in Atlanta that resulted in the formation of the Southern Christian Leadership Conference (SCLC). Its mission was to coordinate and support non-violent direct action as a method of desegregating buses throughout the South. Those events combined to mark the beginning of the mid-twentieth century civil rights movement.[8] In 1960, the Student Non-Violent Co-ordinating Council (SNCC) was formed by students to institutionalize their protest activities that were thought too radical to be contained within the parent organization, SCLC. Thus, the three major historic civil rights organizations mentioned above were expanded to five and, at that time, all believed that the law was finally on their side in support of their advocacy for civil rights. Thus, they all believed that a new day had begun.

Though their public protests for first-class citizenship rights (commonly referred to at the time as racial integration) seemingly had the support of federal law, blacks remained stymied by the power of the various state customs and laws that they were bent on testing all the way to the Supreme Court. That implied the necessity of opposing the unjust state laws on moral grounds while accepting the consequent punishment of being jailed as proof of their respect for law per se.

Thus, in the summer of 1961 the Congress of Racial Equality (CORE) launched an inter-racial interstate "freedom ride" bus protest through the South to protest segregated bus terminals by non-violently disobeying those laws. Their purpose was to test the Supreme Court decision in *Boynton v. Virginia* that racial segregation at bus terminals was unconstitutional. One of the students was twenty-one-year-old John Lewis from Alabama who, along with several others, suffered severe beatings along the way. Undeterred, he continued his studies and eventually became president of Student Non-violent Coordinating Council (SNCC) and the youngest speaker to address the 1963 March on Washington for Equal Rights and Jobs. He later

8. See King, *Stride toward Freedom*.

became Georgia's representative in the US Congress, where he eventually gained the title, "the conscience of the house," because of his undaunted commitment to the philosophy and practice of non-violent resistance, coupled with his persuasive speeches on the floor of the house. Amidst the fire bombings of the buses and bloodied beatings on several subsequent bus rides during that summer, public sympathy along with the appeals of their ally, Attorney General Robert F. Kennedy, the Interstate Commerce Commission finally decided on September 22, 1961, to abolish racial segregation in interstate travel.

Unfortunately, all of the so-called civil rights victories occurred after numerous bombings of homes and buses, many beatings, maimings, and killings of protestors. Those severe costs in both property and lives gradually caused many to doubt the efficacy of advocacy through non-violent protests. In other words, every seeming legal victory seemed to quell the protests while not eradicating the basic cause of systemic racism itself. Rather, racism seemed invariably to morph repeatedly into some new expressive form that rendered credence to Malcolm X's claim that white America's racism was indeed incurable and its laws suggesting otherwise were a joke.

Let us hasten to say, however, that the twentieth-century civil rights struggle began long before the 1954 *Brown v. Board of Education* Supreme Court decision. In 1906, the Niagara movement was formed under the inspirational leadership of W. E. B. DuBois. It soon melted into the National Association for the Advancement of Colored People (NAACP) in 1909, with DuBois as the editor of its official publication, *The Crisis Magazine*, to which most black households throughout the country gradually subscribed. DuBois held that influential position for a quarter of a century while writing many books, as well as assuming the role as pioneer organizer of several Pan-African conferences in London and Paris between 1900 and 1945. Needless to say, however, DuBois was accompanied during all those years by a plethora of men and women, both black and white, whom he viewed as exemplars of his theory of leadership that he called the "talented tenth." It was based on the notion that the top 10 percent of any race constituted its leadership class. In due course, the NAACP parented an auxiliary organization in order to comply with the tax code by separating its strong mission of education and advocacy for civil rights. That new organization was founded in 1940 and named the NAACP Legal and Educational Fund (LDF). It has been called the country's "first and foremost civil and human rights law firm." Then and now, its mission remains the following:

> The NAACP Legal Defense and Educational Fund, Inc. is America's premier legal organization fighting for racial justice.

Through litigation, advocacy, and public education, LDF seeks
structural changes to expand democracy, eliminate disparities,
and achieve racial justice in a society that fulfills the promise
of equality for all Americans. LDF also defends the gains and
protections won over the past 80 years of civil rights struggle
and works to improve the quality and diversity of judicial and
executive appointments.[9]

The most notable achievement of the NAACP Legal Defense Fund was
heralded by its founder and first director-counsel, Thurgood Marshall, who
successfully argued the above stated 1954 *Brown v. Board of Education* Supreme Court decision which became the legal basis for the mid-twentieth
century civil rights movement led by the Rev. Dr. Martin Luther King Jr. We
should note, however, that King was the first black leader to launch non-violent mass protest demonstrations in support of equal civil rights for blacks
and in opposition to the practices of racial segregation and discrimination
that dominated all life in the South as well as large parts of the North.

Clearly, the major difference between the leadership styles of Malcolm
X and Martin Luther King Jr. lay in their opposing judgments about whether or not whites would ever concede to the desires of African Americans
for full citizenship rights. Their different positions on that question were
not due primarily to the obstinacy of two strong willed men, but to the
experiential teachings of two major historical perspectives in the African-
American tradition that date back as far as the days of slavery. Malcolm X
stood in a separatist tradition that was evidenced by all those who sought
freedom by escaping from slavery in search for racially separate environ-
ments where they had no need to fear the terror of bondage. That tradition of flight was long personified by the courageous clandestine work of a
woman named Tubman who, an escaped slave herself, returned to the cauldron of slavery nineteen times to liberate her people via the underground
railroad, a network of safe places to hide during the day while fleeing in
the night. Under her guidance and that of others, countless numbers risked
their lives by following the "north star" in search for freedom in both the
Northern states and central Canada, where they lived in racially segregated
sections of white towns and cities. After the Civil War, some attempted to
form "All Black Towns" or "Freedom Towns," several of which have endured
to the present day.[10]

In addition to the methods of escape and revolt, the separatist tradition in which Malcolm X stood utilized institutional forms that were

9. See the mission statement on the website: www.naacpldf.org/naacp-mission.

10. See Brown, "All-Black Towns across America."

devised and chosen by blacks themselves, rather than imposed on them by whites. Such methods usually aroused the fears of whites, even though their goals of their separatist orientation seemed in some respects to be similar to those of racial segregation. But the two are profoundly different. Racial separation has always been satisfying to blacks because it is chosen by them. Racial segregation was always abhorrent to them because it was imposed on them and thus denied them both dignity and freedom of choice. The separatist tradition found its home in the black churches, black schools, black hospitals, black residential areas, black social clubs, black fraternities, black sororities, black mortuaries, black businesses, black sporting leagues, black newspapers, and black radio stations, to name only a few. Unlike segregation, which was maintained by force, the separatist tradition was nurtured and sustained by choice.

Contrary to the fictional claims of Harriet Beecher Stowe in her famous book, *Uncle Tom's Cabin,* blacks were never content with the system of slavery or with racial discrimination and segregation, because each denied them the dignity of personhood, economic well-being, and the rights and privileges of equal citizenship. As we have seen, the struggle for their humanity necessarily preceded all claims for civil rights, and that struggle was undertaken by themselves for themselves. Apart from their own self-understanding, blacks found affirmation of their humanity in the Christian faith, which they first encountered from white evangelists during the so-called Great Awakenings that began in the early decades of the eighteenth century. By improvising on that inheritance, they gradually made it their own in both form and substance.

Another significant exemplar of the racial separatist tradition in the twentieth century was Marcus Garvey, an immigrant from Jamaica. His Back-to-Africa movement made an indelible mark on the masses of blacks in general, as well as the above-mentioned Elijah Muhammad. Though that movement flourished in the United States for only a short period of time (1915–1922), its memorable impact has been felt up to the present day, mainly because of the emphasis it placed on the beauty and dignity of African peoples and their common ancestral continental homeland, Africa. Most of all, it both advocated for racial self-development and highly praised the capacity of African peoples for their independence, self-reliance, self-initiative, and self-determination as manifested in the world they built under the severe conditions of slavery in American and its cruel societal aftermath. Its matchless contribution, however, was the pride in blackness it created which, in turn, inspired the rise of the Nation of Islam, commonly known in the 1930s as the Black Muslim movement, founded in Detroit by Elijah Muhammad who had migrated north from Georgia. The separatist tradition also influenced the black consciousness movement, as exemplified in the arts movement known as the Harlem Renaissance in the 1930s, the black power movement of the 1960s, black caucuses within white denominations, the demand for African-American studies programs in white colleges and universities, and their ready acceptance of Professor Derrick Bell's critical race theory as a cherished method of inquiry and analysis in higher education.

Unlike the separatist tradition exemplified by Malcolm X, the inclusivist tradition personified by Martin Luther King Jr and his followers has a much shorter history because it did not begin until after the Civil War when the thirteenth, fourteenth, and fifteenth amendments to the constitution were enacted and institutionalized in the federal government during the short period of the Reconstruction era (1865–1877). As stated above, the fall of Reconstruction marked the beginning of the so-called Jim Crow era in American history, where the laws of the Southern states and their customary practices denied blacks all the rights and privileges afforded to whites. For a century following the Civil War, that *ethos* permeated not only the South, but most of the North, as well. Thus, throughout the greater part of American history, racial segregation and discrimination have characterized every dimension of life, including the nation's cemeteries. Those practices remained intact up through the 1960s, when, only then, blacks had the support of the law in adjudicating their grievances and demands for justice.

Gradually, since the late 1960s, the *ethos* underlying racial separation, and threatened for a time by the press for racial integration, has gained respect throughout black America. While not obliterating the implicit values attending racial inclusivism, blacks no longer view the latter as an exclusive intrinsic moral good to be pursued at all cost. Consequently, in the black theological academy and generally in the arts, these two traditions continue to be discussed and debated regularly. Examples of this convergence are seen in the Black Theology movement that emerged in 1969 with the publication of James H .Cone's first book, *Black Theology and Black Power*. Subsequently, the founding of the Society for the Study of Black Religion sought to provide a necessary space for black religious scholars to meet and encourage one another's works in order to strengthen one another for more effective engagement in the predominantly white American Academy of Religion, the Society of Biblical Literature, the Society of Christian Ethics, the Society of Homiletics, and many more both within the religious academy and far beyond.

The various struggles within predominantly white colleges and universities by black students for black faculty, black administrators, and black studies programs, were soon embraced by women and other ethnic groups.

Those activities gradually resulted in the endorsement of racial, ethnic, gender, and even class diversity as a positive value not only in academia, but in all parts of the culture, including the professions, the military, the media, film industry, and the corporate worlds and their various award systems.

In brief, the values implicit in both the black separatist and inclusivist traditions have been sources of creativity, empowerment, and celebration for all concerned. Though both traditions carry on their respective works separately, each is constantly aware of the other from which each draws insight, constructive criticism, and affirmation. More often than not, representatives of each tradition are able to affirm the values implicit in the other without striving to dissolve itself into the other.

While not obliterating the implicit value of racial integration, blacks no longer view racial integration as an unquestioned moral good. In the black theological academy, these two traditions have been discussed and debated incessantly since the Black Theology movement was born in 1969. That movement has sought to unite the two traditions of racial inclusivism and racial separation by affirming the values implicit in each. Yet, insufficient common ground between the two renders any complete union of the two undesirable.

Suffice it is to say that the ongoing separatist tradition continues its goal of racial justice through the empowerment of blacks in all dimensions of their lives. In pursuit of that goal, their advocates support all endeavors that contribute to its actualization and oppose all obstacles along the way. Similarly, the ongoing inclusivist tradition continues to monitor critically all legal structures pertaining to our shared societal life with an eye towards correcting all dents and cracks in that structure that threaten racial justice in any way. Given the long, bitter history of racial injustice, such oversight is necessary to preserve the health and expansion of what has been achieved thus far, such that the inclusivist and separatist traditions in the black experience continue to complement each other and not dissipate.

The rise of the Black Lives Matter Global Network Foundation, Inc., in 2013 constituted a response to the acquittal of young Trayvon Martin's murderer. Its mission is to eradicate white supremacy and build strong local resistance to violence inflicted on the black community by the police and vigilantes. This movement reaches out to an expansive support system in advocating for equal justice for all. After the cruel deaths of George Floyd (May 25, 2020) and Breonna Taylor (March 13, 2020), numerous cities in the United States, Canada, Europe, Brazil, and elsewhere witnessed large numbers of protestors occupying the streets for many weeks during the summer of 2020. The Black Lives Matter movement supports all oppressed groups including women, the LBGTQIA+ folk, those who are undocumented, disabled, and those who have records for having been incarcerated.

Most importantly, the Black Lives Matter Network centers much of its energy on condemning state-sanctioned violence against blacks and all other oppressed groups, which brings it into alignment with nineteenth-century abolitionist groups and non-violent twentieth-century civil rights activists like Representative John Lewis, who days before his death stood in the nascent Black Lives Matter Plaza in Washington, DC, named by Mayor Muriel Bowser after federal law enforcement agents removed peaceful demonstrators in June 2020. The motorcade carrying Lewis's body stopped at the plaza on its way to the Capitol, where it lay in state before going to Atlanta, Georgia, where the funeral was held at the Ebenezer Baptist Church long pastored by the father and grand-father of Martin Luther King Jr.

BIBLIOGRAPHY

Bell, Derrick. *Race, Racism and American Law.* 3rd ed. Boston: Little, Brown and Co., 1992.

Brown, DeNeen L. "All-Black Towns across America: Life Was Hard, but Full of Promise." *Washington Post*, March 27, 2015. https://www.washingtonpost.com/lifestyle/style/a-list-of-well-known-black-towns/2015/03/27/9f21ca42-cdc4-11e4-a2a7-9517a3a70506_story.html.

Camus, Albert. *The Rebel.* Translated by Anthony Bower. New York: Random House, 1956.

Cone, James H. *Black Theology and Black Power.* New York: Seabury, 1969

Evans, Gavin. "The Unwelcome Revival of Race Science." *Guardian*, March 2, 2018. https://www.theguardian.com/news/2018/mar/02/the-unwelcome-revival-of-race-science.

King, Martin Luther, Jr. *Stride Toward Freedom: The Montgomery Story.* New York: Harper and Row, 1958.

Painter, Nel Irvin. *The History of White People.* New York: W. W. Norton and Co., 2010.

Paris, Peter J. *The Social Teaching of the Black Churches.* Philadelphia: Fortress, 1985.

Thomas, Hugh. *The Slave Trade: The Story of the Atlantic Slave Trade, 1440–1870.* New York: Simon and Schuster, 1997.

BEYOND BINARY MORAL
AND POLITICAL ADVOCACY ON ABORTION

Rubén Rosario Rodríguez

INTRODUCTION

IN THE UNITED STATES, no issue highlights the blurring of lines between the theoretical and the practical—ethics and advocacy—more clearly than the battle over abortion. The partisan division along Rural/Urban, Red/Blue, Republican/Democrat, and conservative/liberal lines in the US is not particularly helpful when trying to have a nuanced conversation about abortion. Cultural and religious conservatives who oppose abortion frame the discourse around the inherent dignity and sacredness of human life, while the more politically liberal, who favor legalized abortion, argue from a foundation of constitutionally protected individual freedoms to advocate for women's reproductive rights. One is left with a seemingly insurmountable divide in which *real human suffering* during a time of crisis becomes *secondary* to ideological and political commitments. Theologically and pastorally, reducing a pressing bioethical concern to competing social and political agendas ignores the model of compassionate care embodied by Jesus in the Gospels. It also shifts the focus away from the person in crisis toward abstract principles.

Taking my cue from liberation theology's pastoral and practical emphasis on alleviating human suffering and following the example of Jesus, who focused his ministry around the concrete needs of particular persons, this essay seeks an alternative model of Christian ethics beyond mere *partisan* activism by creating a space wherein genuine conversation can happen outside the dominant polarities. Through an examination of Jesus' example of compassionate care, with its grounding in concrete communal networks of support, the goal is to present a viable and normative approach to Christian ethics and advocacy on abortion that transcends the single-issue politics currently dominating the discourse.

SINGLE-ISSUE POLITICS: BEYOND THE IMPASSE

There is a new orthodoxy in the Democratic Party. Previously, the party articulated a middle ground between pro-life and pro-abortion extremes by working to keep abortion "safe, legal, and rare," a position restated during Hillary Clinton's first presidential bid in 2008: "and by rare, I mean rare."[1] Clinton cautioned we ought not lose sight of abortion as a wrenching personal decision that "should not in any way be diminished as a moral issue."[2] Barrack Obama ran two successful presidential campaigns by winning the crucial (predominately pro-life) Catholic vote in both 2008 and 2012, supporting *Roe v. Wade* yet expressing "moral reservations about abortion itself."[3] Obama's presidency embodied the Clinton ideal of "safe, legal, and rare" by remaining open to additional restrictions on (especially late-term) abortion and focusing on a set of "policies with the purpose of reducing the abortion rate in America, such as paid family leave, workplace protections for parents and pregnant women, increased access to birth control and a strengthened social safety net."[4] Consequently, when Obama left office the abortion rate was at a historic low, which many attribute to a comprehensive strategy that not only sought to keep abortion legal, but also worked to eliminate the need for abortions.[5] In fact, candidate Obama went on record about abortion in 2008 employing terms none of the candidates in the 2016 Democratic primary used:

> I have repeatedly said that I think it's entirely appropriate for
> states to restrict or even prohibit late-term abortions as long

1. Candidate Clinton restated her position as part of an in-depth discussion of religion, faith, and politics hosted by the Sojourners Presidential Forum on the campus of George Washington University in Washington, DC, broadcast as a special edition of CNN's "The Situation Room" on June 4, 2007.

2. Clinton, "The Situation Room."

3. Wear, "Democrats Shouldn't Be So Certain About Abortion."

4. Wear, "Democrats Shouldn't Be So Certain About Abortion."

5. Cha, "Number of abortions in U.S. hit historic low in 2015, the most recent year for which data is available."

as there is a strict, well-defined exception for the health of the mother. Now, I don't think that "mental distress" qualifies as the health of the mother. I think it has to be a serious physical issue that arises in pregnancy, where there are real, significant problems to the mother carrying that child to term.[6]

Unfortunately, when Hillary Clinton ran against Donald Trump in 2016, there was a noticeable shift in both her own position and that of the Democratic Party, which contributed to her not only losing the Catholic vote in 2016, but losing with conservative Christian voters across the board.[7]

This new Democratic orthodoxy appears as absolutist as the extreme right of the pro-life movement, as evidenced by this tweet from the Ohio chapter of NARAL Pro-Choice America: "This is a position—making abortion 'rare'—not supported by pro-choice advocates."[8] The pro-abortion-rights group Shout Your Abortion goes even further, working to undermine the very notion of abortion as a morally debatable decision: "I cannot think of a less compelling way to advocate for something than saying that it should be rare. And anyone who uses that phrase is operating from the assumption that abortion is a bad thing."[9] Perhaps no single moment encapsulates the new Democratic orthodoxy more than the 2016 party line calling for the repeal of the Hyde Amendment, which in the words of Clinton campaign staffers made the 2016 Democratic platform "the most ambitious and progressive our party has ever seen,"[10] and marked the first time the party openly called for an end to the decades-old ban on federal funding for abortion by arguing that the lack of public funding for abortion services disproportionately affects the poor and women of color. It is possible to take a position that supports bringing fetal life to birth and makes abortion rare while supporting public funding for poor persons who are forced to abort. Unfortunately, the way in which the Democratic Party made this shift in policy has been perceived as disregarding public opinion in an effort to appease a vocal and powerful progressive minority within the party.

Since the Supreme Court's 1973 ruling in Roe v. Wade, US voters have been consistently moderate on abortion, with 44 percent of Americans asserting that abortion is morally wrong even as 59 percent of Americans

6. Strang, "Q&A With Barack Obama."

7. Martínez and Smith, "How the faithful voted." CNN, New York Times, and the Pew Research Center all had Trump winning among conservative Christian voters: 81 percent of white evangelical voters, 61 percent of Mormon voters, 58 percent mainline Protestant voters, and 52 percent of Catholic voters.

8. DeSanctis, "How Democrats purged 'safe, legal, rare' from the party."

9. Solis, "Tulsi Gabbard's Stance on Abortion Is Stuck in the '90s."

10. Tatum, "Clinton campaign hails progressive Democratic platform."

support legalized abortion.[11] The polling reveals that Americans have a more nuanced view of the moral complexities of abortion beyond the two dominant advocacy groups (pro-life and pro-choice) that have framed and controlled the public debate. In the words of one pollster, "the public has diverse views on abortion. But it's rarely a split between 'abortion is right' and 'abortion is wrong.'"[12] Despite the push from pro-choice advocates to remove the stigma of abortion, a consistent number of adults—including a sizeable percentage of those who identify as pro-choice—still consider abortion a moral "gray area," as articulated by one of the participants in the 2015 *Vox* poll: "I guess if you're raped or in a desperate situation, then abortion would be the way to go, but if you're just being careless and irresponsible, then I don't think it's the right decision."[13]

Gene Burns in *The Moral Veto: Framing Contraception, Abortion, and Cultural Pluralism in the United States* (2005), offers a historical and sociological analysis of the pro-life and pro-choice movements that seeks to find alternative modes of discourse beyond the ruling binary between both advocacy groups. Burns identifies contradictions running through the twentieth-century history of US reproductive politics, such as the fact that prior to *Roe v. Wade*, "the liberalization of abortion laws sailed through a number of state legislatures."[14] In fact, before this landmark 1973 Supreme Court decision, there was little "grassroots concern for, or even awareness of, abortion as a public issue"; instead, "numbers of liberalizing physicians, lawyers, and clerics advocated new, more lenient laws, the goal of such laws being to allow unhindered the professional and humanitarian practice of medicine."[15] But once the debate entered the public consciousness via *Roe v. Wade*, it did not take long for grassroots advocacy movements on both sides to mobilize large segments of the American electorate. In concord with the data of the 2015 *Vox* poll, Burns' analysis of US reproductive politics presents a more nuanced and diverse set of perspectives or frameworks from which to approach the conversation on abortion. Recognizing how each perspective frames the discussion reveals the guiding values of that particular community or interest group and sets limits about what they are willing to debate and discuss while demarcating that which is beyond debate.

Within this set of competing frameworks, each with distinct narratives, goals, and limiting values, conversation need not die simply because

11. Lipka and Gramlich, "5 facts about the abortion debate in America."
12. Cliff, "What Americans think of abortion."
13. Cliff, "What Americans think of abortion."
14. Burns, *The Moral Veto*, 4.
15. Burns, *The Moral Veto*, 5.

the leading players have conflicting end goals, since the "different sides on an issue are in fact *not* directly negating the position of the other side, but rather that they think that the other side's position is a distraction from the *real* issue."[16] Applying Burns' paradigm to the contemporary abortion debate, it is not constructive to take a position directly opposite one's opponent, choosing instead a strategy that frames the debate in different terms, implying the opponent's position is irrelevant to the issue at hand.

Competing frames naturally attempt to control the public discourse on abortion, but in a pluralistic democratic society—where tolerance and dissensus are valued and even necessary for healthy public discourse—authoritarian attempts to stifle dialogue by imposing absolutist claims tend to fail in the political arena (and even more so in the moral arena).

According to Burns, each framework also has its own potential "moral veto." In a pluralistic society, when an otherwise effective social movement with a long track record of organizing and advocacy fails to attain its ultimate goals—like the Christian pro-life movement's long-sought constitutional amendment to ban abortion and overthrow *Roe v. Wade*—said movement "often has considerable success *vetoing* the goals of its opponents."[17] That is to say, "movements or groups that explicitly promote a moral worldview can serve very effectively as an opposition to the initiatives that it opposes, even when *its own* initiatives are not going anywhere. Its strategic success, then, is primarily negative rather than positive."[18] The polling data bears out Burns's analysis, given that despite almost fifty years of concerted efforts at overturning *Roe v. Wade,* the majority of Americans (61 percent) still believe abortion should be *legal* in all or most cases, while only 38 percent say abortion should be illegal all or most of the time.[19] Thus, despite clear losses in the court of public opinion, the pro-life framework remains a viable and important player precisely because it offers an *alternative* to the politics of choice and reproductive freedom: 48 percent of Americans still believe abortion is morally wrong, even when the same poll shows 55 percent believe abortion ought to remain legal (with some restrictions).[20] In other words, despite the pro-choice movement's efforts to de-stigmatize abortion by focusing either on the constitutional rights of women, or discussing abortion as a purely private medical decision, it remains a morally

16. Burns, *The Moral Veto,* 9.

17. Burns, *The Moral Veto,* 22.

18. Burns, *The Moral Veto,* 22.

19. Lipka and Gramlich, "5 facts about the abortion debate in America."

20. Lipka and Gramlich, "5 facts about the abortion debate in America."

ambiguous choice which in the minds of many still constitutes the death of a (potential) human life.

By moving away from the moderate paradigm of keeping abortion "safe, legal, and rare," the Democratic Party has embraced an absolutist stance that factored heavily in the 2016 presidential election and has the potential of alienating large subsections of the American electorate.[21] Donald Trump, who was behind in all the polling leading up to the November election, attacked the new DNC platform by aggressively presenting Clinton as the "pro-abortion" candidate in the final 2016 presidential debate:

> If you go with what Hillary is saying, in the ninth month, you can take the baby and rip the baby out of the womb of the mother. Just prior to the birth of the baby. You can say that that's OK and Hillary can say that that's OK, but it's not OK with me. Because based on what she's saying and based on where she's going and where she's been, you can take the baby and rip the baby out of the womb. In the ninth month. On the final day. And that's not acceptable.[22]

Despite Hillary Clinton's effort to recast Trump's remarks as "scare rhetoric," her response reiterated the new Democratic hardline on abortion: "This is one of the worst possible choices that any woman and her family has to make. And I do not believe the government should be making it."[23] In doing so, Clinton employed scare rhetoric of her own:

> I've been to countries where governments either force women to have abortions like they used to do in China, or forced women to bear children like they used to do in Romania. And I can tell you, the government has no business in the decisions that women make with their families in accordance with their faith, with medical advice, and I will stand up for that right.[24]

Since his 2016 victory, Donald Trump has appointed two hundred federal judges. Three conservative justices to the Supreme Court (Gorsuch, Kavanaugh, and Barrett) supported a federal ban on all abortions after twenty weeks known as the Pain-Capable Unborn Child Protection Act,[25]

---

21. See DeSanctis, "How Democrats purged 'safe, legal, rare'"; Wear, "Democrats Shouldn't Be So Certain About Abortion"; and Groome, "To Win Again."

22. Jensen, "Clinton, Trump."

23. Jensen, "Clinton, Trump."

24. Jensen, "Clinton, Trump."

25. H.R. 36 also contained these provisos: "unless the abortion is judged necessary to save the life of the mother; is the result of a rape of an adult woman who has received counseling or medical treatment for the rape; or is the result of an act of rape or incest

and threatened to stop federal funding of Planned Parenthood. In a bit of election year theatrics, recalling the time President Obama became the first sitting president to address the national Planned Parenthood Conference,[26] Donald Trump became the first sitting president to speak at the annual March for Life in 2020, declaring: "Unborn children have never had a stronger defender in the White House."[27] Without question, there has been an increased absolutism of the pro-life movement that predated Trump but was emboldened by his 2016 electoral victory, which has sought to restrict abortion, overturn *Roe v. Wade* (within the realm of possibility given the new 6–3 conservative majority on the Supreme Court), and defund Planned Parenthood. But the Democratic strategy of embracing abortion absolutism, given the American public's more moderate views on abortion summarized above, undermines genuine moral discourse. This effort to reframe abortion advocacy aims—as much as possible—at maintaining both the dignity of fetal life and the dignity of women and families in crisis.

Joe Biden was able to narrowly reclaim the Catholic vote in 2020, but much of Biden's electoral success can be attributed to four years of presidential dysfunction—especially during the global COVID-19 pandemic—than to specific policy proposals. Furthermore, exit polls reveal that abortion remains a tipping factor for key segments of the voting public. During the 2020 campaign, Joe Biden reversed his longstanding position in support of the Hyde Amendment in order to appease the new party orthodoxy and court the younger, more progressive wing of the party. This position was reinforced by selecting Kamala Harris, who received praise from Planned Parenthood for her consistent support of reproductive rights and in 2019 a 100 percent "choice rating" by NARAL Pro-Choice America.[28] The new Democratic Party orthodoxy was reiterated by all the candidates during the 2020 presidential primaries: Kirsten Gillibrand declared that the Democratic Party should "be 100 percent pro-choice, and it should be nonnegotiable"; Cory Booker called abortion rights "sacrosanct"; and Kamala Harris tweeted, "As President, I will stop dangerous state laws restricting reproductive rights before they go into effect."[29] In November 2020, the Democratic Attorneys General Association (DAGA) announced it requires candidates to support abortion rights *before* receiving DAGA's endorsement

---

against a minor that has been reported to a law enforcement agency or other government authority." See https://www.congress.gov/bill/115th-congress/house-bill/36/text.

26. See Obama, "Remarks by the President at the Planned Parenthood Conference."

27. Dias et al., "Trump Tells Anti-Abortion Marchers."

28. See Gonzales, "Where Does Kamala Harris Stand"

29. See Murdock, "The Future of the Pro-Life Democrat."

or financial assistance, the first time a Democratic campaign committee has required such an explicitly pro-choice litmus test.[30] A growing number of pro-life Democrats feel marginalized and excluded from the party, including more religiously conservative constituencies still solidly within the Democratic Party faithful (an estimated 21 million pro-life voters).[31] One in three Americans ranked abortion as the top issue heading into the 2020 presidential election,[32] yet at the 2020 Democratic National Convention, Democrats for Life were excluded from the official party platform.

Joe Biden won the 2020 election by relying on traditional Democratic bases like African-American, Latino/a, and Asian-American voters, but a closer look at these constituencies' views on abortion is warranted, especially as there are indications of a growing gap between the party leadership and the party faithful. While the party justifies its opposition to the Hyde Amendment, claiming that a lack of federal funding for abortion disproportionately impacts the poor and women of color, 66 percent of black Democrats support legal abortion as compared to 83 percent of white Democrats, and when asked if "voters should support only candidates who favor legal abortion" 35 percent of white Democrats agree while only a paltry 7 percent of black Democrats answer affirmatively.[33] Dorothy Roberts' milestone study, *Killing the Black Body: Race, Reproduction, and the Meaning of Liberty* (1997), problematizes abortion from a black feminist perspective by arguing that the dominant reproductive rights narrative has focused on white "women's increasing control over their reproductive decisions, centered on the right to an abortion" to the neglect of the harrowing history of "dehumanizing attempts to control Black women's reproductive lives."[34] In light of this social reality, Cherilyn Holloway, founder of Pro-Black Pro-Life, argues that Democrats cannot commit to fighting racism while promoting abortion in black communities: "Do you want to help my community? Stop providing funding to these abortion clinics."[35]

Trump won 35 percent of the historically Democratic Latino/a vote in 2020 (up from 29 percent in 2016), due in large part to his pro-life agenda (though it could be argued "anti-abortion" is a more accurate descriptor). A 2019 survey by the Public Religion Research Institute (PRRI) found that most Hispanics identify as pro-life, with 58 percent of Hispanic Protestants

---

30. Murdock, "The Future of the Pro-Life Democrat."
31. Robles, "Pro-life Dems protest"
32. Murray, "Abortion a Factor in 2020 Vote."
33. DeSanctis, "How Democrats purged 'safe, legal, rare."
34. Roberts, *Killing the Black Body*, 4.
35. Hadro, "We will not be ignored."

(evangelical and non-evangelicals) and 52 percent of Hispanic Catholics responding abortion should be illegal in all or most cases, making Hispanics the only US demographic in which a consistent majority identifies as pro-life.[36]

In 2020, both parties courted the US Latino/a vote, prompting the Rev. Gabriel Salguero, president of the National Latino Evangelical Coalition, to caution that Hispanics are not single-issue voters, but seek a holistic agenda that addresses their concerns as Hispanics *and* evangelicals: "We're pro-life. We want criminal justice reform. We want educational equity. We want a healthy economy. Because we're not one-issue voters, people think if they come to us with talking points they're gonna get us—no."[37]

Like the Latino/a voting block, Asian American and Pacific Islanders (API) constitute a diverse group representing different nations, religious perspectives, and linguistic traditions. While Asian Americans are more religiously diverse than the general US population, Asian-American Christians have similar voting patterns to Latino/a populations.[38] A growing number of Asian-American evangelicals for whom pro-life concerns are important have embraced their political power, and like Latino/a voters, do not want to be perceived as single-issue voters:

> As a Christian, I believe that I am called to a consistent ethic of life, from womb to tomb. I don't believe in being defined by a single issue . . . Everything is interconnected . . . there is no realm of life that is off limits to the work of God. If Jesus is coming to redeem all creation, then God has something to say about all aspects of life.[39]

Given this diversity of perspectives on abortion *within* the Democratic Party, a continued push toward pro-choice absolutism undermines the possibility of a more nuanced ethical argument in support of legalized abortion and public funding for the most disadvantaged populations. African American, Latino/a, and Asian American advocates do not want to be reduced to any single political issue, but neither do they want the moral worth of the most vulnerable lives—be it the unborn fetus or the economically and politically marginalized mother—trampled by either party's absolutist advocacy.

The notion that abortion rights in the US are under assault by pro-life activists, while technically true, is clearly part of the pro-choice framework's

36. PRRI, "The State of Abortion and Contraception Attitudes."

37. Jenkins, "In a close 2020 election."

38. See "Asian Americans: A Mosaic of Faith."

39. Cheng-Tozun, "Chinese American Christians Are Becoming More Politically Engaged."

efforts to absolutize abortion rights by creating a sense of hysteria about a return to the days of back-alley abortionists. Even with the current 6–3 conservative majority on the Supreme Court, the likelihood of *Roe v. Wade* being overturned soon is unlikely, given the chain of events necessary to bring the right kind of case before the court and Chief Justice Roberts' stated commitment to respect past abortion precedents.[40] Couple that with the widespread popular support for legalized abortion—61 percent of Americans continue to say that abortion should be legal in all (27 percent) or most (34 percent) cases—and the opposition to overturning *Roe v. Wade* across party lines (70 percent of all voters, including 50 percent of Republicans).[41] The pro-choice framing narrative that abortion rights face imminent demise quickly fades. By supporting an extreme position of the Democratic base, the party leadership has gambled that the fear of losing ground on reproductive rights outweighs their constituents' qualms about the rights of an unborn fetus. It has the possibility of an open debate about the moral complexities of abortion and diminished the moral elements of the abortion decision. To paraphrase President Barrack Obama, Democrats "aren't expressing the full reality of it."[42]

CHRISTIAN ETHICS IN THE PUBLIC ARENA

In their landmark primer on Christian ethics, *Kingdom Ethics: Following Jesus in Contemporary Context* (2003), Glenn Stassen and David Gushee argue that the academic study of Christian ethics—not to mention Christian churches across the confessional spectrum—evade the teachings and practices of Jesus, especially as encapsulated in the Sermon on the Mount. In doing so, "Jesus' way of discipleship is thinned down, marginalized, or avoided" and Christians risk "serving the purposes of another lord."[43] This reading of contemporary US Christianity, while far from exhaustive, is validated by liberation theology's critique of culturally dominant forms of Christianity. According to the Rev. Dr. William J. Barber II, founder and co-chair of the Poor People's Campaign, American Christianity—especially evangelicalism—is becoming more and more culturally irrelevant as a result of its own idolatrous practices:

40. Ziegler, "How the Supreme Court could overturn Roe."
41. See "U.S. Public Continues to Favor Legal Abortion."
42. Pulliam and Olsen, "Q&A: Barack Obama."
43. Gushee and Stassen, *Kingdom Ethics*, xvi.

I mean, Jesus is very clear. That's the problem for people like Graham and Falwell. They can't debate us publicly because there's no way they can say, "We're against guaranteed health care for all because Jesus was against guaranteed health care for all." Jesus never charged a leper a co-pay! How can you stand up and say God is for the oppression of the poor when Isaiah—in Isaiah 10—says, "Woe unto those who legislate evil and rob the poor of their right and make women and children their prey?"[44]

Barber is not alone in this assessment of US Christianity. As Christianity transitions from a predominately white European and North American religion to a religion of black and brown peoples of the global south, and as increased globalization brings American Christianity into contact with all the diversity of world Christianity, US Christians will have to confront and come to terms with much that they equate with their religion which is, in fact, "serving the purposes of another lord."[45] Recent scholarship has exposed the white nationalism at the heart of the American experiment in democracy, rejecting much of what passes for Christianity in the US as an ideology of white supremacy.[46] According to Miguel De La Torre, "The gospel is slowly dying in the hands of so-called Christians, with evangelicals supplying the morphine drip."[47] Lest we think this idolatrous perversion of the gospel of Jesus Christ is an isolated evangelical or Protestant phenomenon, Fr. Bryan Massingale says this about US Catholicism:

The only reason that racism continues to persist is because white people benefit from it. If we're always going to have conversations that are predicated upon preserving white comfort, then we will never get beyond the terrible impasse that we're in, and we will always doom ourselves to superficial words and to ineffective half-measures. That difficult truth is something that the Catholic Church in America has never summoned the courage or the will to directly address.[48]

44. Marchese, "Rev. William Barber on Greed."

45. Gushee and Stassen, *Kingdom Ethics*, xvi.

46. See Carter, *Race*; Fletcher, *The Sin of White Supremacy*; Weed, *The Religion of White Supremacy in the United States*; Joshi, *White Christian Privilege*; Jones, *The End of White Christian America*.

47. De La Torre, *Burying White Privilege*, 4.

48. Munch, "'Worship of a False God.'"

According to Massingale, the pervasive normative whiteness and Eurocentrism of Roman Catholicism is "a form of idolatry. It's the worship of a false god."[49]

This chapter seeks to create a conversational space to unravel the moral complexities of abortion in a political context defined by ideological partisanship where even Christian communities are divided into pro-life and pro-choice camps and dialogue is viewed with suspicion as a form of moral compromise. Over against the dominant polarity, the teachings and practices of Jesus—succinctly presented in his Sermon on the Mount—are offered as an alternative model of moral discourse in which the Christian community seeks guidance and instruction without imposing pre-conceived moral judgment, and fully cognizant that when it comes to abortion—as with many other contemporary moral problems—we lack an explicit teaching from Jesus. Nowhere in the Christian canon of sacred Scripture, including the Hebrew Bible, is abortion explicitly named or discussed. However, the lack of explicit approval or condemnation of abortion does not mean Christian communities are left without guidance from the biblical sources. Christian ethics as an academic discipline guides the Christian churches' discernment in fidelity to the one and only Lord, Jesus Christ, which means Christian ethicists must strive to overcome personal biases and preferences—even set aside core political commitments—in an effort to *hear* the Word of God rather than dictate the Word of God. Whatever else Christ says that might inform our systematic reflection on the morality of abortion, we can be certain that surrendering to the dominant politics of coercion—by embracing either a pro-life or pro-choice absolutism—entails a fundamental betrayal of the Jesus encountered in the Scriptures.

A liberation understanding of US politics centers on power: *Who has it, who wields it, and to what end?* Donald Trump's dysfunctional presidency exposed the racist and white supremacist core festering in the heart of our culture; a culture that liberationists have worked hard to uncover, and ultimately transform, for over half a century. Liberation theologians view the church as a counterculture, resisting oppression and defending human dignity, even while recognizing that the institutional church has more often served the oppressors instead of the oppressed. As such, the work of liberation is grounded in the shared hope that through communal action, we can make a radical break with the status quo in order to bring about profound social change. Yet, because liberation theology is also guided by the biblical

---

49. Munch, "Worship of a False God." Also see Massingale, *Racial Justice and the Catholic Church*.

teachings and practices of Jesus, its moral praxis and political activism reflects the same humility and compassion Jesus embodied.

An argument can be made that the first ecclesial statements in support of liberation theology were made at the 1968 gathering of the Latin American Episcopal Council (CELAM) in Medellín, Colombia. Deeply influenced by the 1963 encyclical, *Pacem in terris* ("Peace on Earth"), the dogmatic statements proceeding from Vatican II, and the 1967 encyclical, *Populorum progressio* ("On the development of peoples"), the Medellín documents articulate a commitment to work together to create conditions that make life "more human." It calls for defending "the rights of the poor and oppressed according to the gospel commandment, urging our governments and upper classes to eliminate anything which might destroy social peace: injustice, inertia, venality, insensibility."[50] Pope Francis, the first Latin-American pope and a friend and supporter of liberation theologians, describes the church's ministry in these terms: "we must accompany people, and we must heal their wounds."[51] Recognizing the church's limited resources when addressing the enormity of human suffering, Francis compares the church to a field hospital during wartime:

> I see clearly that the thing the church needs most today is the ability to heal wounds and to warm the hearts of the faithful; it needs nearness, proximity. I see the church as a field hospital after battle. It is useless to ask a seriously injured person if he has high cholesterol and about the level of his blood sugars! You have to heal his wounds. Then we can talk about everything else. Heal the wounds, heal the wounds . . . And you have to start from the ground up.
>
> The church sometimes has locked itself up in small things, in small-minded rules. The most important thing is the first proclamation: Jesus Christ has saved you. And the ministers of the church must be ministers of mercy above all.[52]

Embracing this image of the church as field hospital, with its ministries of compassion a form of triage, the bishops' call at Medellín to work together to make life "more human" becomes a liberationist entry point for discussing abortion.

50. See Hennelly, *Liberation Theology,* 89–119.
51. Spadaro, "A Big Heart Open to God."
52. Spadaro, "A Big Heart Open to God."

TOWARD A CONSISTENT ETHIC OF SOLIDARITY

Reproductive rights advocates in the US call for an end to the Hyde Amendment, arguing that the lack of public funding for abortion services disproportionately impacts the poor and women of color. At first glance, this argument seems consistent with a liberationist perspective that seeks to advocate on behalf of the poor and marginalized. Undoubtedly, women have been marginalized and excluded from the dominant political circles, especially economically disadvantaged and ethnic minority women. As the Latin-American bishops concluded in the documents of the third Latin American Episcopal Council (Puebla, 1979), a point reiterated at the fifth Latin-American Episcopal Council (Aparecida, 2007), if the poor of Latin America are the oppressed, poor women trapped in a *machista* and patriarchal culture are "doubly" oppressed.[53]

Considering that many Latin-American nations do not recognize marital rape as a crime, a majority of rapes go unpunished, and gender-based murders (femicide), often characterized by post-mortem humiliation of the victim, are commonplace, the United Nations identified Latin America as the most dangerous region to be a woman.[54] Therefore, in the Latin-American context, where abortion is completely prohibited in some countries, severely restricted in most countries, and selective abortion is only legal in four countries—Cuba, Guyana, Uruguay, and (as of December 2020) Argentina—the argument can be made that women's struggles for liberation include a comprehensive push for legalized abortion.[55] Still, even in the Latin-American context, a liberationist perspective also tells us children, especially the unborn, ought be considered the *triply* oppressed given their marginalized and exploited status. As stated in the final document of Aparecida (a conciliar document informed and guided by the preferential option for the poor), "One cannot remain indifferent to the suffering of so many innocent children."[56] At the same time, while the church seeks to protect the dignity and inalienable rights of children, it seeks to do so "without detriment to the legitimate rights of parents."[57] Thus, even in a situation

53. See "Preferential Option for the Poor," in *Puebla and Beyond*, ¶1135, n297; Bergoglio, *The Aparecida Document*, ¶454.

54. See Essayag, *From Commitment to Action*.

55. According to the World Health Organization, in 2008, approximately "4.2 million abortions were conducted in Latin America and the Caribbean, almost three-fourths of them in South America. Virtually all these procedures were illegal and many were unsafe." In 2011, unsafe abortions accounted for 31 percent of the maternal mortality rate in Argentina. See Kulczycki, "Abortion in Latin America."

56. Bergoglio, *The Aparecida Document*, ¶439.

57. Bergoglio, *The Aparecida Document*, ¶441d.

where women are systemically and unremittingly repressed and violated, the moral worth of the unborn child cannot be eliminated from the moral calculus. So, when the conversation shifts to the United States—Christian ethics ought not unilaterally dismiss the right to life of the fetus. The absolutist position that focuses solely on reproductive rights intentionally glosses over the moral worth of the fetus and fails to express the full reality of abortion (Obama).

Despite efforts by the leading advocacy groups on both sides of the issue to frame the conversation in absolute terms, abortion poses a moral dilemma precisely because both the fetus and the mother have moral worth and their interests are in direct competition. The discipline of Christian ethics seeks to help Christian believers navigate this difficult situation by providing guidance that draws on the teachings and practices of Jesus Christ, which necessitates affirming the inherent worth and dignity of both the fetus and the mother as made in the image of God. Because abortion is a morally ambiguous situation, the pro-life Christian believer ought to enter the conversation willing to concede that there are situations where abortion is permissible. By the same token, the pro-choice Christian believer ought to have enough respect for the inherent humanity of the unborn fetus to accept legal restrictions to abortion, especially after the point of fetal viability.

Although there is no direct biblical teaching on abortion, abortion by definition involves the termination of a (potential) human life. It follows that what the Scriptures say about the taking of human life can guide our moral reasoning on abortion. Gushee and Stassen focus on what Jesus had to say about killing and violence in three passages from the Sermon on the Mount: Matthew 5:21–26, 38–42, and 43–48. In these verses,

> . . . we are taught to stop killing/harming one another, offered a diagnosis of how we get stuck in patterns leading us to keep killing and harming, and taught several transforming initiatives that can bring us back into an obedience that preserves and cherishes human life—all human life, which we must honor and consider sacred just as the Father in heaven does (Mt 5:45, 48).[58]

In the first pericope (Matt 5:21–26), Jesus offers his wisdom on what the Mosaic Law says about murder, then proceeds to equate anger with murder, commending forgiveness as a way past the anger that leads to violence—and murder—toward reconciliation. In the Torah, the commandment against murder is given as a moral absolute and the punishment for murder is death: "Whoever sheds the blood of a human, by a human shall that person's

---

58. Gushee and Stassen, *Kingdom Ethics*, 418.

blood be shed; for in his own image God made humankind" (Gen 9:6). Yet for all the fear of hell and damnation (Matt 5:22), Jesus—who in this same sermon reminds us, "Do not think that I have come to abolish the law or the prophets; I have come not to abolish but to fulfill" (Matt 5:17)—also knows that the first murderer was spared death despite the severity of God's command. Though the Law prescribes death as the punishment for murder, God transcends the Law, and offers Cain forgiveness and life (Gen 4:1–16). In the second pericope (Matt 5:38–42), Jesus continues to offer constructive advice on coping with anger and avoiding violence by commending nonviolence: "But I say to you, Do not resist an evildoer. But if anyone strikes you on the right cheek, turn the other also" (v. 39 NRSV), which culminates in the third pericope (Matt 5:43–48) with Jesus' commandment to "Love your enemies and pray for those who persecute you" (v. 44 NRSV).

In the Christian tradition, capital punishment and just war are two instances in which the teachings of Jesus from the Sermon on the Mount have been scrutinized in order to provide moral instruction on the taking of human life. While there is a strong defense of pacifism grounded in the historical example of Jesus of Nazareth, this exegetical convention eventually gave way to a more pragmatic position often traced to the writings of Augustine of Hippo (354–430 CE).[59] Some of Augustine's earliest comments on war are found in *Contra Faustum*, where he argues that God in the Scriptures employs war as a just means of countering evil:

> What is the evil in war? Is it the death of some who will soon die in any case, that others may live in peaceful subjection? This is mere cowardly dislike, not any religious feeling. The real evils in war are love of violence, revengeful cruelty, fierce and implacable enmity, wild resistance, and the lust of power, and such like; and it is generally to punish these things, when force is required to inflict the punishment, that, in obedience to God or some lawful authority, good men undertake wars, when they find themselves in such a position as regards the conduct of human affairs, that right conduct requires them to act, or to make others act in this way.[60]

Augustine, like most early Christians, believed that Jesus' teachings were incompatible with violence and warfare, yet drew a distinction between pacifism as a personal philosophy and the divinely established power of the sword given to the state that *sometimes* requires legitimate applications of

---

59. See Wynn, *Augustine on War*, 9–32, 213–64.
60. Augustine, *Contra Faustum*, 301.

political violence. Thus, when his Manichean opponents raised up Christ's admonition to "turn the other cheek" (Matt 5:39), Augustine replied:

> If it is supposed that God could not enjoin warfare, because in after times it was said by the Lord Jesus Christ, "I say unto you, That ye resist not evil: but if any one strike you on the right cheek, turn to him the left also" [Matt 5:39], the answer is, that what is here required is not a bodily action, but an inward disposition. The sacred seat of virtue is the heart, and such were the hearts of our fathers, the righteous men of old. But order required such a regulation of events, and such a distinction of times, as to show first of all that even earthly blessings (for so temporal kingdoms and victory over enemies are considered to be, and these are the things which the community of the ungodly all over the world are continually begging from idols and devils) are entirely under the control and at the disposal of the one true God.[61]

By distinguishing between the different desires motivating political violence, Augustine transformed Christian thought on just war, concluding that political violence is not necessarily an evil, but could—under very strict conditions—be understood as the morally preferable choice endorsed by God's sovereign authority. Legitimate political violence originates in the "double" love of God and neighbor (Matt 22:36–40) that demands action when such evil threatens to cause greater harm if unopposed. Not only must "just" war be waged by the good "in obedience to God or some lawful authority," but also "right conduct requires them to act, or to make others act in this way."[62] According to Augustine, war and other forms of political violence are unavoidable aspects of the human condition, but they are things neither to be desired nor lightly entered into.

Applying Christian moral reasoning on just war to the question of abortion is problematic but can yield productive guidelines for the contemporary conversation. If the taking of human life is done in self-defense or to prevent greater loss of life, then it is morally justified, and for Augustine constitutes love of neighbor, and even love of one's enemy (Matt 5:44). Distilling Jesus' teachings and practices from the Sermon on the Mount, Augustine identifies practical moral precepts guiding Christian moral reasoning:

> Now God, our master, teaches two chief precepts, love of God and love of neighbour; . . . For this reason, he will be at peace, as far as lies in him, with all men, in that peace among men, that ordered harmony; and the basis of this order is the observance

61. Augustine, *Contra Faustum*, 301.
62. Augustine, *Contra Faustum*, 301.

of the two rules: first, to do no harm to anyone, and, secondly, to
help everyone whenever possible.[63]

The problem when discussing abortion is that by definition someone is
always harmed—in the case of the aborted fetus, irreparably harmed—no
matter the course of action taken. Consequently, it becomes all the more
vital to scrutinize the motivations and intentions that lead to aborting a
fetus. Extrapolating from what Augustine has said concerning just war, we
can safely conclude that some justifications for abortion are morally questionable: say, for example, a young couple who engage in sexual intercourse
without adequate birth control despite the widespread availability and ease
of use of modern means of birth control. At the same time, we can easily
imagine a situation where the termination of the fetus is warranted in order
to save the life of the mother. Inevitably, there are moments of crisis that demand a choice between the life of the mother and the life of the fetus when
we are unable to "do no harm," but the reality of abortion is greater and far
reaching. Therefore, we need to expand our moral calculus to consider the
myriad ways we can act "to help everyone whenever possible."

John Calvin also used the Sermon on the Mount as the lens through
which to refract the whole of Scripture, so when interpreting the sixth commandment, "You shall not murder" (Exod 20:13 NRSV), Calvin, like Augustine, encountered a consistent and comprehensive Christian ethic:

> . . . the Lord has bound mankind together by a certain unity;
> hence each man ought to concern himself with the safety of all.
> To sum up, then, all violence, injury, and any harmful thing at
> all that may injure our neighbor's body are forbidden to us. We
> are accordingly commanded, if we find anything of use to us
> in saving our neighbors' lives, faithfully to employ it; if there
> is anything that makes for their peace, to see to it; if anything
> harmful, to ward it off; if they are in any danger, to lend a help-
> ing hand.[64]

A consistent Christian ethic on abortion recognizes the inherent dignity
all human beings possess, which entitles every human life—even potential
life—be treated as image of God with the appropriate respect and care. If we
understand *oppression* as social structures that enable one group to control
and limit the self-determination of another group, and define *liberation* as
empowering the victims of oppression to become the agents of their own
self-determination, we cannot continue to embrace absolutism on the

---

63. Augustine, *City of God*, 873.

64. Calvin, *Institutes of the Christian Religion*, 2.8.39.

matter of abortion. Instead, we ought to move forward with great humility and compassion to make life "more human" by doing as *little* harm as possible while helping *everyone* whenever possible.

CONCLUSION

Regrettably, those who most strongly defend the right to life of the fetus often do so with little or no regard for the plight of the pregnant mother. Some abortion rights opponents have begun to develop more holistic approaches for addressing unwanted pregnancies. They recognize the need to radically restructure the societal networks necessary to adequately care for women and children. Even so, most pro-life advocates lack credibility with those concerned with women's liberation. Pro-choice activists are equally delinquent when it comes to holistic support for women in crisis pregnancies. They frame their discourse solely in terms of reproductive rights. Informed by years of pastoral work in the parish and as a hospital chaplain, rarely have I been consulted by a parishioner prior to deciding whether or not to abort her fetus, yet on numerous occasions, I had to counsel women who years after the fact still experienced loss and guilt over their decision to abort.

A liberative theological framework on abortion—properly grounded in the teachings and practices of Jesus Christ—ought to begin moral reasoning with an accounting of the relationships of mutuality between the mother and the unborn child, the mother and the father, and the immediate biological family and the greater community. Any call for liberation that ignores the fullness of human experience by denying the covenantal responsibilities of all parties involved (recognizing that such relationships do not exist or have been grossly violated in cases of rape and/or incest) risks further alienating women at a time when they are physically, emotionally, and spiritually vulnerable. While arguments for the autonomous and unilateral right of a woman to abort a fetus run contrary to the comprehensive and consistent ethic here described, faith communities ought to ask themselves why so many women find liberation in the choice to abort a fetus. How have the Christian churches failed women in crisis? How has our culture failed by creating a social reality in which abortion is considered liberative? And what strategies does the church bring to help make society "more human"?

Gustavo Gutiérrez envisions the church as a universal sacrament of salvation in human history and challenges the church to "uncenter" itself by ceasing to consider "itself the exclusive place of salvation and orient itself towards a new and radical service of people."[65] By affirming the sacramental

65. Gutiérrez, *A Theology of Liberation*, 143.

dimension of the work of human liberation—a universal sacrament that extends Christ's redemptive work to *all* humankind by means of the Holy Spirit—Gutiérrez challenges the church to alter its concrete existence to become "a place of liberation," in recognition that the sacrament is itself a "sign of the liberation of humankind."[66] The fellowship initiated and preserved by the work of the Spirit *cannot* take place without "a real commitment against exploitation and alienation," and in a society *without* solidarity and justice, "the Eucharistic celebration is an empty action, lacking any genuine endorsement by those who participate in it."[67]

The church is confronted with an existential decision, and liberation theology insists the church must choose sides. Though the phrase "preferential option for the poor" was not officially endorsed by any magisterial document until 1979, Gutiérrez quickly points out that Medellín (1968) contained in its final documents a call for the church to give "preference to the poorest and most needy sectors and to those segregated for any cause whatsoever."[68] Accordingly, the Latin-American bishops confronted the historical reality of a deeply divided church in which fellow Christians were

> among the oppressed and persecuted and others among the op-
> pressors and persecutors, some among the tortured and others
> among the torturers or those who condone torture. This gives
> rise to a serious and radical confrontation between Christians
> who suffer from injustice and exploitation and those who ben-
> efit from the established order.[69]

The consequent scandal breaches the union in Christ that makes *ecclesia* ("assembly," "gathering") possible in the first place: "Participation in the Eucharist, for example, as it is celebrated today, appears to many to be an action which . . . becomes an exercise in make-believe."[70] From a liberationist perspective, the church has no choice but to divest itself from the centers of political and economic power and put its social weight behind the transformation of the dominant culture on the side of the poor and oppressed. Inevitably, "The groups that control economic and political power will not forgive the Church for this."[71]

66. Gutiérrez, *A Theology of Liberation*, 147.

67. Gutiérrez, *A Theology of Liberation*, 150.

68. Gutiérrez, *A Theology of Liberation*, xxv. Gutiérrez cites paragraph 9 of the "Document on the Poverty of the Church" from the Medellín conference. See Hennelly, *Liberation Theology*, 114–19.

69. Gutiérrez, *A Theology of Liberation*, 75.

70. Gutiérrez, *A Theology of Liberation*, 75.

71. Gutiérrez, *A Theology of Liberation*, 151.

As a liberation theologian, I am fully cognizant that I am engaged in a utopian project grounded on an eschatological promise that might never be realized. Nevertheless, hope remains because rather than expending energy in debating old theological arguments, liberationists embrace Marx's eleventh thesis on Feuerbach about *changing*, not just interpreting the world. This approach analyzes and critiques inequalities of class, gender, and race in order to create more just social structures informed by the biblical promise of what Dr. Martin Luther King Jr. called the Beloved Community—a normative ethical vision of an inclusive and interracial society grounded in our shared humanity as creatures made in the image of God (Gen 1:26–27)—where all people are challenged to relate peacefully across all boundaries that divide us:

> We have inherited a large house, a great "world house," in which we have to live together—black and white, Easterner and Westerner, Gentile and Jew, Catholic and Protestant, Moslem [sic] and Hindu—a family unduly separated in ideas, cultures, and interests, who, because we can never live again apart, must learn somehow to live with each other in peace.[72]

In the context of our affluent society, where abortion is a choice of convenience for the well off and more often than not a financially untenable option for the economically deprived, liberation theology must adapt its tools of social analysis in order to ask and answer some very difficult questions: Why is it that in our culture, abortion is often seen as the most convenient—if not the only—solution to an unwanted pregnancy? How is it that in our culture, we have "unwanted pregnancies"? Why has the church's discussion of abortion focused on legislating private sexual behavior while ignoring systemic issues of poverty, racism, and sexism that have perpetuated a culture in which women and children are treated as less than human? If as Christians we value justice and seek to defend the rights of the oppressed, why are we afraid to name unborn children "victims" of oppression? Christian ethics and advocacy must wrestle with these questions in its efforts to articulate a theology of liberation for women and the unborn.

There are many ways in which Christian churches can take action to protect and preserve the dignity of all life. The church can challenge sexist and patriarchal structures that exclude women from the political process by modeling inclusion in its own governance. Christian communities can provide women with economic and emotional support during a crisis pregnancy. Churches can support economically disadvantaged parents by providing (and subsidizing) affordable childcare and after-school programs for

72. King, "Where Do We Go from Here?," 617.

children. Denominational bodies can work to diminish barriers to adoption so that adoption becomes a viable alternative to abortion. For only after providing real-world solutions to the problems raised by abortion does it make sense for the church to take up its political vocation and seek to shape public policy in ways that transform the world in the image of God's kingdom.

My own immediate and extended family faced some very difficult decisions concerning two so-called "unwanted pregnancies." In both cases, the extended family came together to support the mothers and, to whatever extent possible, hold the fathers accountable. I am not trying to paint an idyllic picture of Latino/a family life—these two pregnancies created division and strife and much time had to pass and healing happen before familial relationships returned to previous levels of trust and mutuality—but a guiding principle of my "churched" Latino/a upbringing is the fact that as a member of a large, extended family (and a larger, even more far-reaching church community), I was raised to consider how my personal choices impact the whole community. Raised bilingual and bicultural in a US context, one of the most difficult aspects of navigating the highly individualistic North American culture after spending my childhood in Latin America was coming to terms with the fact that as far as my family and my church was concerned, no decision is ever a purely private choice. The community feels entitled and empowered to act whenever an individual behaves in ways that are injurious to the community. As a teenager, I rebelled hard against this intrusion into my private life, but as an adult I have come to recognize much of the wisdom contained therein.

No one in my family was thrilled that prevalent Latino/a stereotypes—young unwed mothers, sexually promiscuous fathers, children on public assistance—had become embarrassing realities, but these two children were born into an extended family that cared for them and made sure they were always wanted and valued. Sadly, not all unplanned pregnancies become wanted children. Furthermore, children born into poverty are more likely to remain in poverty, to receive a subpar education, and to be excluded from the power structures that continue to govern and shape society. Consequently, when we embrace a theological framework that respects the dignity of all human life—that seeks to liberate those who are oppressed—God's preferential option demands that we act in the best interest of the least powerful. In some instances, that might entail allowing—even funding—abortion for economically disadvantaged women, in other cases it might mean advocating for the right to life of the unborn fetus. A consistent Christian ethic recognizes there are no moral absolutes—Christian teaching allows for the taking of human life through capital punishment and just war so it can reasonably justify abortion in extreme circumstances—but such an ethic advocates first and foremost for compassion, guided by the Christian values of preserving life and helping those in need whenever possible.

BIBLIOGRAPHY

"Asian Americans: A Mosaic of Faiths." *Pew Research Center*, July 19, 2012. https://www.pewforum.org/2012/07/19/asian-americans-a-mosaic-of-faiths-overview/.

Augustine. *City of God*. Translated by Henry Bettenson. New York: Penguin, 1984.

———. *Contra Faustum*. In vol. 4, *Nicene and Post-Nicene Fathers*. Edited by Philipp Schaff. Translated by Richard Stothert. New York: Cosimo Classics, 2007.

Bergoglio, Jorge Mario, SJ. *The Aparecida Document*. Scotts Valley: CreateSpace Independent Publishing Platform, 2013.

Burns, Gene. *The Moral Veto: Framing Contraception, Abortion, and Cultural Pluralism in the United States*. Cambridge: Cambridge University Press, 2005.

Eunjung Cha, Ariana. "Number of abortions in U.S. hit historic low in 2015, the most recent year for which data is available." *Washington Post*, November 21, 2018. https://www.washingtonpost.com/health/2018/11/21/number-abortions-us-hits-historic-low/.

Calvin, John. *Institutes of the Christian Religion*. Edited by John T. McNeill. Translated by Ford Lewis Battles. Louisville: Westminster/John Knox Press, 1960.

Carter, J. Kameron. *Race: A Theological Account*. Oxford: Oxford University Press, 2008.

Cheng-Tozun, Dorcas, "Chinese American Christians Are Becoming More Politically Engaged—and More Divided." *Christianity Today*, October 27, 2020. https://www.christianitytoday.com/news/2020/october/chinese-american-christian-voters-asian-divided-trump-biden.html.

Cliff, Sarah. "What Americans think of abortion." *Vox*, April 8, 2015. https://www.vox.com/2018/2/2/16965240/abortion-decision-statistics-opinions.

"The Situation Room." *CNN*, June 4, 2007. http://transcripts.cnn.com/TRANSCRIPTS/0706/04/sitroom.03.html

De La Torre, Miguel A. *Burying White Privilege: Resurrecting a Badass Christianity*. Grand Rapids: Wm. B. Eerdmans, 2019.

DeSanctis, Alexandra. "How Democrats purged 'safe, legal, rare' from the party." *Washington Post*, November 15, 2019. https://www.washingtonpost.com/outlook/how-democrats-purged-safe-legal-rare-from-the-party/2019/11/15/369af73c-01a4-11ea-8bab-0fc209e065a8_story.html.

Dias, Elizabeth, Annie Karni, and Sabrina Tavernise. "Trump Tells Anti-Abortion Marchers, 'Unborn Children Have Never Had a Stronger Defender in the White House.'" *New York Times*, January 24, 2020. https://www.nytimes.com/2020/01/24/us/politics/trump-abortion-march-life.html.

Eagleson, John, and Philip J. Scharper. *Puebla and Beyond: Documentation and Commentary*. Translated by John Drury. Maryknoll, NY: Orbis, 1979.

Essayag, Sebastián. *From Commitment to Action: Policies to End Violence Against Women in Latin America and the Caribbean*. Panamá: UNDP and UN Women, 2017.

Fletcher, Jeannine Hill. *The Sin of White Supremacy: Christianity, Racism, & Religious Diversity in America*. Maryknoll, NY: Orbis, 2017.

Gonzales, Erica. "Where Does Kamala Harris Stand on Abortion and Reproductive Rights?" *Harper's Bazaar*, November 9, 2020. https://www.harpersbazaar.com/culture/politics/a34284404/kamala-harris-stance-on-abortion/.

Groome, Thomas. "To Win Again, Democrats Must Stop Being the Abortion Party." *New York Times*, March 27, 2017.

Gushee, David P., and Glenn H. Stassen. *Kingdom Ethics: Following Jesus in Contemporary Context*. 2nd ed. Grand Rapids: Wm. B. Eerdmans, 2016.

Gutiérrez, Gustavo. *A Theology of Liberation: History, Politics and Salvation*. Edited and translated by Sister Caridad Inda and John Eagleson. Rev. ed. Maryknoll, NY: Orbis, 1988.

Hadro, Matt. "'We will not be ignored': Pro-lifers rally at Democratic National Convention." *Catholic News Agency*, August 17, 2020. https://www.catholicnewsagency.com/news/we-will-not-be-ignored-pro-lifers-rally-at-democratic-national-convention-62533.

Hennelly, Alfred T., ed. *Liberation Theology: A Documentary History*. Maryknoll, NY: Orbis, 1990.

Jenkins, Jack. "In a close 2020 election, could a Hispanic evangelical swing vote be key?" *National Catholic Reporter*, October 28, 2019. https://www.ncronline.org/news/politics/close-2020-election-could-hispanic-evangelical-swing-vote-be-key.

Jensen, Kurt. "Clinton, Trump spar over abortion issue as final debate opens." *National Catholic Reporter*, October 20, 2016. https://www.ncronline.org/news/politics/clinton-trump-spar-over-abortion-issue-final-debate-opens.

Jones, Robert P. *The End of White Christian America*. New York: Simon and Schuster, 2017.

———. *White Too Long: The Legacy of White Supremacy in American Christianity*. New York: Simon and Schuster, 2020.

Joshi, Khyati Y. *White Christian Privilege: The Illusion of Religious Equality in America*. New York: New York University Press, 2020.

King, Martin Luther, Jr. *A Testament of Hope: The Essential Writings and Speeches of Martin Luther King, Jr.* Edited by James Melvin Washington. New York: Harper Collins, 1990.

Kulczycki, Andrzej. "Abortion in Latin America: Changes in Practice, Growing Conflict, and Recent Policy Developments." *Studies in Family Planning* 42.3 (September 2011) 199–220.

Lipka, Michael, and John Gramlich. "5 facts about the abortion debate in America." *Pew Research Center*, August 30, 2019. https://www.pewresearch.org/fact-tank/2019/08/30/facts-about-abortion-debate-in-america/.

Marchese, David. "Rev. William Barber on Greed, Poverty and Evangelical Politics." *New York Times Magazine,* December 29, 2020. https://www.nytimes.com/interactive/2020/12/28/magazine/william-barber-interview.html.

Martínez, Jessica, and Gregory A. Smith. "How the faithful voted: A preliminary 2016 analysis." *Pew Research Center*, November 9, 2016. https://www.pewresearch.org/fact-tank/2016/11/09/how-the-faithful-voted-a-preliminary-2016-analysis/.

Massingale, Bryan N. *Racial Justice and the Catholic Church*. Maryknoll, NY: Orbis, 2010.

Munch, Regina. "'Worship of a False God': An Interview with Bryan Massingale." *Commonweal*, December 27, 2020. https://www.commonwealmagazine.org/worship-false-god.

Murdock, John. "The Future of the Pro-Life Democrat." *National Affairs* 45 (Fall 2020). https://www.nationalaffairs.com/publications/detail/the-future-of-the-pro-life-democrat.

Murray, Patrick. "Abortion a Factor in 2020 Vote." *Monmouth University Poll*, June 25, 2019. https://www.monmouth.edu/polling-institute/reports/monmouthpoll_us_062519/.

Obama, Barrack. "Remarks by the President at the Planned Parenthood Conference." *Office of the Press Secretary*, April 26, 2013. https://obamawhitehouse.archives.gov/the-press-office/2013/04/26/remarks-president-planned-parenthood-conference.

Pulliam, Sarah, and Ted Olsen. "Q&A: Barack Obama." *Christianity Today*, January 23, 2008. https://www.christianitytoday.com/ct/2008/januaryweb-only/104-32.0.html.

Roberts, Dorothy E. *Killing the Black Body: Race, Reproduction, and the Meaning of Liberty*. New York: Pantheon, 1997.

Robles, Kevin Christopher. "Pro-life Dems protest party's abortion policy: 'If we lose, it's going to be because of this issue.'" *America: The Jesuit Review*, August 18, 2020. https://www.americamagazine.org/politics-society/2020/08/18/pro-life-democrats-protest-abortion-democratic-national-convention.

Solis, Marie. "Tulsi Gabbard's Stance on Abortion Is Stuck in the '90s." *VICE*, October 16, 2019. https://www.vice.com/en/article/43k5db/tulsi-gabbards-stance-on-abortion-is-stuck-in-the-90s.

Spadaro, Antonio, SJ. "A Big Heart Open to God: An interview with Pope Francis." *America: The Jesuit Review*, September 30, 2013. https://www.americamagazine.org/faith/2013/09/30/big-heart-open-god-interview-pope-francis.

"The State of Abortion and Contraception Attitudes in All 50 States." *Public Religion Research Institute*, August 13, 2019. https://www.prri.org/research/legal-in-most-cases-the-impact-of-the-abortion-debate-in-2019-america/.

Strang, Cameron. "Q&A With Barack Obama." *Relevant Magazine*, July 8, 2008. https://www.relevantmagazine.com/current/2726-qaa-with-barack-obama/.

Tatum, Sophie. "Clinton campaign hails progressive Democratic platform." *CNN Politics*, June 25, 2016. https://www.cnn.com/2016/06/25/politics/hillary-clinton-campaign-praises-democratic-platform-draft/index.html.

"U.S. Public Continues to Favor Legal Abortion, Oppose Overturning Roe v. Wade." *Pew Research Center*, August 29, 2019. https://www.pewresearch.org/politics/2019/08/29/u-s-public-continues-to-favor-legal-abortion-oppose-overturning-roe-v-wade/.

Wear, Michael. "Democrats Shouldn't Be So Certain About Abortion." *New York Times*, July 14, 2019. https://www.nytimes.com/2019/07/13/opinion/sunday/abortion-roe-2020-democrats.html.

Weed, Eric. *The Religion of White Supremacy in the United States*. Lanham: Lexington, 2017.

Wynn, Phillip. *Augustine on War and Military Service*. Minneapolis: Fortress, 2013.

Ziegler, Mary. "How the Supreme Court could overturn Roe—while claiming to respect precedent." *Washington Post*, July 1, 2020. https://www.washingtonpost.com/outlook/how-supreme-court-could-overturn-roe/2020/07/01/51fe4a2c-bb1e-11ea-80b9-40ece9a701dc_story.html.

—PART 4—

Pedagogical Strategies

DOING ETHICS AND ADVOCACY IN CATHOLIC HIGHER EDUCATION

Darlene Fozard Weaver

THIS ESSAY CONSIDERS THE relationship between ethics and advocacy from a Catholic perspective and with a particular focus on the context of Catholic higher education. Ethics aims to determine how we ought to live and whether our judgments in these matters are justified. Advocacy is active support for a particular moral cause or on behalf of a particular person, group, or non-human entity. Advocacy is an expression of ethical conviction aimed at practical—very often political—outcomes. However important the relationship between ethics and advocacy is, it is not always an easy alliance in practice, nor is the exercise of either ethics or advocacy automatically ethically good. Why look at higher education? It is where the bulk of academic ethics is done and where professional ethics are introduced to students preparing for practice in various fields such as business, nursing, and science. It is also a locus for civic education, providing opportunities for community-based learning and research, as well as exposing students to different persons and new ideas. Higher education is where students' positions on social issues can be informed or altogether overturned, and where some experiment with forms of advocacy, perhaps for the first time.

Nevertheless, a variety of dynamics complicate matters. "Cancel culture" deploys public shaming and social pressure to ostracize persons or organizations through social media trends, pressure to boycott business or drop sponsorships, and so forth, sometimes dismissing advocates due to prior mistakes or identifying moderates as cowards or worse.[1] Moreover,

1. Mishan, "The Long and Tortured History." See also Italie, "Everywhere and nowhere."

demographic and financial trends in higher education and historical features of Catholic ethics pose additional challenges. Furthermore, the fact of moral diversity and development, the necessity of addressing moral failure, and the occasional value of the "art of the possible" as compared to the impossibility of the preferable, all require nuance and skill for the practice of advocacy.

This essay explores the various factors that make it difficult to practice advocacy with moral skill in the context of Catholic higher education. It looks to an unlikely case study for guidance and argues that the differentiation of roles among higher education constituents is necessary. Finally, the essay argues that a number of virtues are needed to manage life together and explores what these might mean for advocacy in Catholic higher education.

CONTEMPORARY CATHOLIC HIGHER EDUCATION

The context of contemporary Catholic higher education impacts the practice of both ethics and advocacy. Scholarship and teaching in ethics obviously instantiate an institution's mission, as can the practice of advocacy within a university or by executive leadership on behalf of the institution. As we will see, however, the fight for institutional sustainability, contested questions about Catholic identity on campuses, and intra-Catholic polarization can make fidelity to mission fraught. Moral courage is needed, but so are a host of other virtues.

Survival Mode

The first factor to note is the difficulty of enrollment management for tuition-dependent colleges and universities. Catholic institutions face the same intense competition for students that most other institutions confront.[2] Declining birthrates are yielding significantly smaller pools of traditionally aged high school graduates. In the US, birthrates have been below replacement levels for decades.[3] The Great Recession caused a marked drop in births between 2007 and 2012 that will depress enrollments for many colleges and universities by double digit percentages, only to be followed by further downward trends since 2015 and what appears to be, for 2019, the lowest annual birthrate in over three decades.[4] Consequently, higher edu-

2. O'Loughlin, "Is Catholic identity hurting enrollment?"
3. Galvin, "U.S. Births Continue to Fall," para. 1.
4. Galvin, "U.S. Births Continue to Fall," para. 1.

cation enrollments are trending downward, and the number of collegiate mergers and closures are increasing.[5] The COVID-19 pandemic has only exacerbated these problems.

To navigate competition for tuition dollars, many Catholic colleges and universities attempt to distinguish themselves by appealing to their mission.[6] Why pay tuition for a private university, even those which are more selective and highly ranked, when one can earn the same degree for a lower price? These institutions argue that their Catholic identity lends distinctiveness to the academic and student life experiences they provide. Jesuit institutions, for instance, promote *cura personalis*, a commitment to the whole person, as a core value in Ignatian spirituality and pedagogy. Many students report selecting Catholic colleges and universities for reasons other than their Catholic identity.[7] To be sure, there are some institutions, such as Ave Maria University and Franciscan University in Steubenville, which attract a population of Catholic students for whom the Catholicity of the institution is vigorously defined as "authentic" over against what they take to be the suspect orthodoxy of other Catholic institutions. But this student population is comparatively small and certainly insufficient to sustain adequate levels of enrollment for Catholic higher education in general. Other students (Catholic or not) are looking for colleges or universities (again, Catholic or not) with different campus cultures.

What Does It Mean to Be a Catholic University?

Notwithstanding any linkage between mission-related marketing and enrollment, a second feature of Catholic higher education concerns the way developments in Catholicism and in higher education have raised questions about Catholic identity. Prior to Vatican II (1962–65), the majority of faculty members were members of the religious orders, which often sponsor Catholic colleges or universities. From the mid-1960s into the 80s, the composition changed as enrollments surged and more lay faculty were hired for content expertise rather than their familiarity with the Catholic intellectual tradition. The task of explicating the Catholic intellectual tradition and stewarding the religious identity of the institution still fell to members of the sponsoring congregations, even as vocations to these orders were declining. As Gallin notes, at the same time, leadership of Catholic colleges and

5. Adams and Smith, "The demographic cliff is here," para. 1.

6. Lehman, "Mission Officers."

7. Parrott, "How 2600+ students and parents perceive Catholic colleges today," lines 30–33.

universities was being shaped by a number of forces.[8] For example, Vatican II ushered in theological and ecclesial changes, including a call to engage the "signs of the times," respect for individual conscience, and an affirmation of religious liberty and the dignity of other religions. Moreover, governmental regulations surrounding public funding for higher education required Catholic colleges and universities to present themselves as Catholic yet nonsectarian in order to be eligible for funding. These institutions also needed to demonstrate their compliance with expectations for academic freedom and accreditation standards. In such a context, leaders from US Catholic universities gathered in 1967 at Land O'Lakes, property owned by the University of Notre Dame, and wrote a position paper that has since been called the *Land O'Lakes Statement*. The statement asserts: "to perform its teaching and research functions effectively, the Catholic university must have a true autonomy and academic freedom in the face of authority of whatever kind, lay or clerical, external to the academic community itself."[9] The statement also asserts that a Catholic university is one in which its Catholicity is *"perceptibly present and effectively operative."*[10] In sum, "the task . . . Catholic colleges and universities faced was to adapt to the standards of American higher education, meet legal demands consequent on government funding, satisfy the expectations of students, parents, faculty and alumnae/i, and do all this without losing their Catholic character."[11] The increased laicization of faculty, not to mention board governance, along with the impact of Vatican II, public funding, and evolving standards in American higher education, raised questions about mission that simply would never have occurred before.[12]

Catholic colleges and universities are integrally related to the Church. As the Association for Catholic Colleges and Universities puts it, "born from the heart of the Church, the Catholic college or university advances a common love of knowledge and wisdom in its research, teaching, and service. Participating in the wisdom of the past and casting a discerning gaze on the knowledge of every age, the Church and academy are united in the endeavor of advancing the common good of humanity."[13] This relationship is a source of the vitality of Catholic higher education, animating a legacy of academic excellence and innovation for the sake of the common

---

8. Gallin, *Negotiating Identity*.

9. *Land O'Lakes Statement*, 4.

10. *Land O'Lakes Statement*, 5.

11. Gallin, *Negotiating Identity*, xii.

12. Lehman, "Mission Officers," 14–26.

13. *The Catholic Intellectual Tradition*, 5.

good. While the *Land O'Lakes Statement* is sometimes represented as a de-clarative rejection of the Catholic university's ecclesial bonds, the statement in fact seeks to safeguard academic freedom from ecclesial intrusion while describing the Catholic university in terms of a lively culture nourished by the integration of faith and reason. Nevertheless, reaetions to the statement reflected larger intra-Catholic tensions concerning the reception of Vatican II. By 1990, the apostolic exhortation *Ex corde Ecclesiae* sought to re-affirm the integral relationship between the Church and Catholic colleges and uni-versities, recognizing the importance of academic freedom but also "recog-nition of and adherence to the teaching authority of the Church in matters of faith and morals."[14] The practice of ethics as an academic discipline and advocacy as an expression of ethics occur within this tension between au-tonomy and integral relation, academic freedom and adherence to Church teaching.

Intra-Catholic Polarization and the Rise of Alt-Catholicism

Another important feature in the context of Catholic higher education is the increasing polarization within Catholicism in the United States.[15] Intra-Catholic polarization is due in part to the contested reception of Vatican II. Pope Benedict XVI, for instance, described this reception in terms of oppos-ing interpretations: on one side are those who interpret the council through a hermeneutic of continuity or reform, and on the other side are those who interpret the council through a hermeneutic of rupture in relation to pre-conciliar Catholic tradition.[16] In his study of Vatican II, John O'Malley describes Vatican II as a "language event" shaped by deliberate choices of themes and vocabulary. These themes include a focus on the human person, articulation of a universal call to holiness, respect for individual conscience and religious liberty, and a call for the Church to engage the world.

American Catholics reflect similar attitudes to that of the general American public on issues like abortion, same-sex marriage, immigra-tion, and government responses to climate change and economic disparity. Notably, "when it comes to specific policy issues, Catholics are often more aligned with their political party than with the teachings of their church."[17] When asked if abortion should be legal in all or most cases, nearly two thirds (64 percent) of Democratic Catholics agree and roughly four out of ten (39

14. John Paul II, *Ex corde Ecclesiae.*
15. Konieczny et al., *Polarization in the US Catholic Church.*
16. Benedict, "Address."
17. Smith, "8 facts."

percent) Republican Catholics agree.[18] On same-sex marriage, majorities of Republicans (59 percent) and Democrats (76 percent) express support.[19] The fact that Catholic attitudes on contested moral questions largely reflect those of non-Catholics results partly from the internal diversity of American Catholicism, but surely also raises questions about the efficacy of Catholic ethics education.

Intra-Catholic polarization is aided and abetted by the increased opportunities for Catholic organizations and individual influencers to shape Catholic opinion, political engagement, and exert public pressure on Catholic institutions. While much more investigative and scholarly research needs to be done, a number of scholars and journalists are beginning to grapple with the rise of "alt-Catholicism" in the US.[20] Alt-Catholicism refers to a "small group of militant far-right dissenters who distort and damage the U.S. church on a daily basis."[21] Alt-Catholicism represents the convergence of Catholic media, right-wing Catholic social media influencers, and Catholic resistance to Vatican II and/or to Pope Francis. It is increasingly influenced by conspiracy-driven Republican sub-cultures that combine Steve Bannon's anti-globalism and the QAnon conspiracy, which holds that the Democratic party is a satanic cabal of pedophiles and cannibals. Says Robert Christian, alt-Catholics have

> set up their own alt-magisterium, one that permits them to reject church teaching on a range of subjects . . . These alt-Catholic individuals who claim to be more orthodox and more Catholic than the pope . . . have used social media (including troll armies filled with anonymous accounts) and the Catholic press to magnify their favorite narratives and conspiracy theories, despite the small number of U.S. Catholics (and miniscule number of global Catholics) who embrace this approach.[22]

While alt-Catholics comprise a minority in the American Catholic population, they reflect the overall tenor of Catholic media and social media, which is increasingly venomous, partisan, and weaponized, and have an oversized impact. The problem is significant enough that the third encyclical from Pope Francis, *Fratelli Tutti*, repeatedly discusses the problem of

---

18. Lipka and Smith, "Like Americans overall."

19. Lipka and Smith, "Like Americans overall."

20. Wetzel, "The rise of the Catholic Alt-Right." See also Joyce, "Deep State, Deep Church."

21. Christian, "The Roots of American Catholic Polarization," § 25.

22. Christian, "The Roots of American Catholic Polarization," § 24.

digital campaigns of hatred and aggression and devotes an entire chapter to calling for a "better kind of politics."[23]

While alt-Catholicism is a fringe element, social media provides it a megaphone that amplifies its voice and impact, providing interest groups opportunities to pressure Catholic organizations and even bishops. Even short of full-blown conspiracy theorists, media outlets and social media influencers (on the left and the right) can create public relations issues for Catholic colleges and universities. They protest speakers who are brought to campus, turn internal decisions regarding student organizations or programming into national news, and even expose faculty, staff, or students to threats of violence. The challenges posed by opportunistic external agents are not unique to Catholic higher education, but they find there good soil in which to flourish, given the contested character of Catholic identity, and struggles to attract and retain sustainable student enrollments.

In sum, the context of Catholic higher education is fraught. Some institutions are in a high-stakes fight for enrollments and tuition dollars to ensure their long-term sustainability. It would be a mistake to paint their boards and senior leaders with a single and uncharitable brush as prioritizing profit over people or eroding the goods of liberal education in order to turn institutions into trade schools.[24] That is not to say that such decision-makers are beyond reproach. Rather, we must acknowledge that the economic realities of higher education make it very difficult for tuition-dependent institutions to be agile, and the process of reconfiguring financial models will unavoidably be disruptive and painful. In such a context, the practice of ethics and of advocacy can be selling points to attract faculty, staff, and students, as well as occasions for criticism from unhappy internal members, bishops, alumni, donors, and others. Such pressures do not justify deliberate wrongdoing or omission, but they do summon particular skills and dispositions and point to important topics for ethics.

CATHOLICISM AND ADVOCACY

Catholicism in the United States has a long history of advocacy. The Catholic pro-life movement comes readily to mind. Less known, or perhaps less remembered, is Catholic advocacy around labor issues and for peace. As Sharon Erikson Nepstad notes, early Catholic responses to the injustices wrought by the industrial revolution took the form of charity. "However, by the 1880s, many workers believed that charity was merely a short-term

23. Francis, *Fratelli Tutti*, no. 43.

24. Furstenberg, "University Leaders Are Failing."

measure that did not address the underlying problem. What workers really needed was a transformed economic system."[25] While Catholic support for labor unions was by no means unanimous,[26] Pope Leo XIII's encyclical *Rerum Novarum* took a clear position on the dignity of human labor and the rights of workers, including the right to organize. *Rerum Novarum* "marked the public emergence of a Catholic social conscience," acknowledging "that contemporary social issues have a moral dimension, to which the church must respond," and "that the Catholic Church's primary role is to educate people to act fairly and justly."[27] While *Rerum Novarum* affirms the rights of workers and criticizes laissez-faire capitalism at the same time it rejects dangerous forms of collectivism. *Rerum Novarum* inaugurates the modern encyclical tradition of Catholic Social Teaching and marks coordinated advocacy by religious and laity to shape policy on select issues.

Catholic advocacy for international peace provides another instructive example. Catholic teaching has long affirmed the possibility of waging a just war.[28] The just war tradition identifies criteria that must be met in terms of reasons for waging war and for the conduct of warfare. More recently, the just war tradition has come to include criteria to shape post-war conditions and conduct.[29] Despite this teaching, Catholic advocacy for peace flourished in the latter half of the twentieth century. As with labor issues, Catholic positions on war and peace were not monolithic. Some members of the Catholic Worker movement, for example, disagreed with the pacificism of Dorothy Day.[30] Brothers Daniel and Philip Berrigan, along with Trappist monk Thomas Merton, organized across faith traditions to oppose the Vietnam War, but while Daniel Berrigan wound up in jail for pouring blood on draft records, Merton argued against forms of advocacy that use "spectacular tricks" or "forms of protests that are merely odd and provocative" in the pursuit of "immediate visible results."[31]

Indeed, David O'Brien identifies three varieties of "public Catholicism," which he calls immigrant, republican, and evangelical.[32] The immigrant form is more sectarian, motivated by concerns about "absorption into

25. Nepstad, *Catholic Social Activism*, 21–22.

26. Nepstad, *Catholic Social Activism*, 22.

27. Nepstad, *Catholic Social Activism*, 25.

28. Literature on the just war tradition is considerable. The origins of the tradition lie in Augustine's *City of God*.

29. Allman and Winright, "Growing Edges of Just War Theory," 173–91.

30. Nepstad, *Catholic Social Activism*, 53.

31. Merton, *Blessed Are the Meek*, 98–100.

32. O'Brien, "Public Catholicism."

a comfortable non-denominationalism," and therefore emphasizing the distinctiveness of Catholic identity through forms of separatism.[33] O'Brien sees expressions of the immigrant approach in "lobbying for Catholic interests, support for community organizing, single issue advocacy which pays little attention to the positions of other groups or the needs of the community at large."[34] The republican form rejects the sectarianism of the immigrant approach. It affirms the separation of church and state, but also seeks to shape a public church and counteract the marginalization of religious perspectives in public debate. The republican approach affirms the value of religious liberty and pluralism, and seeks to learn from secularization. The third style, the evangelical, "sought a reintegration, personal, communal and public, by means of a complete commitment to the Gospel, expressed in profound religious faith, and interiorization of the spiritual life, and a dedication to serving the poor and healing the wounds besetting society."[35] O'Brien points to the Catholic Worker movement as an example. O'Brien argues that

> bishops would be wise to nourish all three [kinds of public Catholicism], for each reflects some fundamental realities about the church's presence in this kind of society, and each constitutes an appropriate and responsible stance for some members of the community of faith. Given the right kind of forums, they can be mutually correcting and enriching.[36]

Maureen K. Day recently built upon O'Brien's work by identifying a fourth style of public Catholicism, what she calls the discipleship style.[37] The discipleship approach is "personalist," by which Day means more individualistic than civic and including a concern for personal meaning and growth through service. Accordingly, the discipleship approach also emphasizes "individual-level solutions, such as lifestyle changes, rather than . . . ways of becoming involved in macro-level change."[38] Finally, the discipleship approach locates moral authority in the individual: "American Catholics have increasingly come to understand themselves as sources of moral authority while decreasingly relying on the Catholic hierarchy for moral guidance."[39]

The history of Catholicism in the US also includes institutional failures and largely hidden forms of resistance to them. In her work on black

33. O'Brien, "Public Catholicism," 89.
34. O'Brien, "Public Catholicism," 94.
35. O'Brien, "Public Catholicism," 94.
36. O'Brien, "Public Catholicism," 95.
37. Day, *Catholic Activism Today*.
38. Day, *Catholic Activism Today*, 3.
39. Day, *Catholic Activism Today*, 3–4.

Catholic nuns, Shannen Dee Williams details the way these sisters challenged racism both within and beyond the Catholic Church. Their history
is rarely if ever incorporated into formal or informal education in the faith.
Williams describes their history as a dangerous memory, since sharing this
history requires confronting the complicity of the Catholic Church in the
sinful structures of slavery and racism.[40] In addition to such failures, the
US Catholic record of advocacy also includes blameworthy instances of
lukewarm and middling responses to select social issues. For example, the
recent pastoral letter on racism from United States Conference of Catholic
Bishops (USCCB), their first statement on racism in forty years, was both
welcomed as an overdue attention to the sin of racism and, by some, poorly
received as a soft response more concerned about the possibility of offend-
ing white Catholic communities than with laying bare the horror of racism
or the Catholic Church's complicity in it.[41] However collegial the USCCB
may be, differences among the bishops mean that the conference's own advocacy bears the marks of being done by committee. Furthermore, whatever
the force of formal statements from episcopal leadership in the US, the issue
of implementation within individual parishes and schools is yet another
matter. According to Olga Segura, only 42 diocese out of 197 reported some
formal programming on racism, 12 which predated the pastoral letter and
30 in response to it.[42]

Direct engagement with work by historians of Catholicism will yield
far more insight into the Catholic record with regard to advocacy. For the
purposes of this essay, we can highlight several points. The very fact that
there is a robust tradition of advocacy in US Catholicism is a testament to
the theological, ethical, and pastoral bonds between Catholic faith and public engagement. Despite significant agreement that the Church should "stay
out of politics,"[43] Catholicism is hospitable to advocacy. As Pope Francis puts
it in *Fratelli Tutti*, "all things human are our concern."[44] Second, magisterial
teaching on social issues tends to carve out mediating approaches that do
not align neatly with polarized American political options. Third, there are
diverse approaches to advocacy which reflect differing understandings of
the relationship between the Church and the state, different theologies, and
different ecclesiologies. There is usually something to attract and something
to disappoint just about anyone. Finally, whatever is morally admirable in

---

40. Williams, "Forgotten Habits, Lost Vocations."

41. United States Catholic Conference, *Open Wide Our Hearts*.

42. Segura, "I Reached Out to Every US Diocese."

43. Smith, "8 Facts."

44. Francis, *Fratelli Tutti*, no. 278.

the Catholic record of advocacy, that record also includes culpable omissions, blameworthy lukewarmness, and outright complicity in sinful behaviors, attitudes, and structures. Unflinching honesty about the practical limitations and moral failings of Catholic engagement on social issues like racism is absolutely essential.[45] It is also, for reasons we discuss below, a difficulty within a tradition that has permitted concern over causing scandal to foster a culture of silence regarding systemic forms of abuse.

PARTICULAR CHALLENGES FOR THE PRACTICE OF ETHICS AND ADVOCACY

Advocacy is a good and necessary moral practice. While ethics without advocacy becomes hypocrisy, an ivory tower exercise that abandons our responsibilities to cultivate the common good, advocacy without ethics easily goes amiss. The practice of advocacy within Catholic colleges and universities must navigate dynamics of cancel culture and the tensions that mark Catholic higher education. Moreover, several additional challenges impact ethics and advocacy therein.

Moral Diversity

The first challenge is moral diversity. Ethics and advocacy presume there is moral diversity and disagreement. Ethics assesses the adequacy of diverse positions and endeavors to reduce errors and integrate insights so as to better understand and articulate how we ought to live or, put theologically, love the Lord our God with all one's heart, mind, and strength, and one's neighbor as oneself (Matt 22:34–40). So why make special note of it here? A primary reason is that the way individuals and communities respond to moral diversity is itself morally significant. In addition, moral diversity gives rise to ethical issues within higher education. Students, faculty, and staff will disagree on virtually anything and can inflect this disagreement with moral stakes. Decisions about allocating resources reflect priorities that some will find objectionable. Adjustments to policies can become litmus tests for whether an institution is faithful to its mission. In the context of Catholic higher education, moral disagreements are also conflicts over how to understand and live out the institution's Catholic identity and how to respect academic freedom and shared governance. Moreover, when it comes to advocacy within or by the institution, internal debates about

45. Francis, *Fratelli Tutti*, no. 249.

particular forms of advocacy are made more heated and more challenging due to moral diversity, even before any external media outlets might amplify the issue.

Moral diversity poses fundamental challenges for any community, including the distinctive sort of communities formed by institutions of higher education. On the one hand, there is the imperative of nurturing a culture of hospitality, inclusion, respect, and equity. On the other hand, there is the necessity of enforcing expectations and redressing wrongs, which includes meting out sanctions. Indeed, this practice of justice is ingredient to the work of sustaining a hospitable, inclusive, respectful, and equitable culture. The difficulty, of course, is that there will be different viewpoints regarding which behaviors will be tolerated and which will not. I am not speaking about classroom debates regarding the morality of capital punishment or gun culture, so much as instances like having one student tell another student that they will go to hell because they are gay, or a faculty member offering extra credit for student participation in a pet cause that is wholly unrelated to the course subject. Both of these examples, which differ in their gravity, are instances of moral wrongdoing (which we will discuss next) motivated by each agent's moral commitments. They are also instances in which different constituents at the university may view the matter as a proxy for divergent ways of understanding what it means to be a Catholic university or as justified under the banner of "mission."

The practice of ethics in a context of moral diversity should equip persons and communities to navigate that diversity and manage disagreements with confidence and humility, rigor and graciousness, integrity and forgiveness. These dispositions and virtues will in turn foster morally good practices of advocacy.

Moral Development, Moral Failure, and Forgiveness

A second particular challenge for the doing of ethics and advocacy concerns the dynamics of moral development and human wrongdoing. These issues are even more acute in a context of higher education, Catholic or otherwise. Traditionally aged undergraduate students are legally adults, but most of them are also living away from home for the first time and coming to terms with heretofore unknown degrees of freedom. They make poor choices, even undeniably horrifying ones. They also exercise advocacy in ways that can range from the morally courageous to misguided.

Any workable, let alone good, human community requires due recognition that we are each imperfect and unfinished moral agents, and therefore diligence in mustering constructive responses to moral failure and cultivating practices of forgiveness. Members of all constituencies in a university—faculty, staff, and students—are capable of wrongdoing and displaying vices. They all bring psychosocial issues to their work and studies, too. Like any human community, colleges and universities are comprised of people who continue to change, whose lives transpire amidst dynamics of sin and grace. The fact of ongoing moral development and the inevitability of human moral failure require virtues of patience and forgiveness to be practiced. These can be hard to come by in cancel culture. While ethics includes literature on forgiveness, forbearance, reconciliation, and moral development, more work is needed on these topics, especially in the context of a "cancel culture."

The Art of the Possible in a Scorched Earth Environment

A final particular challenge confronting the doing of ethics and doing advocacy concerns moral compromise and the "art of the possible." There is scant work in ethics on the morality of compromise. In some instances of advocacy, one finds the practice of compromise and willingness to work for and accept what is possible even when it falls well short of one's true aspirations. And yet, "political polarization demands more and more complete commitment to a tightly defined partisan agenda, and political leaders cannot compromise without losing credibility with the all-important base. Politics, which used to be defined as 'the art of the possible,' depends now on the appearance of ultimacy."[46]

Two important elements of Catholic moral tradition that both inform and complicate approaches to moral diversity and moral failure are teaching cooperation with evil and the avoidance of scandal. Catholic ethics distinguishes cooperation with evil in terms of formal and material cooperation.[47] Formal cooperation is when someone directly authorizes or knowingly facilitates or wills another's sin. Material cooperation with evil occurs in degrees depending on the proximity and directness of material assistance in another's wrongdoing. Catholic teaching about cooperation with evil helps us consider the presence and degree of culpability that may attend our interaction with others' moral failure. This can include complicity with sinful structures, as when I knowingly purchase goods that involve exploitative labor practices. However, the framework for cooperation with evil can also be applied selectively, as in single issue voting. Considering how enmeshed

---

46. Lovin, "Faith and Politics."
47. Rubio, "Cooperation with Evil Reconsidered."

our lives are and how complex human behavior is, Catholic teaching about cooperation with evil requires serious rethinking with regard to structural injustice or, put theologically, social sin.[48]

Another related feature of Catholic moral tradition concerns scandal. In Catholic ethics, scandal is a technical term. It designates more than shock, outrage, or disillusionment in response to another's conduct. The *Catechism of the Catholic Church* defines scandal as "an attitude or behavior which leads another to do evil."[49] Scandal is not about my emotive reaction to your offense, but my responsibility for inducing another to sin. Catholic teaching about scandal characterizes the relationship between my own freedom and responsibility for my neighbors. As the *Catechism* says, "the person who gives scandal becomes his neighbor's tempter. He damages virtue and integrity; he may even draw his brother into spiritual death. Scandal is a grave offense if by deed or omission another is deliberately led into a grave offense."[50] My cooperation with another's evil can cause scandal, but so can "laws or institutions, . . . fashion or opinion."[51] Moreover, the gravity of scandal is linked to the authority of the one scandalizing, such that more damage can be done by undermining trust in those charged with responsibility for the good of a community. It is not difficult to see how such an account of scandal contributed to institutional culture that aided and abetted sex abuse in the Catholic Church.

Is Catholic teaching about scandal adequate at a cultural moment characterized by such moral diversity and polarization, when it seems so many of us are so often offended by others and so easily tempted to respond uncharitably? How can Catholic teaching about cooperation with evil accommodate imperfect forms of compromise or collaboration with unlikely partners on issues of common concern? Without losing the insight operative in these two areas of teaching, can we articulate a place for respect for the conscience and moral competence of others? Or must we forsake piecemeal progress in our advocacy for the sake of some notion of purity?

Diane Yeager and Stewart Herman have written a stimulating essay forging an ethics of compromise.[52] In their view moral compromise is neither "a gross betrayal of one's principles nor . . . the least worst option in a fallen world but rather . . . a fully virtuous ethical engagement with otherness

---

48. McRorie, "Rethinking Moral Agency in Markets."

49. *Catechism of the Catholic Church*, 2284.

50. *Catechism of the Catholic Church*, 2284.

51. *Catechism of the Catholic Church*, 2286.

52. Yeager and Herman, "The Virtue of 'Selling Out.'"

in the context of pluralism."[53] According to Yeager and Herman, an ethics of compromise consists of two imperatives. The first is to recognize the moral competence of others, to respect their capacity for considered moral judgments and choices. If the other also respects one's own moral competence, this mutual respect provides a framework for compromising. The second imperative is to negotiate a compromise in good faith, to pursue forms of social cooperation that are mutually agreeable. Not all compromise is good, but neither is it always a lesser evil. Rather, morally good compromises reconstruct the locus of moral assessment from the individual agent to the interactions between agents. Bringing an ethics of compromise into engagement with Catholic teaching about cooperation with evil and scandal can bear fruit for ethical assessment of advocacy.

When it comes to the ethics of advocacy, the question of whether we are willing to abide injustice any longer meets the question of what is possible for us to accomplish now. The latter too often provides moral cover for those who prefer to be like the "white moderates" of Dr. Martin Luther King Jr's *Letter from a Birmingham Jail*, those who counsel the oppressed to bide their time and choose less disruptive tactics. In such hands, concerns about causing scandal provide extra protection. That said, scorched earth approaches to advocacy can forego meaningful, if imperfect, progress or opportunities for collaboration on shared issues of concern. They let the perfect become the enemy of the good.

ROLE DIFFERENTIATION AND VIRTUE

Guidance is available in an unlikely case study. M. Cathleen Kaveny's essay "Virtuous Decision-Makers and Incompetent Patients: The Case of the Conjoined Twins" examines the contested positions of parents, physicians, and the judge in a 2000 legal case involving surgery for conjoined twins.[54] The essay concerns the nature of role-related obligations in medical moral decision-making, particularly in cases involving incompetent patients. The particular case under consideration involved conjoined twin girls born in England in 2000. The girls shared a torso and a bladder, but otherwise had their own organs. One girl's heart and lungs were deformed, however, and she, Mary, was surviving by drawing on her sister Jodie's circulatory system. Doctors predicted both girls would die before their first birthday if they were not separated. Surgical separation would result in Mary's death while her sister was likely to have a normal life expectancy after separation. The

53. Yeager and Herman, "The Virtue of 'Selling Out,'" 3–4.
54. Kaveny, "Virtuous Decision Makers."

parents, both Catholic, refused to approve of the surgery, believing such a decision would mean willing the death of one of their children. The court authorized the surgery over the parents' objection. The surgery was performed and Mary died as expected while Jodie survived.

Kaveny published several articles that consider different features of this case from legal and ethical perspectives. In this particular essay, her focus is on making decisions for incompetent patients. Advocates are not surrogate decision-makers, but there is wisdom in Kaveny's analysis of the case that we can apply to the ethics of advocacy. She argues that agents are not fungible:

> They are particular human beings, with particular strengths and weaknesses, called to be faithful to particular relationships and particular vocations. Their moral obligations are in part determined by the particular roles they inhabit. Not only the actions, but also the habits, thoughts and feelings required of them are to some degree determined by the exigencies of those roles.[55]

Roles are socially defined ways for agents to participate in specific practices, with all of the goods internal to those practices.[56] As such, roles shape our moral identity and confer responsibilities and privileges upon some that do not apply to others. It does not follow that a role gives someone permission to do morally that which is wrong for anyone to do. However, a role may morally prohibit an action that is permissible for others outside that role. It is this line of argument that Kaveny follows to argue that in the case of the conjoined twins, the court and parents occupy two different roles, each with distinct obligations sometimes in tension and both of which are important to protect the children, despite the tension. The court and parents should not be treated as fungible decision-makers, each charged to protect the children's best interests in an undifferentiated way.[57] For Kaveny, the parents act rightly as parents when they determine they cannot approve of the surgery. But she thinks the court also acts rightly when it authorizes the surgery. The parents and the courts occupy distinct roles with different role-related obligations in relation to the best interests of the twins. To be sure, these roles are in tension with one another in this case, but for good reasons.

What lessons may we draw from Kaveny's essay for the work of ethics and advocacy? She locates moral decision-making within relational contexts that have normative import for the agents who inhabit them. Her

55. Kaveny, "Virtuous Decision Makers," 347.

56. Kaveny, "Virtuous Decision Makers," 347–50.

57. Kaveny, "Virtuous Decision Makers," 358.

argument indicates that our examination of ethics and advocacy in higher education can profit from consideration of the differentiated roles that faculty, students, and academic leaders play, and the virtues that are integral to those roles.

MANAGING LIFE TOGETHER

Ethics and advocacy matter because our lives together matter. To do both ethics and advocacy well, we must cultivate a variety of skills and dispositions—virtues, really—to manage our lives together. Virtues will assist us in negotiating moral diversity and disagreement, supporting others' moral development, responding appropriately to moral failure and practicing forgiveness, as well as discerning the ways to retain both prophetic and pragmatic dimensions of ethics and advocacy.

We can outline these virtues in conversation with Pope Francis's *Fratelli Tutti*. Pope Francis begins the encyclical noting "signs of a certain regression," the increase of inequality and concentration of power and wealth in the hands of the few, the further marginalization and disrespect for vulnerable persons, distorted views of globalism and nativism, and the deterioration of communication into more shallow and aggressive forms, to name only a few.[58] He calls for a "rebirth of a universal aspiration to fraternity."[59]

The chief virtue *Fratelli Tutti* exhorts is love. Love is the ultimate measure of the moral value of one's life,[60] as well as the fulfillment for which we are created.[61] God's love encompasses all, and just so, human love impels us to a universal communion.[62] Political love is a "decisive commitment to devising effective means" to a social friendship that includes everyone, and "any effort along these lines becomes a noble exercise of charity."[63] Love seeks to be efficacious in responding to others' needs and changing social conditions that contribute to their suffering.[64] For this reason, love exercises a preferential option for the poor and vulnerable. Love is also closely related to hope. Francis states that one of his goals for the encyclical is to invite people to travel "paths of hope."[65] He stresses the boldness of hope in its

58. Francis, *Fratelli Tutti*, no. 11.
59. Francis, *Fratelli Tutti*, no. 8.
60. Francis, *Fratelli Tutti*, no. 92.
61. Francis, *Fratelli Tutti*, no. 68.
62. Francis, *Fratelli Tutti*, no. 95.
63. Francis, *Fratelli Tutti*, no. 180.
64. Francis, *Fratelli Tutti*, no. 186.
65. Francis, *Fratelli Tutti*, no. 54.

aspirations and readiness to persevere. Hope is integral to loving fraternity because it believes the others have "reserves of goodness" which can be engaged through patient cultivation of encounter and a dialogue that seeks fundamental consensus. Hope also trusts in the efficacy of action, believing that efforts to tend to others' needs and accomplish solutions to the problems that beset them, however partial those solutions might be, can continue to bear fruit in the future.[66]

Solidarity[67] is a steadfast and mature commitment to needs and interests of others, however distant.[68] It means "thinking and acting in terms of community."[69] Francis contrasts solidarity with the illusion of unity provided by communications technology and forms of globalization.[70] *Fratelli Tutti* calls for new international networks of solidarity, with policies of cooperation to support the development of all peoples.[71] But Francis also asserts that solidarity requires subsidiarity,[72] opportunities for individuals and groups to participate in society. The sheer complexity of the challenges we face and the moral failures we observe can undermine our will to forge solidarity.[73] But Francis writes repeatedly that the fraternity he exhorts is not an abstraction. It requires an urgent commitment to use all the tools at our disposal to devise and implement pragmatic solutions for problems like hunger, human trafficking, and terrorism. Finally, solidarity requires the practice of forgiveness[74] so that we can respond to conflict and forms of injustice in a way that restores and sustains the bonds of fraternity.

Finally, Francis notes that wisdom is needed. He distinguishes wisdom from mere information or data. "True wisdom demands an encounter with reality,"[75] but this markedly contrasts with our ability to create our own social and informational echo chambers, to sequester ourselves from whatever we do not like "and exclude all that we cannot control or know instantly and superficially."[76] The search for a basis for consensus across our differences can lead us to wisdom, the wisdom that every human being is valuable and

---

66. Francis, *Fratelli Tutti*, no. 196.

67. Francis, *Fratelli Tutti*, nos. 114–17.

68. Francis, *Fratelli Tutti*, no. 117.

69. Francis, *Fratelli Tutti*, no. 116.

70. Francis, *Fratelli Tutti*, no. 36.

71. Francis, *Fratelli Tutti*, nos. 132, 137.

72. Francis, *Fratelli Tutti*, no. 187.

73. Francis, *Fratelli Tutti*, no. 75.

74. Francis, *Fratelli Tutti*, nos. 243, 249.

75. Francis, *Fratelli Tutti*, no. 48.

76. Francis, *Fratelli Tutti*, no. 49.

inviolable. Francis also speaks of the benefit of religions for society in terms of the gift of faith, but also the accumulated wisdom that religions transmit.

Fratelli Tutti speaks to the particular challenges noted above, each of which makes the practice of ethics and advocacy more difficult. Much of *Fratelli Tutti* addresses the dignity of others, welcoming and seeking a genuine encounter with them. An important instance of such hospitality is migration. In the course of discussing migration, Francis says, "the arrival of persons who are different from us becomes a gift when we receive them with open hearts and allow them to be true to themselves."[77] For Francis, love exceeds acts of benevolence. It includes a genuine regard for the other, "considering them of value, worthy, pleasing and beautiful beyond their physical *or moral* appearance."[78] Francis notes that the appearance of virtue is possible. What distinguishes apparent virtue from authentic virtue is whether they foster openness and union with others.[79] Openness to the "moral other" is not the same as relativism or the reduction of morality to group consensus or the judgment of those in power.[80] Francis urges dialogue, through which persons might discover fundamental values, values which "transcend our concrete situations and remain non-negotiable" but which we can always better understanding through the dynamic reality of building consensus.[81]

Fraternity must also contend with the inevitability of moral failure and the need to forgive. Without minimizing moral fault or ruling out measures of justice, Francis writes that "we should never confine others to what they may have said or done, but value them for the promise that they embody, a promise that always brings with it a spark of new hope."[82] We must reckon with one another's limitations and failure in the truth.[83] And we must strive to be open to the other, for "the path to social unity always entails acknowledging the possibility that others have, at least in part, a legitimate point of view, something worthwhile to contribute, even if they were in error or acted badly."[84]

77. Francis, *Fratelli Tutti*, no. 134.
78. Francis, *Fratelli Tutti*, no. 94. Emphasis mine.
79. Francis, *Fratelli Tutti*, no. 91.
80. Francis, *Fratelli Tutti*, nos. 206–210.
81. Francis, *Fratelli Tutti*, no. 211.
82. Francis, *Fratelli Tutti*, no. 228.
83. Francis, *Fratelli Tutti*, no. 226.
84. Francis, *Fratelli Tutti*, no. 228.

In *Fratelli Tutti*, Francis offers grand exhortations such as "Never again war!"[85] but he is also mindful of the slow and partial progress that usually marks political life. As Merton warned against a fetishism of immediate visible results, so does Francis remind us that "constantly achieving great results" is not always possible, and cautions against mistaking politics for a quest for power. Even partial good done in love is not wasted. "For this reason, it is truly noble to place our hope in the hidden power of the seeds of goodness we sow, and thus to initiate processes whose fruits will be reaped by others. Good politics combines love with hope and with confidence in the reserves of goodness present in human hearts."[86] Moreover, such political love is not the province of elected or appointed officials, but all persons who have a "co-responsibility in creating and putting into place new processes and changes. Let us take an active part in renewing and supporting our troubled societies."[87] The Pope reminds us that love and solidarity are not achieved once and for all; they have to be built day by day.[88]

PRACTICING ETHICS AND ADVOCACY IN CATHOLIC HIGHER EDUCATION

Bearing these lessons in mind, we can conclude with some brief reflections on practicing ethics and advocacy in Catholic higher education.

Ethics Scholarship and Teaching

Ethics education, whether in a religiously affiliated context or not, must prioritize the navigation of a morally diverse world by equipping students to evaluate moral arguments, provide reasons for their own positions, and integrate knowledge and insight drawn from diverse sources. These sources include other disciplines, the world's religions, and the experiences from vulnerable and marginalized communities.

In the context of Catholic higher education, confidence in the compatibility between faith and reason undergirds a robust culture of academic freedom. Catholic colleges and universities are sites of great innovation, the creation of cultural treasures, and the primary engines for entire fields of human inquiry and knowledge. They are and must remain intellectual

85. Francis, *Fratelli Tutti*, no. 258.
86. Francis, *Fratelli Tutti*, no. 196.
87. Francis, *Fratelli Tutti*, no. 77.
88. Francis, *Fratelli Tutti*, no. 11.

communities open to the unpredictable, animated by the love that drives scholarship, prepared to be drawn in directions they cannot predetermine. Catholic colleges and universities are communities of hope, confident in human capacities for discovery, creativity, and improvement. They are also communities of solidarity, formed through processes of peer review, which provides mechanisms for accountability through criticism, correction, and integration. And like all human communities, they are sites where we can assist one another to grow in wisdom, striving to form the kind of culture of encounter that Francis describes.

Respectful engagement with Catholic moral tradition is a vital part of ethics scholarship and teaching in Catholic higher education. Critical assessment and rigorous analysis are part of respectful engagement. Ethicists play a vital role in the mandate of Vatican II to interpret the signs of the times and bring the Church into deeper dialogue with the world.[89] Climate change—along with the forced migration, public health, and resource-related conflicts it is already sparking—raises urgent moral challenges. The resurgence of white nationalism, massive increases in economic disparity, the extension of human power through rapid technological developments, and the global fire of misinformation and disinformation require assiduous efforts from ethicists and other content experts. Catholic intellectual tradition brings insights and resources, as well as a stalwart defense of the dignity of each human life and a rich vision of the common good.

University Ethics

Curiously, though colleges and universities produce the vast majority of ethics scholarship and, of course deliver instruction in ethics, there is no formal professional ethics for those who work in higher education. James Keenan rightly notes that "professional ethical standards are not constitutive of the commerce of university life and this stems from the university's lack of any serious, conscious engagement with ethics."[90] Ethics is, of course, baked into accreditation standards, research protocols, and administrative policies. These provisions address issues such as informed consent for research subjects, requirements for purchasing and reporting expenses, compliance with legal regulations, and expectations for academic integrity, civility, and so forth.

Keenan explores several aspects of university ethics. He looks at issues surrounding adjunct faculty, cheating, other forms of student misconduct,

89. Second Vativan Council, *Gaudium et Spes*, no. 4.
90. Keenan, *University Ethics*, 6.

forms of injustice related to gender and race, commodification, class, and athletics. Keenan, a Jesuit priest, writes that his work on university ethics was prompted in part by the Catholic sexual abuse scandal. He argues that universities have been left to monitor themselves and given the benefit of the doubt that they conduct their affairs ethically. While Keenan's argument does overlook the way university ethics is embedded in accreditation compliance, policies, and training established by human resources and other institutional codes of conduct, he is correct that there is no professional code of ethics for the academy or standardized training. Practices within the same institution, much less across institutions, can vary widely. Moreover, colleges and universities are de-centralized in many ways. Individual faculty enjoy considerable autonomy, and some faculty also have the protection of tenure. This can breed an environment for inconsistency and limit reporting of problematic behavior.

Colleges and universities should heed Keenan's call for comprehensive ethics reviews and action. Ethicists and those who do scholarship on teaching and learning should build on Keenan's work to develop a literature on university ethics.

Advocacy and the Role of Faculty

The practice of advocacy by faculty falls under academic freedom, but also an institution's particular administrative policies. Faculty enjoy constitutional rights to free speech. Academic freedom extends to teaching and research. Administrative policies may stipulate certain expectations regarding faculty speech; for example, by requiring faculty to refrain from portraying their own opinions as those of the institution. Forms of advocacy engage students in co-curricular opportunities for learning, enhance their civic education, and teach them skills for facilitating social change.

Faculty shape their students' practice of advocacy by teaching them information literacy, content expertise, and in some cases specific skills associated with advocacy, such as community organizing practices or how to write an op-ed. Faculty can go awry if their own practice of advocacy or their work with students on specific issues fails to respect the power dynamics between them. It is one thing for faculty to support students as advisors to organizations that may advocate on campus for specific issues, or to advocate for student concerns to administration, and another thing to enlist students to fight battles on one's behalf. Faculty need to be attentive to potential conflicts of interest in engaging with students on issues of advocacy and safeguard assessment of student work from situations that might give even the appearance of evaluating student learning on any grounds apart from their work in a given course.

Ethical expectations about faculty conduct and public advocacy are likely addressed in faculty handbooks and administrative policies, but expectations regarding faculty interaction with students in advocacy may be informal and uncodified. The latter can be especially murky. Faculty and students may be drawn to shared advocacy because of similar values, interests, and passions. Faculty may wish to ensure students feel supported and have opportunities to be heard by the administration. They may be seeking to serve the interests of students on campus. In contexts of concern and mentoring, it can be difficult to discern when ethical boundaries may be crossed. Colleges and universities should foster opportunities to discuss these issues in order to developed shared ethical standards.

Advocacy and University Leadership

University leaders need to claim the distinctive space of Catholic higher education, not only as a rationale for advocacy that aligns with the ethical commitments embedded in their missions, but also as a strategy for negotiating the challenges associated with the practice of advocacy. Catholic colleges and universities are more than producers of knowledge, they are communities for human development and civic formation. They provide space and time and resources and relationships to support students' development. While there are certainly behaviors that cannot be tolerated, whether by students or tenured faculty or senior leadership, colleges and universities are also important places for making mistakes and learning from them, places where peer review, in its many expressions, provides accountability and spurs improvement. They are distinctive cultures, with norms, values, structures, and chains of command that are not readily understood from outside, even by those who have earned or are currently working towards degrees. When instances of advocacy within or by the university meet with backlash, when moral disagreements arise, or when a particular moral failure requires formal response, university leaders can find wisdom not only in the Catholic mission and identity of the institution, but also in the peculiar kind of environment a university is.

Advocacy and the Role of Anchor Institutions

Colleges and universities also contribute to the common good through the activities that are proper to higher education, most especially through their essential activities of instruction, research, and scholarship. Catholic colleges and universities inform and shape public discourse and practice on a host of issues, often aligned with the strengths of their faculty and historic areas of emphasis. Moreover, they can recruit, develop, and advance—or launch—scholars and professionals who can be leaven for their communities or for particular causes. My own institution, for example, has recently convened a cohort of undergraduates to teach them grant-writing skills. The students themselves sought this opportunity so that they could begin to secure funding to invest in their communities of origin.

In addition, Catholic colleges and universities play varied and important roles in the communities where they are located. They are "anchor institutions." Emily Sladek defines anchor institutions as "important place-based engines that play key roles in local economies."[91] She rightly notes that "it is one thing to be an anchor institution. It is another to consciously and intentionally adopt an anchor mission, leveraging all available institutional and operational resources for community benefit."[92] That kind of corporate advocacy requires a strategic plan, with clear goals and messaging to units across the university. If Catholic colleges and universities are to live out their mission as local institutions, they can exercise forms of advocacy across their areas of impact. Universities, for example, are employers. Their hiring practices can be pipelines for diversifying a workforce and providing economic opportunity for underserved populations. Universities are consumers and producers. They contract with suppliers for goods and services. In all of these activities, they can commit themselves to sustainable and ethically sourced goods and screen third party service providers for their own ethical practices. Universities also partner with other regional units—governments, businesses, foundations, and charities, to accomplish shared goals. A city and a university might work together to accomplish goals for sustainability or workforce readiness or to coordinate a shared response to immigration policies.

CONCLUSION

The exercise of ethics and of advocacy in general, and in the context of Catholic higher education more particularly, require skills and dispositions that seem to be increasingly rare in public life. The appearance of virtue through the exercise of advocacy can tempt people away from the hard work of authentic forms of solidarity. Cancel culture can tempt people

91. Sladek, "The Transformative Power," 3.
92. Sladek, "The Transformative Power," 3.

away from the more difficult, patient, and messy work of restorative justice, partial progress toward goals, pastoral support of young persons, or respect for others across moral differences. Doing advocacy within Catholic higher education means taking up these challenges in an environment that is further complicated by intra-Catholic polarization and amidst a fight for institutional survival.

Institutions of higher education should be catalysts for the kinds of change we require. As we noted at the outset, higher education produces the overwhelming majority of ethics scholarship and teaching, and is closely related to the development and dissemination of ethics in various professional fields. Moreover, the practice of advocacy is frequently connected to and undertaken within colleges and universities. They are therefore important incubators for critical reflection on kinds of advocacy and for the moral and civic formation of advocates.

Any college or university faces challenges for navigating the practice of advocacy in an era of increased competition for students and the temptations presented by cancel culture. Catholic colleges and universities confront even more challenges since they must preserve both academic freedom and fidelity to the Catholic magisterium. Nevertheless, they have a special responsibility to foster the skills and dispositions needed for managing life together in a morally diverse world. This patient and complex work requires due attention to the differentiated roles and attendant virtues for faculty, staff, and students.

BIBLIOGRAPHY

Adams, Megan and Samantha Smith. "The demographic cliff is here—and it's about to get worse." *EAB* May 28, 2020. https://eab.com/insights/expert-insight/enrollment/the-demographic-cliff-is-already-here-and-its-about-to-get-worse/.

Allman, Mark J., and Winright, Tobias L. "Growing Edges of Just War Theory." *Journal of the Society of Christian Ethics* 32.2 (2012) 173–91.

Augustine. *City of God*. London: Penguin, 2003.

Benedict XVI. "Christmas Greetings." December 22, 2005. http://www.vatican.va/content/benedict-xvi/en/speeches/2005/december/documents/hf_ben_xvi_spe_20051222_roman-curia.html.

Catechism of the Catholic Church. New York: Catholic Book, 1994.

The Catholic Intellectual Tradition: Core Principles for the College or University. Washington, DC: Association of Catholic Colleges and Universities, 2017.

Christian, Robert G., III. "The Roots of American Catholic Polarization." *Church Life Journal*, April 1, 2019. https://churchlifejournal.nd.edu/articles/the-roots-of-american-catholic-polarization/.

Day, Maureen K. *Catholic Activism Today: Individual Transformation and the Struggle for Social Justice*. New York: New York University Press, 2020.

Francis. *Fratelli Tutti: On Fraternity and Social Friendship*. Enyclical letter. October 3, 2020. http://www.vatican.va/content/francesco/en/encyclicals/documents/papa-francesco_20201003_enciclica-fratelli-tutti.html.

Furstenberg, François. "University Leaders Are Failing." *Chronicle of Higher Education*, May 19, 2020. https://www.chronicle.com/article/when-university-leaders-fail.

Gallin, Alice. *Negotiating Identity: Catholic Higher Education Since 1960*. Notre Dame: University of Notre Dame Press, 2000.

Galvin, Gaby. "U.S. Births Continue to Fall, Fertility Rate Hits Record Low." *U.S. News and World Report*, May 20, 2020. https://www.usnews.com/news/healthiest-communities/articles/2020–05-20/us-births-continue-to-fall-fertility-rate-hits-record-low.

Second Vatican Council. *Gaudium et Spes*. In *Vatican Council II: The Conciliar and Postconciliar Documents*, edited by Austin Flannery, 163–282. Northport: Costello, 1975.

Italie, Hillel. "Everywhere and nowhere: The many layers of 'cancel culture.'" *AP News*, July 26, 2020. https://apnews.com/article/nfl-george-packer-media-football-social-media-9090804abf933c422207660509aeef22.

Joyce, Kathryn. "Deep State, Deep Church: How QAnon and Trumpism Have Infected the Catholic Church." *Vanity Fair*, October 30, 2020. https://www.vanityfair.com/news/2020/10/how-qanon-and-trumpism-have-infected-the-catholic-church.

Kaveny, M. Cathleen. "Virtuous Decision Makers and Incompetent Patients: The Case of the Conjoined Twins." In *Just & True Love: Feminism at the Frontiers of Theological Ethics: Essays in Honor of Margaret A. Farley*, edited by Maura A. Ryan and Brian F. Linnane, SJ, 338–67. Notre Dame: University of Notre Dame Press, 2008.

Keenan, James F., SJ. *University Ethics: How Colleges Can Build and Benefit from a Culture of Ethics*. London: Rowman and Littlefield, 2015.

Konieczny, Mary Ellen, Charles C. Camosy, and Tricia C. Bruce. *Polarization in the US Catholic Church: Naming the Wounds, Beginning to Heal*. Collegeville: Liturgical, 2016.

Land O'Lakes Statement. Privately published by Cushwa Center, 1967.

Lehman, Joseph John. "Mission Officers in Catholic Higher Education: Responsibilities and Competencies." PhD dissertation, Boston College, 2014.

Lipka, Michael, and Gregory A. Smith. "Like Americans overall, U.S. Catholics are sharply divided by party." PEW RESEARCH CENTER, January 24, 2019. https://www.pewresearch.org/fact-tank/2019/01/24/like-americans-overall-u-s-catholics-are-sharply-divided-by-party/.

Lovin, Robin. "Faith and Politics: An Augustinian Reflection." *Occasional Paper* 29 (2013) 1–17.

McRorie, Christina. "Rethinking Moral Agency in Markets: A Book Discussion on Behavioral Economics." *Journal of Religious Ethics* 44.1 (March 2016) 195–226.

Merton, Thomas. "Blessed Are the Meek." *Passion for Peace*. New York: Crossroad, 2006.

Mishan, Ligaya. "The Long and Tortured History of Cancel Culture." *New York Times Style Magazine*, December 3, 2020. https://www.nytimes.com/2020/12/03/t-magazine/cancel-culture-history.html.

Nepstad, Sharon Erickson. *Catholic Social Activism*. New York: New York University Press, 2019.

O'Brien, David. "Public Catholicism." *U.S. Catholic Historian* 8.4 (Fall 1989) 89–99.

O'Loughlin, Michael. "Is Catholic identity hurting enrollment at Catholic colleges?" *America*, May 16, 2018. https://www.americamagazine.org/politics-society/2018/05/16/catholic-identity-hurting-enrollment-catholic-colleges.

Parrott, Sarah. "How 2600+ students and parents perceive Catholic colleges today." *EAB*, February 4, 2019. https://eab.com/insights/blogs/enrollment/how-2600-students-and-parents-perceive-catholic-colleges-today/.

Paul, John, II. *Ex corde Ecclesiae: Apostolic Constitution on Catholic Universities.* Washington, DC: United States Catholic Conference, 1990.

Rubio, Julie Hanlon. "Cooperation with Evil Reconsidered: the Moral Duty of Resistance." *Theological Studies* 78.1 (2017) 96–120.

Segura, Olga. "I Reached Out to Every US Diocese. Here Are the Ones Implementing the 2018 Pastoral Letter on Racism." *America Magazine* November 21, 2019. https://www.americamagazine.org/faith/2019/11/21/i-reached-out-every-us-diocese-here-are-ones-implementing-2018-pastoral-letter.

Sladek, Emily. "The Transformative Power of Anchor Institutions." *Metropolitan Universities* 30.1 (2019) 3–4.

Smith, Gregory A. "8 facts about Catholics and politics in the U.S." *Pew Research Center*, September 15, 2020. https://www.pewresearch.org/fact-tank/2020/09/15/8-facts-about-catholics-and-politics-in-the-u-s/.

United States Catholic Conference. *Open Wide Our Hearts: The Enduring Call to Love—A Pastoral Letter Against Racism.* Washington, DC: United States Catholic Conference, 2018.

Wetzel, Dominic. "The rise of the Catholic Alt-Right." *Labor and Society* 23.1 (March 2020) 31–55.

Williams, Shannen Dee. "Forgotten Habits, Lost Vocations: Black Nuns, Contested Memories, and the 19th Century Struggle to Desegregate U.S. Catholic Religious Life." *Journal of African American History* 101.3 (2016) 231–60.

Yeager, D. M., and Stewart Herman. "The Virtue of 'Selling Out': Compromise as a Moral Transaction." *Journal of the Society of Christian Ethics* 37.1 (2017) 3–23.

A WOMANIST REFLECTS ON TEACHING
AS MORAL ADVOCACY

Marcia Y. Riggs

INTRODUCTION

AT THE BEGINNING OF every ethics class I teach, I ask students to describe the sociomoral context in which we live. I do so to impress upon them that the descriptive task precedes analytical and normative tasks of ethical reflection. They must acknowledge that their ethical questions derive from the context. In this essay, I reflect upon what it means to be a teacher who practices advocacy for her students in terms of my pedagogical choices. I make these choices because of the way I describe the sociomoral context in which we live.

A DESCRIPTION OF THE SOCIOMORAL CONTEXT

Post-9/11, nationalist grief and anxiety along with its militant rhetoric has provided fertile ground for domestic fear and anxiety about the direction of the United States. As reported in *The Divide Over America's Future: 1950 or 2050?*, "Pessimism about the direction of the country is higher today (74 percent) [2016] than it was at this time during the 2012 presidential race, when 57 percent of the public said the country was off on the wrong track."[1]

---

1. Jones et al., *The Divide Over America's Future*, 7.

Also, these pessimistic respondents think that the country has been on the wrong track for some time (since the 1950s).[2]

Furthermore, the political divide during the Bush-Obama years increased more dramatically than the division of US society based on race, gender, class, and education differences.[3] This partisan polarization is illustrated well by a debate over the proper motto of the United States: *E pluribus unum* (Out of Many, One) or "In God We Trust." The debate surfaced during President Obama's tenure in the White House and later during the presidential campaign of Hilary Clinton; both President Obama and presidential candidate Hilary Clinton used the motto *E pluribus unum* in their speeches. *E pluribus unum* emanates from the founders' discussion of a seal for the United States in 1776, and it has been considered a *de facto* national motto. For political liberals, it suggests openness to the pluralism of the nation, including religious diversity. However, "In God We Trust" was officially adopted as the national motto in 1956. Political conservatives contend that failure to use this motto disregards the history of struggle to found this "Christian" nation and God's providential oversight in that struggle.[4]

With the election of President Donald Trump, there is no longer a debate over the motto and the evolution of a culture of absolutism is stark. President Trump has affirmed "In God We Trust" as the country's motto and its consonance with his campaign slogan, "Make America Great Again." He asserts this in his own words from the first State of the Union Address:

> Tonight, I want to talk about what kind of future we are going to have, and what kind of Nation we are going to be. All of us, together, as one team, one people, and one American family. We all share the same home, the same heart, the same destiny, and the same great American flag. Together, we are rediscovering the American way. In America, we know that faith and family, not government and bureaucracy, are the center of American life. Our motto is "in God we trust."[5]

Following the election of Donald Trump, we are a national community embroiled continuously in vicious claims and counter-claims about important

2. Jones et al., *The Divide Over America's Future,* 27–28.

3. See "Partisan Polarization Surges in Bush, Obama Years."

4. Foster, "'In God We Trust' or 'E Pluribus Unum'?"; Niose, "'E Pluribus Unum' Becomes Controversial"; Daigle, "Meaning of America's Phrase 'In God We Trust' and Why It Is Important Today"; Stone, "Clinton Replaces 'In God We Trust' with 'E Pluribus Unum'"; Smith, "Trump replaces 'E Pluribus Unum' with 'Make America Great Again' on presidential coin."

5. Trump, *2018 State of the Union Address,* 54.

matters such as health care, immigration, gun control, criminal justice, and the list goes on.

In sum, the debate had not been simply about the country's motto; it was deeply rooted in anger about the direction of the country and fear that the white Christian majority was becoming a minority.[6] "Make America Great Again" resonated as a clarion call to return to the greatness of the 1950s. Although a majority of white evangelical Christians affirm that the country is going in the wrong direction, "nearly six in ten white mainline Protestants (59 percent) and white Catholics (57 percent) also believe the American way of life has taken a turn for the worse over the past 60 years."[7] Likewise, political partisanship held sway in churches as support for presidential candidates Hilary Clinton and Donald Trump tended to cluster into either largely Democratic or Republican congregations. Thus, the election of President Trump signaled not only a win for conservative politicians in the national motto debate, it sanctioned the anger and fear of many white evangelical Protestants and some mainline Protestants and Catholics that had been just under the surface.

Anger and fear are anchoring our political and religious life. That anger and fear have warped our sense of how to be a national and religious community that is a moral community.[8] Political discourse is uncivil; religious discourse is confrontational. Whether members of congress are holding their party's line or members of denominations are holding a doctrinal line, there is partisan polarization. At the heart of this polarization is an absolutist morality. Political or religious convictions based upon absolutist morality are binary, rigid, non-empathetic, and/or non-adaptive. My womanist ethical analysis of the sociomoral context contends that social, cultural, political, and religious ethical polarities are the crux of a culture of absolutism that drives the failure of moral community in both national and ecclesial life.

Polarized thinking mires us in anger, fear, and hatred. For some, these emotions masquerade as patriotism, wherein love of country and love of the Christian God are the same. For others, anger, fear, and hatred fuel a

---

6. See Jones et al., *The Divide Over America's Future*; Jones, "The Rage of White, Christian America."

7. Jones et al., *The Divide Over America's Future*, 28.

8. I am using this understanding of moral community: "Moral community refers to the network of those to whom we recognize an ethical connection through the demands of justice, the bonds of compassion, or a sense of obligation. The moral community for most of us lies somewhere in between, reaching beyond the immediate limits of family and friends to include those who share our gender or race, class, profession, religion, nationality, and, possibly, our humanity" (Spohn, "Who Counts?").

religio-political idealism and essentialism that asserts that if we see one another as disembodied human beings, we can tolerate one another because we are essentially the same. In both instances, we experience exclusion as normative. Likewise, the moral failure of churches is bypassing incarnation and focusing solely on crucifixion as the full (or, at least, the most important) meaning of how to understand redemption. In other words, it is our focus on the sacrificial suffering of Jesus' death rather than Jesus' life and ministry as the ethical imperative of his death to be the New Creation and live into the gift of a ministry of reconciliation (2 Cor 5:11–21).

Moral community cannot thrive in national or ecclesial life without revised interpretations of what it means to be a nation or a community of faith and concrete practices for living as a moral community. The clarion call today is to respect and affirm the intersectional and multi-variegated ways we must live as moral community. The clarion call is not to settle for toleration, colorblindness, or redemptive suffering as means to address the conflicts of violence and counterviolence. The clarion call is to break our complicity in these conflicts of violence (harms inflicted through hate speech or physical assaults or exploitation of confessional claims) that is hindering moral community in this twenty-first century sociomoral context.

Most importantly, polarization is the crux of our culture of absolutism. In order to counter that polarization, we need to cultivate the role of imagination in ethics. My womanist moral imagination insists that we abandon the binary between rationalism and relativism and focus instead upon how to foster a continuum of ethical thinking and responses that we construct through our intercultural encounters with one another. My contention here is that perceived rational (objective or impartial) moral principles or norms (even arrived at through intersubjective moral argumentation) can engender a morality that is polarizing when we seek the rational because we believe it will bring order to perceived chaos. Such attempts at rationalized order diminish our ethical capacity to respond constructively to twenty-first century ethical questions and issues, i.e., competing social and economic needs, political and religious pluralism, state-sanctioned violence, hate crime, and hate speech. Moral advocacy in this polarized, absolutist context is subverted. I will explicate ideas from an article on moral advocacy and moral discourse to unpack this statement.

SUBVERSION OF MORAL ADVOCACY IN A
CULTURE OF ABSOLUTISM

The journal article that I engage is "Advocacy as Moral Discourse" by Thomas I. Shaffer. The article opens thus:

> Advocacy at its best is a form of reconciliation. It reconciles the advocate with those whose champion he proposes to be. It reconciles the advocate with its hearers. It reconciles the person whose cause is advocated with persons who hear advocacy. It brings to community life a new sense of the interests of those the community neglects. It seeks to make things better. It is moral discourse.[9]

Shaffer speaks of two forms of advocacy: (1) public interest, advocacy in the name of justice on behalf of the community, and (2) advocacy on behalf of a particular client, such as a lawyer does. Although he asserts that both forms can be practiced as moral discourse, Shaffer importantly distinguishes moral discourse from adversary discourse. He offers this definition and features of moral discourse:

> Advocacy radiates into the community, into consideration of social justice, because of four features that distinguish moral discourse from adversary discourse: (1) Moral discourse is interpersonal; (2) Moral discourse argues from the person of the client; (3) Moral discourse is addressed to the conscience of those who hear it; (4) Moral discourse, because it is a form of reconciliation, binds the community together.[10]

Finally, Shaffer offers a discussion of advocacy addressed to conscience through his interpretation of the biblical story of Jesus and the woman caught in adultery in the Gospel of John. Jesus disrupts the group consensus ("an obstacle both to advocacy and justice") about the woman by not arguing about Mosaic Law, but by "bear[ing] witness against the rules in order to give purpose to the rules."[11] The idea that the rules may be unjustly applied seems far from the minds of those individuals and groups today who claim that they support "law and order" when they challenge any protest of the deaths of black women and men at the hands of police. Their position upholds that the law is sacrosanct even if there is video evidence to the contrary. Those espousing this position do so with certitude in the rightness

---

9. Shaffer, "Advocacy as Moral Discourse," 647.

10. Shaffer, "Advocacy as Moral Discourse," 661–62.

11. Shaffer, "Advocacy as Moral Discourse," 665.

both of their position and the actions of the police. Then when (if) a case is brought against the police involved in the killing, the police officers are most often not charged. Instead, a state's attorney general informs a grand jury or the public that there are no charges that can be brought that can be proved, i.e., can be upheld in a court of law. Is there no room in the judicial process to "bear witness" against the law in order to effect a just outcome?

Likewise, Shaffer's discussion of moral advocacy supports my assertion that in the current culture of absolutism, there is a subversion of moral advocacy. Individuals and groups use adversary discourse as they assert the rightness of their positions in defense of single-focused moral issues; for example, arguments against abortion. Although many persons or communities of faith maintain that their argument derives from biblically based principles, their arguments are not concerned with the persons (women as individuals or a social group) and the conditions of women (e.g., sexual violence, poverty) who deliberate and make a decision to have an abortion. Moreover, if anti-abortion or pro-life arguments are rigid, binary, and nonadaptive, then they are not interpersonal. Such arguments do not address the conscience of those who hear them, and do not bind the community together. Moreover, anti-abortion advocates are not the only persons captive to the culture of absolutism; pro-life advocates commonly take absolutist positions that attest to their political allegiances. Both groups rarely make persuasive appeals to the heart and minds of the other party. Polarized thinking is the engine of a culture of absolutism, thus what is touted as moral advocacy is adversary discourse.[12]

The micro-sociomoral context of a classroom mirrors the dynamics of the macro-sociomoral context. This is not simply the case because our students come to us as citizens and persons of faith in communities of faith who have been raised and live in the culture of absolutism. This is the case because western education teaches students how to argue positions; students have not been taught how to be in dialogue in ways that we engage different positions for the purpose of understanding. We teach students to debate, to win an argument. Within this sociomoral context of absolutism and Western education, teachers must discern what moral advocacy means in an educational context. The teacher's advocacy has two dimensions: (1) institutional and (2) pedagogical.

---

12. See the essay in this volume by Rueben Rosario Rodriguez for a full discussion of the pitfalls of binary moral and political advocacy on abortion. Rodriguez offers a "normative approach to Christian ethics and advocacy for abortion that transcends the single-issue politics currently dominating the discourse" that respects dialogue as important to advocacy.

TEACHER AS MORAL ADVOCATE

The discussion here is in conversation with ideas in this article: "Moral Positionality in Social Justice Advocacy and Leadership" by Jonathan O'Brien. O'Brien asserts that character grounds ethical professional practice, and in his ethical leadership framework, character refers to "the will and courage to act."[13] Likewise, he contends advocacy should be counted among the competencies for student affairs professionals because advocating for students is at the heart of their work. I maintain that advocacy is equally important to the vocation of professor, as an employee of an educational institution and as a teacher in a classroom.[14]

Being an advocate institutionally can take several forms. O'Brien highlights three: (1) martyrs (those who are left socially and politically isolated), (2) sellouts (those who eventually submit to the status quo), (3) madvocates (those who "try to change minds through anger, righteous indignation, guilting, gossiping, and moral outrage").[15] However, authentic advocates respect the different moral positions of their colleagues and enter into dialogue about these differences. Disclosing one's moral positionality is precursor to such dialogue. "Moral positionality [is] the location from which we are advocating our opinion on a given issue within a dynamic field of conflicting possibilities for ethical action."[16]

O'Brien offers a fourfold typology of moral positions. First, there is the pragmatic idealist; this position is characterized by making ethical decisions with reference to their impact on people. Second, a principled realist makes and judges ethical decisions in terms of following the rules, and rules determine responsibility and consequences. Third, the principled idealist affirms enduring principles as foundational to actions; thus, they support the status quo. Fourth, there is a pragmatic realist who makes strategic ethical choices so as not to challenge authority directly. These moral positions are "sites, any of which individuals may occupy, more than once, as they discern the best approach to resolve a specific conflict or concern."[17] Unlike the dynamism and discernment that O'Brien suggests regarding moral positions, conflict ensues because colleagues act out these various moral positions with

13. O'Brien, "Moral Positionality," para. 5.

14. See the essay "Doing Ethics and Advocacy in Catholic Higher Education" by Darlene Fozard Weaver in this volume for a discussion that informs a position regarding doing advocacy as an employee. My primary focus is on teaching as a practice of advocacy in the classroom.

15. O'Brien, "Moral Positionality," para. 11.

16. O'Brien, "Moral Positionality," para. 14.

17. O'Brien, "Moral Positionality," paras. 31–35.

uncompromising rigidity, unable to hear and be in dialogue with one another. Conflict is not the issue per se; the issue is whether colleagues engage in their conflicts destructively or generatively.

Professors exercise their responsibility to be moral advocates via institutional governance and the curriculum. With respect to institutional governance, professors serve on committees and advocate for policies and structures that support equity and justice as fairness, thus creating a context in which all constituents (administration, faculty, staff, and students) can flourish. With respect to the curriculum, professors advocate pedagogically for methods and contents for teaching and learning. The questions are these: Will professors advocate for curriculum that will prepare students primarily for a profession that upholds institutions as they are? Or, will we advocate for curriculum that prepares students for a profession with capacities to serve courageously in a world filled with diversities and injustices linked to racial, ethnic, gender, class, sexual, physical ability, and cognitive ability, to name a few?

I am an African-American woman employed in a seminary that has historical entanglements in Southern slavery from which it has reaped present-day benefits. I accepted a letter of appointment to the faculty in 1991, and I was the first person of color to be appointed to a full-time position, tenured, and promoted to full professor. Being an institutional advocate in the seminary has had mixed outcomes mostly because of the inability of my colleagues to own their moral positions; the practice of forced consensus is preferred to engaging in moral discourse. Adversary discourse thus prevails. In the remainder of this essay, I will *not* focus on being an institutional advocate. *I will argue for teaching as moral advocacy.* An exercise that I use with my students is the point of departure.

TEACHING AS MORAL ADVOCACY

Students in my classes often complete a circle of oppression exercise.[18] In the seminary classroom, I have students complete the circle by positioning themselves and those persons who they serve in a ministry context on the circle; they are to observe points of intersection and where there are no intersections. The circle of oppression has at its hub a space to name the dominant group ideology operative in the ministry context. Students are sometimes surprised by the multiple intersections between themselves and the people they serve that shows up the homogeneity of the group. Other students are dismayed by the lack of intersections between themselves and

18. Russo and Fairbrother, "Using the Circle of Oppression," 8.

the people they serve when it shows up as an elitism separating them from their congregants.

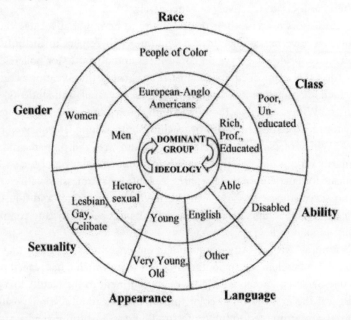

My question to the first group of students is this: Are you concerned about a lack of diversity? My question to the second group is this: Are you concerned about how to bridge the gap? Each group answers yes to their respective question because of a similar concern: they are unprepared to lead. On one hand, they want to do ministry with a diverse group of people, but they are unsure about how they will get their congregation to invite others unlike themselves to join. On another hand, they want to do ministry with a diverse group of people, but they are unsure about handling "all of the conflict that comes with diversity" (their words).

In the larger context of the theological educational institution, the dominant ideology/theology and power resides in the trustees and administrators. In the micro-context of the classroom, the professor as teacher is at the center, and they must choose how they inhabit that center. Either professors inhabit the center as (1) employees who align our teaching and learning practices to that of the institution and its dominant ideology and theology, or (2) pedagogical power brokers whose dissent from institutional ideology is driven by personal theological commitments and pedagogical choices.

We make choices about our moral positionality from our location at the center of power in the classroom. Alongside O'Brien's fourfold typology of moral advocacy, I think that there are two overarching types of teaching as advocacy. First, there is content advocacy: teachers maintain that there is a canon of texts that must be taught; their priority is teaching these texts for the sake of transmitting subject content that must anchor the student's professional development. This canon of texts reinscribes the dominant culture's ideology and theology. Teaching is moral advocacy that benefits the status quo. Second, there is community advocacy: teachers affirm an open canon; their priority is teaching diverse texts as resources for analytical, constructive thinking that prepares students to interpret their profession contextually. This open canon of texts brings the canonical texts into dialogue with texts/voices of peoples who have been marginalized, minoritized, and erased—subjugated knowledges become canonical. Teaching is moral advocacy for just inclusion. If we take seriously O'Brien's idea that moral positions are sites for making ethical choices, then content and community advocacy might be engaged dialogically instead of oppositely.

What happens in the classroom pertains to both what is studied and how students interact and learn in the classroom. The oppression circle exercise pushes us to recognize that teaching and learning must attend to the way teachers and students challenge one another consciously and unconsciously as we share our lives and learn new ideas. Importantly, we engage in the social construction of knowledge.

When the professor places themself on the circle, you can see where you and everyone else is located at the intersections of identity. From the center of power, you choose whether this is a classroom where acknowledgment and recognition of everyone in their particularity and diversity are valued and essential to teaching and learning subject content. Or, you choose that this is a classroom where ignoring diversity and particularity is the best way to ensure that teaching and learning subject content is not hindered. Teaching as moral advocacy requires that we intentionally choose the former or the latter because what happens in the classroom pertains to both what is studied and how students interact and learn in the classroom.

We are located at the center of power in the classroom, and our choice is the type of advocacy our teaching will take. When we enter the classroom, we cannot leave our embodied sociohistoric selves behind and neither can our students. We professors embody personal and social group histories that inform and/or bequeath us our current social status as professors. Even if our current social status as professors is marked by power and privilege that may not align with our outsider status or minoritized place in society because of our race, ethnicity, gender, class, sexual identity, citizenship, and/or (dis)ability, we are at the center of power in our classrooms. As an African-American womanist ethicist, I am an outsider-insider whose personal and theological commitment lead me to transgress the claims of the institution's ideological and theological commitments. From my location at the center of power in the classroom, my teaching practices create dialogue about social justice because I am preparing students to live in a world filled with injustices. Accordingly, I teach to nurture ethical capacities in my students that will enable them to recognize injustices and to lead empathetically and justly. The capacities are nonviolent and intercultural communication, conflict transformation, dialogue, and moral imagination. I nurture these capacities in students to integrate character with skills in my students.

THEOLOGICAL EDUCATION
AND THE CULTURE OF ABSOLUTISM

Teaching as moral advocacy is about exposing all of our captivity to a culture of absolutism. Political groups and religious groups define themselves based upon values, principles, and norms that confirm who is in or out of such groups. These different values, principles, and norms can be simply markers of distinctiveness, but more often they are boundaries of exclusivity. In a culture of absolutism, exclusion becomes the norm by which values and practices of community are ordered. This norm of exclusion is both definitional and prescriptive. When the norm is both definitional *and* prescriptive, it renders some persons/groups forever outside of a community because who the community is and how its members live together establishes a boundary that some are never to cross. Whereas when the norm of exclusion is solely definitional it sets forth what is distinctive about a community in the hope that others may choose to join because of sharing that community's commitments. In today's context, we exclude by definition *and* practices, thus failing as moral community. This failure as moral community distorts and circumscribes the scope of justice consistent with democratic ideals about equality and justice and religious beliefs about justice and love. Most importantly, though, a culture of absolutism with its dynamics of partisan polarization obstructs practices necessary to nurturing and sustaining moral community. The culture of absolutism is based in moral conflict rooted deeply in values and norms that derive from what is of ultimate concern, from what is religious. Persons and groups identified broadly as the Left, the Center, and the Right. The Left values freedom, the Center values compromise, and the Right values conformity. As each person or group holds tenaciously to its core value and offers interpretations of political, social, and/or theological issues, destructive conflict and violence ensues. Such rigid interpretations turn the nation and its institutions into places of moral conflict.[19] Moral conflict becomes intractable as individuals and groups insist that their position is right or the Truth.

As educational institutions for leaders and members of faith communities that are also socialization systems for the nation's citizens, schools of theological education are not immune to the culture of absolutism. The purpose, the curriculum, and practices of teaching and learning must be refocused through a relationality paradigm that engages the dominant rationality paradigm dialogically. Theological education as a dialogue between relationality and rationality would bring heart and mind together authentically as the crux of theological formation for doing ministry in faith communities, society, and the world.

Is the purpose of theological education the continuation of denominations and the historic understandings of the traditions of those denominations? Or, is the purpose of theological education to nurture ministerial capacities and moral agency for leading, teaching, and healing in communities of faith, theological institutions, societies, and the world? It seems to me that theological education must answer both questions affirmatively and dialogically. Schools must regard traditions as repositories of resources for addressing twenty-first-century challenges, rather than as historical artifacts to be revered or as depositories of the Truth. Theological education must have the twofold purpose of mediating the historical and the present in ways that nurture moral imagination.

Theological education with the purpose of nurturing moral imagination is invitational. The term, invitational, suggests a posture of openness to, valuing of, and respect for particularity and diversity (e.g., diversity of theological interpretations, denominations, spiritualities, social groups, learning abilities, physical abilities, race, ethnicity, gender, and economic groups). From this posture of openness, the institution ensures the teaching and learning is about educating everyone for constructive engagement of diversity and its accompanying conflicts.

Teaching and learning in a school of theological education that is aware of its potential to be a place of intractable moral conflicts operates from the following presuppositions of teaching as advocacy:

1. Teaching and learning must expose and analyze biases.

2. Teaching must create a moral community of learning in which self-criticism and mutual criticism challenge attitudes that support oppression and violence.

19. See Maiese, "Moral or Value Conflicts."

3. The classroom must be a just space, and teaching is a practice of jus-tice-making so that classrooms become nonviolent spaces.

4. Teaching and learning must facilitate intercultural encounter.

5. Knowing the body of learners is as important as the body of knowl-edge that is the subject of the teaching and learning process.

6. Classrooms are spaces of intercultural encounter.

7. Classrooms are spaces of conflict.

8. Teachers mediate tensions of difference and particularity.

9. Teachers shift energies of conflict from destructive to generative.[20]

Teaching as advocacy happens each time you decide what you will teach and create a course syllabus. You choose whether you will teach from a position that promotes content advocacy or community advocacy. As Bell Hooks writes:

> Dominator culture [absolutist culture] has tried to keep us all afraid, to make us choose safety instead of risk, sameness instead of diversity. Moving through that fear, finding what connects us, reveling in our differences; this is the process that brings us closer, that gives us a world of shared values, of meaningful community.[21]

Teaching as advocacy requires that you choose risk, diversity, and connec-tion on the way to meaningful moral community.

20. See Riggs, "Loves the Spirit." My theoretical discussion in that essay informs these presuppositions.

21. Hooks, *Teaching Community*, 198.

BIBLIOGRAPHY

Daigle, Katherine. "Meaning of America's Phrase 'In God We Trust' and Why It Is Important Today." *PolitiChicks*, July 19, 2015. https://politichicks.com/2015/07/meaning-of-americas-phrase-in-god-we-trust-and-why-it-is-important-today/.

Foster, Thomas A. "'In God We Trust' or '*E Pluribus Unum*'?: The American Founders Preferred the Latter Motto." *Origins*, November 9, 2011. https://origins.osu.edu/history-news/god-we-trust-or-e-pluribus-unum-american-founders-preferred-latter-motto.

Hooks, Bell. *Teaching Community: A Pedagogy of Hope.* New York: Routledge, 2003.

Jones, Robert P. "The Rage of White, Christian America." *New York Times*, November 10, 2016. https://www.nytimes.com/2016/11/11/opinion/campaign-stops/the-rage-of-white-christian-america.html.

Jones, Robert P., Daniel Cox, Betsy Cooper, and Rachel Lienesch. *The Divide Over America's Future: 1950 or 2050?: Findings from the 2016 American Values Survey.* Washington, DC: Public Religion Research Institute, 2016.

Maiese, Michelle. "Moral or Value Conflicts." *Beyond Intractability,* July 2003. https://www.beyondintractability.org/essay/intolerable-moral-differences.

Niose, David. "'E Pluribus Unum' Becomes Controversial." *Psychology Today,* March 13, 2011. https://www.psychologytoday.com/us/blog/our-humanity-naturally/201103/e-pluribus-unum-becomes-controversial.

O'Brien, Jonathan. "Moral Positionality in Social Justice Advocacy and Leadership." *Developments* 13.2 (Summer 2015).

"Partisan Polarization Surges in Bush, Obama Years." *Pew Research Center,* June 4, 2012. https://www.pewresearch.org/politics/2012/06/04/partisan-polarization-surges-in-bush-obama-years/.

Riggs, Marcia. "'Loves the Spirit': Transformative Mediation as Pedagogical Practice." In *Conflict Transformation and Religion: Essays on Faith, Power, and Relationship,* edited by Ellen Ott Marshall, 111–124. New York: Palgrave MacMillan, 2016.

Russo, Pat, and Anne Fairbrother. "Using the Circle of oppression to Understand Teaching about Social Justice." *Just in Time* 8.2 (June 2012) 8–12.

Shaffer, Thomas I. "Advocacy as Moral Discourse." *North Carolina Law Review* 57 (1978–1970) 647–70.

Smith, Allan. "Trump replaces 'E Pluribus Unum' with 'Make America Great Again' on presidential coin." *Business Insider,* December 22, 2014. https://www.businessinsider.com/trump-makes-changes-to-presidential-coin-2017-12.

Spohn, William. "Who Counts?: Images Shape Our Moral Community." *Santa Clara University.* https://legacy.scu.edu/ethics/publications/iie/v7n2/spohn.html.

Stone, Michael. "Clinton Replaces 'In God We Trust' with 'E Pluribus Unum.'" *Patheos: Progressive Secular Humanist,* July 29, 2016. https://www.patheos.com/blogs/progressivesecularhumanist/2016/07/clinton-replaces-in-god-we-trust-with-e-pluribus-unum/.

Trump, Donald. *2018 State of the Union Address: January 30, 2018.* In *Historic Documents of 2018,* edited by Heather Kerrigan, 52–61. Thousand Oaks: Congressional Quarterly, 2019.

ETHICS AND ADVOCACY IN PEDAGOGY

An Example in Poverty Studies

Harlan Beckley

THE RELATIONSHIP BETWEEN ETHICS and advocacy applies to pedagogy as well as scholarship. Ethics in this essay is understood broadly to include second order reflection on arguments bearing on a moral cause, and advocacy as arguments for a moral cause. This essay offers one example of pedagogy: undergraduate and professional education focused on poverty, also broadly defined to include barriers to minimally acceptable opportunities for individual and community or group well-being. The essay is not argumentative, although the description incorporates reasons for why the particular pedagogy evolved as it did. It describes limitations as well as strengths for this approach to education in support of the moral cause of diminishing poverty.

The description and assessment of the pedagogy proceeds in four sections: the inchoate origins of a multi-school pedagogy focused on poverty; expansion from a few schools to a poverty studies consortium, now twenty-five schools; the evolution to a more mature pedagogy at the school where I taught; and the implications, including observations about the strengths and weaknesses of this pedagogy for relating ethics and advocacy.

PEDAGOGY TO DIMINISH POVERTY:
AN EARLY EXPERIMENT

I was a principal among faculty, students, and administrators who initiated a poverty studies program at Washington and Lee University in the mid-1990s. The program was envisioned as appropriate for undergraduates from any major and for law students preparing for most aspects of law. It was not a research program focused on poverty or a program in politics and poverty or poverty policy. The hope was and is that graduates understand how any career and many areas of civic and political leadership and involvement impact poverty and can have a role in diminishing it. The program incorporates a blend of philosophical and religious ethics, literature and the arts, and social sciences and sciences that incorporate policy issues and remedies while examining causes and obligations bearing on poverty.

Measured by student and faculty participation, the program flourishes after twenty-plus years. The Shepherd Program on Interdisciplinary Study of Poverty and Human Capability, or Shepherd Program as it has come to be called in recognition of a benefactor couple who contributed funds and nurturing advice, enrolls a hundred undergraduates in an interdisciplinary introductory course on poverty each year. The course, branded "Poverty 101" by students, engages just over 20 percent of Washington and Lee's graduating seniors. The Shepherd Program graduates the most minors—twenty-five to thirty each year—of any department or program and supports approximately forty undergraduate and law students in eight-week (or longer) summer internships working directly with impoverished individuals and communities in the US and globally. The internship, as well as one-credit community engagement courses for undergraduates, which enroll about fifty students annually, and a capstone interdisciplinary seminar for nearly thirty undergraduate and law students are part of the minor. The minor also includes a variety of discipline-based courses related to poverty, courses taught by departmental faculty mostly in the social sciences. Some students, especially those interested in health professions and environmental issues and poverty, also draw heavily on their studies in the sciences for research components of their capstone course and occasional community-based research projects.

Twenty-five affiliate faculty from beyond the Shepherd Program, approximately fifteen per year, offer discipline-based and interdisciplinary courses for minors and other interested students. Nearly 350 students enroll in these courses annually, a far more poverty-focused curriculum than existed in 1997.[1] The Shepherd Program employs five full-time persons: a director who is a professor, two associate directors (one executes the internships and a small post-graduate fellowship with alumni and alumnae support and one supervises a Bonner Foundation Program and is an instructor in poverty studies), an assistant director who supports publicity for all

---

1. Data supplied by the Shepherd Program staff at Washington and Lee University for 2017–18 academic year and remains approximately accurate though 2019.

activities and a variety of community-engagement programing; and a coordinator for a campus kitchen who also supervises community-engagement and community-based-research pertaining to food and nutrition. When the program began in 1997, I was the senior-faculty director. There was a half-time administrative assistant and no affiliated faculty or discipline-based courses explicitly associated with poverty studies. As will become apparent, this growth in faculty and staff and affiliate faculty has been pedagogically significant well beyond the mere expansion of personnel devoted to poverty studies at Washington and Lee.[2] The program has undoubtedly changed the university curriculum, and some would say has changed the student culture.[3]

There is more. Although these developments were not part of our initial vision, the Shepherd Program at Washington and Lee did not stay at Washington and Lee. Initially, it did not even include summer internships, but someone reminded us that studying poverty in the classroom is like studying "scum" on a pond. The criticism seared. Academic study alone tends to relegate poor persons and communities to a distant problem, not self-respecting equals. The organizers of the initial poverty studies program—aware of liberation theology and other sources that introduced the "epistemological privilege" of the poor and other victims of injustice—were alert to the pitfalls of the relatively well-off and largely white suburban students at Washington and Lee being taught exclusively by comfortably situated faculty. Attempts to compensate for that shortcoming included a carefully planned and sustained internship. We believed that the internship should include direct engagement with persons hindered by limited employment opportunities, low wages, poor education, segregated neighborhoods, family instability, the criminal justice system and incarceration,

2. The very term "poverty studies" is controversial for some observers because it can associate a group of persons with a negative, stigmatizing label. Furthermore, it is rarely associated with learning through community engagement and community research. As will become apparent, there are reasons for using this vivid term, rather than some more abstract designation like inequality, social justice, or marginalized, and for incorporating community engagement integrated with various facets of traditional academic courses. There are certainly reasons for avoiding "the poor" and "persons in poverty" in some contexts, but there are also good reasons for keeping the focus of this education on persons and communities deprived of minimal opportunities or the "capability" for a decent level of well-being. Terms such as injustice may refer to racial, sexual, and other moral abuses to and among students and education professionals, but all students and teachers are relatively privileged.

3. This program has benefitted admissions at Washington and Lee and has shaped the blend of class and race diversity at a school that does not stand out as diverse in these respects. Exact numbers for this area are necessarily uncertain estimates, but entering students and admissions officers verify significant effects.

lack of healthcare, inadequate housing and homelessness, and more. Internships in policy research or exclusively devoted to funding or administrating non-profits would not enable knowledge of the struggles and obstacles to opportunities nor the strategies to deal with these obstacles. Hence, we proposed internships in which students interested in education, law, healthcare, business, policy, politics, and specific vocations work for eight weeks with and alongside communities and persons encountering obstacles to their well-being.

Poverty studies moved beyond Washington and Lee in another important respect. Washington and Lee interns joined interns from colleges and students informed by quite different experiences: Berea, Spelman, and Morehouse. I wish we could claim that reaching out to these schools was for strictly pedagogical reasons. It should have been, but it became apparent that asking for internship funding for W&L students alone was unlikely to succeed. Funders were much more likely to support student interns from diverse colleges. The Alliance has continued with Berea for over twenty years and has been woven into a national poverty studies consortium with twenty-five schools. More about that momentarily.

Part of the initial motivation for this Alliance was to enhance funding and expand poverty studies to other institutions, but we also foresaw plausible pedagogical benefits. Participation in internships required applications and interviews at each participating school. At Washington and Lee, eligibility to apply required enrollment in the introductory course on poverty. Applicants at each school were expected to indicate how their studies and experiences prepared them for the internship. All applicants needed to articulate how their internship placements could inform their career choices and possible work or civic activity.

Equally important, interns were brought together in an opening conference to prepare for internships and become acquainted, especially with those with whom they would live and work for eight weeks. They were housed together in a variety of urban or rural locations and encouraged to live on a *per diem* budget—funding provided—that nearly ensured that they eat mutually prepared meals and talk with each other. The purpose was for students from dramatically diverse backgrounds—sometimes even those from the same school—to become acquainted and learn from each other as they were exposed to the suffering, aspirations, capabilities, and hopes of people facing barriers to personal, family, civic, and economic well-being. The interns, regardless of their college or circumstances before college, possessed privileges many persons with whom they work do not have. The interns were also required to participate in a closing conference at which they continued to interact and begin to establish a network for later communication. Over time, we incorporated other means to promote interaction among students from different schools and backgrounds. Interns were expected to learn from agency supervisors, partners, and persons in the community throughout the summer. They were encouraged to learn from each other. The number of participants from all schools has ranged from approximately two-dozen in the first year to nearly 130 in 2018 and 2019. (Unfortunately, the COVID-19 virus required severely truncated internships in 2020 and 2021 with much more restricted interaction between students and with communities.)

Most participating schools have required interns to present what they learned to faculty and students at their school, and we have invited students to submit essays focused on what they learned about the causes and plausible remedies for aspects of poverty. These essays were shared with current and future interns in order to promote additional interaction.

Returning interns at Washington and Lee are encouraged to consider additional courses and a capstone seminar as part of a minor.

A HIGHER EDUCATION CONSORTIUM FOR POVERTY STUDIES

The Shepherd Program on poverty studies has transcended Washington and Lee—as well as the Alliance with Berea, Spelman, and Morehouse—in another way. In 2012, a group of schools, including Berea and Spelman, formed a 501-c-3 educational consortium that incorporates pedagogical elements of the Shepherd Program at Washington and Lee. Called the Shepherd Higher Education Consortium on Poverty to further honor the inspiration, donations, and nurturing support of Tom and Nancy Shepherd, the Consortium schools offer introductory courses prior to an internship, and like the earlier Alliance, a common internship followed by post-internship community engagement and courses, often constituting a minor. All Consortium schools provide a capstone experience to bring together previous coursework and community engagement in a study that builds toward the students' post-graduate career, civic, and policy interests to diminish poverty. I reiterate that these schools, like the earlier Alliance schools, do not offer a poverty studies major. The minor offers flexibly with almost any major or career vocation students select.

As of 2021, the Shepherd Consortium consists of twenty-five schools—and several additional schools have initiated poverty studies programs on similar models. The Consortium and its predecessor—the Shepherd Alliance formed in 1998—has supported over 1,250 domestic internships in direct engagement. (Several of the member schools also sponsor international internships addressing poverty; the Consortium internship collaboration focuses on US poverty.) The Consortium staff has two full-time, one half-time, and intermittent part-time employees. It has a governing board, and sponsors conferences and symposia that focus on relevant topics such as criminal justice and incarceration, childhood literacy and nutrition, and family structure and policy support for families.

Consortium members have adopted a common strategic plan focused on a sustained education as distinct from service or pure advocacy; they share the assumption that the education is about diminishing poverty. Hence, consideration of economic growth, labor markets, education, environmental sustainability, family formation, housing, policing and criminal justice; race, ethnic, and gender discrimination, and community organizing are all considered in relation to causes of and diminishing poverty. Ethics and normative concerns are prominent at most member institutions, but so are other humanities, social sciences, and sciences. Consortium schools share a commitment to preparing graduates for diminishing poverty, regardless of their career choice or special civic, policy, or political interests. The Consortium does not seek to produce community organizers, poverty researchers, social workers, or a particular kind of political advocate, although graduates may choose these vocations. Many have.

As the Consortium examines long-term assessment, it will consider how its educational programming shapes graduates' professional and civic activity. The Consortium will not limit its assessment to the quality and influence of particular courses and internships, including agency supervisors' judgments regarding the value of the interns' work. Nor can assessment be limited to student satisfaction with the educational programming. The assessment of the effects of pedagogy on graduates' work and civic engagement has to this point been mostly qualitative and anecdotal; for example, a hundred-plus self-reporting essays by graduates on the Consortium website.[4] Although I am now retired, the current Consortium leadership agrees an accurate assessment of the extent to which poverty studies education actually diminishes poverty in the US is not feasible.[5] The variables to judge such a causal relationship would be daunting. The Consortium can,

4. See https://www.shepherdconsortium.org/alumni/alumni-essays/.

5. My colleague, David Bradley, executive director of the National Community Action Program, once ventured that sustained poverty studies education at a hundred schools with fifteen graduates each year would do as much to diminish poverty as any policy change since the mid-seventies. David, to be sure, intending to inspire the formation of the Consortium made this remark prior to the Affordable Care Act and the expansion of SNAP after the 2008 recession. He offered no quantitative measures.

however, assess more systematically and quantitatively the extent to which its graduates approach their work and civic and political activity relative to poverty differently than they would have absent a sustained and integrated poverty-focused education.

Although Shepherd Consortium member schools have much in common, a qualitative assessment by the Curry School of Education at the University of Virginia shows that the Consortium members differ in the disciplinary emphases within their interdisciplinary approaches and in the extent to which they seek to measure success by specific attitude and values outcomes of their courses and comprehensive poverty studies education.[6] Some are based more in economics and less in explicit religious, philosophical, theoretical, or even normative ethical approaches. Some seek results measured by attitudes about poor persons or the common culture's view of poverty or by where students stand on issues, policies, or structural impediments to overcoming poverty. The Consortium has favored flexibility in these pedagogical approaches, justifiably in my opinion, but the differences do bear on the roles of both ethics and advocacy within poverty studies education, even assuming the common cause of diminishing poverty.

MORE REFINED DESCRIPTION AND ASSESSMENT

I simplify this essay with a finer-grained description of the pedagogical approach I know best: the one developed at Washington and Lee University for a program that I directed for seventeen years. It manifested several pedagogical features that distinguish the ways in which ethics and advocacy are related. While it differs from the pedagogy at other Consortium schools and evolving currently at Washington and Lee's program under the able leadership of my successor, we can, I think, learn from both the strengths and possible weaknesses of its prominent pedagogical features.

First, students are not supported for internships, community-based engagement in their campus communities, or community-based research projects prior to an interdisciplinary course on poverty.[7] The course is comprehensive. The readings and discussions start with definitions and measurements of poverty and go on to consider causes and moral obligations related to poverty before examining plausive remedies and their prospects

6. Pusser and Steinmetz, "Evaluation of the Shepherd Higher Education Consortium on Poverty."

7. While my pedagogy had its idiosyncrasies, this requirement for a course prior to the internship is a goal for all Consortium schools and is realized in practice by most schools.

for diminishing poverty. The course is not limited to specific aspects, e.g., race and poverty or labor markets, and considers remedies through inter-disciplinary academic criticism that proffers many options. Moral resolu-tions to poverty are considered plausible as informed by social sciences and factual data about poverty and what causes it. A distinction between ethics as evaluative description and as norms and principles is relevant here.[8] The social scientific analysis of definitions, measurements, and causes of poverty are evaluative, but they are more descriptive than normative and are not direct advocacy.

The course exposes students to multiple points of view and requires that they explicate the reasons for views they advocate. The only moral as-sumption is that all enrollees are committed to reducing poverty and pro-hibited from concluding that some poverty is good[9] or deserved; hence, no particular efforts to reduce it are required as part of the course. The course does not advance advocacy or encourage advocacy without critical social scientific scrutiny and proffered ethical justifications from multiple points of view. Normative ethics or moral justifications must be supported by so-cial science and science. Advocacy for policies and prophetic stances are encouraged, but the students are obliged to defend their points of view or, if they remained indecisive, their uncertainties. For these and other reasons, it does not qualify for what Miguel De La Torre describes as "ethics from the margins"[10] or fully qualify as a form of liberation theology and the pedagogy of the oppressed.[11]

8. This reference to ethics including evaluative descriptions is informed by James Gustafson's distinctions among four basepoints in ethics, both theological and philo-sophical, delineated throughout his corpus. While Gustafson's view of evaluative descriptions of circumstances is complex and related to his other basepoints, such as moral norms and principles, my simple point in this context is that descriptions of the circumstances and causes of poverty are a part of ethics and profoundly informed by social sciences. The descriptions are value laden, although they do not constitute norms, principles, or virtues. See Gustafson, *Ethics from a Theocentric Perspective*, 333–37, for one account of what he intends by "evaluative descriptions" in ethics. Evaluative descriptions as a dimension of moral discernment should not be confused with de-scriptive ethics that describes and compares different ethical theories. This distinction is also consonant with Matthew Petrusek's account (following William Schweiker) in this volume of the dimensions of ethical inquiry. See also Otati's article in this volume.

9. Note again that poverty is defined as obstacles to opportunities for minimum well-being and not as minimum income or material possessions, which could be part of a "vow of poverty."

10. De La Torre, *Doing Christian Ethics from the Margins*. See note 14 for further elaboration of differences.

11. See note 22 for a more nuanced distinction with Gustavo Gutierrez and Pablo Feire.

Furthermore, these students, privileged in multiple ways, are not, while taking the course, directly informed by the observations and values of poor persons or communities. They read firsthand narrative accounts of poverty but rarely have direct exposure to poverty or poor persons based on sustained work in an educational, housing, criminal justice, or health clinic setting. Some students have limited direct exposure for two or three hours per week. (A few students, even at Washington and Lee, have experienced poverty, including homelessness, firsthand, and offer observations as they choose to do so.) The students do, of course, read arguments that understanding poverty is not possible for privileged persons without sustained exposure to and some form of solidarity with impoverished communities.

Requiring this kind of course prior to an internship assumes that some rigorous academic study should precede and inform intense firsthand participant observation. For example, students who have read about and discussed the causes of low wages or of racial inequality in incarceration are better able to assess firsthand experience of labor markets or a criminal justice system.

None of these students is required to have a fully engaged internship following the course or even a part-time volunteer experience during the course. However, all are encouraged to pursue community-based learning to supplement their academic study of poverty. Many do. Some do not. For better or worse, a significant percentage of the one hundred students per year who take "Poverty 101" at Washington and Lee do not have an opportunity to engage with poor persons and communities via a formal and sustained firsthand experience during their college years. One task for assessment is to determine as objectively as possible how this strictly academic and largely momentary study of poverty manifests itself later in work life, civic involvement, and attitudes, values, and advocacy for diminishing poverty. It would be informative to compare and contrast students who continue to the internship and minor and those who end their poverty studies with the introductory course.

Second, students who complete the introductory course are strongly encouraged and provided incentives—using course credits, a transcript designation for a minor, and covering expenses and even opportunity costs for students who need summer employment to defray their accumulating college debt—to apply for and participate in an eight-week summer internship. The incentives alone are not decisive; other reasons may motivate some students to apply. Many apply and participate in this selective and rather onerous internship because they think it enriches their education and credentials for the kind of professional work and civic leadership the program encourages. Several features of this internship are relevant to the relationship between ethics and advocacy against poverty.

First, applicants must submit essays explaining how a described placement in a specific line of work (e.g., in healthcare, criminal justice, education, community development) and in a specific geographical location (e.g., the Mississippi Delta; Appalachia; Camden, New Jersey; Harlem) could advance their education. We seek students who will connect their internship experience with tentative plans for work or civic involvement after graduation. Some, of course, say that they want to go to New York or Washington because they had never been there before or to be at the DC Public Defenders Office or a health clinic because they believe these assignments will enhance their credentials for law or medical school. Others indicate their eagerness to serve others. These applicants are not selected, regardless of outstanding academic records or leadership and service activities.[12] Our purpose is not to burnish credentials or offer opportunities for service, but to facilitate earnest students seeking to know more about how their future work or civic participation can address the realities of poverty. Not so incidentally, interns who think they are headed to medical school are sometimes persuaded to go into public health, and interns contemplating legal practice are occasionally diverted to focus on criminal justice policy.

All internship placements incorporate significant direct involvement with the realities of people suffering from poverty. (Some students are encouraged and do follow up with second internships in policy, politics, or grant writing, but these types of internships do not offer the direct engagement deemed suitable for a first internship.)

This pedagogical judgment is explicitly informed by literature in liberation ethics on the epistemological privilege of poor and marginalized and vulnerable persons and by an emphasis on solidarity with these groups. Placements are chosen on the basis of agencies' work with persons and communities rather than on serving others. The Consortium does not denigrate

12. We cannot claim perfect success in the filtering process. One young woman who interned in a medical setting in Dorchester, Massachusetts, wrote several years later that she applied for the internship to burnish her credentials for medical school. The internship, she later observed, redirected her focus to primary care for children and research on the health problems of children in impoverished areas. She also succeeded in improving her credentials. She is on the medical school faculty at the University North Carolina. No less significant and no longer surprising, her research and teaching focus on social factors and determinants of health, especially for children and for LGBTQ patients and their parents. For part of this story, see Schaaf, "The Remarkably Direct Path from Poverty 101 to Pediatrician Advocate." She demonstrates that internships can shape a student's career and civic aspirations, as well as help learn firsthand about aspects of poverty.

service to others. The purpose, however, emphasizes education and solidarity with persons from different backgrounds and struggles.

Second, interns from diverse schools and sometimes diverse economic, racial, ethnic, educational, and cultural backgrounds within the same school are assigned housing together and immersed as much as feasible in communities in which they work. As previously noted, intern subsidies, housing, and social connections are structured to encourage them to interact with each other. The hope is that somewhat diverse interns—all privileged as college students—living and dining together in common housing in community neighborhoods and encouraged to use public transportation learn about the realities of poverty from firsthand experiences and discussions with each other. Neither we nor the interns are so naïve as to believe that eight weeks in this environment equates with a family living for years in similar circumstances. That said, this exposure to the realities of different types of poverty differs markedly from a two-day service plunge or reading a narrative account by Alex Kotlowitz, Jason DeParle, Adrian Nicole LeBlanc, David Shipler, Wes More, or Barbara Ehrenreich,[13] all of whom students have read at one time or another in the introductory course in poverty studies.

Interns' working eight weeks in these communities does not constitute solidarity with nor even adequate direct knowledge about poverty and poor persons. For one thing, eight weeks is insufficient time. Both interns and the people with whom they work frequently complained about the difficulty of the interns' abrupt departures and that eight weeks is too brief. We persistently insist that internships are not efforts to remedy the poverty that interns encounter or to establish long-term solidarity with the communities. The interns work with agencies, communities, and persons who welcome them, and while they take initiatives approved by others, they cannot imagine themselves eradicating poverty for others. They contribute to ongoing projects. This interaction enables but does not ensure what Paulo Friere calls "dialogic" dialogue (see note 22 below). We do expect the interns to learn from listening to others and experiencing their struggles and triumphs and to achieve something akin to empathy or Dietrich Bonhoeffer's ideal of internal substitution as articulated in a recent paper by Howard Pickett, my successor as director of the Shepherd Program at Washington and Lee.[14]

13. See bibliography for full publication information.

14. Pickett, "Taking the Place of Another." The practices and goals of the internship long pre-date Pickett's paper and were not based on Bonhoeffer or other formulations of empathy or substitution, but these conceptual formulations nevertheless articulate the intentions of these pedagogical practices.

Although the interns' exposure enables learning from victims of injustice, it is not based on exclusive epistemological privilege for the poor nor on an assumption that interns can absorb or fully embrace the views of those with whom they work. This modesty regarding a full embrace of the perspective of those who are impoverished arises for multiple reasons. First, there is no assumption that persons enmeshed in particular aspects of poverty agree with each other. They do not have a monolithic perspective on the causes or the ethics of poverty. Second, poverty studies interns interpret and assess what they learn in their internships in light of prior and continued courses on poverty and many other influences on their judgments. Third, the interns, although all privileged as college students, come from different class, racial, ethnic, religious, and family backgrounds. A few have experienced poverty and marginalization. Most have not. Fourth, we try to respect the agency of the interns and their capacity for interpreting and applying what they learn from experience.[15]

Third, these internships incorporate summer seminars among the students in specific geographical areas, journaling reports to each other and faculty at a joint closing conference for all Consortium interns, intern essays voluntarily submitted to the Consortium staff for review and website publication if accepted by the reviewer after revisions, and presentations via poster sessions and talks at the interns' home institutions. These focused educational exercises further distinguish the internships from service events. The interns are asked to talk and write about what they have learned pertaining to an aspect of poverty from their firsthand experiences. They are given free rein as long as the essays and oral presentations are informed, critical, and coherent. They are not expected or encouraged to agree with their agency supervisors or faculty and are actually discouraged from making their comments and essays public relations pieces for their supervising agencies, the Consortium, or their school's poverty studies program. They are neither encouraged nor discouraged from focusing more on descriptive analysis or normative moral advocacy and political or community remedies.

15. These observations about the limitations of interns adopting the epistemology and ethics of those with whom they work are also informed by Howard Picket's comments about the potential and limitations of empathy of Bonhoeffer's inner substitution of the life of impoverished persons. Here again, this pedagogy falls far short in many respects of Miguel De La Torres's summary of ethics from the margins in his "Epilogue." We do not assume a unified view among those at the margins; we do not assume a binary division of privilege and lack of privilege between those at the margins and those some distance from the margins; all college students are privileged in ways that many other persons are not; finally, we do not discourage—in fact we encourage—interns to exercise their own agency to interpret their experience in light of a variety of contemporary ethical and social scientific claims. See De La Torres, *Margins*, 329–30.

They are encouraged to give reasons for their views, whether descriptive or more normative advocacy. These shorter pieces are not propitious occasions for serious ethical justifications of their normative positions.

These internships and educational exercises do not ensure that the interns have learned exclusively from poor persons and communities or adopt specific attitudes or norms for advocacy. The interns are not even discouraged from criticizing the values and behavioral patterns of those with whom they work. Few interns offer such criticism, and they frequently express astonishment at the challenges with which persons and communities cope and the positive attitudes among those persons. Nonetheless, the interns are encouraged to bring their coursework, experiences, and moral and descriptive reasoning to bear on their observations regarding persons with whom they work, their agencies, and the larger culture, institutions, and policies that bear on the lives of persons.

I will illustrate with an impressive essay from a future physician, a young white woman in this case, written after her 2017 internship in Atlanta. She was struck by what she learned about the theoretical concept of privilege from the setting and persons with whom she worked. Working in an institution for recovering homeless and abused (mostly black) women—all of them exploited in some way—exposed that lack of privilege, the intern observed, can be a matter of life and death, as it rarely is for anyone in a college setting. This intern was also informed by her college courses, other college and pre-college experiences, and her capacity for critical ethical reasoning. She does not grant the women with whom she worked exclusive epistemological privilege, but she does claim to learn from them what she could not have learned from college courses alone, from medical school, or even the staff at the agency where she interned. She may not yet be ready to advocate for specific policies and practices, but she is confident that SNAP (protected from those willing to purchase "stamps" from vulnerable addicted recipients at a discount) is essential to help overcome the devastation these exploited women experienced as they strived to benefit their children whom they love. The intern was not coolly clinical or academic. Following a morning listening to abuse-survivors tell their stories, she wrote: "Today could be filed under several headings: aggressively horrible . . . , the only time I've wanted to cry at work (the only time I have cried about work), testing the limits of compartmentalization, or simply: sadness."[16] I doubt that an academic argument, a second-hand narrative about poverty, or weeks of direct service to others could have evoked that observation.

---

16. Jones, "Privilege and Inequality," para. 5.

Third, students who have completed the introductory course and internship are encouraged to minor in poverty studies and to sustain community-based learning, including focused community-based research. The vast majority of Shepherd Program students who complete the internship do minor. This "third leg" of poverty studies requires faculty and staff advice for students with a variety of majors and diverse career trajectories and civic interests. Faculty and staff advise regarding volunteering for non-credit bearing community activities in areas such as nutrition, housing, education, immigration, and criminal justice. Some of the courses are in theological or philosophical ethics. Most are in the social sciences or law and address topics such as health and education policy, gender and poverty, race and poverty, economic issues, education practices, social entrepreneurship, families and children, the media, homelessness, criminal justice, and the culture of poverty. Faculty advice helps poverty studies minors integrate poverty-related courses and community-based learning with their majors, career trajectories, and long-term civic interests. Hence, these courses and engagement experiences feature distinct characteristics: They are tailored to the particular interests of the students. They are more descriptive than normative ethics. They seek to integrate each individual's total poverty studies education; and they shape potential advocacy without promoting particular advocacy.

The minor—for undergraduates only—culminates with a required capstone seminar—or research project—with a variety of readings regarding ethics, institutions, practices, and policies—both global and domestic. The capstone enrolls upper-level undergraduates and law students and includes sustained research and an essay on a topic or a community-based-research project chosen by students in consultation with faculty. These papers guided by tutorials (often with faculty from multiple disciplines) frequently include descriptive and normative ethics and occasionally efforts to justify moral norms and principles. They have included short stories or critical analyses of a literary figure like Faulkner and can interpret or assess the work of a particular theologian or philosopher. The research essays infrequently attempt to justify a moral "truth" regarding poverty. Despite being tutored by ethicists (usually) and readings with a heavy dose of normative and applied ethics, there is no demand—except by example and gentle advice—that the essays are ethics driven. Students who have taken a course or two in theology or theoretical or applied ethics often apply this knowledge in their papers. They always include some type of advocacy for theory, policies, practices, or revising institutions to better address aspects of poverty. The authors are always required to give social scientific, scientific, literary, and usually some ethical reasons, or at least normative reasons, for their advocacy.

It might be helpful to illustrate how ethics and advocacy can be integrated in a capstone essay. A senior came to ask if she could write about breastfeeding and its implications for poverty. She planned to enroll in medical school, which she later did, had a summer internship working with young children and families in Thailand, and had volunteered at the local community health clinic for mostly indigent patients. I readily consented to her proposal. She was a biology major with courses in chemistry as well as poverty studies and a few in social sciences. Her paper started with data showing that income-poor mothers, mothers with less formal education, and African-American mothers in the US are much less likely to breastfeed than other mothers, especially Europeans. She drew on scientific and psychological data to show that breastfeeding usually, not always, has positive physical and mental health effects for mothers and infants. She was committed to the view that the decision to breastfeed should be made by each mother, but when considering whether lower instances of breastfeeding among these groups resulted from autonomous individual decisions, she concluded they do not. Mothers from these groups have historically been provided baby formula by Women Infants and Children (WIC) without adequate information on the benefits of breastfeeding. Medical professionals have provided insufficient information and counsel to discuss the advantages of breastfeeding. Public policy and employers in the US discouraged impoverished mothers from taking time away from work to establish breastfeeding in a comfortable environment.

The scientific and social scientific evaluative descriptions along with an elementary understanding of moral principles of autonomy and beneficence persuaded this future medical student to advocate for changes in public legislative and administrative polices (especially for WIC), in practices by medical professionals, and in employer practices relative to low-income employees. Despite her conservative political instincts (at the time), she advocated for mandatory paid maternity leave sufficient to encourage breastfeeding and rejected what she views as a superficial individualistic understanding of autonomy. Her conception of autonomy was forged more by working through this project than by a formal study of ethics. Her advocated positions emerged from research and reasoning, although I confess concurring with her judgments.[17] Advocacy was the end point for a project

---

17. Petry, "Breastfeeding and Socioeconomic Status." I should report that Rachel ended up as a surgeon and pharmacist, not an OB/GYN or Pediatrician. She reports a continuing deep interest in healthcare practice and policy relative to poverty. I also need to indicate that I advised research papers that argued against any minimum wage in the US and that emphasized personal responsibility in the distribution of healthcare treatment. In sum, the teacher did not always concur with the students' advocacy.

that involved interdisciplinary research, including descriptive and normative ethics, with some attention to justifying conceptions of autonomy and
beneficence and their relationship.

IMPLICATIONS FOR ETHICS AND ADVOCACY

Advocacy

This pedagogy does not begin with assumptions about advocacy except for
the focus on diminishing "poverty." We should not understate the importance of this stipulation.

Moral Norms, Practices, and Policies

First, the assumption commits academic institutions and students who
enroll in the poverty studies education to intense scrutiny of poverty as a
negative moral reality. Poverty as a social and moral problem has not received equal attention from undergraduate and, to a lesser extent, professional education as other social issues such as the environment, gender,
race and ethnicity, peace and justice, social justice, and human rights. The
very existence of poverty studies offering a sustained education for students
in almost any major and on nearly all professional trajectories advocates
for greater attention to this social problem within the academy. Although
students in higher education vary markedly in various forms of privilege
and in the extent to which they have backgrounds defined by poverty, their
futures are far less likely to be determined by poverty than by the other
social problems to which academic institutions have given more attention.
Concerns about the environment, race and gender inequalities, and other
social problems bear heavily on poverty, but, as the Shepherd intern from
Atlanta reminds us, the lack of privilege associated with poverty is *sui generis* and less existential for college students than for persons thwarted by
various forms of poverty. Students in poverty studies may retroactively consider the ethics of a sustained focus on poverty that relegate other social and
cultural problems less central. However, the moral merits of the emphasis
on poverty are assumed without prior ethical analysis. That emphasis also
demands attention to related injustices that exacerbate poverty.

Second, some persons—both academics and those who live and work
in impoverished communities—find the label poverty associated with an
identifiable group of people stigmatizing, even demeaning. Certainly,
the word can be used that way. Those who have taught courses and led

internships in poverty studies must be sensitive to how the language is used in essays and papers, and they must admonish interns to be cautious in their use the term during the time of their engagement in an impoverished community. Hence, some would prefer to use other terms to define the problem, e.g., social justice or inequality. This caution about the term is informed by listening to those about whom it is used.

On the other hand, terms like inequality, social injustice, or environmental injustice—even racial and gender injustice—do not fully capture the realities that persons, families, and communities who lack minimal opportunity for well-being encounter. These alternative subject matters deserve attention in their own right, as well as for their impact on poverty, but they can divert attention away from a focus on practices, institutions, and policies that constitute impediments to minimal opportunity. We may, for example, unjustly be denied equality in promotions or adequate access to recreational areas without being impoverished. These other injustices are real, but they are different from poverty. In addition, the poverty studies described above, while leaving latitude for a lively critical scrutiny of the best definitions and measurements of poverty, assumes that poverty cannot be adequately defined as low capacity for earnings or even low income. While retaining a focus on poverty, the Shepherd Program and Consortium adopted the language of promoting human capability, as advanced especially by Amartya Sen and Martha Nussbaum, to accentuate that poverty is more than income levels or inadequate capacity to function. It is society's failure to support minimal capability for well-being.[18] Thinking about poverty in relation to capability falls short of precise definitions but allows for a broad understanding of possibilities for overcoming poverty as well as societal responsibility for enabling individual and community opportunity for decent minimal well-being. The assumption that an absence of capability and poverty are connected does not determine advocacy, but it provides moral grounds for advocating for societal practices and policies.

Third, poverty-studies at its various stages provides educational and emotional means and encourages students to advocate for moral norms, social practices, and public policies. As descriptions and examples of the various elements of poverty studies reveal, students do evolve to advocate in specific ways; however, nothing in the program demands or even leads directly to advocacy for particular positions. Nor is there much unity in what students advocate for, let alone in the sophistication of their advocacy. These disavowals of specific kinds of advocacy should not be confused with

18. See, for example, Nussbaum and Sen, *The Quality of Life*, especially the "Introduction," 1–6; "Capability and Well-Being," 30–53; Beckley, "Capability as Opportunity."

denying the possibility that ethics, rigorous interdisciplinary study, and engagement with persons and communities encumbered by poverty lead to some common advocacy. Research papers advocating for eradication of minimum wage policy, withdrawing all support for single-parent families, or high levels of personal responsibility for health are rare. On the other hand, we do not find uniform agreement about universal basic income, guaranteed jobs, public housing with no behavioral conditions, or support for marriage. The success or failure of the poverty studies program as constituted could not be measured by how many students finish by embracing a particular set of norms, social practices, or public policies. The program is founded on the view that, in the long run, informed and thoughtful citizens disagreeing will produce better results in diminishing poverty than a uniformity of views that follow faculty expectations.

There is an assumption that ethical study of poverty, broadly construed to include evaluative descriptions from literature and the arts and from the social and natural sciences, will change moral norms and advocacy for policies and practices. The study does not have to culminate with the "moral truth" about poverty in order to affect norms and advocacy in particular ways. A carefully constructed assessment of how the totality of the poverty studies changes the moral norms, policy positions, and practices of graduates and alumni/ae would help to establish that poverty studies affects advocacy. The assessment would have to compare poverty studies students, especially minors, to a carefully selected control group of similar students who did not happen to enroll in poverty studies. We certainly believe that the ethics and other dimensions of poverty studies should shape the content of advocacy, even if it does not produce uniform advocacy. In this way, ethics in poverty studies programs shape advocacy.

Careers and Civic Life

Neither does this pedagogy for poverty studies advocate for specific career or civic vocations. It is designed to inform students in most careers and help them make choices about what civic and political activities can be meaningful and satisfying. Students, especially those who participate in the internship and complete the minor, are clearly amply encouraged to consider how their professional and civic (including political) lives impact on poverty, but students are not directed into particular careers or civic activities. Diminishing poverty requires educators, lawyers, businesspersons, health professionals, and curators and artists, as well as community organizers, social workers, leaders in public policy, and poverty researchers. We assume that the efforts of graduates will be more effective if they, informed by courses and community engagement, are responsible for making connections between their poverty studies education and their vocations. They may not even explicitly consider their work and civic activity a vocation rather than a mere career, but the education certainly encourages a sense of calling.

The success of this advocacy and flexibility regarding lifetime work can only be measured by accurate assessment of how and to what extent the poverty studies education manifests itself in the lives of graduates over a long period of time. We have primarily anecdotal information in the form of more than one hundred essays by selected Consortium graduates.[19] A well-conceived and well-executed assessment of alumni/ae at different ages, including comparison to control groups and objective rather than merely self-reported data, could help determine the extent to which these poverty studies—and different specific elements of poverty studies—shape work-life and civic-life, including political involvement. These assessments will be complicated because we know anecdotally that job descriptions alone can be misleading and that graduates change career paths over time. Finally, these assessments can provide clear evidence that poverty studies impact careers and civic and even political life without demonstrating it also diminishes poverty. I accentuate that de-emphasizing the significance of career paths is not indifference regarding self-understandings of vocation within a career.

I remain dubious that assessments can demonstrate that poverty studies reduces poverty. The variables are too complex for such a demonstrable result; nevertheless, diminishing poverty remains the end goal.

Ethics as Part of the Interdisciplinary Study

Ethics in this pedagogy is clearly broadly defined. In addition to evaluative descriptions informed by multiple disciplines,[20] it incorporates what interns learn from people affected by poverty, as well as applied and at least partially justified moral norms and principles and conceptions of human agency. Scant attention is given to theoretical ethical reasoning and almost none to metaethics. No effort is made to arrive at moral truth before students and graduates apply ethics to achieve advocacy.[21]

19. See Shepherd Consortium website: https://www.shepherdconsortium.org/alumni/alumni-essays/. Brian Pusser, our early evaluator, mused to me that the plural of anecdote is data, an observation I use often with a humble smile.

20. Recall, for example, the paper on breastfeeding and poverty.

21. This pedagogy seems to fall far short of Matthew Petrusek's argument for ethics—and especially meta-ethics—having priority over advocacy. See Petrusek,

While the introductory course and the capstone seminar for the minor were usually taught by ethicists and draw on readings in normative and to some extent theoretical ethics, both religious and philosophical, they also draw heavily on social science and political philosophy—and to some extent the natural sciences and literature. The ethics informs students' reasons and judgments for advocating particular positions. The students engage varied, even incompatible ethical arguments before coming to their own judgments about advocacy. They give varying degrees of weight to the ethical and social scientific arguments and to what they learn from firsthand experience. The student products are not evaluated on the sophistication of the ethical arguments alone, but on how coherently ethical arguments are intertwined with other arguments that may be more descriptive than normative—or normative with minimal attention to justifying the norms and principles. An interdisciplinary approach allows for different weighing of a discipline's findings. In this interdisciplinary pedagogy, ethics is important, not determinative.

The internships and other community engagement experiences shape the academic ethics as a degree of epistemological privilege of poor persons and communities and solidarity with oppressed and vulnerable persons inform the design of the internships. Although these internships do not include formal readings or discussions of ethics, the internships are designed to encourage participants to learn about justice by disciplined and penetrating observations and by listening to others talk about their lives and communities. It would be a gross exaggeration to claim that the intern education described earlier fully incorporates epistemological privilege and solidarity as promoted by some advocates for social justice. Insofar as students interpret what they hear and observe from the perspective of their courses in poverty studies and other areas and draw on their own backgrounds, there

---

"Retrieving (Meta)Ethics in an Age of Advocacy," in this volume. Poverty studies students in the Shepherd Program, of which Petrusek was one, are not urged to justify the truth of advocacy that they undertake, but they are encouraged to justify their premises for what Petrusek, following William Schweiker, calls descriptive, normative, practical, and fundamental ethics. The differences may be less dramatic than appears because this program expects that these ethical and interdisciplinary claims, short of meta-ethical justification, offer partial justifications of moral truth and leave open the possibility that the students and graduates will advance their ethical inquiries to consider additional justifications without suspending advocacy until that inquiry is complete. Petrusek, as a Shepherd Program student, is evidence of the latter possibility. Most graduates are not, of course, assumed to become ethicists but to pursue work, civic and political involvement informed by ethics or moral reasoning broadly defined. Furthermore, Petrusek, at points appears to be open to various forms of advocacy short of conclusive meta-ethical justifications of moral truth.

are limits on how what they learn from impoverished communities shapes their ethics or their advocacy.

On the other hand, the discipline they gain about listening and learning from others shapes their approaches to ethics and to advocacy. We view these internships and engagement experiences as essential components of a poverty studies education. The concluding reports and essays by interns are one means for assessing this influence,[22] and longer-term assessments, necessarily mostly self-reported, of graduates with poverty studies minors also measure the significance of these learning experiences.[23]

22. See   https://www.shepherdconsortium.org/about-internships/internship-essays/ for intern essays accepted for posting from 2013 through 2018.

23. Latin-American liberation theology has clearly shaped the role and design of the mandatory student internships and other for-credit and not-for-credit community engagement activities. Although the epistemological privilege of the poor was not an explicit theme in early liberation theology, Gustavo Gutiérrez, in his 1988 introduction to *A Theology of Liberation*, writes that the poor have been "'absent'" from society (and the church) because they have not had "the opportunity to give expression themselves to their sufferings, their comraderies, their plans, their hopes" (Gutiérrez, *A Theology of Liberation*, xx). Internships in which students are fully engaged with agencies that seek to promote the well-being of impoverished persons and communities as well as with the people offer what Gutierrez calls a "new presence of the poor" (xxv) and a "preferential attention" (xxviii) to the poor. These internships encourage and enable but do not assure "solidarity" that constitutes a "protest against the conditions under which [poor persons] suffer" (xxv). They even fall further short of engaging what Gutiérrez and Pablo Freire call the "conscientization" of the poor for liberating "praxis" in solidarity with poor communities (see Freire, "Conscientization as a Way of Liberating"). We make no focused effort to promote the conscientization of the interns or poor communities, in part because the agencies and impoverished communities are not selected to ensure that interns participate in communities that fit Freire's description of a community in the process of conscientization proceeding to praxis for liberation. Nevertheless, the pedagogy rooted in internships of this kind bears resemblance to Freire's conception of a "dialogic" dialogue between those who are poor and not-poor, leading to united action to liberate from oppression. Importantly, Freire does not conceive this dialogue as foisted on or imparted to poor communities nor passively consenting to the judgments of those in poor or oppressed communities. It is a "co-investigation" of reality (see Friere, *Pedagogy of the Oppressed*, 96–97, 106). The program and Consortium pedagogy focus on poverty, which may be and is likely due in some measure to oppression. Freire, by contrast, focuses on the oppressed. Interns are warned against the view that their service will end poverty or that they can "deposit" (Friere, *Pedagogy of the Oppressed*, 109) wisdom in the communities where they work. Our pedagogy accentuates learning from the agencies and people with whom the interns work, but it does not teach or assume that engagement and listening will be fully "dialogic" and a process of conscientization leading to liberating practice in solidarity with poor or oppressed communities. On the other hand, some students, not all, come to levels of consciousness regarding injustice visited on poor communities and form solidarity with those persons and communities that are fully compatible with Freire's hope. See Sara Jones account cited in note 15. Neither Gutiérrez nor Freire imply an exclusive epistemological privilege of the poor. In that respect, the poverty studies pedagogy complies with their views. It differs from an

In sum, ethics as a prominent component in an interdisciplinary and engaged education focusing on poverty prepares students for advocacy to diminish poverty. As part of an integrated education that assumes that all are committed to diminishing poverty and should consider reducing poverty a crucial part of multiple careers and different forms of civic and political involvement, the ethics in this pedagogy shapes advocacy in multiple ways. The pedagogy does not lead to a specific career or civic choices or to a unified set of moral norms or policies. Nor does it hope for justifications for a moral truth. That it has a substantial effect on advocacy for many graduates is indisputable; time and more effective longitudinal assessment will show how widespread and profound that effect can become.

EFFECTIVE?

Whether or not this pedagogy is the most effective method for relating ethics and advocacy in focusing on poverty depends on the criteria by which it is judged.

It cannot be fully effective measured by advocacy for specific institutions, practices, and policies, because there is no intention to achieve such unanimity. It is undoubtedly effective in shaping this specific advocacy, and those of us who promote the pedagogy believe that the sophistication, richness, and diversity of the specific advocacy is likely to generate a greater impact in diminishing poverty than a unified advocacy.

Neither the Shepherd Program nor the Consortium strategic plans seeks to promote particular vocations, professional or civic. They seek to inform students in all majors and influence graduates in all career and civic leadership trajectories. That is the reason no Shepherd Consortium school has to date established a poverty studies major. It would discourage students from combining poverty studies with other majors as preparation for a variety of careers. Thus, the effectiveness of poverty studies in promoting work and civic life that impact poverty must be assessed by the extent to which

---

exclusive epistemological privilege of persons in either poor or oppressed communities for a least two reasons. First, it relies, though not exclusively or uncritically, on traditional ethical theory and reasoning to inform listening and dialogical dialogue with impoverished communities. Second, the agency of students from all socio-economic groups and informed by ethics and social sciences addressing poverty enables interns to observe, listen, interpret, and evaluate what they learn from those with whom they work. I believe this approach is compatible, although not identical, to Gutiérrez's continuing engagement with ethics and theology and Freire's dialogic dialogue respecting an informed self-understanding for all persons, but, as previously noted, I expect that those who propose ethics exclusively from the margins as Miguel De La Torre does (see note 14) will find this pedagogy objectionable, not merely lacking.

graduates in education, healthcare, business, law, community organizing, philanthropy, public policy, politics, and even academia demonstrate the influence of their sustained poverty studies. This influence is not obvious by the type of work or even civic leadership graduates undertake. Nor is it obvious during all periods of a graduate's life. It should not be measured only by actions and practices that we believe effective in reducing poverty. The goal is to encourage and inform practices that the students and graduates believe effective. The assessment is necessarily complex, but the effects across time and many dimensions of work and civic life may be much more significant than could be known by identifying particular work positions or civic activities that obviously address poverty. We know that some poverty studies graduates do not hold jobs that are palpably related to diminishing poverty, but only a longitudinal assessment that reports on graduates' work life, civic participation, and political involvement can accurately measure the effectiveness.

These poverty studies programs can do much more than they have thus far to assess the influence of ethics and poverty studies on graduates' advocacy for particular positions and on work and civic vocations. We can learn more about the effectiveness of ethics and poverty studies based on these outcomes. We can only hypothesize, informed by reasoned judgment, that promoting ethically informed diversity in advocacy for positions and in career and civic vocations will effectively help reduce poverty. There are no practical means to determine if the relation between ethics and advocacy in this pedagogy is most effective in reducing poverty—however it is measured. That is the ultimate goal of the pedagogy. We can have a reasonable hope, but the contribution to that goal, though plausible, cannot be decisively demonstrated.

BIBLIOGRAPHY

Beckley, Harlan. "Capability as Opportunity: How Amartya Sen Revises Equal Opportunity." *Journal of Religious Ethics* 30.1 (Spring 2002) 105–35.

De La Torre, Miguel. *Doing Christian Ethics from the Margins.* 2nd ed. Maryknoll, NY: Orbis, 2014.

DeParle, Jason. *American Dream: Three Women, Ten Kids, and A Nation's Drive to End Welfare.* New York: Penguin, 2004.

Ehrenreich, Barbara. *Nickel and Dimed: On (Not) Getting By in America.* New York: Metropolitan, 2001.

Freire, Pablo. "Conscientization as a Way of Liberating." In *Liberation Theology: A Documentary History*, edited by Alfred T. Hennelly, SJ, 5–13. Maryknoll, NY: Orbis, 1989.

Freire, Pablo. *Pedagogy of the Oppressed.* Maryknoll, NY: Orbis, 1993.

Gustafson, James M. *Ethics from a Theocentric Perspective*. Vol. 1, *Theology and Ethics*. Chicago: University of Chicago Press, 1981.

Gutiérrez, Gustavo. *A Theology of Liberation: History, Politics and Salvation*. Translated and edited by Sister Caridad Inda and John Eagleson. Maryknoll, NY: Orbis, 1988.

Jones, Sara. "Privilege and Inequality: Where Theory Meets Reality." *Shepherd Higher Education Consortium on Poverty*, December 28, 2017. https://www. shepherdconsortium.org/privilege-inequality-theory-meets-reality/.

Kotlowitz, Alex. *There Are No Children Here: The Story of Two Boys Growing Up in the Other America*. New York: Anchor, 1992.

LeBlanc, Adrian Nicole. *Random Family: Love, Drugs, Trouble, and Coming of Age in the Bronx*. New York: Scribner, 2004.

Moore, Wes. *The Other Wes More: One Name. Two Fates*. New York: Random House, 2011.

Nussbaum, Martha C., and Amartya Sen, eds. *The Quality of Life*. New York: Oxford University Press, 1993.

Petry, Rachael. "Breastfeeding and Socioeconomic Status: An Analysis of Breastfeeding Rates Among Low-SES Mothers." Capstone essay, Poverty and Human Capability Studies, Washington and Lee University, Lexington, VA, 2013.

Pickett, Howard. "Taking the Place of Another: Is Dietrich Bonhoeffer's Ethics Substitution Oppressive?" Unpublished Paper delivered at annual meeting of the Society of Christian Ethics, Louisville, KY, January 5, 2019.

Pusser, Brian, and Christian Steinmetz. "Evaluation of the Shepherd Higher Education Consortium on Poverty." Unpublished and confidential report delivered at University of Virginia Curry School of Education Faculty, Charlottesville, VA, May 2016.

Schaaf, Emily Vander. "The Remarkably Direct Path from Poverty 101 to Pediatrician Advocate." *Shepherd Higher Education Consortium on Poverty*, March 15, 2016. https://www.shepherdconsortium.org/the-remarkably-direct-path-from-poverty-101-to-pediatrician-advocate/.

Shipler, David. *The Working Poor: Invisible in America*. New York: A. Knopf, 2004.

Index of Names

Index of Subjects